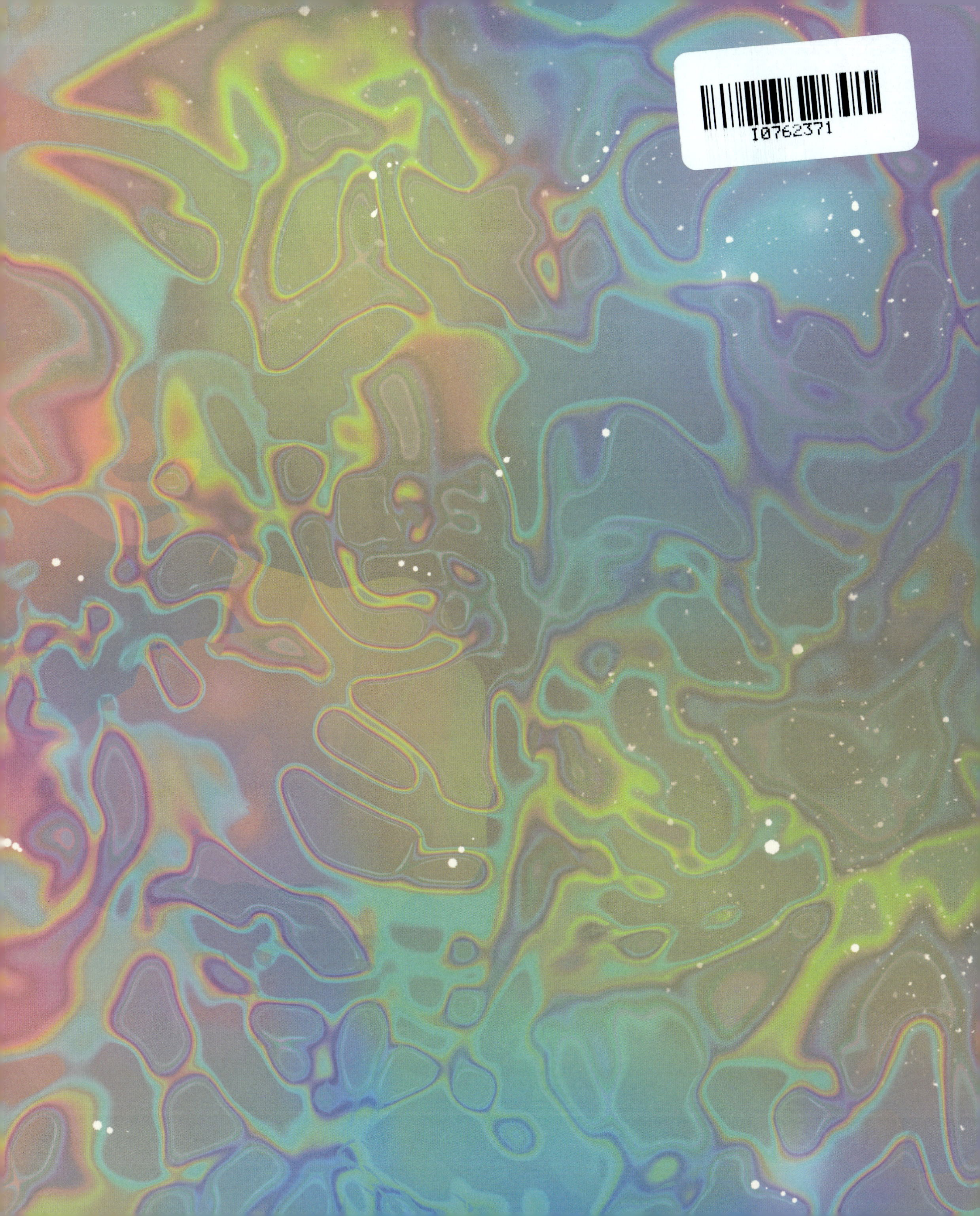

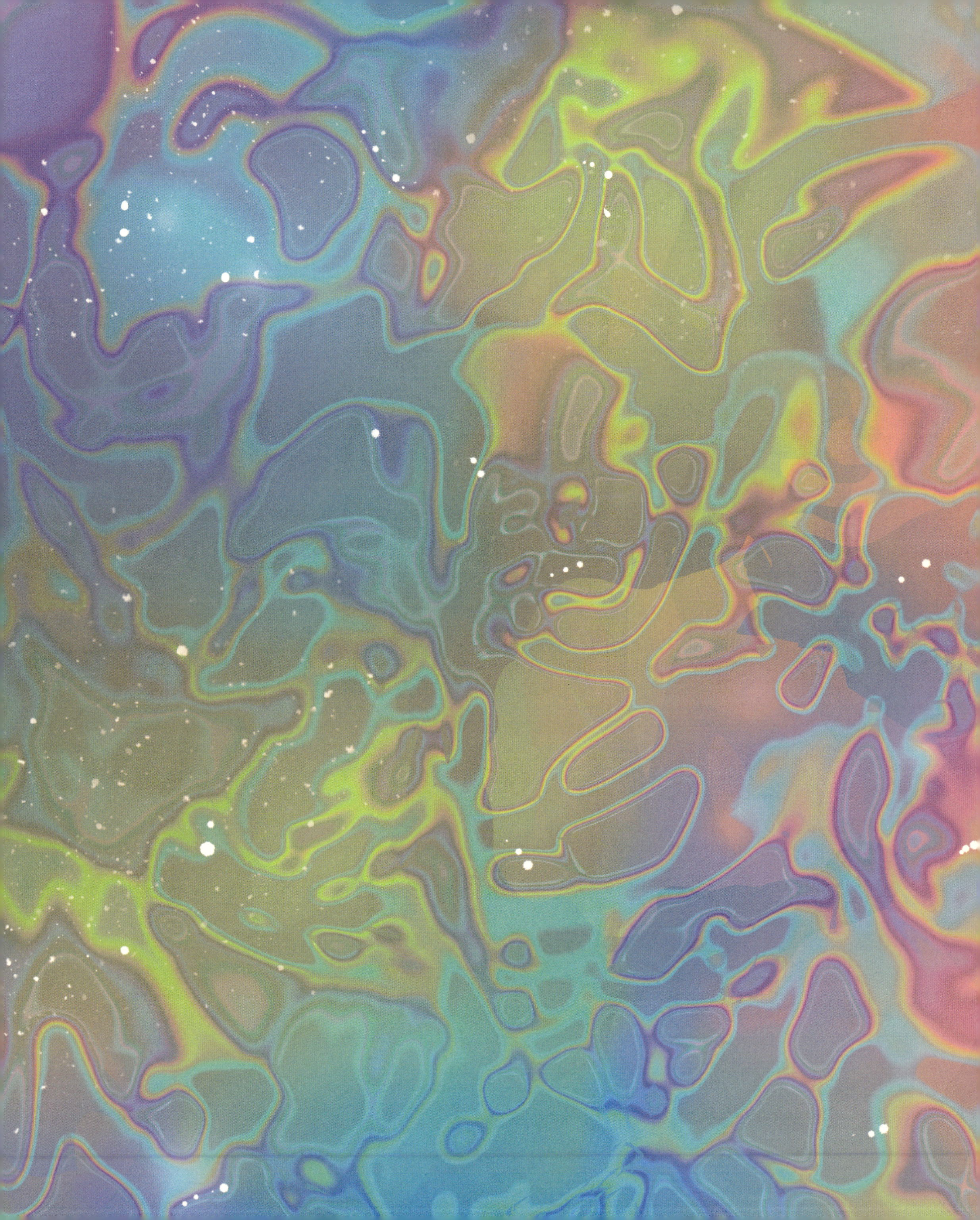

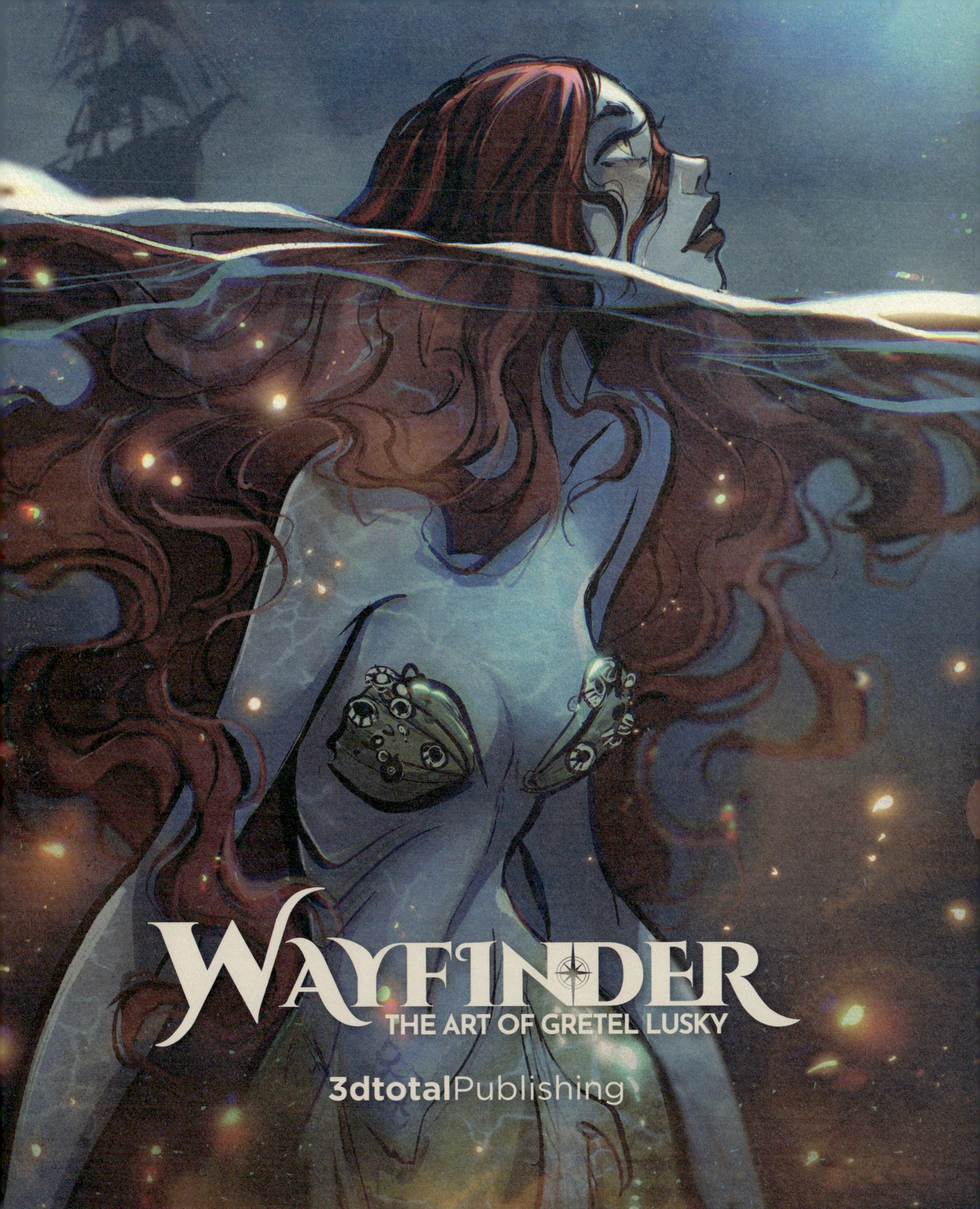
WAYFINDER
THE ART OF GRETEL LUSKY
3dtotalPublishing

3dtotal Publishing

Correspondence: **publishing@3dtotal.com**
Website: **store.3dtotal.com**

First published in the United Kingdom, 2023, by 3dtotal Publishing.

Reprinted in 2024 by 3dtotal Publishing.

Address: 3dtotal.com Ltd, 29 Foregate Street, Worcester WR1 1DS, United Kingdom.

Hard cover ISBN: 978-1-912843-79-4

Printed and bound in China by C&C Offset Printing Co., Ltd

Visit **store.3dtotal.com** for a complete list of available book titles.

Managing Director: Tom Greenway
Studio Manager: Simon Morse
Lead Designer: Joseph Cartwright
Lead Editor: Samantha Rigby
Editorial Project Manager: Rhiannon Joseph

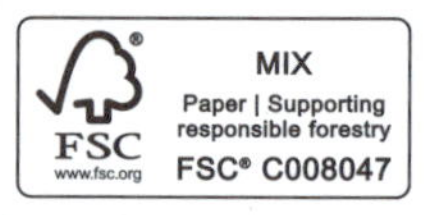

CONTENTS

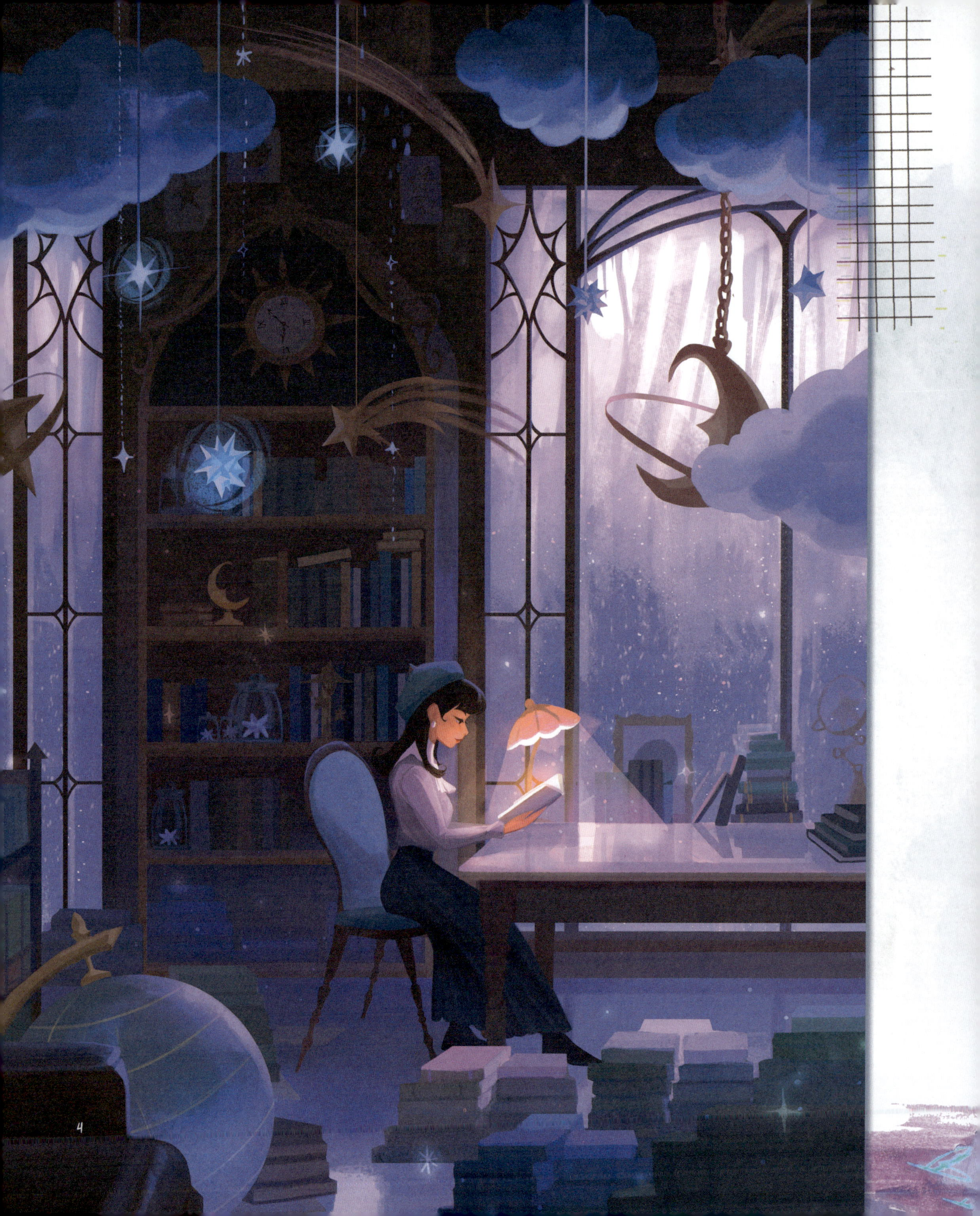

FOREWORD

I had the pleasure of meeting Gretel in person at Lightbox Expo 2022. Though our friendship bloomed through our Instagram conversations over the years, when we finally met, we immediately connected and felt like old friends.

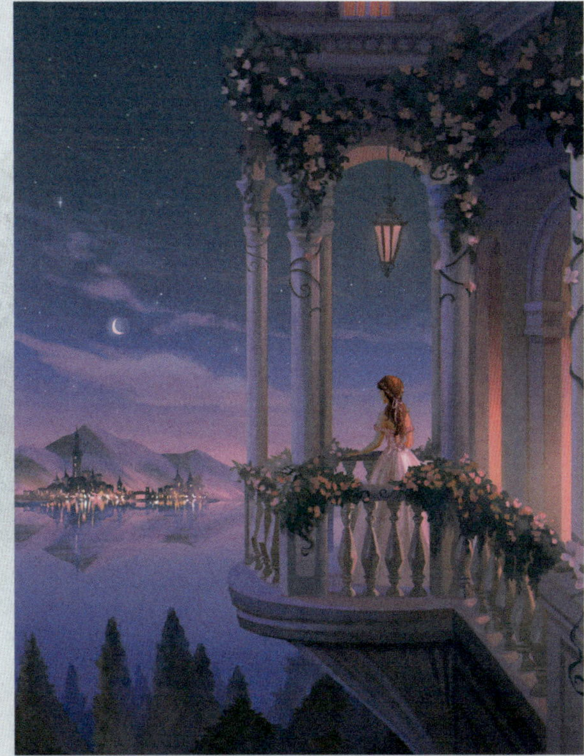

Meeting Gretel in Pasadena was one of the highlights of my trip. Besides sharing our love for art and experiences as artists, we made plenty of jokes and told heartfelt stories. We also learned about each other's cultures and taught one another fun words and greetings in our native tongues. Gretel is truly just as amazing, inviting, and lovely as her art. She has always been an inspiration to me and so many others, and I am very happy to call her my friend!

One of the many things I have always admired about Gretel's work is her process. Many artists can fall into a thought process that makes them focus heavily on the outcome rather than the creation. Allowing myself to let go of perfectionism is something that I still struggle with in my work, but seeing Gretel's process unfold is a reminder to freely embrace the feelings and acts of making art because that's when the magic happens.

Her mastery of infusing her style in both traditional and digital mediums is not to be overlooked either. I have nothing but the utmost respect for her constant exploration of each medium: inks, gouache, markers, and watercolours all beautifully showcase her immense dedication to her craft.

Gretel has masterfully created a unique style that exudes an energy, emotion, and vibrancy that seems almost effortless. Watching her artistic journey throughout the years has been nothing short of inspiring. Each work she creates is filled to the brim with heart and passion. I am always amazed by her incredible ability to create characters that metamorphose into a life of their own. She captures them with bold, raw, and confident markings that all converge to create a series of fresh, dynamic pieces.

In her latest works, you will find an array of gorgeous spreads reminiscent of a sketchbook's explorative nature. Her characters convey an intense mood and emotion, while the bursts of colour, eccentric details, and sprinkles of glitter all spark a sense of joy.

I invite you to feast your eyes on a sea of vivid hues and energetic brushstrokes found abundantly in Gretel's art. Immerse yourself in the world of her imagination. From quirky, fashionable witches to fantastical characters, alluring mermaids to playful animals, all come bearing rich narratives. Each beautifully curated page is an experience in and of itself, full of intrigue, playfulness, and of course, magic!

- Maxine Vee

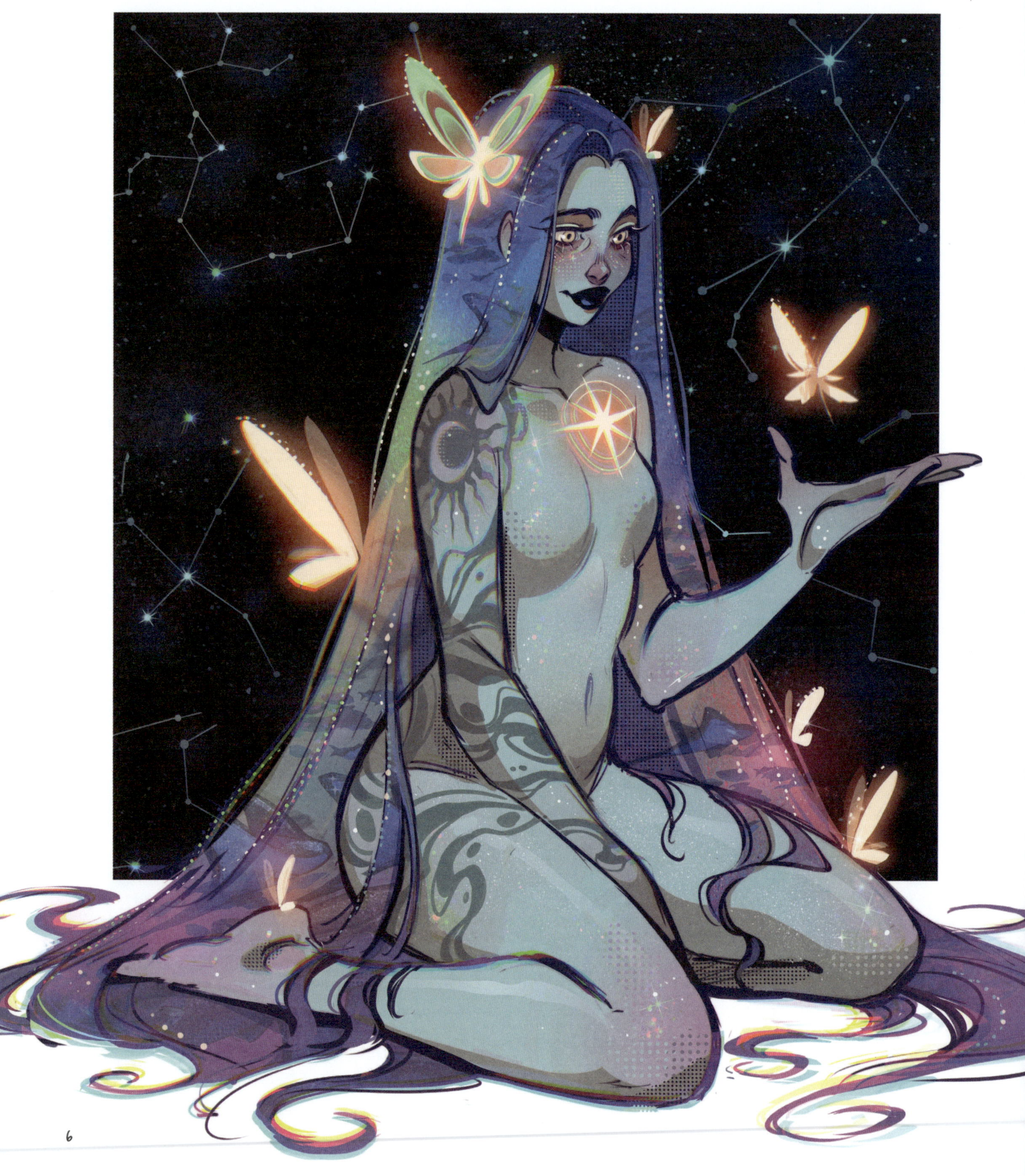

INTRODUCTION

I was one of those kids who didn't want to grow up.

Adjusting to the natural course of things (like leaving high school to venture into the unknown) felt like the end of the world. I just couldn't understand how everyone else embraced all the changes life was throwing at them so easily. It's probably why I liked cartoons so much, and why I stuck to them throughout my teen years when being a nerd wasn't cool like it is nowadays. I didn't know back then, but those silly stories were safe spaces for me – the starting point of my true passion.

As a result, drawing is one of the only things I've ever been consistent with. What started as a fun thing to do slowly evolved into my own way of seeing the world and expressing myself. Without even realizing it, drawing became as natural to me as breathing, so I kept doing it. Eventually, art turned into the core thing that made me who I am today. It allowed me to navigate through life in a way I didn't even know was possible.

Today, I love creating art that feels whimsical and a little bit eerie. I like playing around with fantasy elements and concepts that people can interpret, but I also love making experimental pieces with no big meaning. Whether it's a profound message or just something pretty, I'm always trying to find different ways to communicate through my work and hopefully make people feel something.

I've been sharing my art online for more than ten years now, but I never had the chance – or took the time – to delve deeper into the person behind my work. As an avid book collector, making an art book packed with all the things closest to my heart is a dream come true and a huge achievement in my career, to say the least. Even though I've self-published a few smaller books in the past, I've never poured so much of myself into anything else before, and I'm very excited to take the chance to share it with you all!

Making this book presented a big challenge for me, too. Being an artist, I've always struggled to find my way through words. Much of my art comes to me in a very instinctive way, which makes it hard to explain or even understand myself. It's like trying to describe a colour that doesn't exist. Gut feelings have always played an important role in my artistic journey; doing something just because it feels right without thinking or planning too much. I think for that reason, my work is often described as messy or unhinged. For the past few years, I've been trying to embrace that messiness, and I hope this book will help you find beauty in the raw and spontaneous, just like when we were kids.

Whether you've followed my work for a long time, or stumbled across it recently, thank you so much for picking up this book. It's because of you that I was given this opportunity to share my story. I truly hope you can find inspiration within these pages, but above all else, I hope you will discover a deep, burning love for creating art that is not afraid of failure.

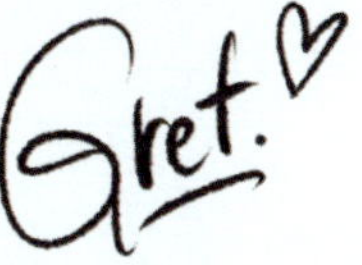

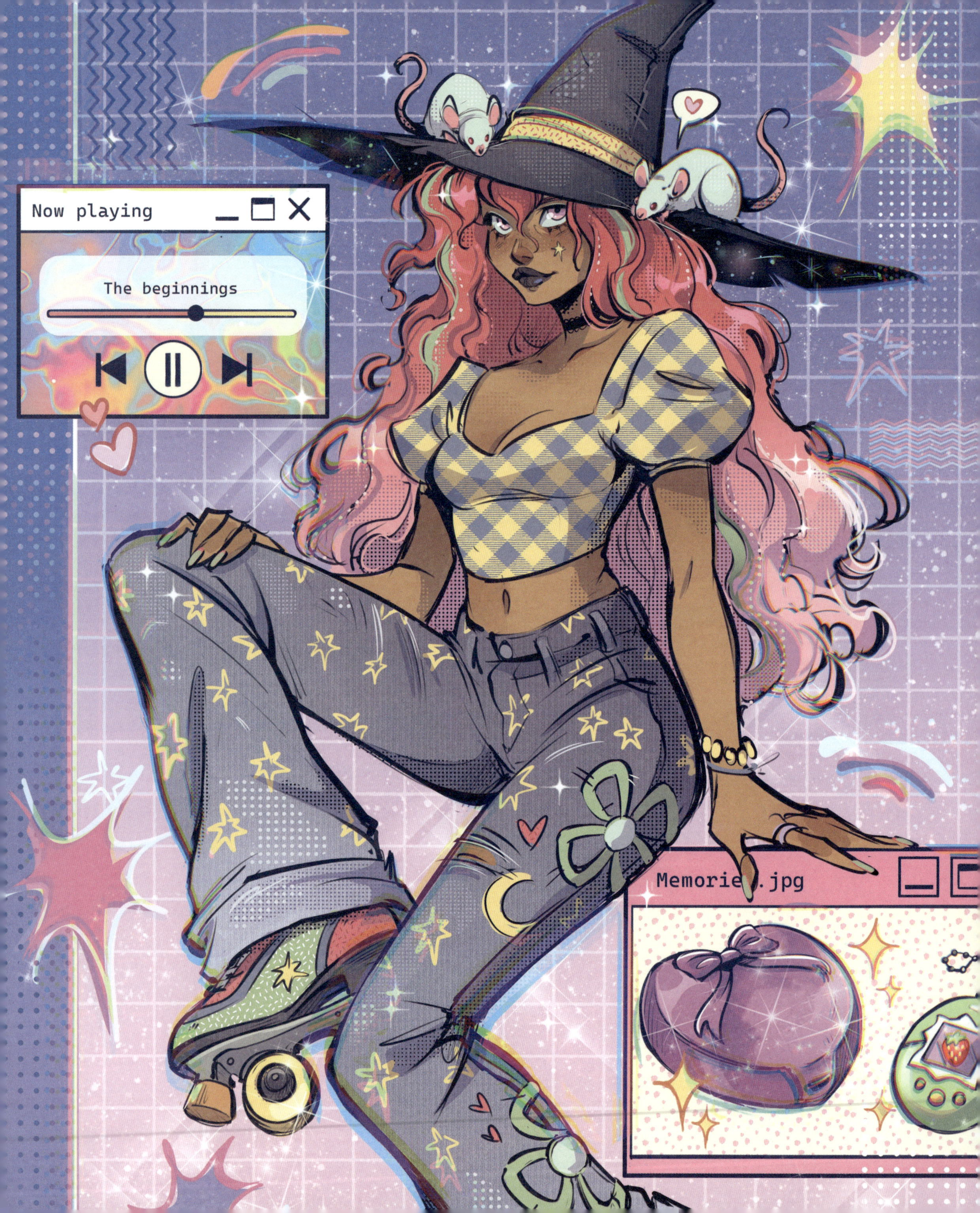
Now playing
The beginnings
Memorie .jpg

ARTISTIC JOURNEY

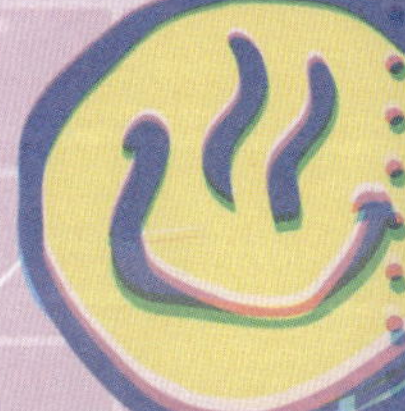

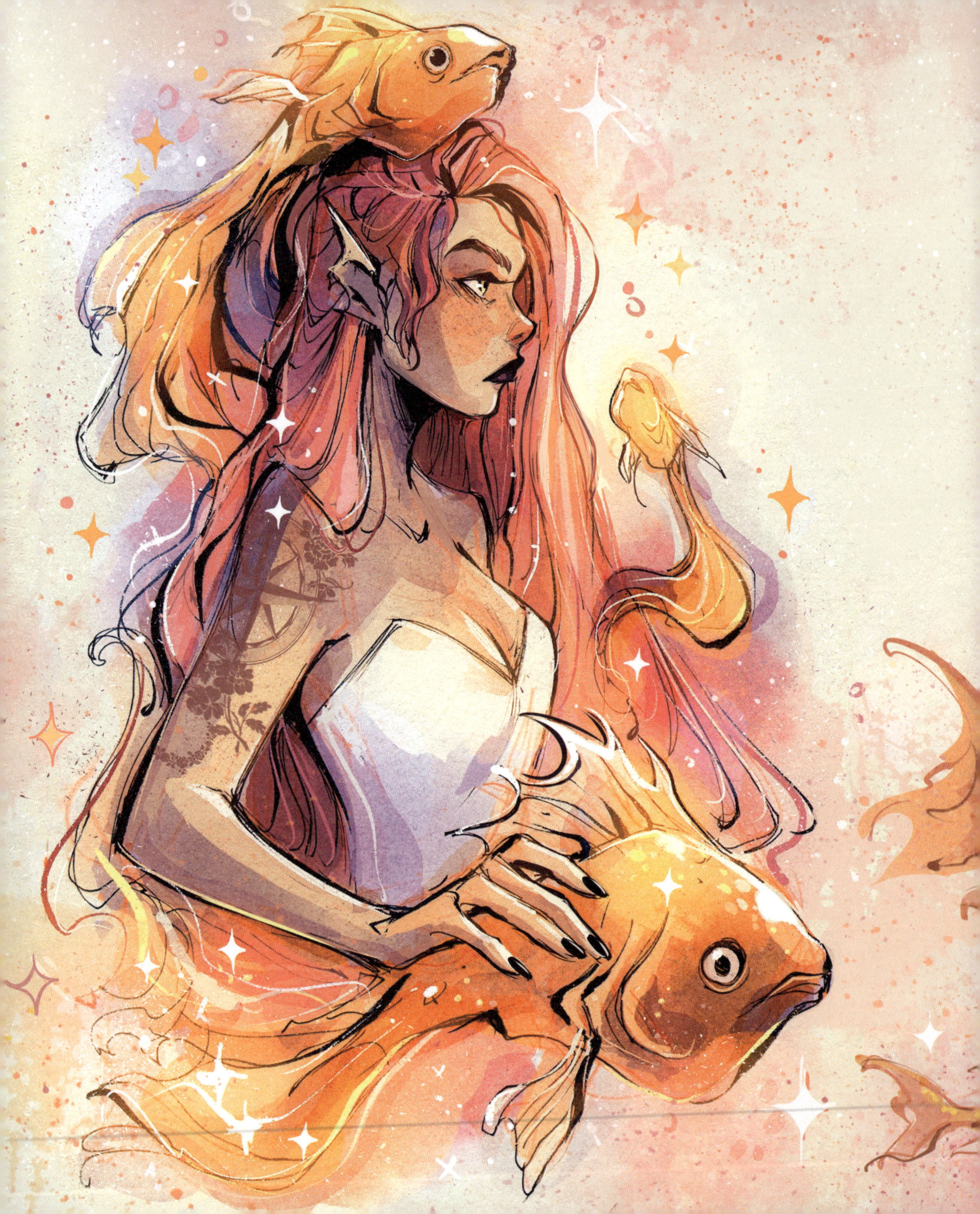

EARLY YEARS

My very first memory of drawing goes back to when I was eight years old. I used to design comics of me and my childhood dog, Lucky, as superheroes. They were short, silly stories about friendship and fighting the bad guys together, who just so happened to be my older sister and our other dog, Bandida. Those comics were a way for me to stand up to my sister, if only in my imagination. As you might have already guessed, we didn't exactly have the best sibling relationship when we were younger.

I'm not sure why I chose comics to document those experiences. I wouldn't say that art runs through my family, but it's always been present in one way or another. My sister liked to draw from time to time, and I'd sometimes steal her drawings to copy them. My mom always enjoyed writing, while my uncles are both photographers. But besides that, there wasn't a huge artistic influence in the family to look up to. That's why I've always considered cartoons to be the spark that ignited my passion.

Abuela was the only member of my family with cable TV, and although I was always happy to see my grandma, I was also excited to sit on the couch and discover loveable characters and captivating stories. Looking back, when I was at home and didn't have a way to watch my cartoons, I found that I could still rekindle the stories I loved so much by drawing them myself.

Eventually, we got cable TV and I watched Cartoon Network religiously, as well as most Disney movies from that time, copying their styles as best as I could. As a result, the stories and comics I created were a mishmash of them all. However, everything changed when I turned twelve years old, when my mom bought me my first *W.I.T.C.H.* comic. The fantasy-art style blew my little tween mind away! I read the monthly issues over and over, staring at the artwork for hours before trying to recreate the elements that captured my attention. Though I copied much of it, I also tried to come up with my own characters and ideas.

From then on, illustrating became a crucial part of me. At first, it was all about the joy I found in creating imaginary worlds. I loved losing myself in the flow of creativity, where time seemed to slip away. As the years went on, drawing became a way for me to document my life and thoughts, and helped me cope with my feelings whenever reality felt too overwhelming.

But above all else, drawing became something I simply loved doing; something I could not go long periods without. I never pressured myself to learn anything I didn't want to, and I never believed that I wasn't good enough to do something I really wanted to do. Who cared, really? Drawing was fun, and I did it for myself, and myself only.

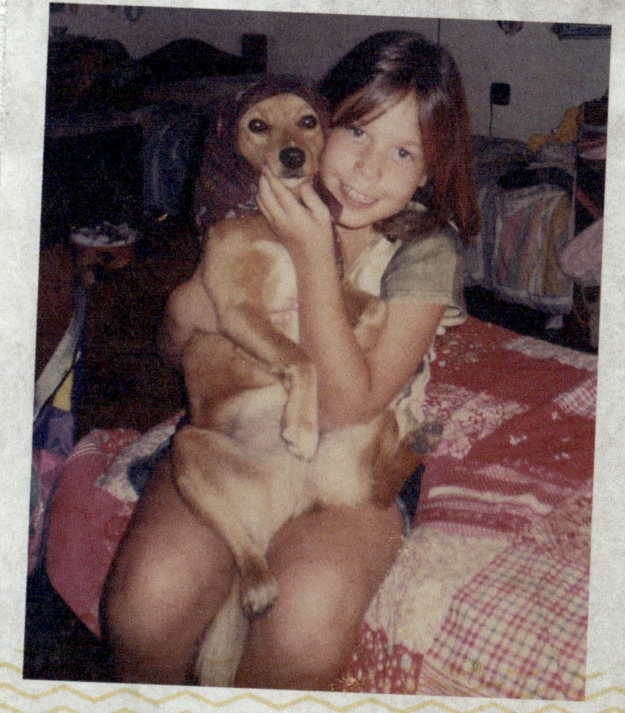

Lucky and me

We adopted her from the streets in 2001 and we became inseparable!

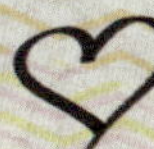

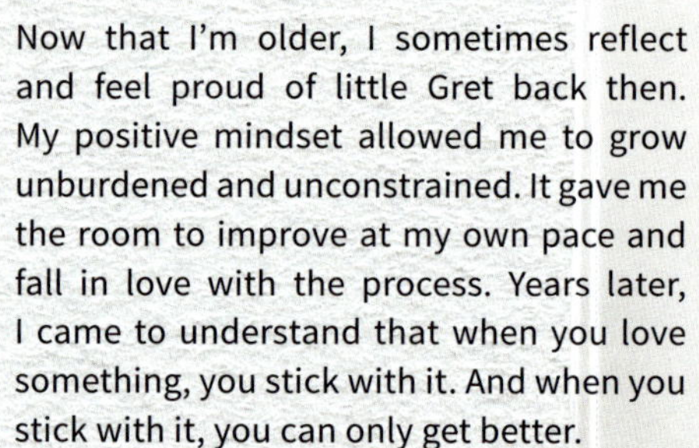

Now that I'm older, I sometimes reflect and feel proud of little Gret back then. My positive mindset allowed me to grow unburdened and unconstrained. It gave me the room to improve at my own pace and fall in love with the process. Years later, I came to understand that when you love something, you stick with it. And when you stick with it, you can only get better.

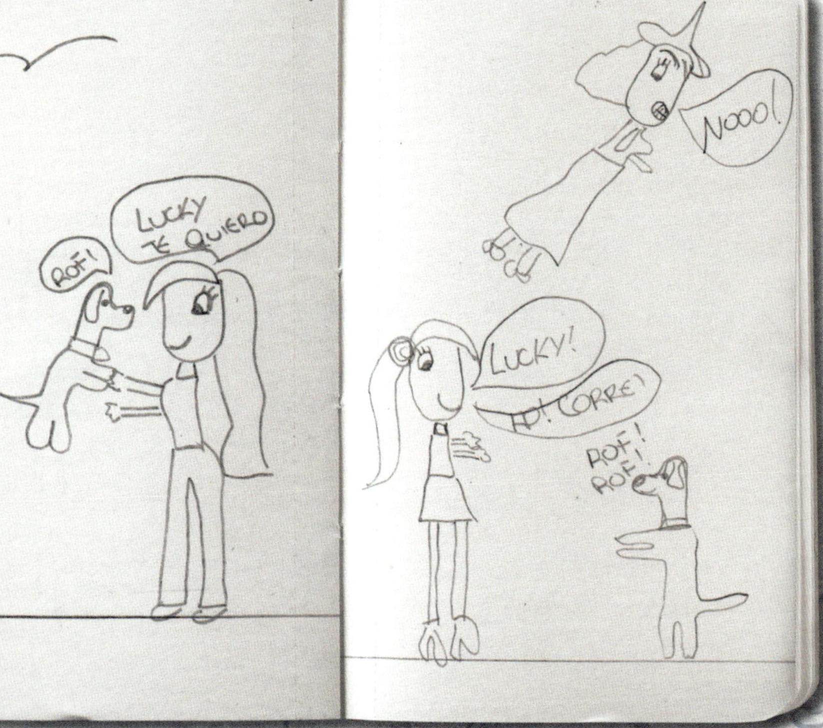

My first comics were called *Las Aventuras de Lucky Supertrepadora y Chica 10*

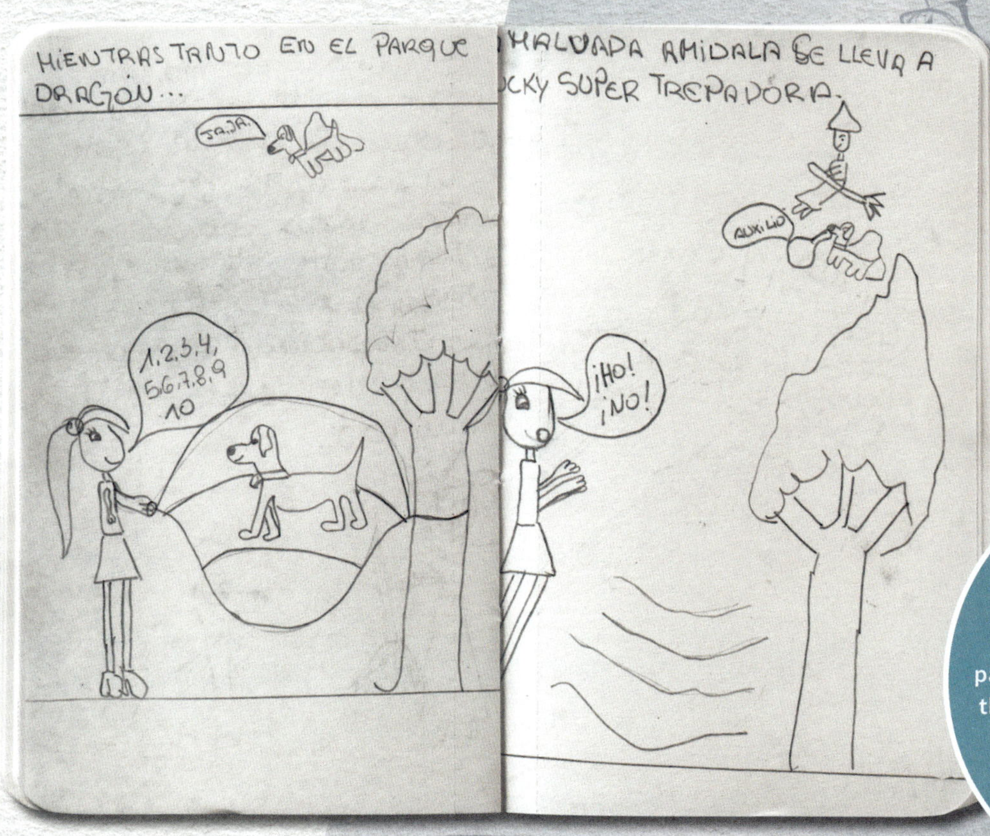

My relationship with my sister has improved since we've grown up. She jokingly takes credit for my passion for drawing, claiming she's the reason for it all. I always laugh sarcastically and deny it, but deep down, I know she might be on to something.

CHOOSING ART

Both of my parents have always been extremely supportive and helped me however they could throughout my journey. Whenever I asked my mom to sign me up to drawing classes, she always did. Even though I'm mostly self-taught, topics like anatomy seemed really daunting at the time, so having someone guide me through the basics made everything much easier to tackle.

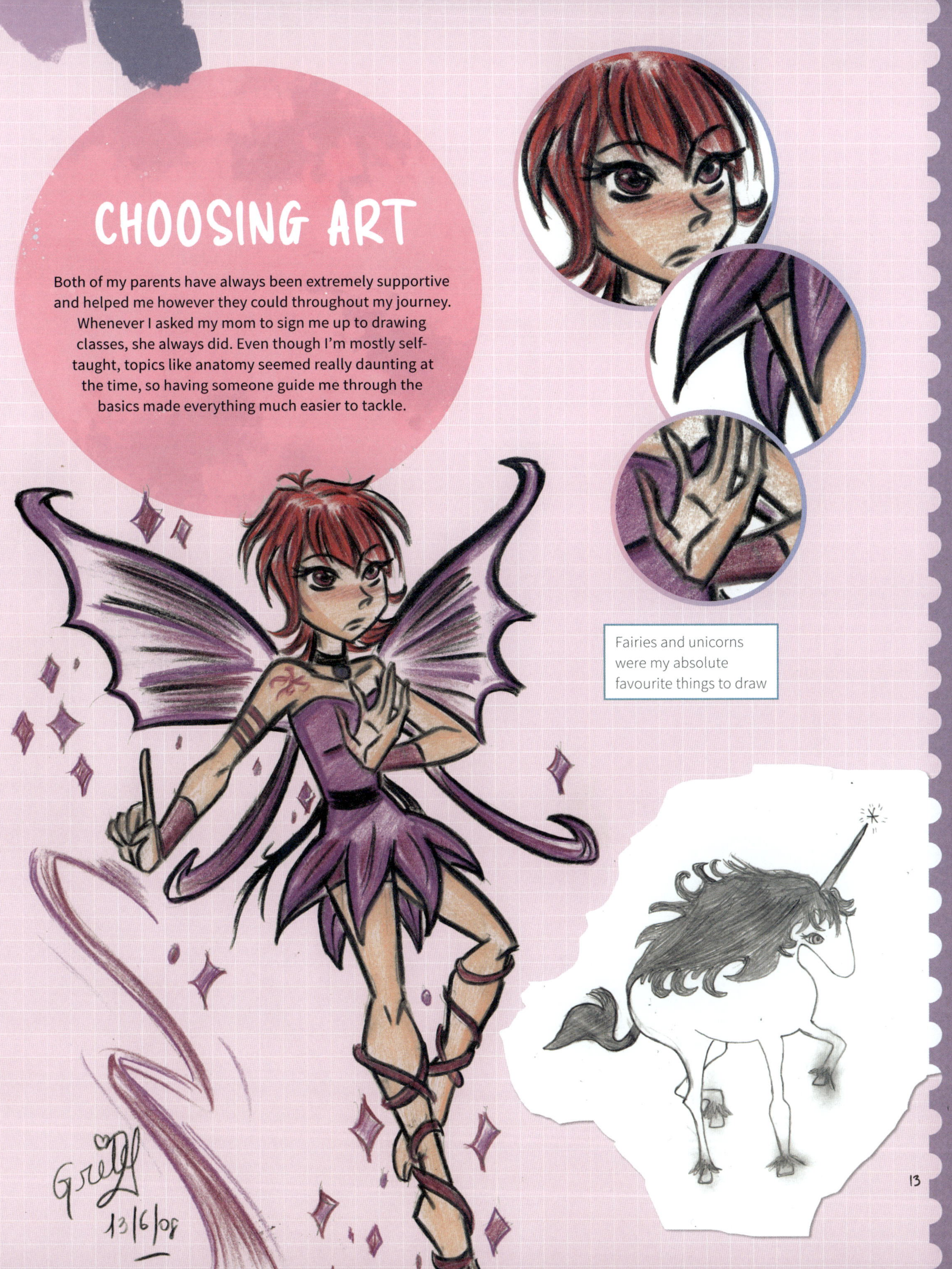

Fairies and unicorns were my absolute favourite things to draw

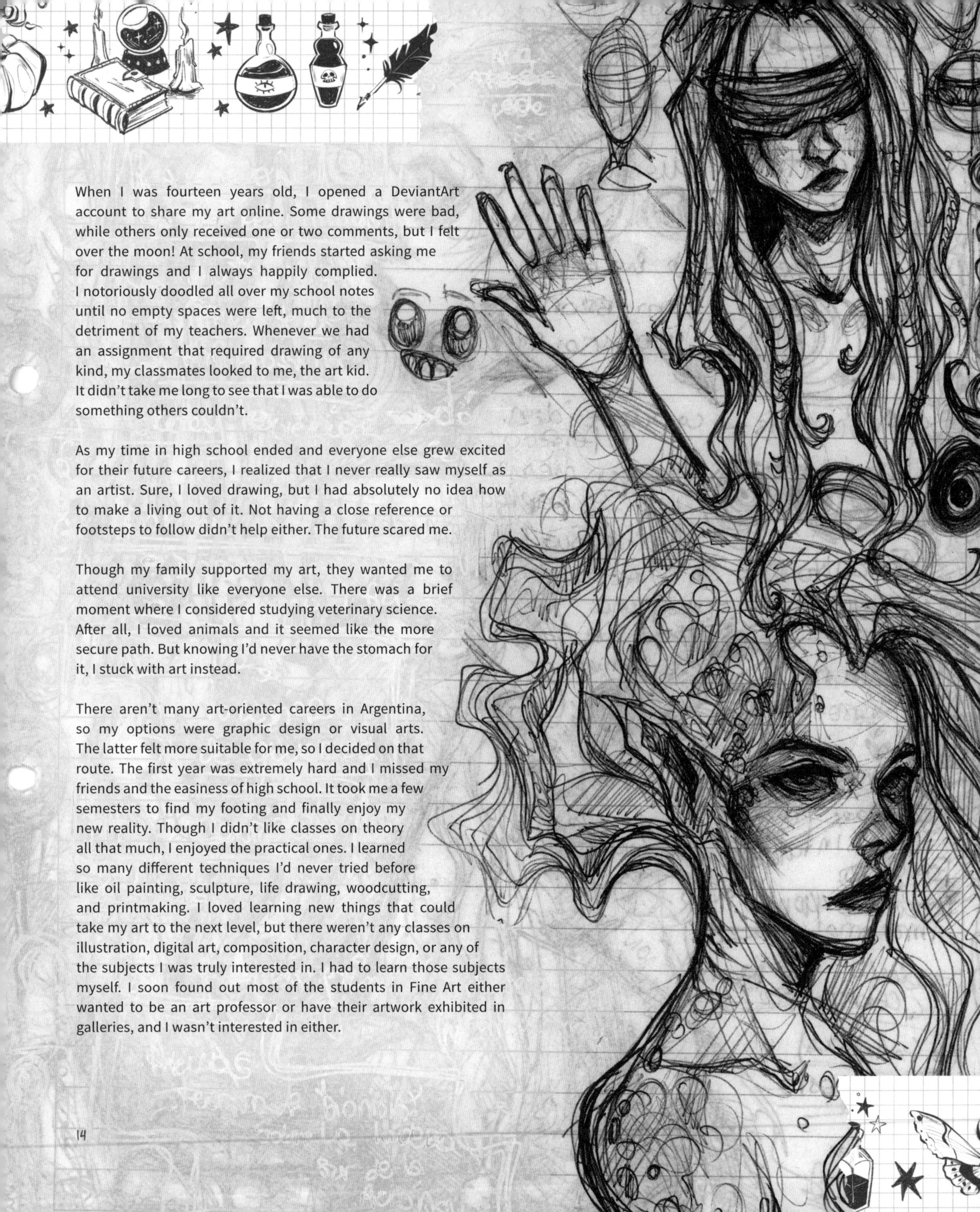

When I was fourteen years old, I opened a DeviantArt account to share my art online. Some drawings were bad, while others only received one or two comments, but I felt over the moon! At school, my friends started asking me for drawings and I always happily complied. I notoriously doodled all over my school notes until no empty spaces were left, much to the detriment of my teachers. Whenever we had an assignment that required drawing of any kind, my classmates looked to me, the art kid. It didn't take me long to see that I was able to do something others couldn't.

As my time in high school ended and everyone else grew excited for their future careers, I realized that I never really saw myself as an artist. Sure, I loved drawing, but I had absolutely no idea how to make a living out of it. Not having a close reference or footsteps to follow didn't help either. The future scared me.

Though my family supported my art, they wanted me to attend university like everyone else. There was a brief moment where I considered studying veterinary science. After all, I loved animals and it seemed like the more secure path. But knowing I'd never have the stomach for it, I stuck with art instead.

There aren't many art-oriented careers in Argentina, so my options were graphic design or visual arts. The latter felt more suitable for me, so I decided on that route. The first year was extremely hard and I missed my friends and the easiness of high school. It took me a few semesters to find my footing and finally enjoy my new reality. Though I didn't like classes on theory all that much, I enjoyed the practical ones. I learned so many different techniques I'd never tried before like oil painting, sculpture, life drawing, woodcutting, and printmaking. I loved learning new things that could take my art to the next level, but there weren't any classes on illustration, digital art, composition, character design, or any of the subjects I was truly interested in. I had to learn those subjects myself. I soon found out most of the students in Fine Art either wanted to be an art professor or have their artwork exhibited in galleries, and I wasn't interested in either.

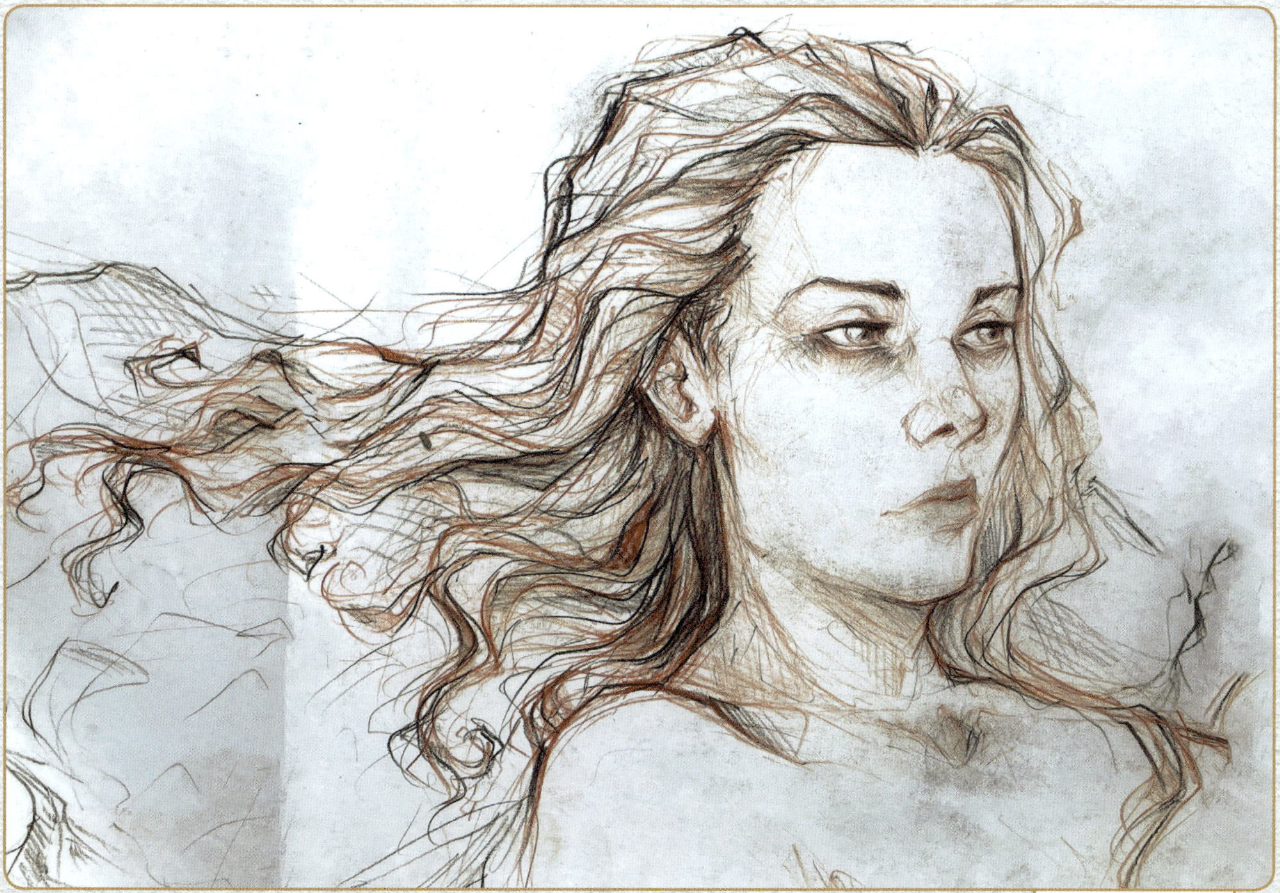

One of the many figure drawings I did in college, 2014

As the years passed, my art style felt more out of place than ever. The time and effort I was investing in college seemed to be leading nowhere and it became a heavy weight on my shoulders, but since I needed the degree, I kept going. That didn't mean I wasn't searching for a new future plan in the meantime. I considered the only other career I thought would allow me to earn money and stay true to my art style: tattoo artistry. After signing up to a tattooing course, I met someone who saw potential in my work. He told me I had talent and that it would be a shame to waste it, which I thought was an odd thing to say to someone you just met.

He put me in contact with a friend who worked in animation. I wasn't sure what I was doing, but later that day, I sent them my portfolio.

A few months after finishing the tattoo course, I received an email from the animation studio asking me to complete a few character-design tests. I sent them in, keeping my expectations very low, but I was wrong to doubt myself – they offered me a job!

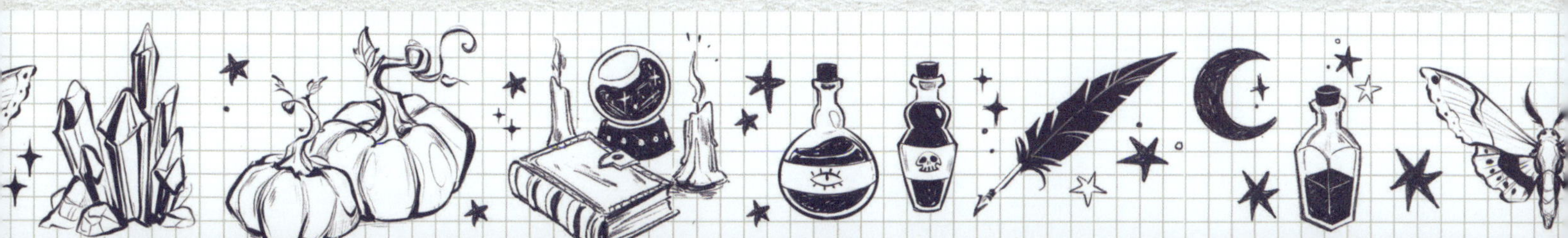

BUILDING A PROFESSION

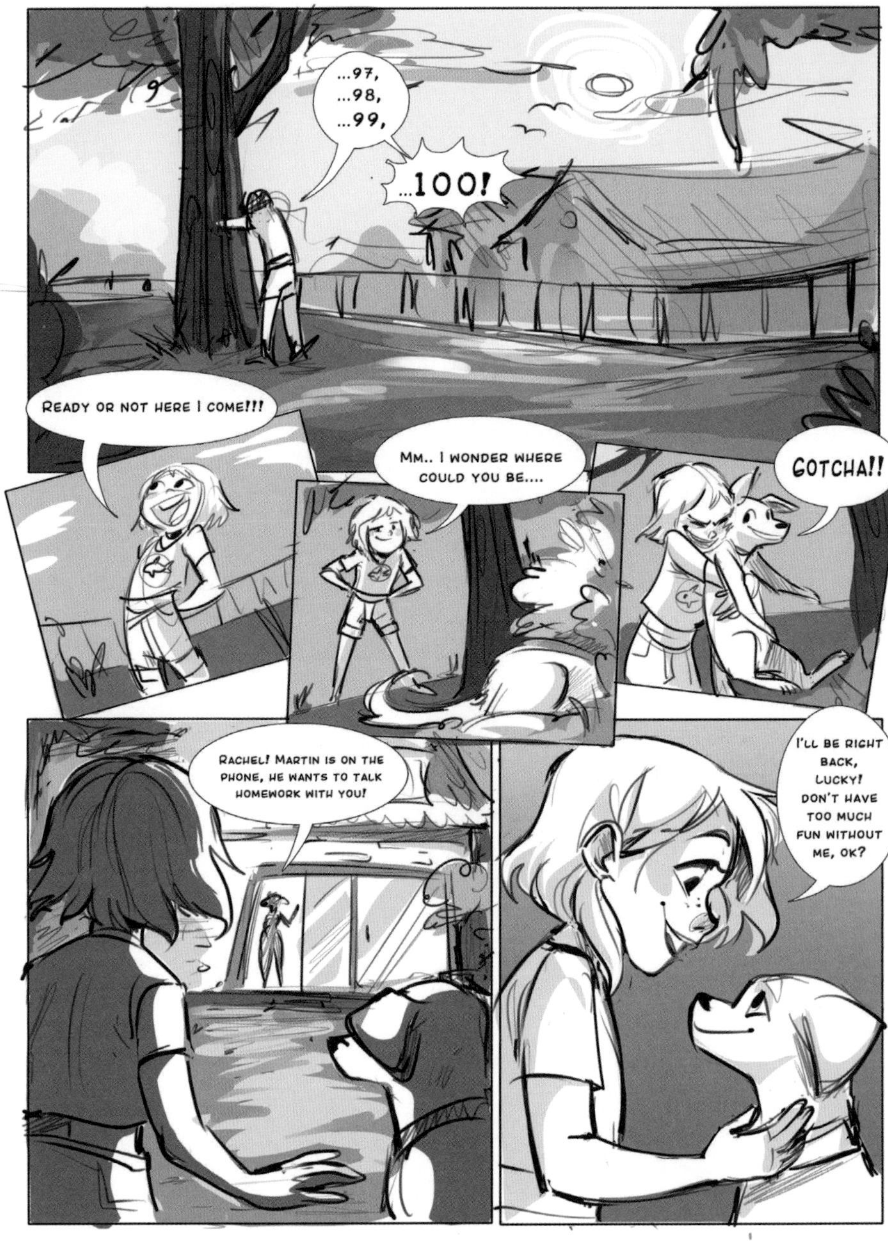

At the age of twenty-one, character designing became my first official job. Before then, I had only taken a few personal commissions here and there. Juggling work and college was difficult in the beginning, especially when work started taking over my life. The studio quickly became my priority – I loved designing characters and being surrounded by like-minded people.

Working in animation was a pivotal point in my life. It opened my eyes to a world of new possibilities and gave me the confidence that I could, in fact, make a career out of my art. It taught me to be more efficient, to adapt to a client's needs, and to understand the importance of deadlines. I learned about teamwork and building a workflow. It also made me realize that I wasn't as good as I thought I was, and I still had much to learn. I was very lucky to have an amazing art director and awesome colleagues to learn from and rely on. Everything just felt right. Suddenly, the future didn't seem so scary anymore.

During my fifth year of university, I dropped out to focus entirely on work. Although my family didn't think it was the best idea at first, they understood that it was the right thing for me to do at the time.

But here's the catch with animation: you're just a small cog on an enormous wheel. Most of the time, the line blurs where your work ends and another's begins. It's a completely collaborative industry, and although I was grateful for my position, I wanted to stamp projects with my own style. I craved being in charge of my own creative decisions. After two years in the studio, I started searching for alternative jobs to explore, so I sent my portfolio to various publishers and took on small freelance projects illustrating book covers in my spare time. I also participated in a few local conventions for the first time. By the fourth year at the studio, I moved to the visual-development department and mainly drew props and assets. I soon understood that I had already absorbed everything I was interested in learning from animation, and I was ready to turn the page. However, letting go of a stable job without a plan B sounded like a bad idea.

Sharing my artwork online always came very naturally to me. I hadn't stopped uploading to DeviantArt, and at some point, I shifted to Tumblr before moving to Instagram. It was something I did for years because it was fun, but I also had the hope of getting discovered by potential clients. One night, after a long day in the studio, I checked my emails, and to my surprise, there was a message from DC Comics. I didn't believe the email was legit at first. It couldn't be – I hadn't drawn a comic page in years. After staring at it for a hot minute, I called my boyfriend and said, 'Someone who says they work at DC wants me to do some character-design tests for a graphic novel. It's a scam, right?' It took him all of ten seconds to read the email and say, 'Gret, this is huge!'

He hyped me up so much that I started to believe it was true. I'd stumbled across my dream job – after all, creating comics was how my love of art first started. I wanted that job more than anything, so I put my heart and soul into those tests. I needed to demonstrate that I was able to create sequential art, but I didn't have a single sample at the time, so my partner helped me put together a short story. I wanted the comic pages to be about my dog, Lucky, so we took my childhood comics and drew up three pages, alongside my character designs. Lucky had passed away the year before, and it was such a bittersweet moment to reconnect with her through those drawings, just like when it all started.

It took him all of ten seconds to read the email and say, 'Gret, this is huge!'

The sequential-art samples I made for DC, based on my comics of me and Lucky, 2018

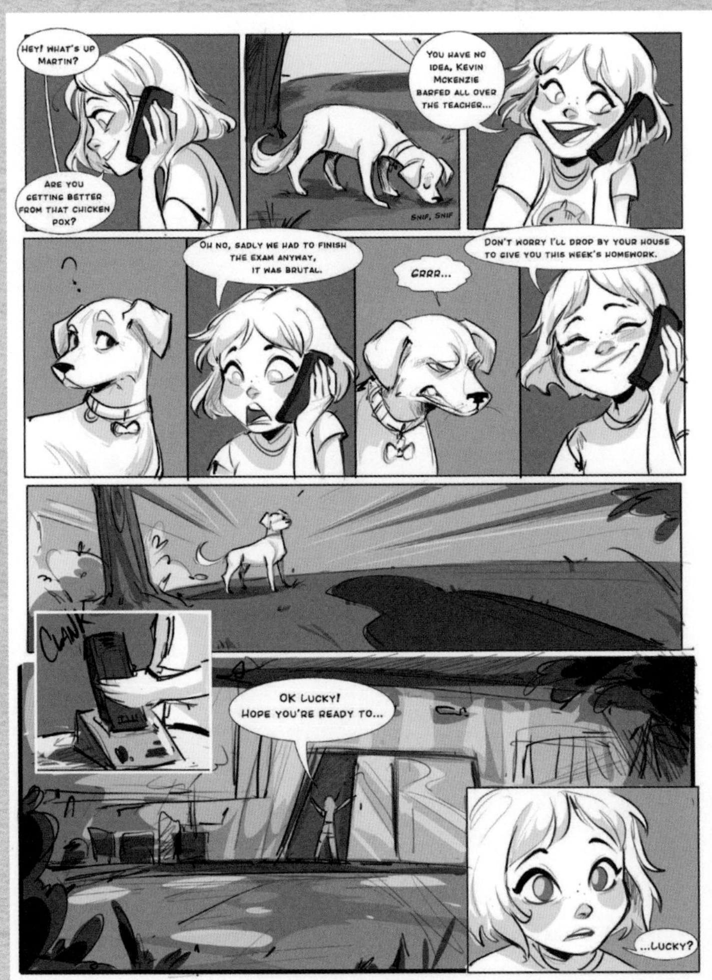

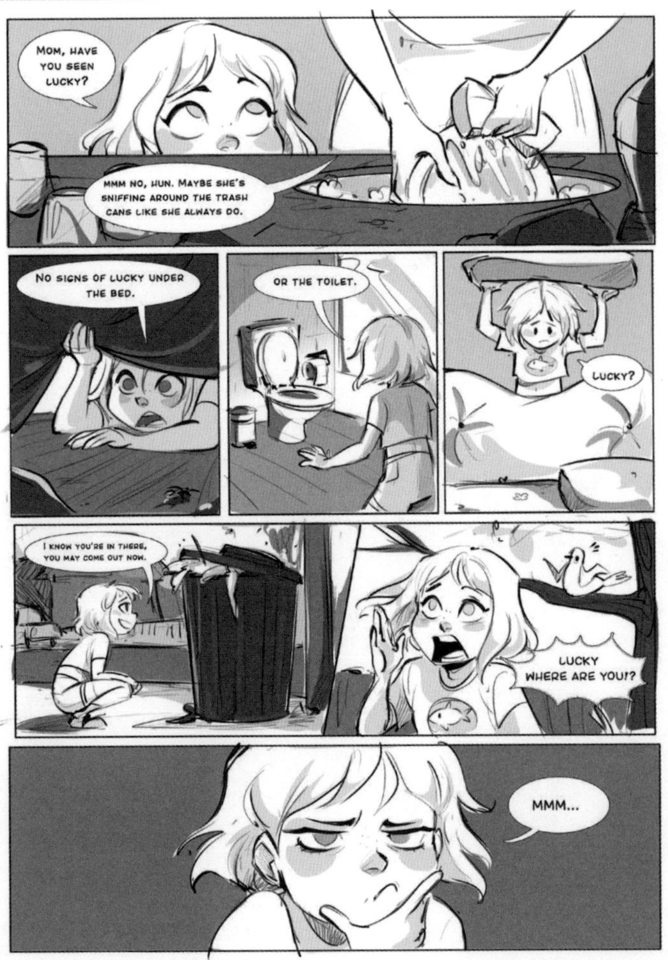

I quit animation and launched into my freelance career the moment DC confirmed I was hired for the project. It took me a while to consider myself a comic artist, and even to this day I don't quite feel like I completely own that title. I know that's silly because if you do comics, you're a comic artist. There's just so much I have yet to learn.

Comics are no piece of cake, and freelancing isn't either. Being your own boss comes with a unique array of challenges such as managing your own time, overworking yourself, or not taking enough breaks. After a couple of years freelancing, I'm still trying to figure out how to maintain a healthy work-life balance. I think artists struggle with that throughout their lives, but I'm okay with it. I'll always be grateful for how things turned out for me, knowing I'm able to do what I love for a living.

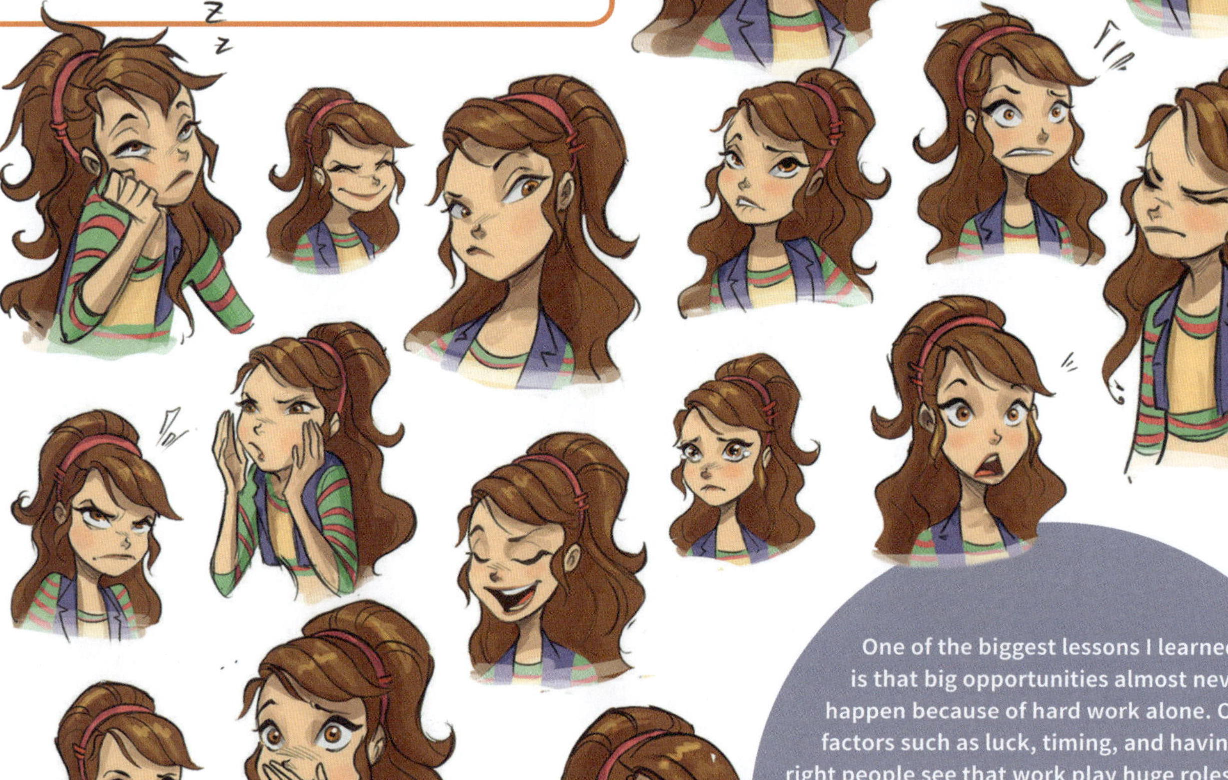

One of my favourite tasks at the studio was creating character-design sheets and playing around with different expressions. Mundoloco CGI, 2015

One of the biggest lessons I learned is that big opportunities almost never happen because of hard work alone. Other factors such as luck, timing, and having the right people see that work play huge roles as well. I think all we can do is put in our best effort and be as prepared as possible for when an opportunity presents itself. I know it can feel really scary to put yourself and your art out there, but I strongly believe that as long as we follow what we're passionate about, we will always find our way. Trust the process!

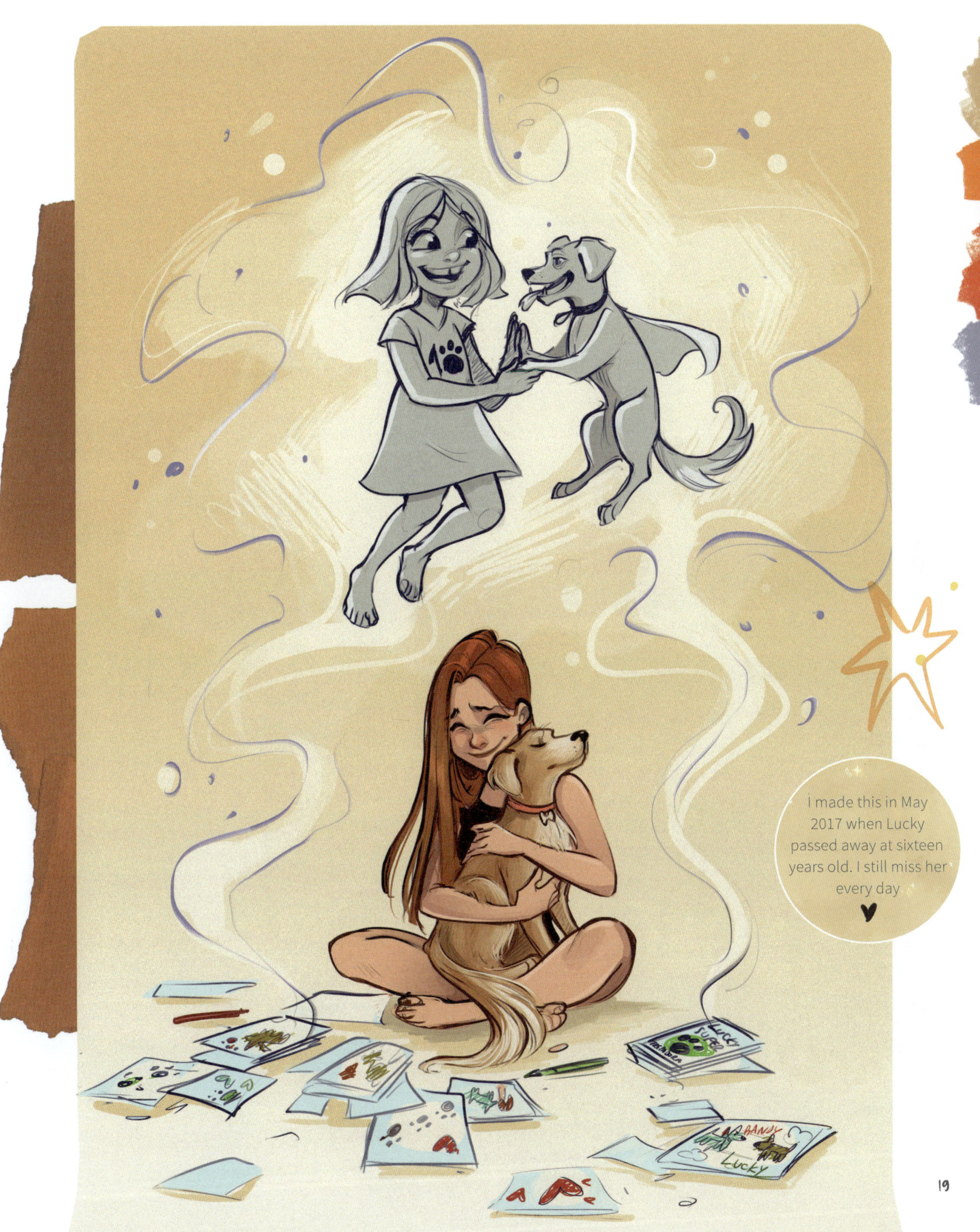

I made this in May 2017 when Lucky passed away at sixteen years old. I still miss her every day ♥

ART-STYLE DEVELOPMENT ♡

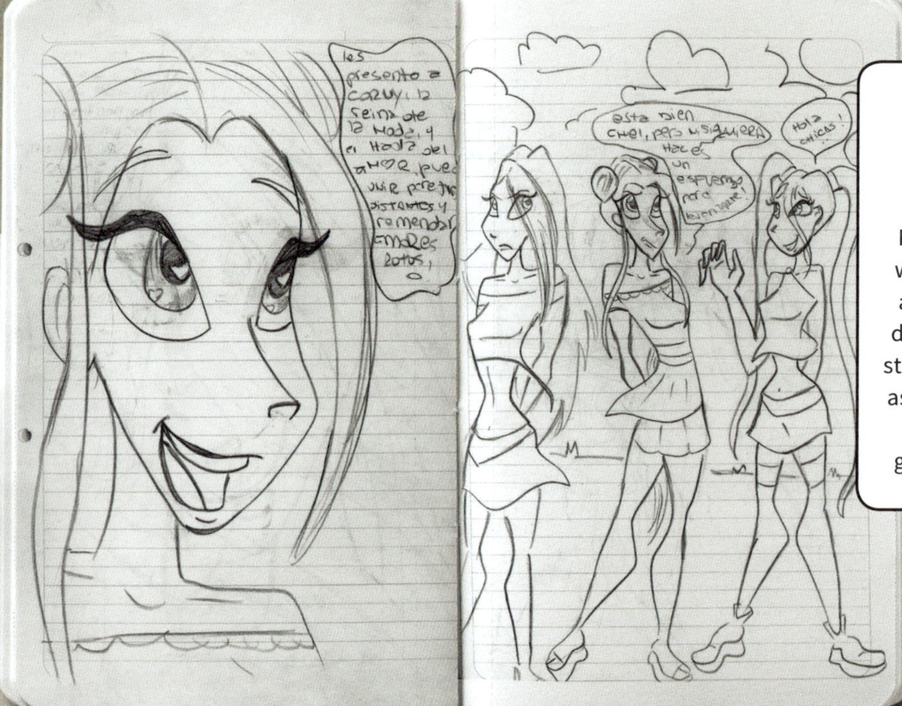

2006, 12 years old

I was simply obsessed with writing and drawing comics at this age. I filled over two dozen spiral notebooks with stories of my favourite shows, as well as random characters I'd created. I only used graphite pencils for a while.

2009, 15 years old

I remember being pretty happy with my art during this year. It was the first time I started incorporating colour and I had a lot of fun using coloured pencils. I shifted from notebooks to single A4 sheets of paper and made tons of drawings I was proud of. Although fan art was still my main focus, I made many original illustrations as well. This was also the time when things started to click with me – I found myself making more conscious decisions.

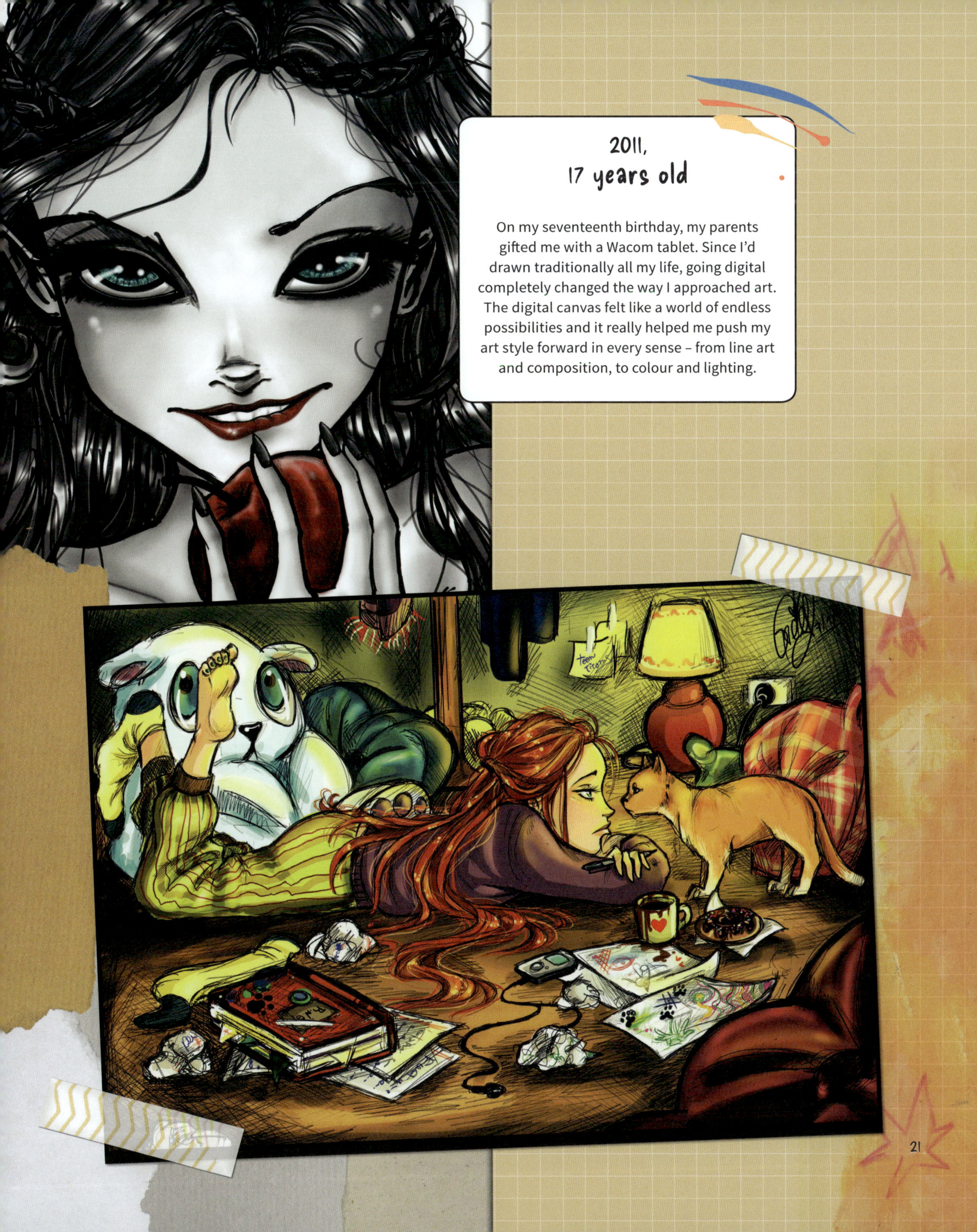

2011,
17 years old

On my seventeenth birthday, my parents gifted me with a Wacom tablet. Since I'd drawn traditionally all my life, going digital completely changed the way I approached art. The digital canvas felt like a world of endless possibilities and it really helped me push my art style forward in every sense – from line art and composition, to colour and lighting.

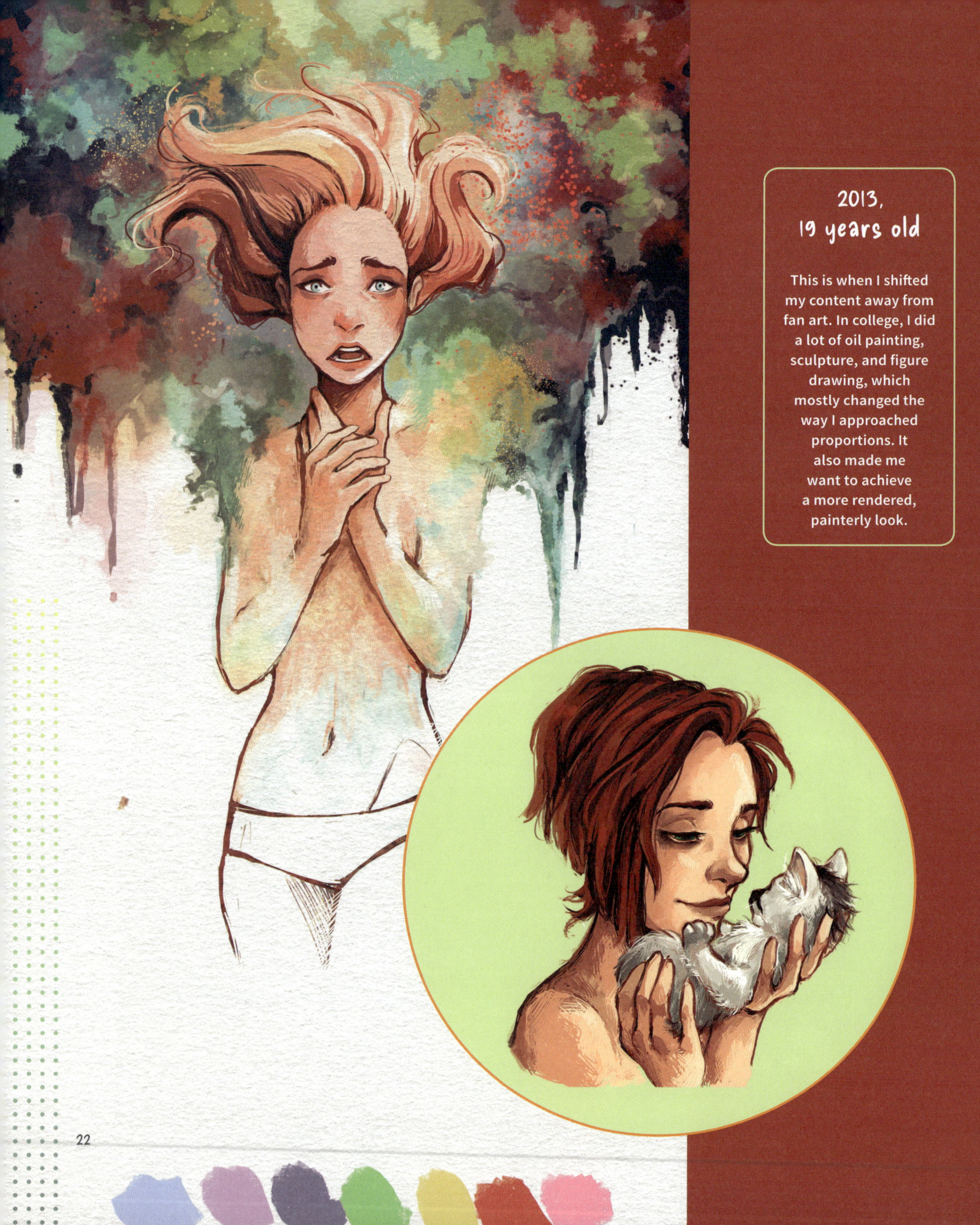

2013, 19 years old

This is when I shifted my content away from fan art. In college, I did a lot of oil painting, sculpture, and figure drawing, which mostly changed the way I approached proportions. It also made me want to achieve a more rendered, painterly look.

2016,
22 years old

Working in animation full-time left me almost no energy to make digital illustrations for myself, which lasted a couple of years. To compensate for that, I decided to buy a small Moleskine sketchbook that I took everywhere with me.

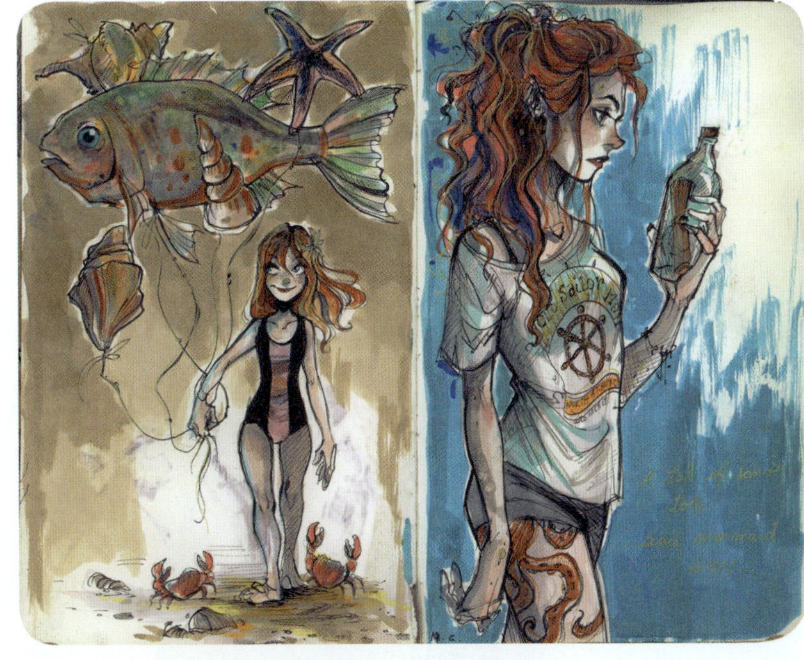

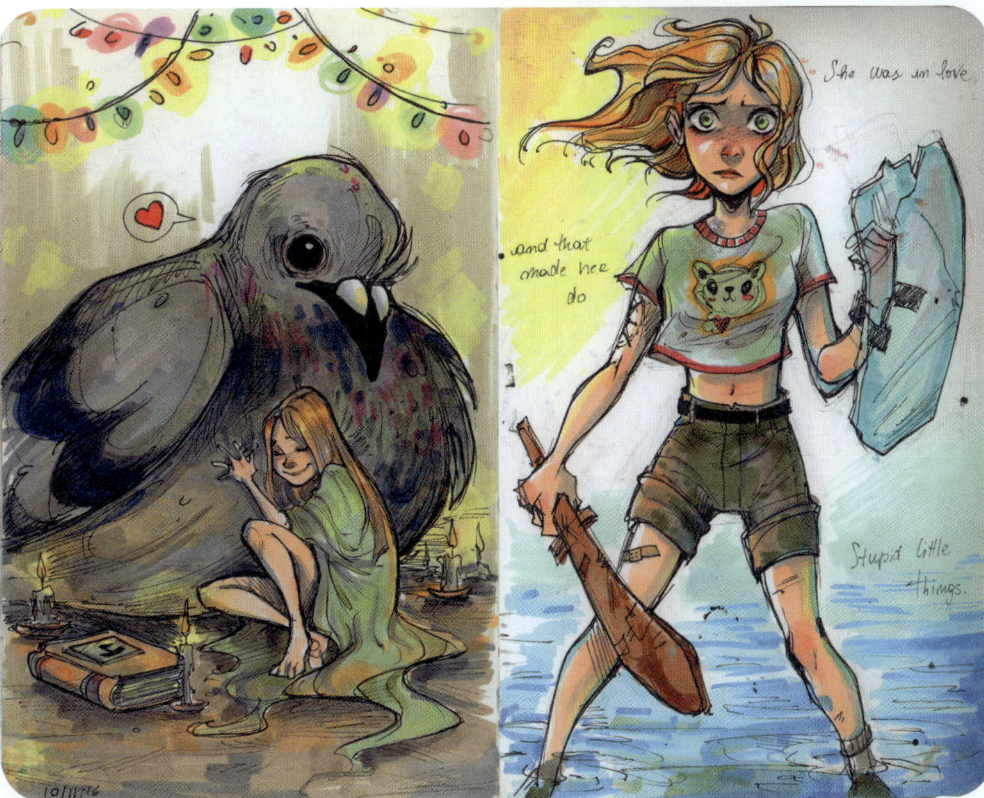

I fell completely in love with watercolours and the idea of having all my drawings – good and bad – gathered in a single book. I started to fill out one sketchbook each year from then onwards.

2020, 26 years old

This year was very experimental for me. I understood that my true love wasn't exclusively digital or traditional, but rather somewhere between them both. I discovered that I enjoyed playing around with different tools and mixing mediums. It felt right to not always follow the same formula to achieve the results I wanted.

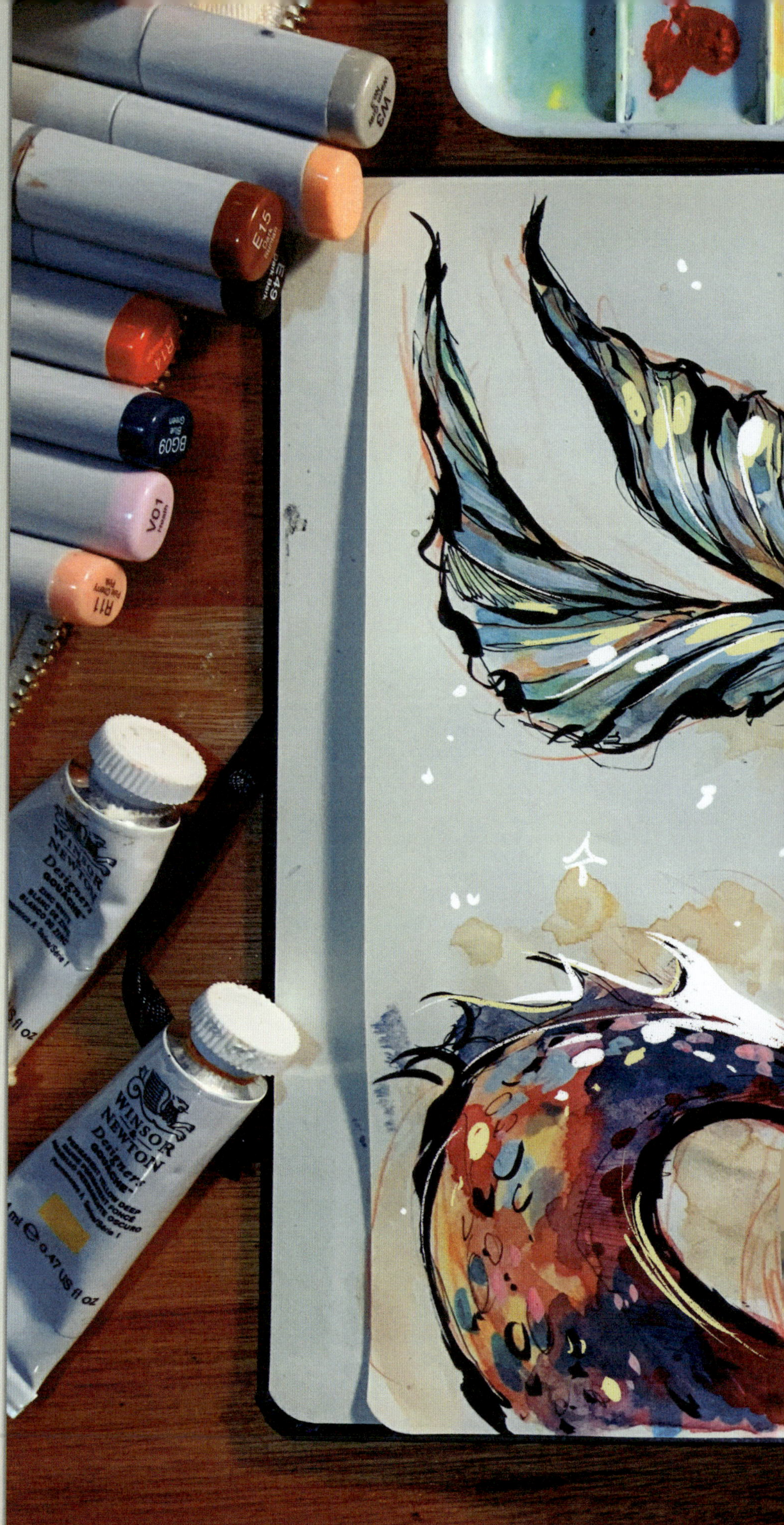

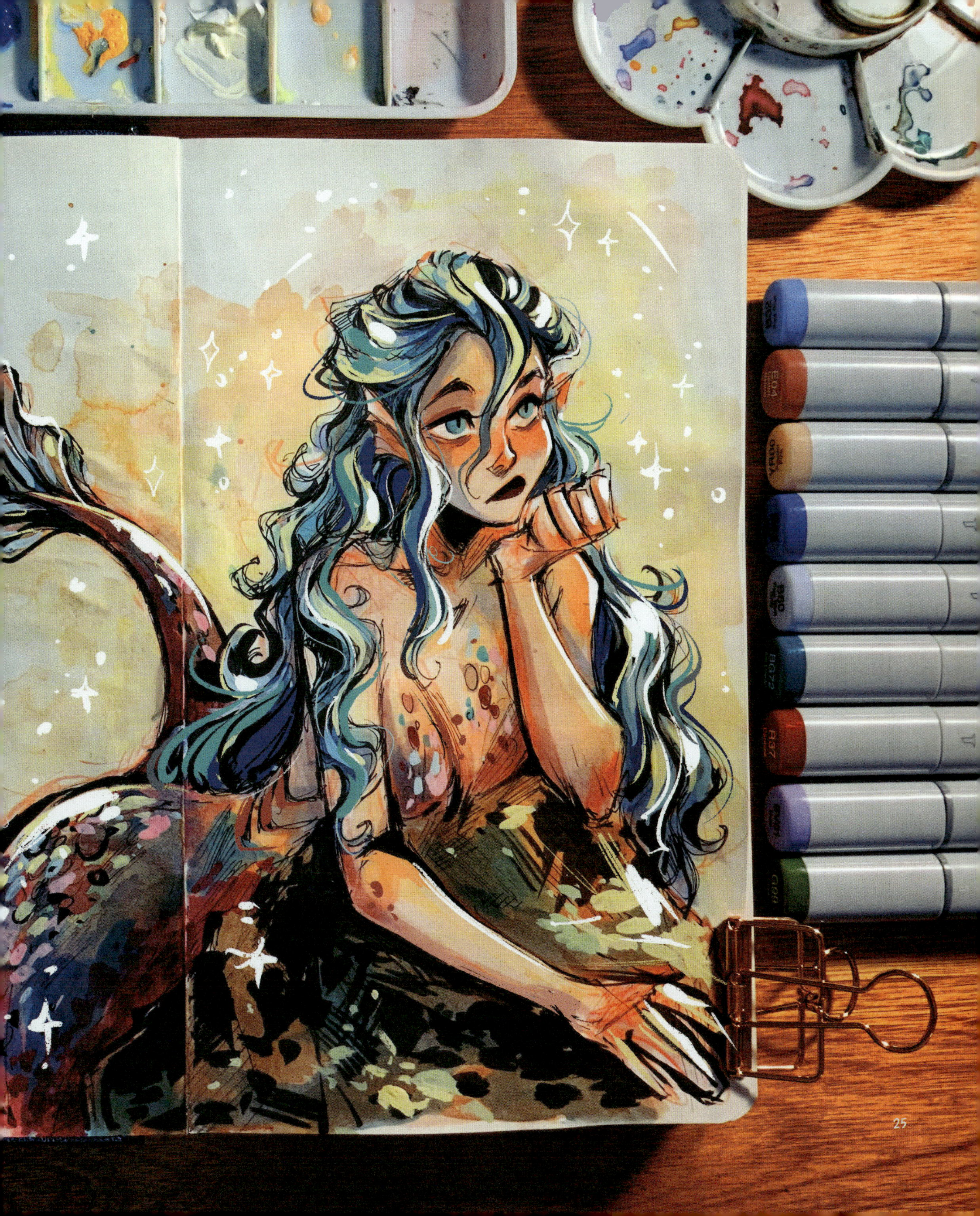

Sometimes, the best way to see how much we've improved is by redrawing old art.

It's such a fun, heart-warming exercise that can provide a big boost of motivation. I created these two fairies in the eighth grade and I was really proud of them back then. My fourteen-year-old self would be thrilled to see how far we've come!

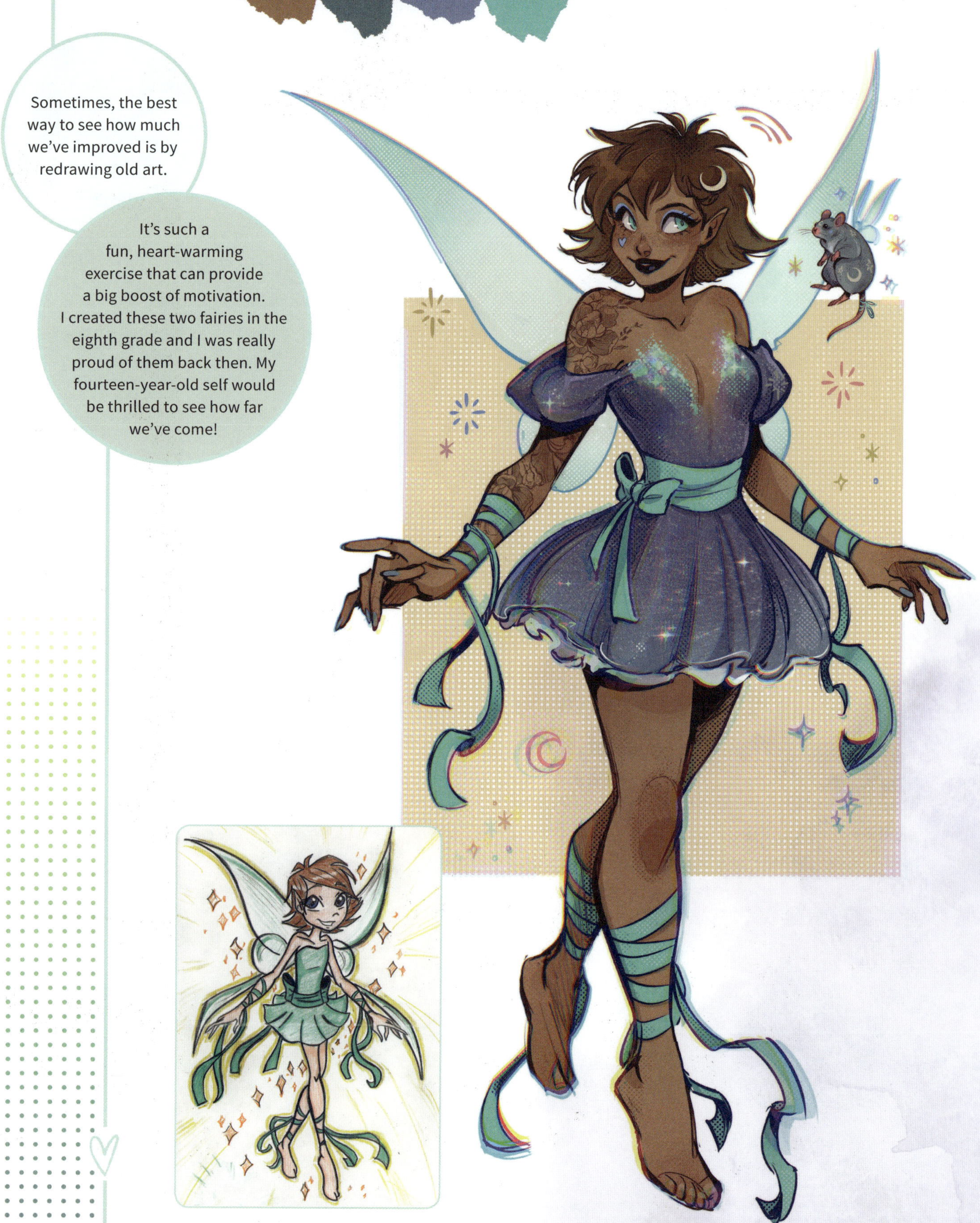

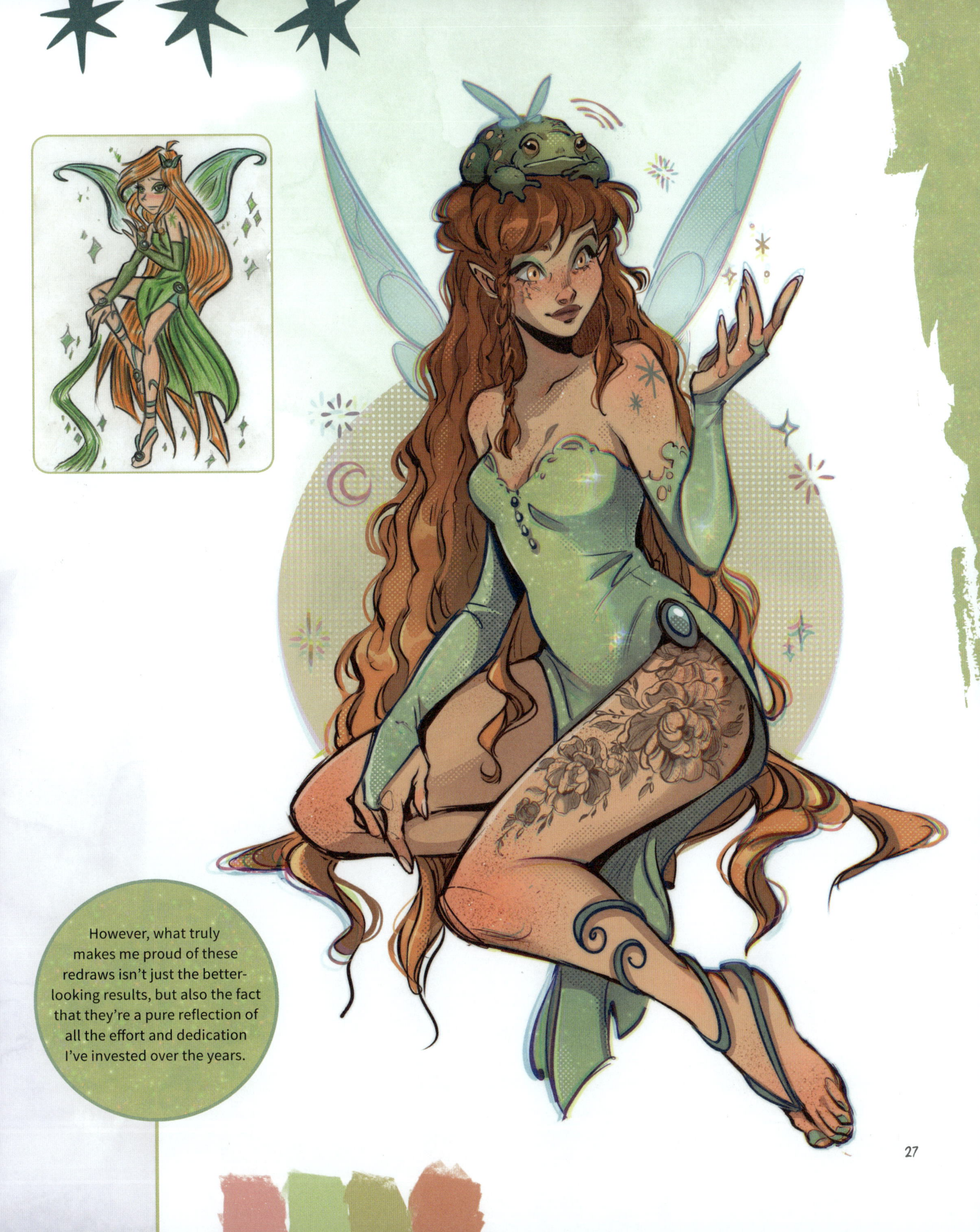

However, what truly makes me proud of these redraws isn't just the better-looking results, but also the fact that they're a pure reflection of all the effort and dedication I've invested over the years.

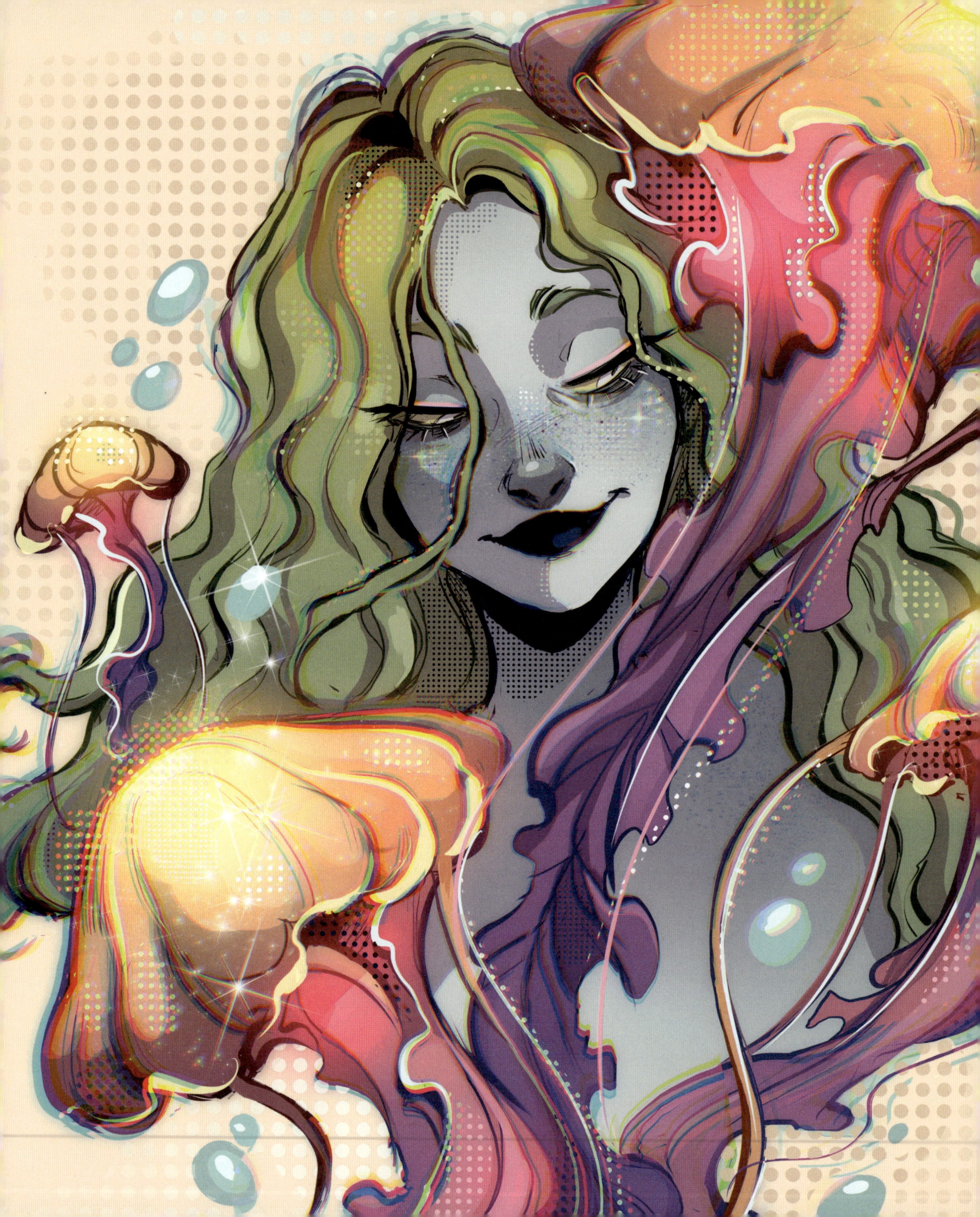

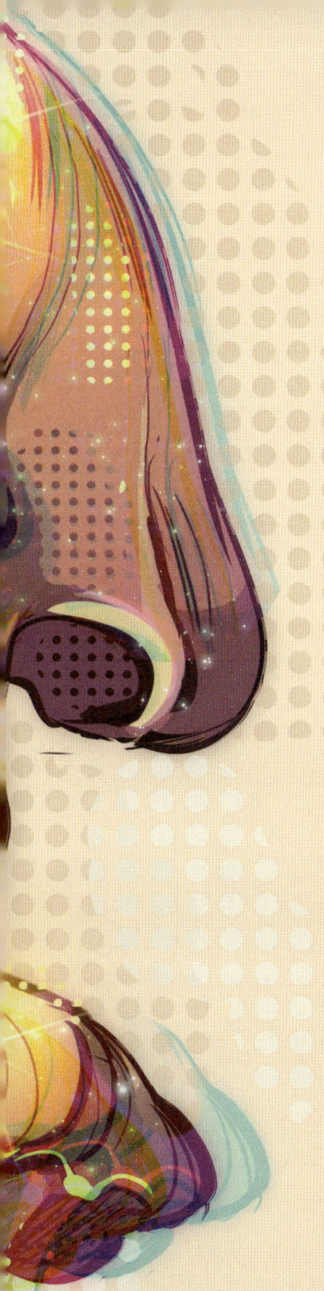

GALLERY: FANTASY FOCUS

I tend to draw things that are far removed from reality. I don't feel connected with realism as a style and I suppose the same goes for the topics I gravitate towards. I've always loved fantasy and all things magical: fairies, mermaids, and mythical creatures. For me, it's all about drawing characters that are colourful yet mysterious, as well as places that feel otherworldly, sometimes bordering the line between beautiful and unsettling. Hidden messages and experimenting with concepts, or little details that can be interpreted in different ways, have been some of the things I enjoy doing the most.

It's hard to put into words *why* I feel so driven to make illustrations that are often connected to the sea, but I know my dad is definitely one of the reasons I find it so fascinating. He has a very unique professional background; he was a scuba diver and worked on shipwreck sites when he was very young, and has also participated in more than fifty Antarctic expeditions. Naturally, my sister and I grew up hearing all about his stories – the places he visited, the things he saw, and the animals he studied.

Each summer, before he left to work away for a couple of months, we took time off as a family to go to the sea or lakes in southern Argentina. I remember being terrified of the depths at first because my imagination was constantly envisioning different creepy creatures that could've been lurking beneath my feet. Nevertheless, I always tried to push myself, learning how to hold my breath for longer and swim deeper. I started to enjoy the adrenaline that came with exploring the unknown and discovering the ocean wildlife. Leaving the city behind to spend two weeks surrounded by nature became the thing I most looked forward to each year.

When I'm far away from the sea – which, sadly, is the majority of the time – I feel an endless longing. I guess my drive to paint maritime stuff comes from that melancholic place; a mix between home and adventure.

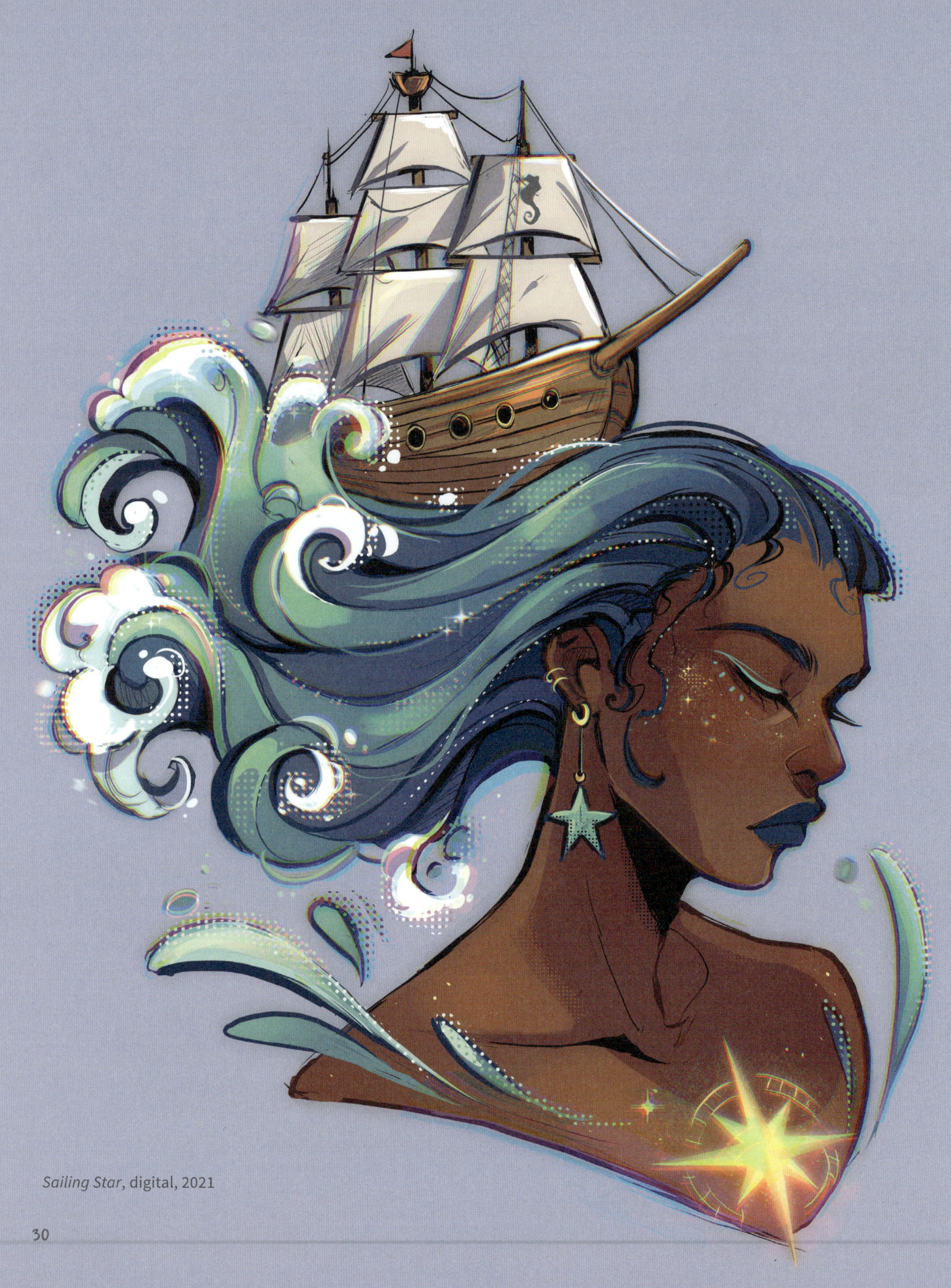

Sailing Star, digital, 2021

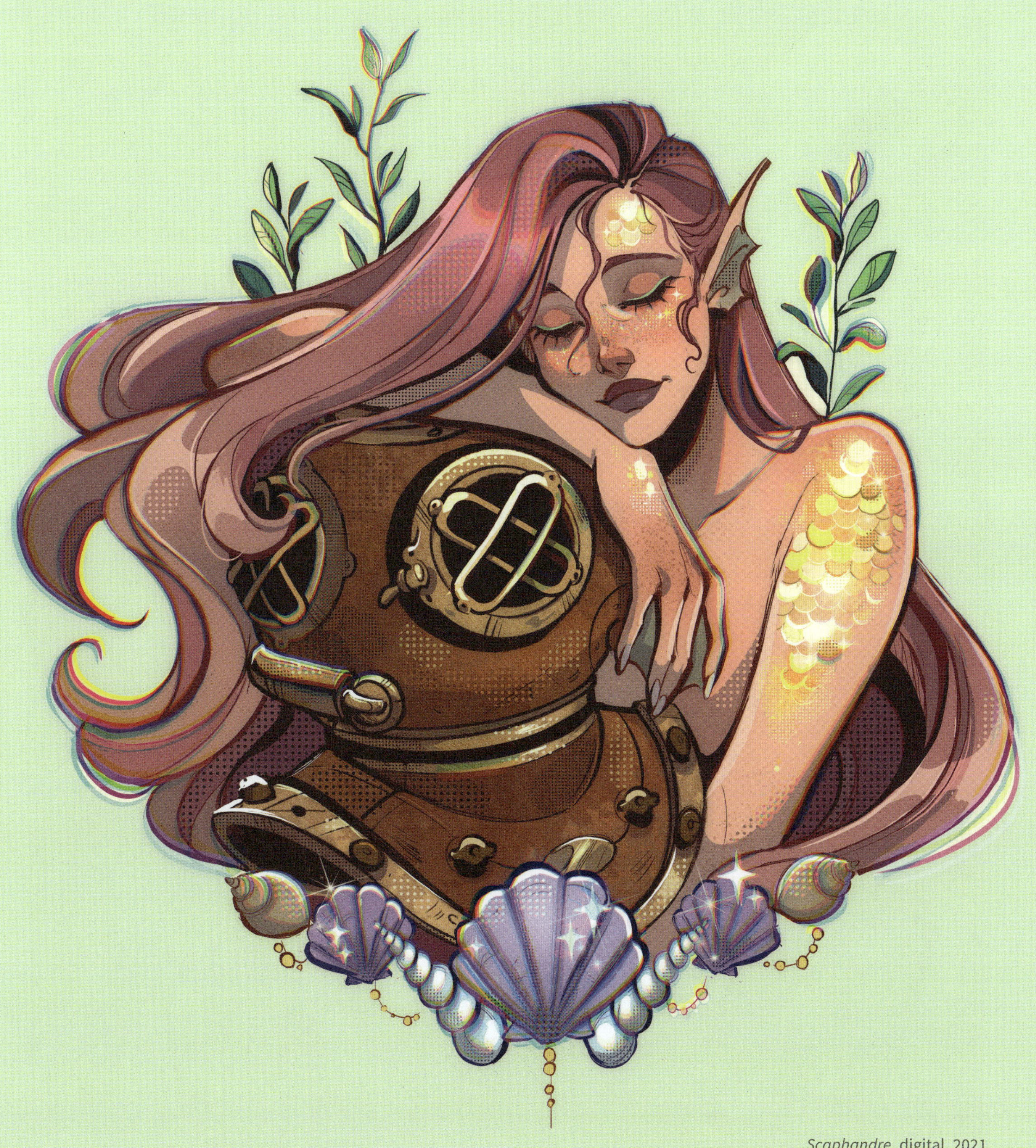

Scaphandre, digital, 2021

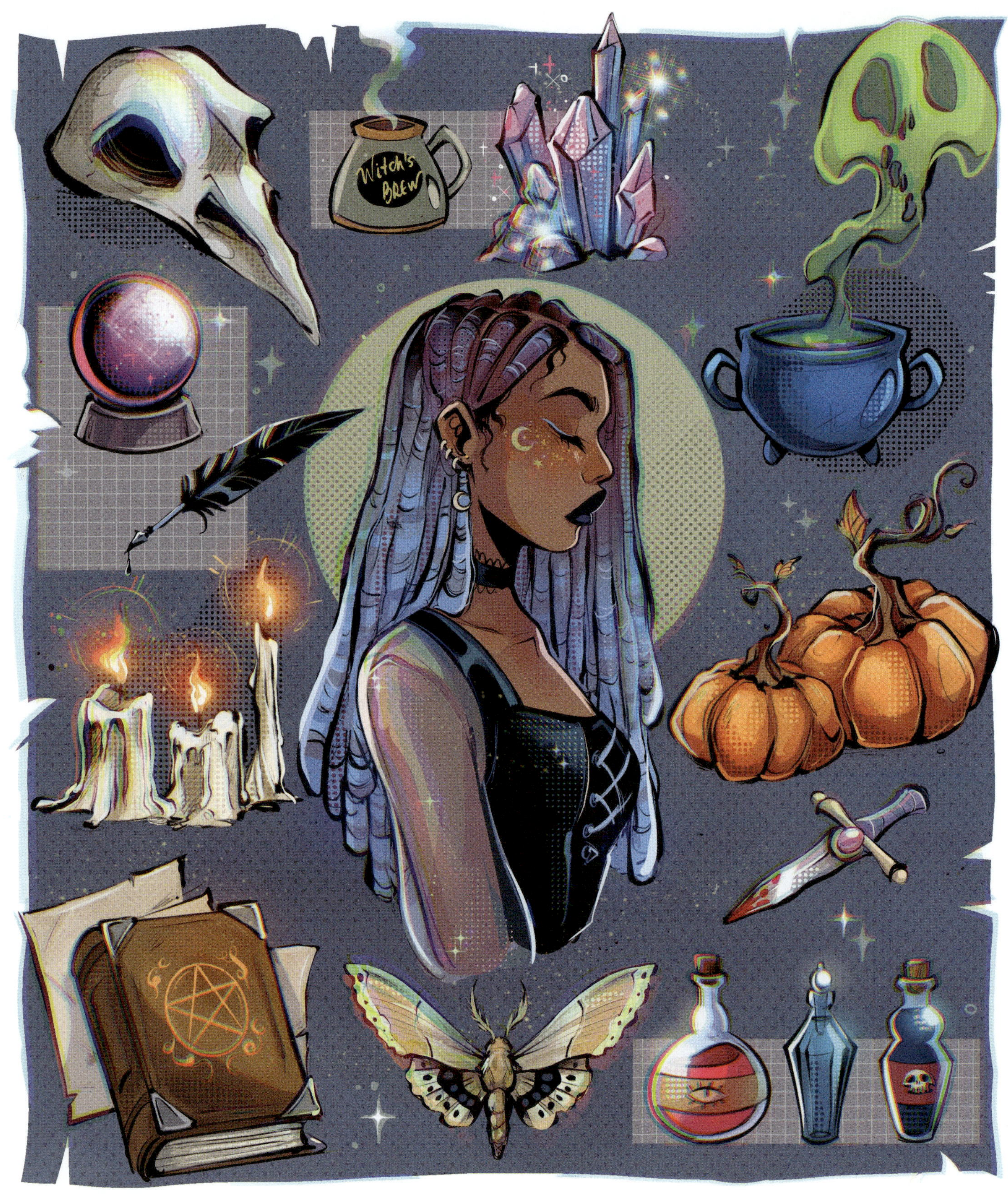

Witchy Moodboard, digital, 2021

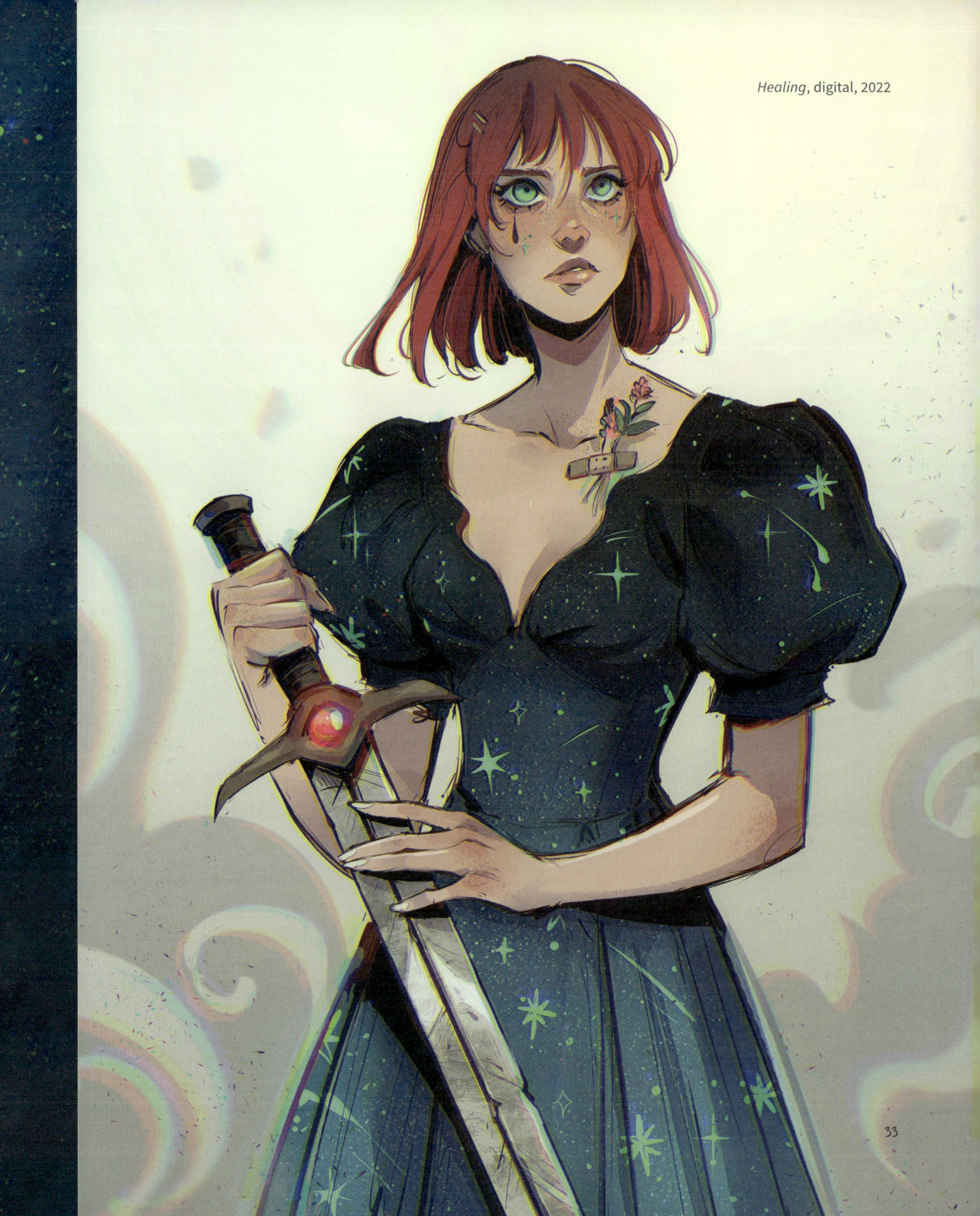

Healing, digital, 2022

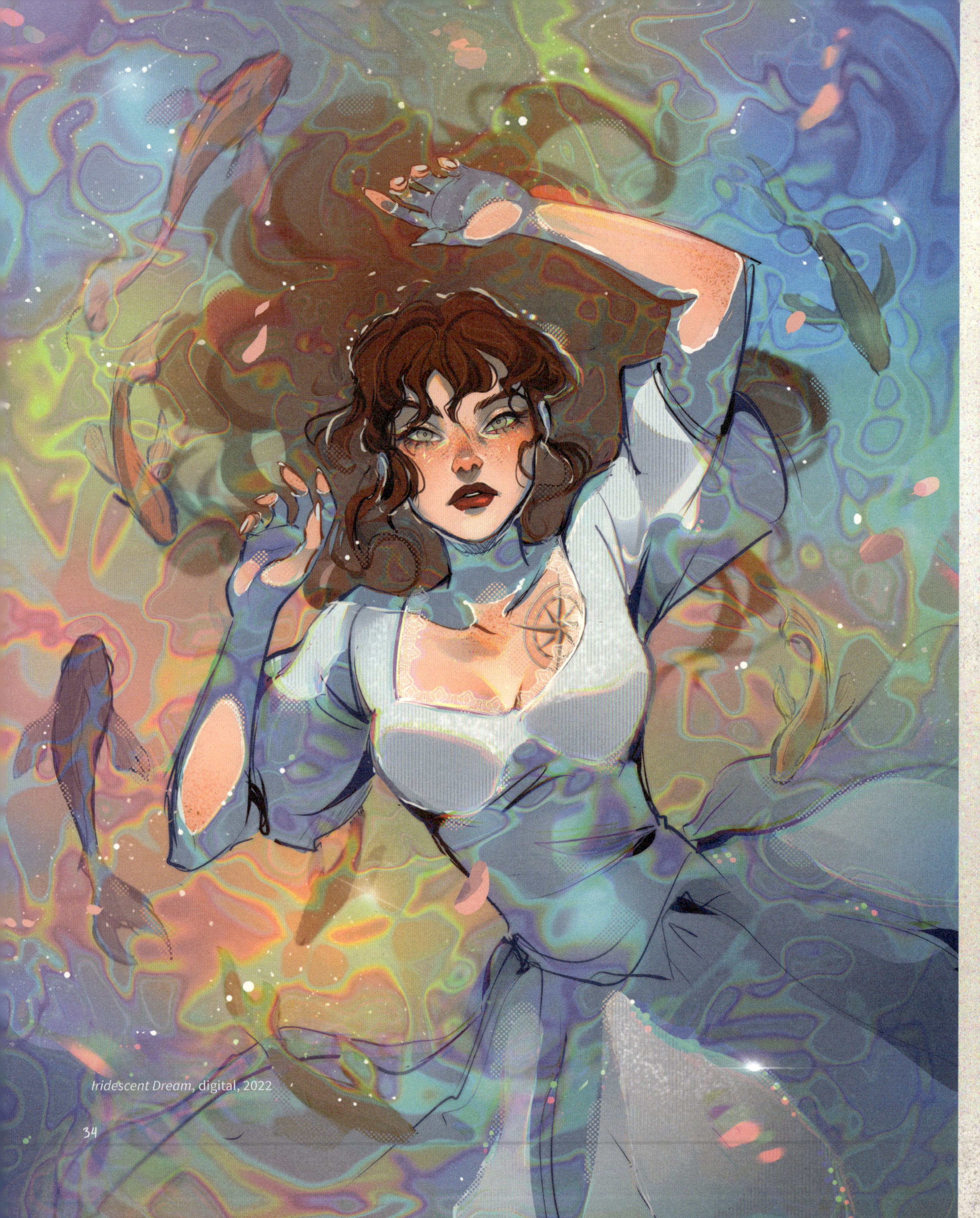

Iridescent Dream, digital, 2022

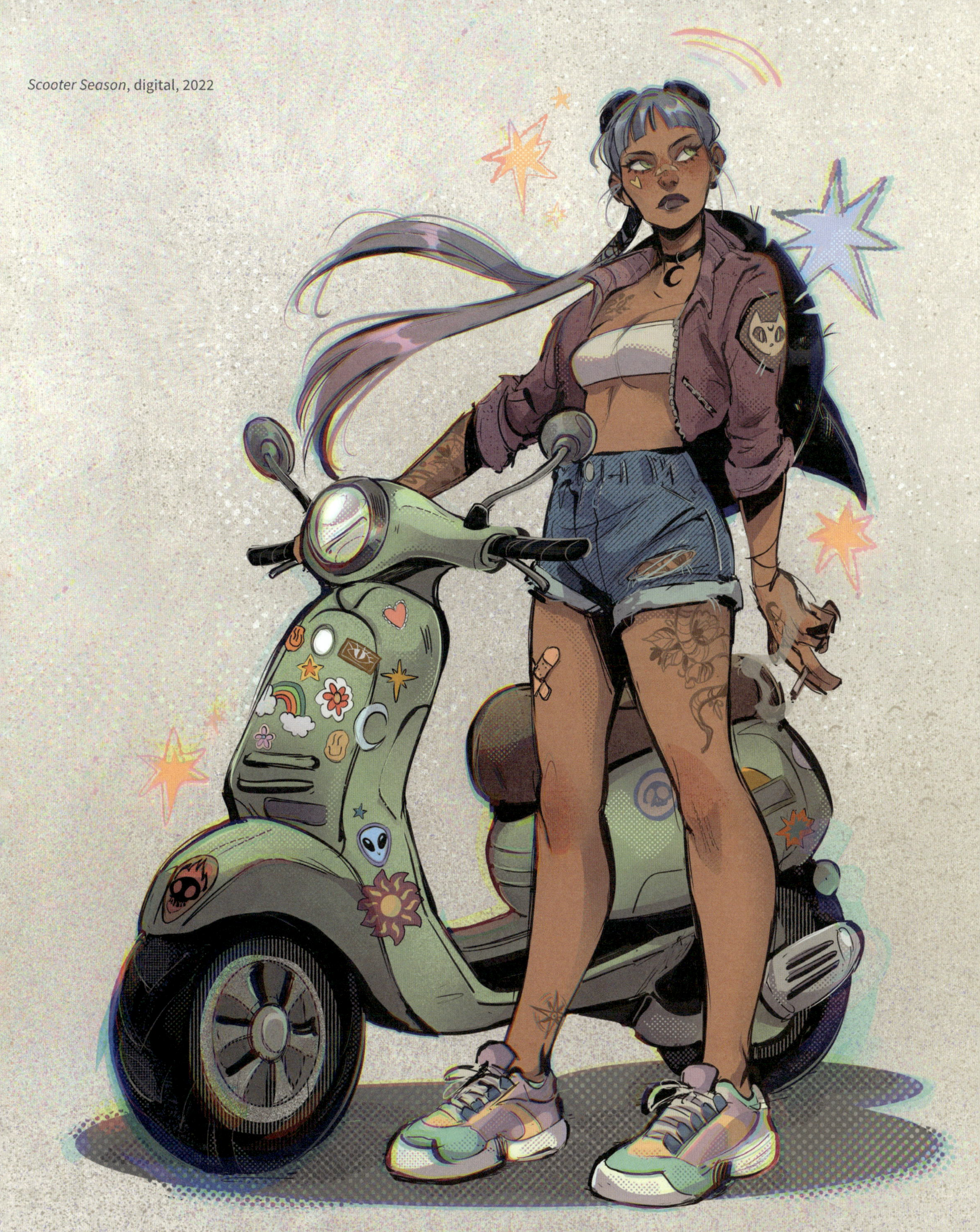

Scooter Season, digital, 2022

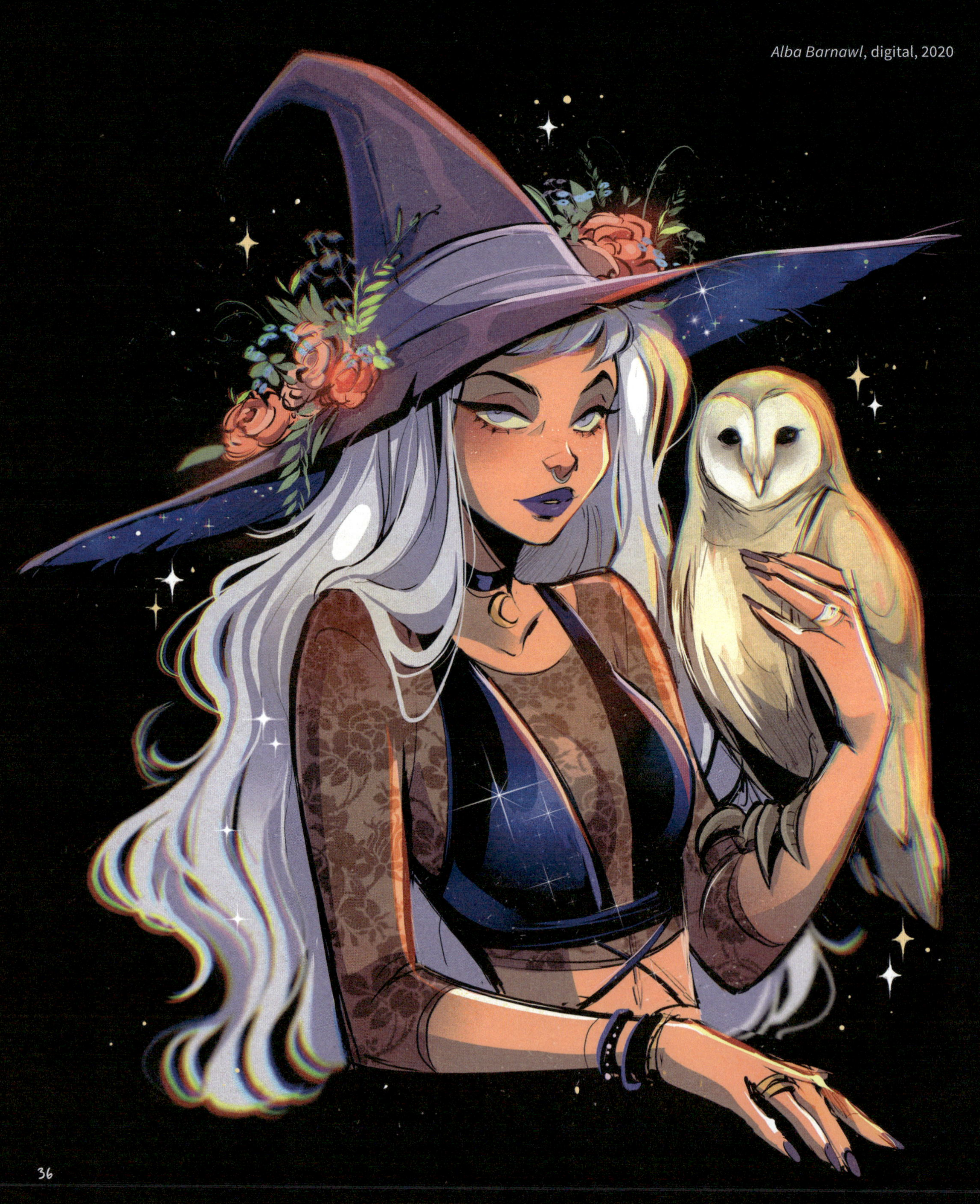

Alba Barnawl, digital, 2020

Witch's Study at Night Light, digital, 2022

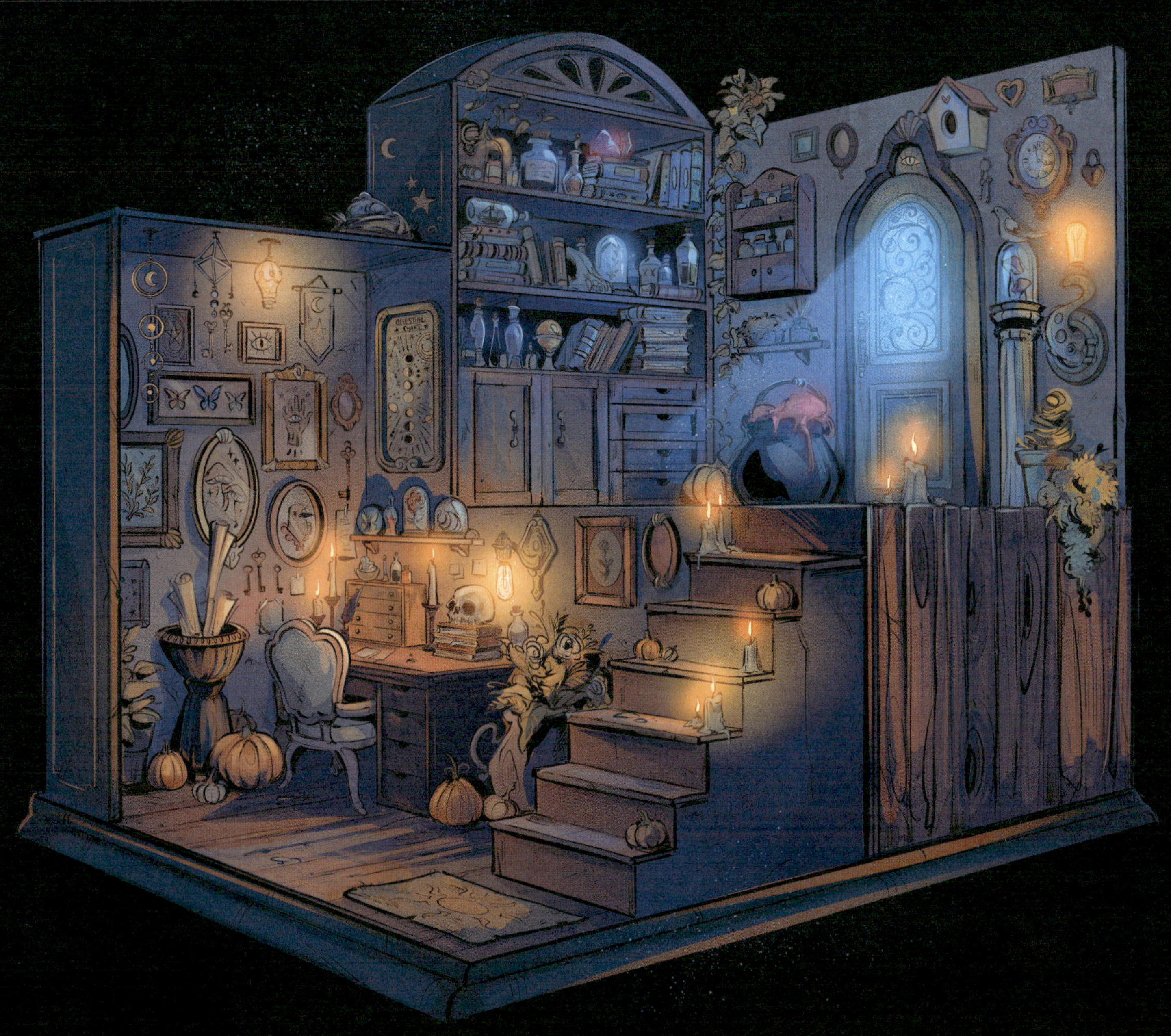

Barracuda, digital, 2021

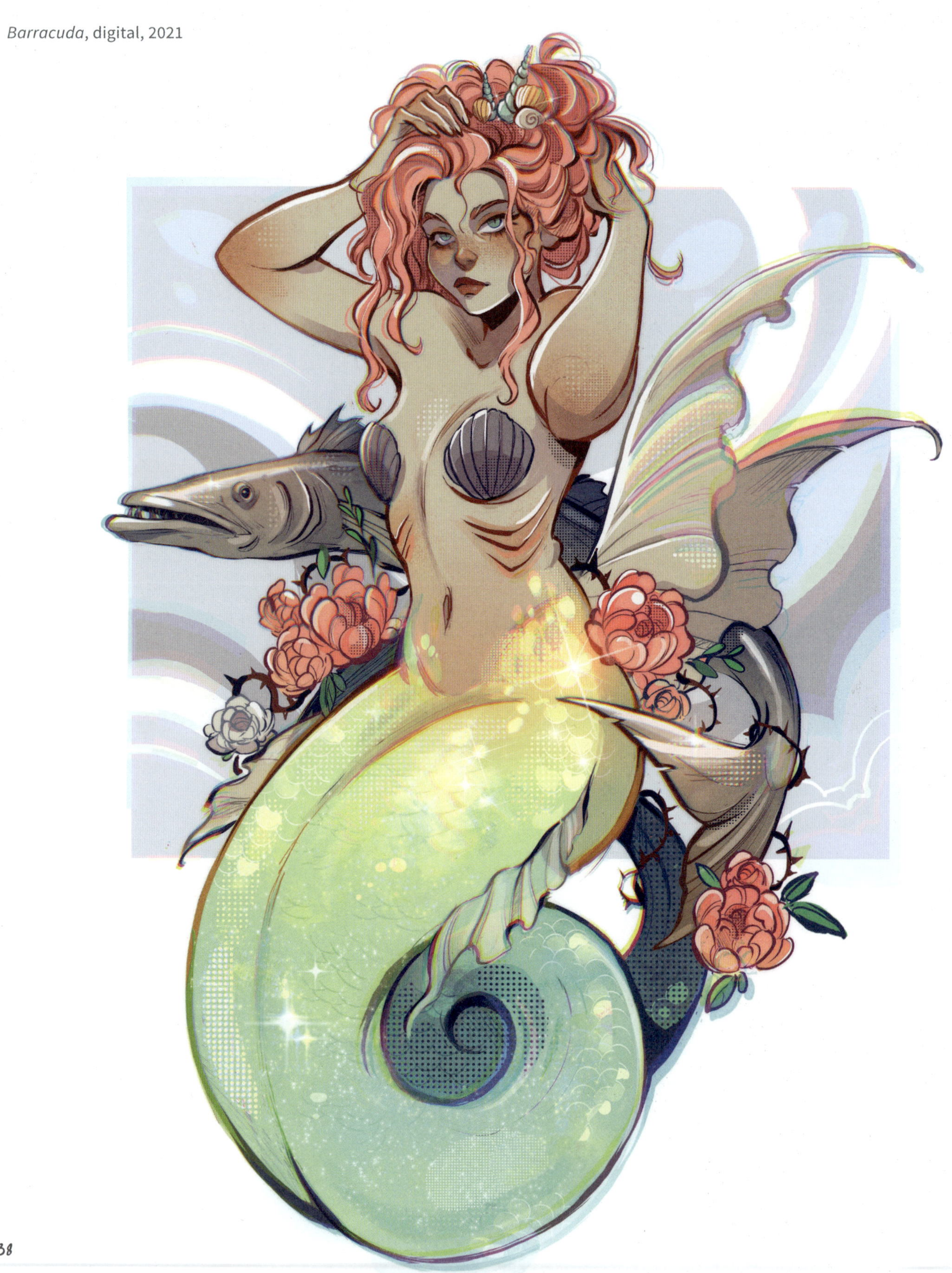

Witch's Study at Day Light, digital, 2022

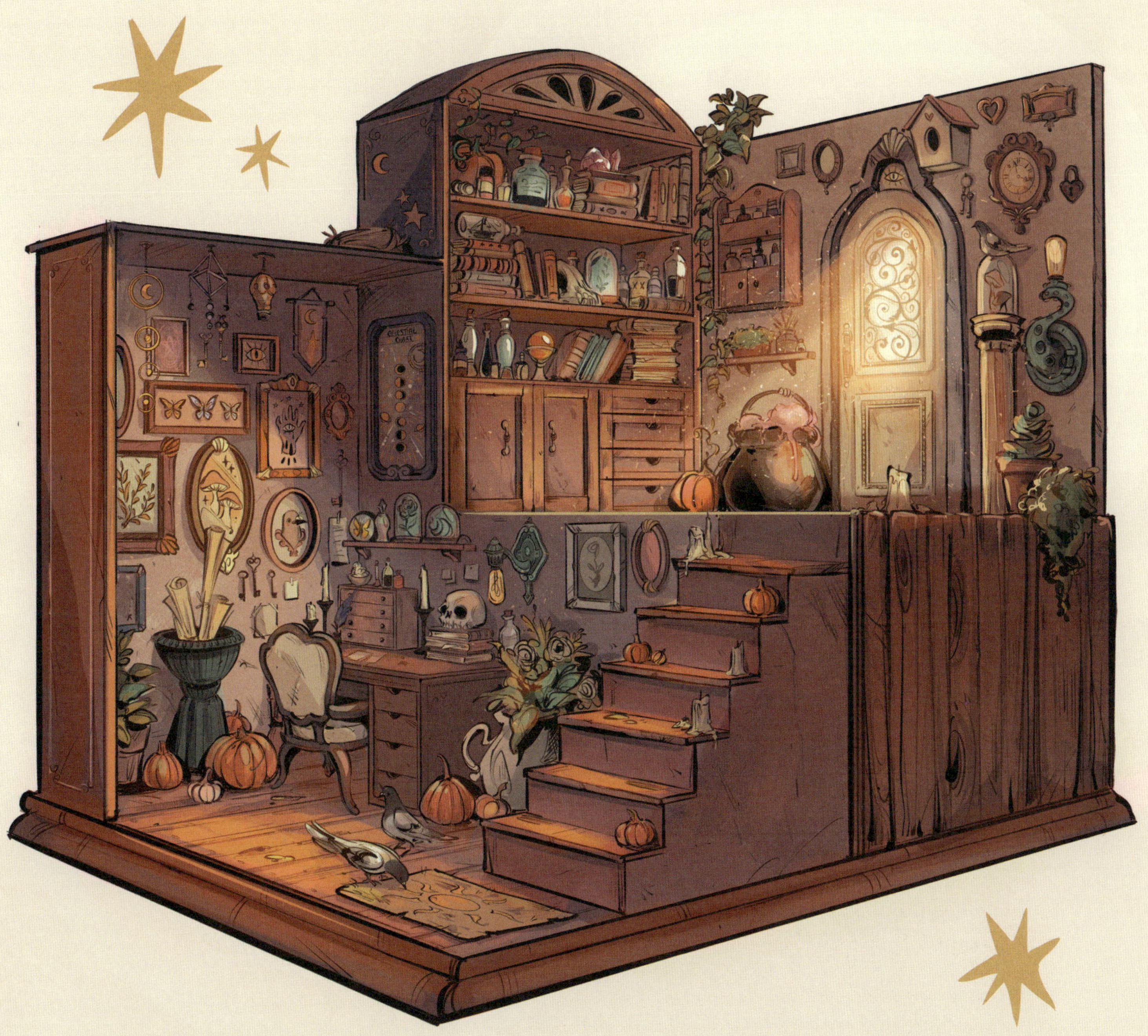

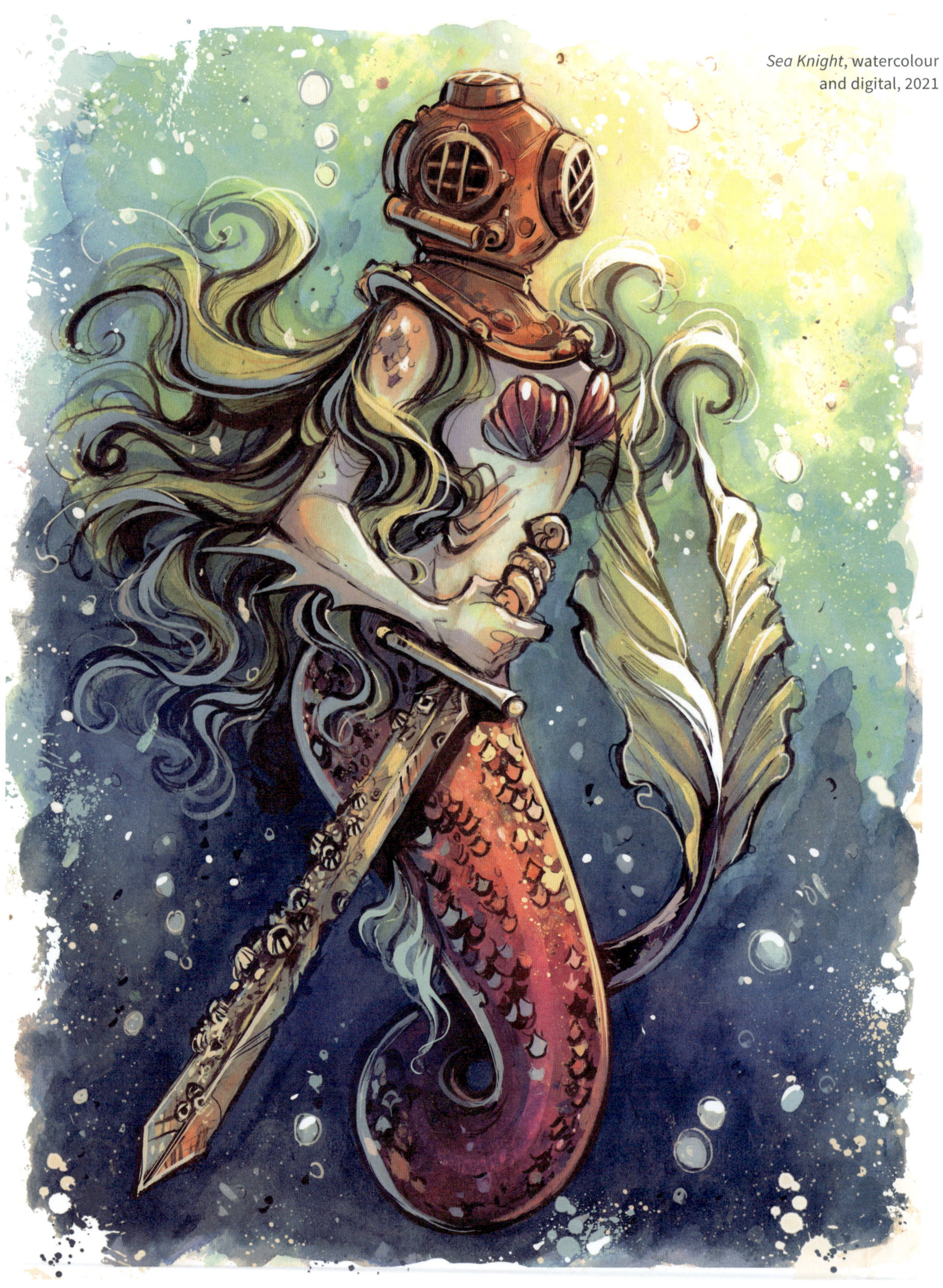

Sea Knight, watercolour and digital, 2021

Lily Pad Mystery, watercolour and digital, 2021

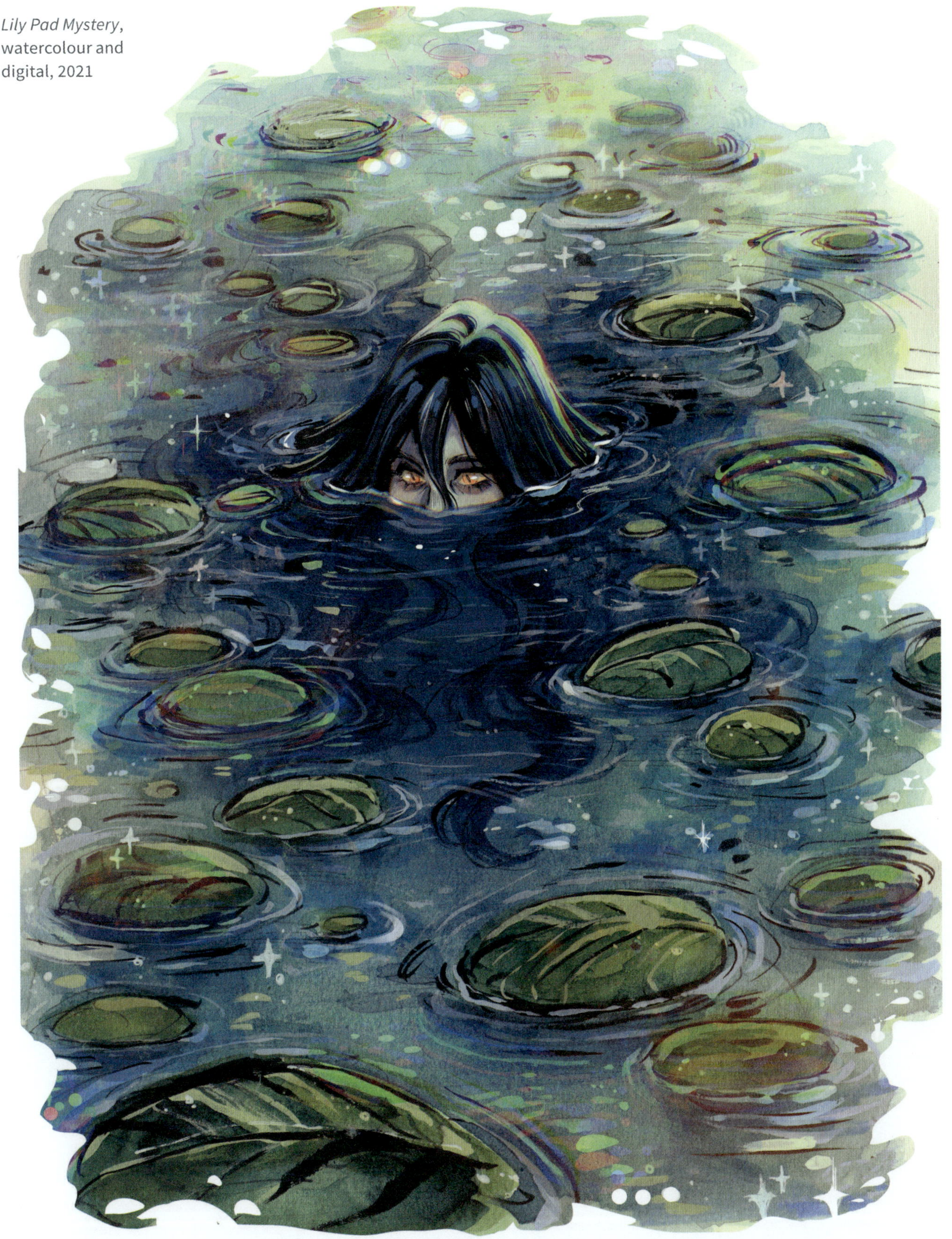

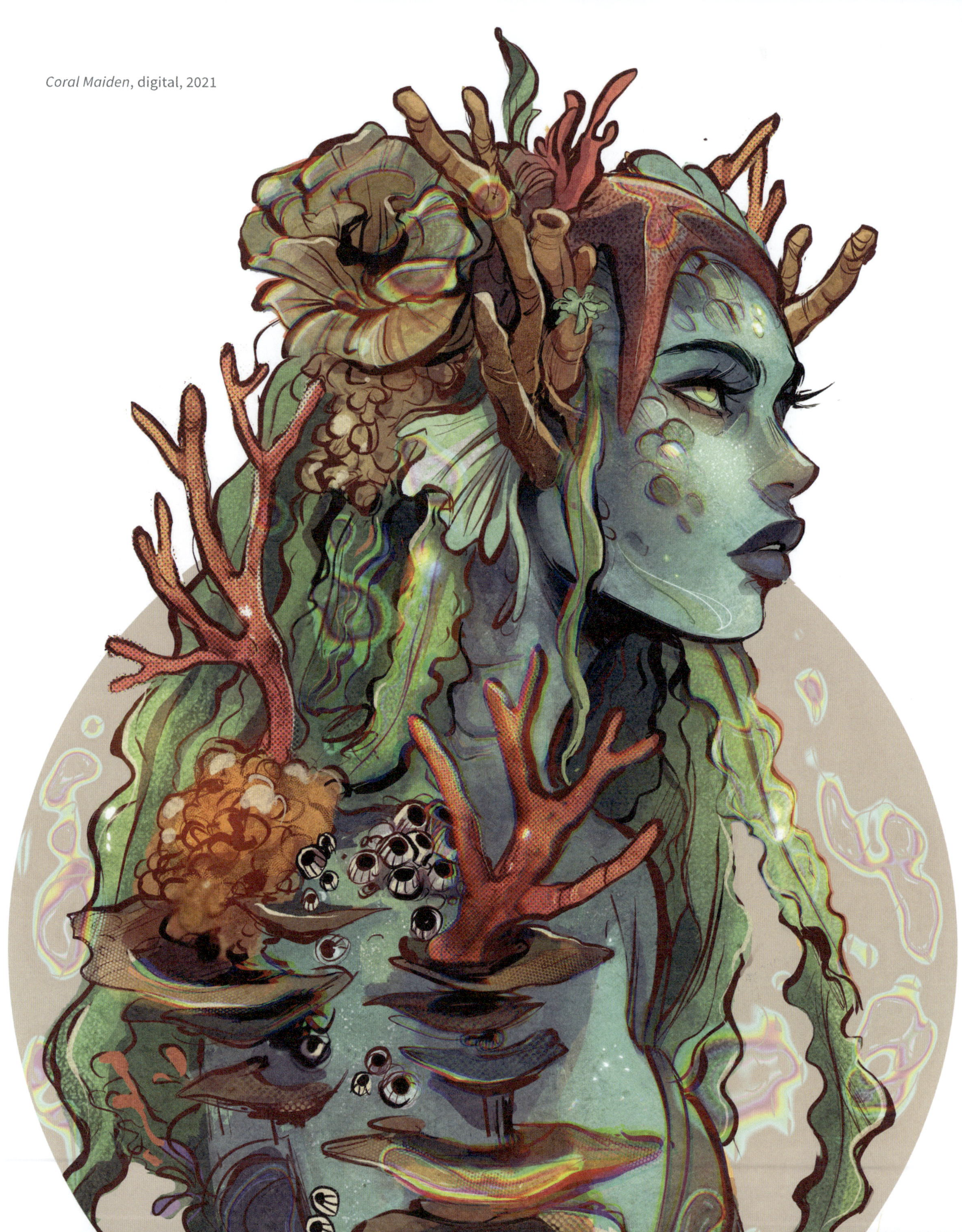

Coral Maiden, digital, 2021

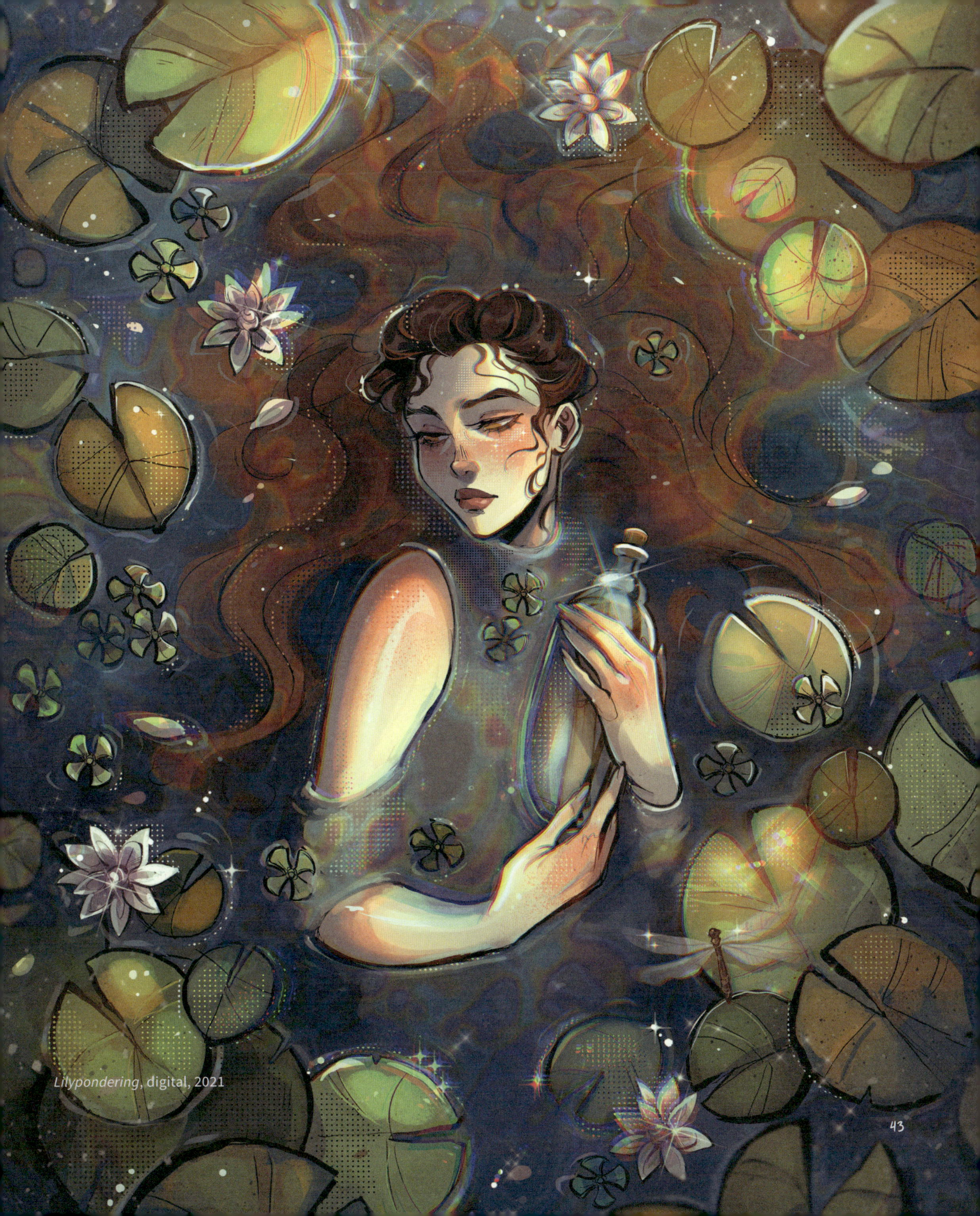

Lilypondering, digital, 2021

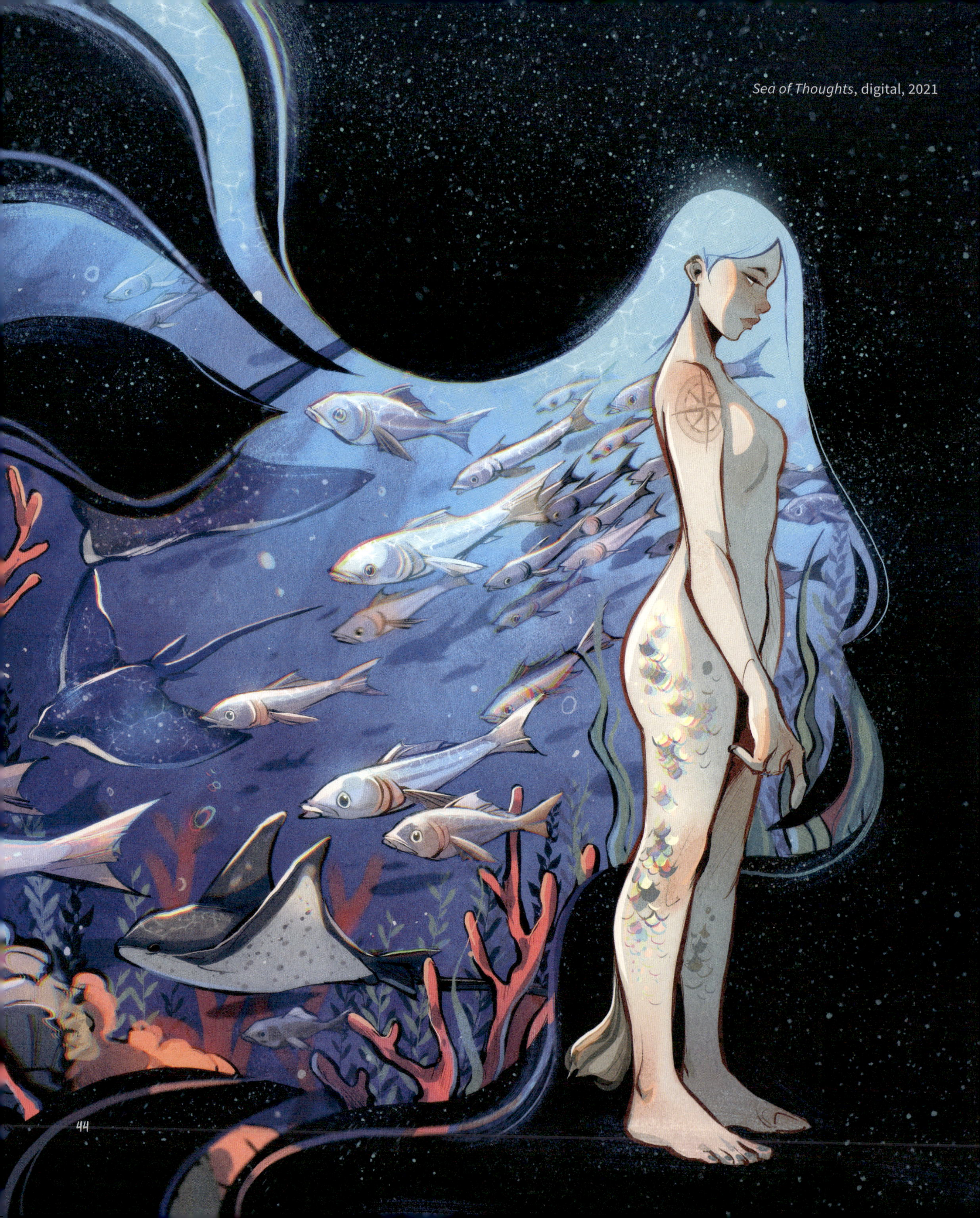

Sea of Thoughts, digital, 2021

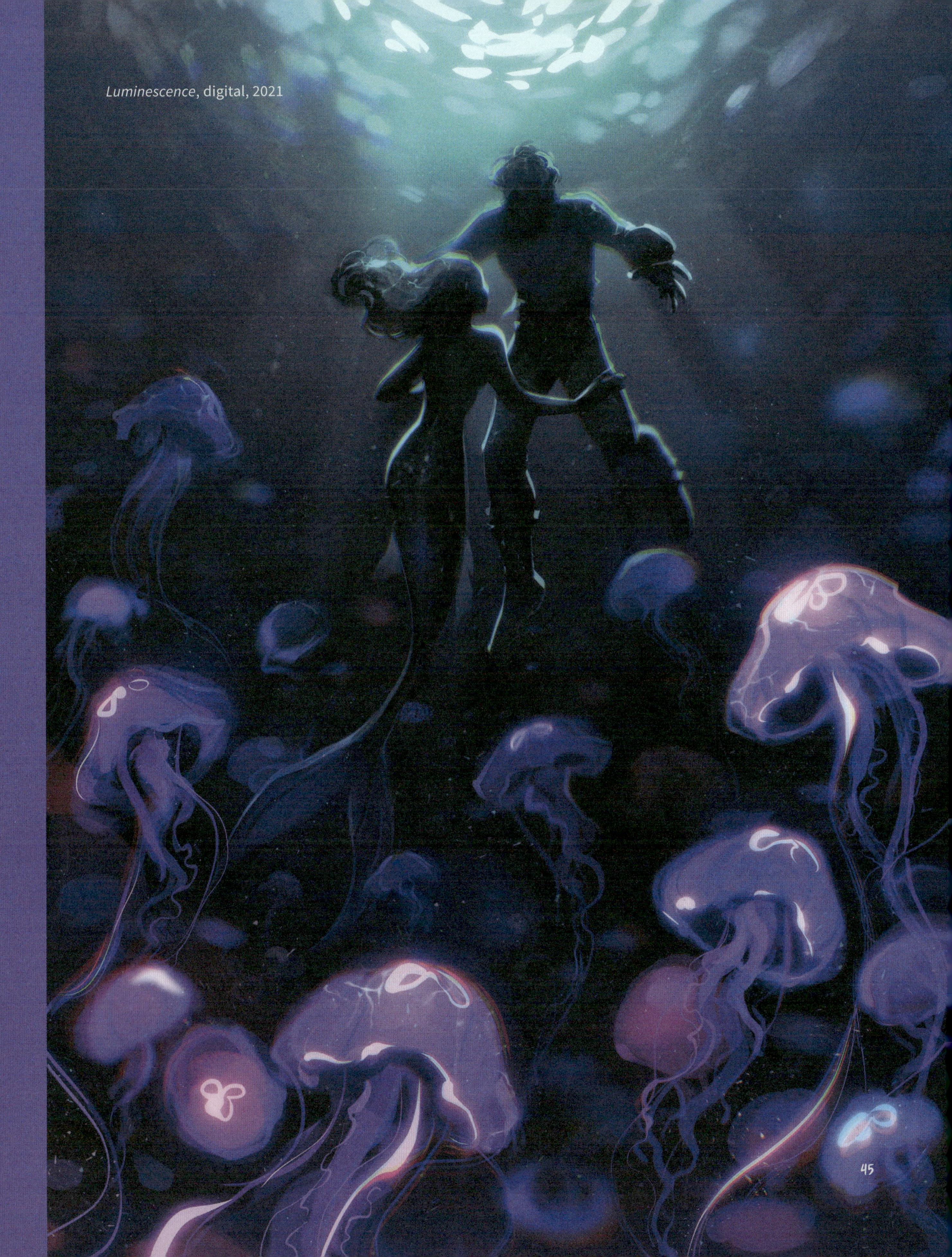

Luminescence, digital, 2021

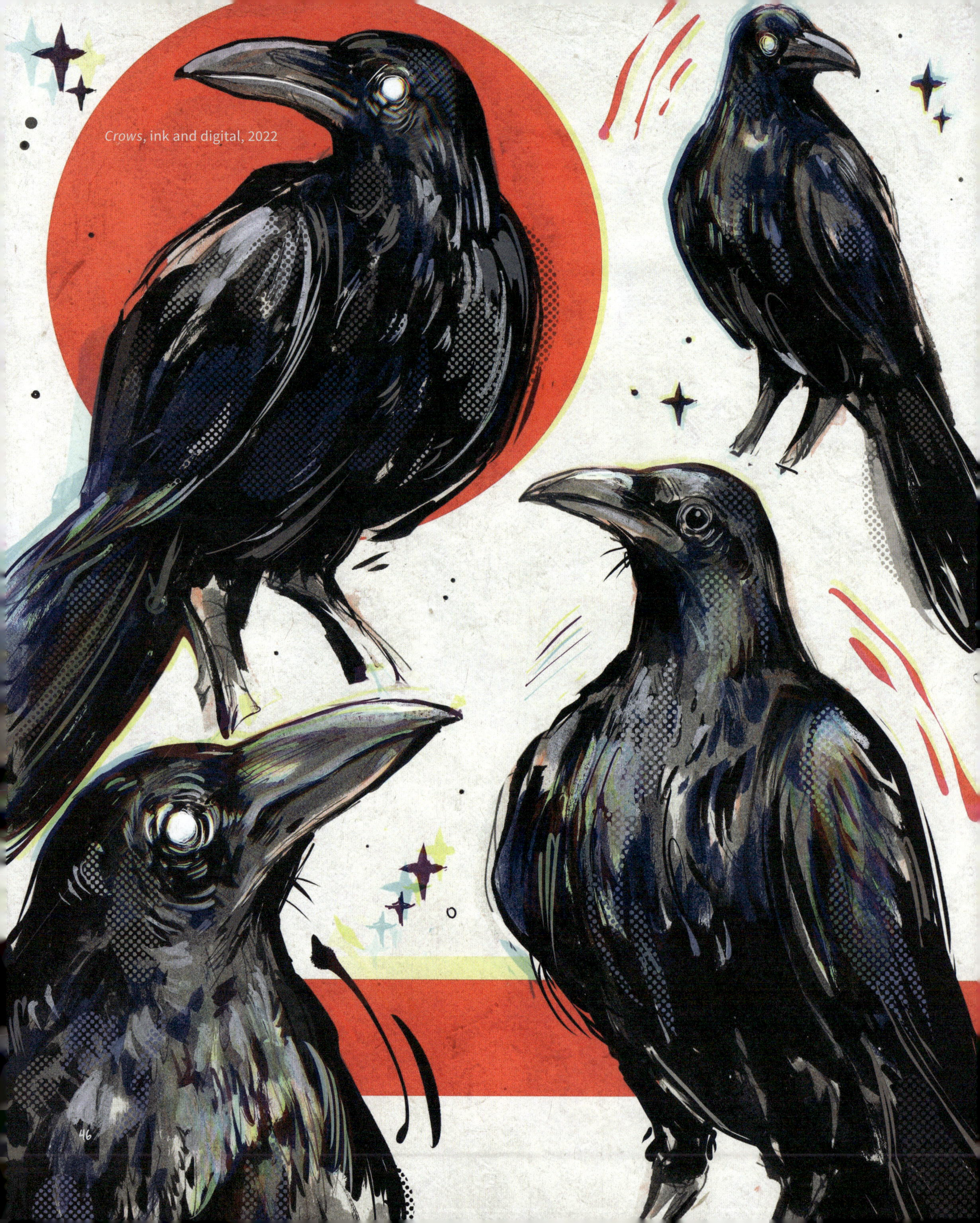

Crows, ink and digital, 2022

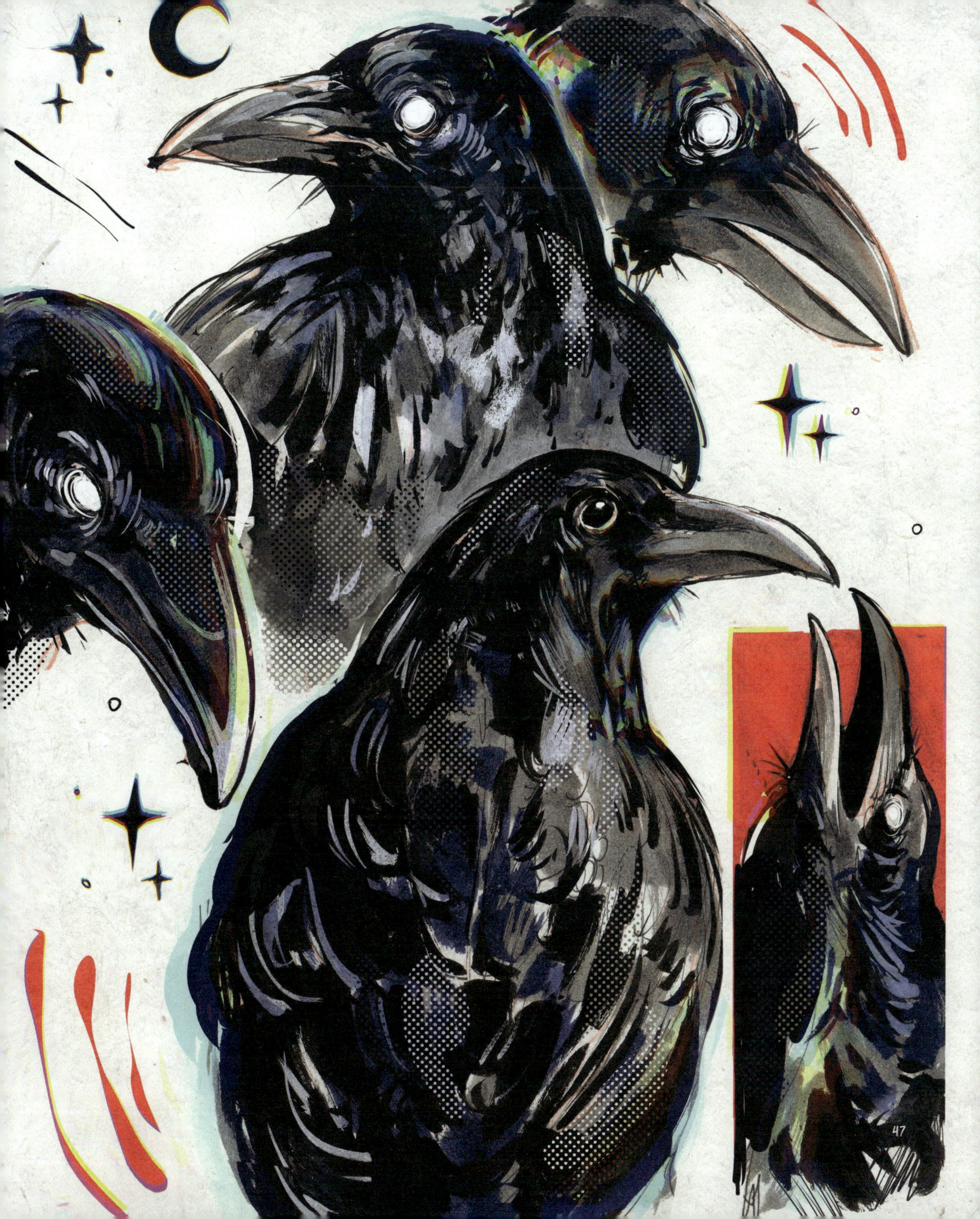

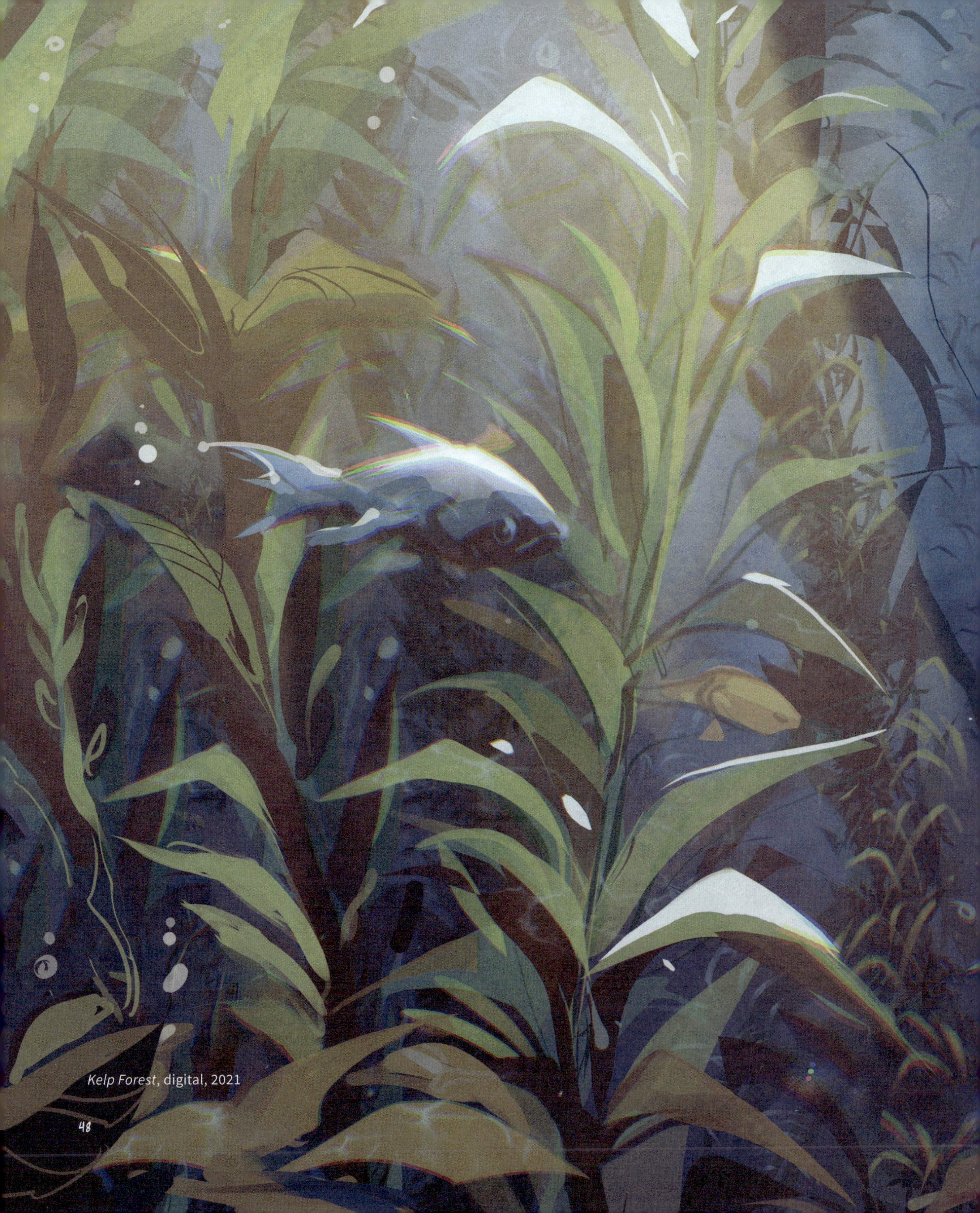

Kelp Forest, digital, 2021

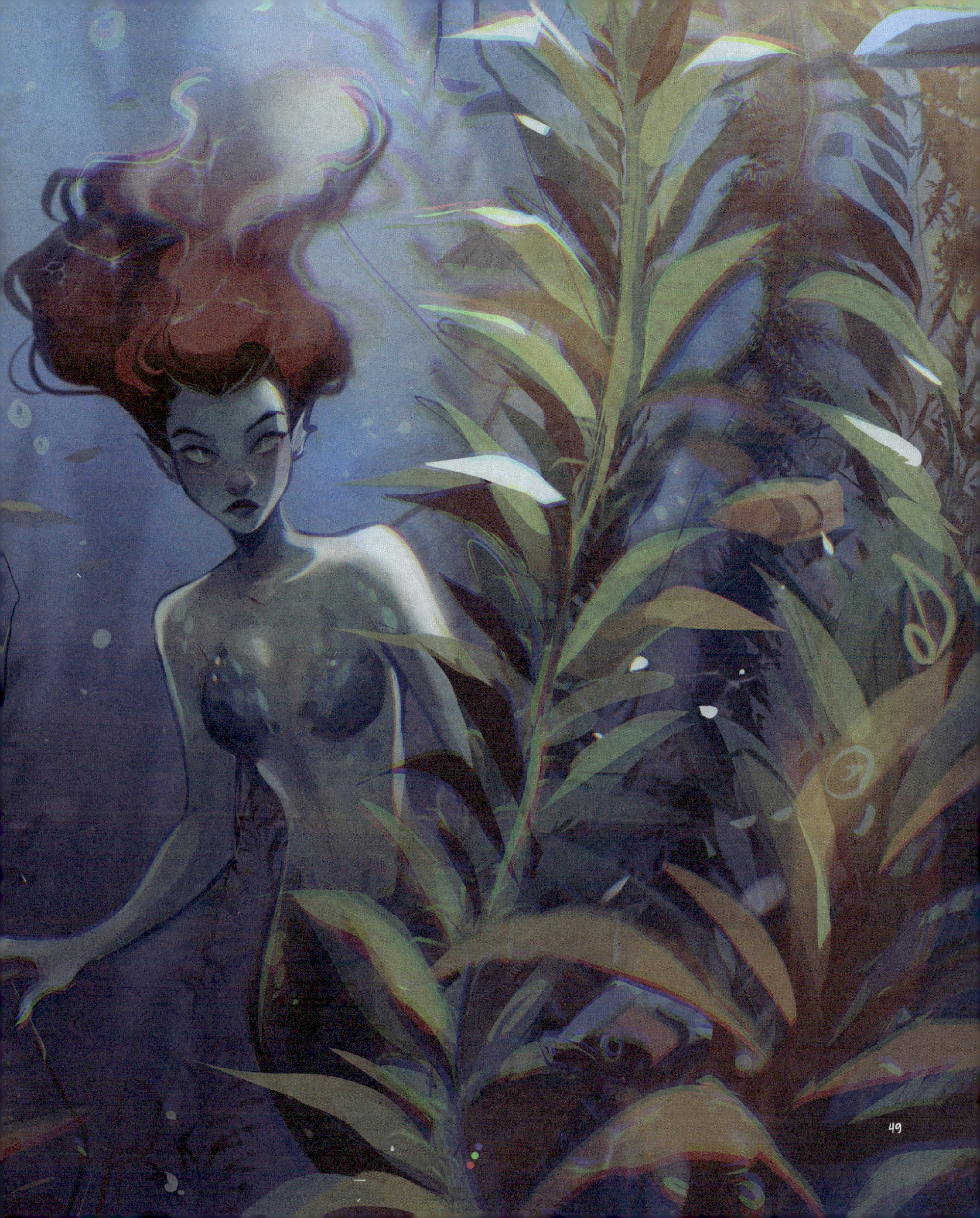

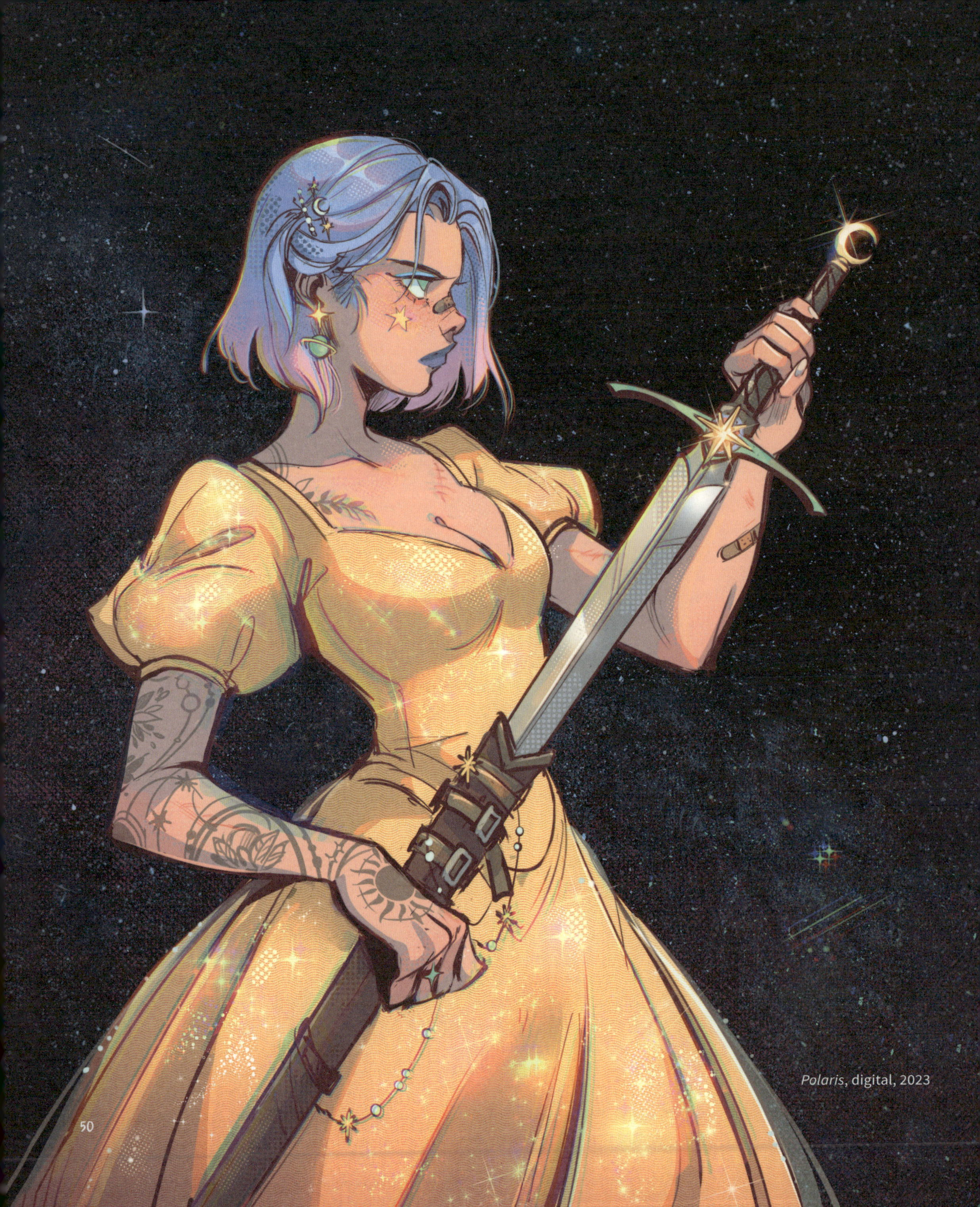

Polaris, digital, 2023

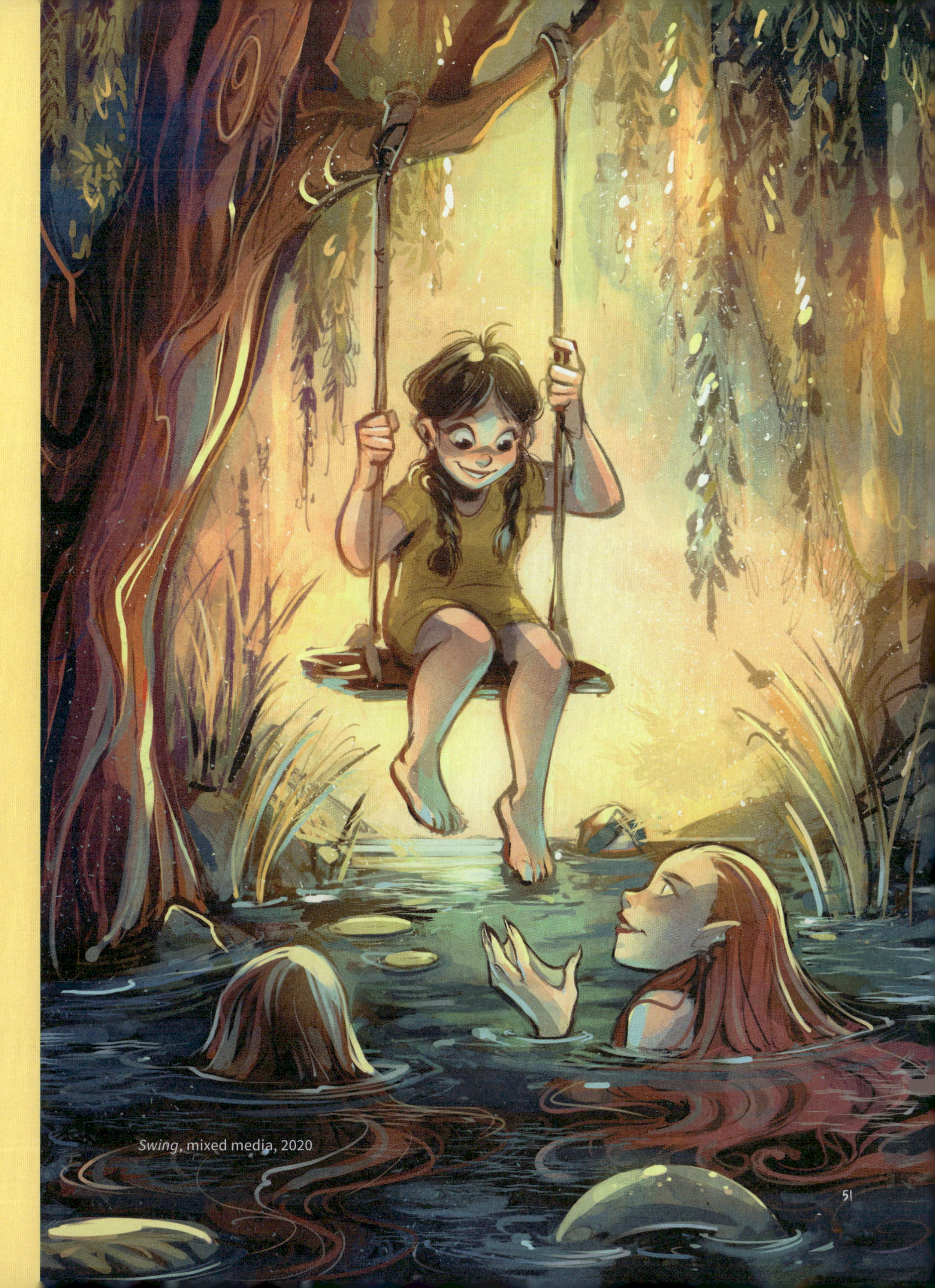

Swing, mixed media, 2020

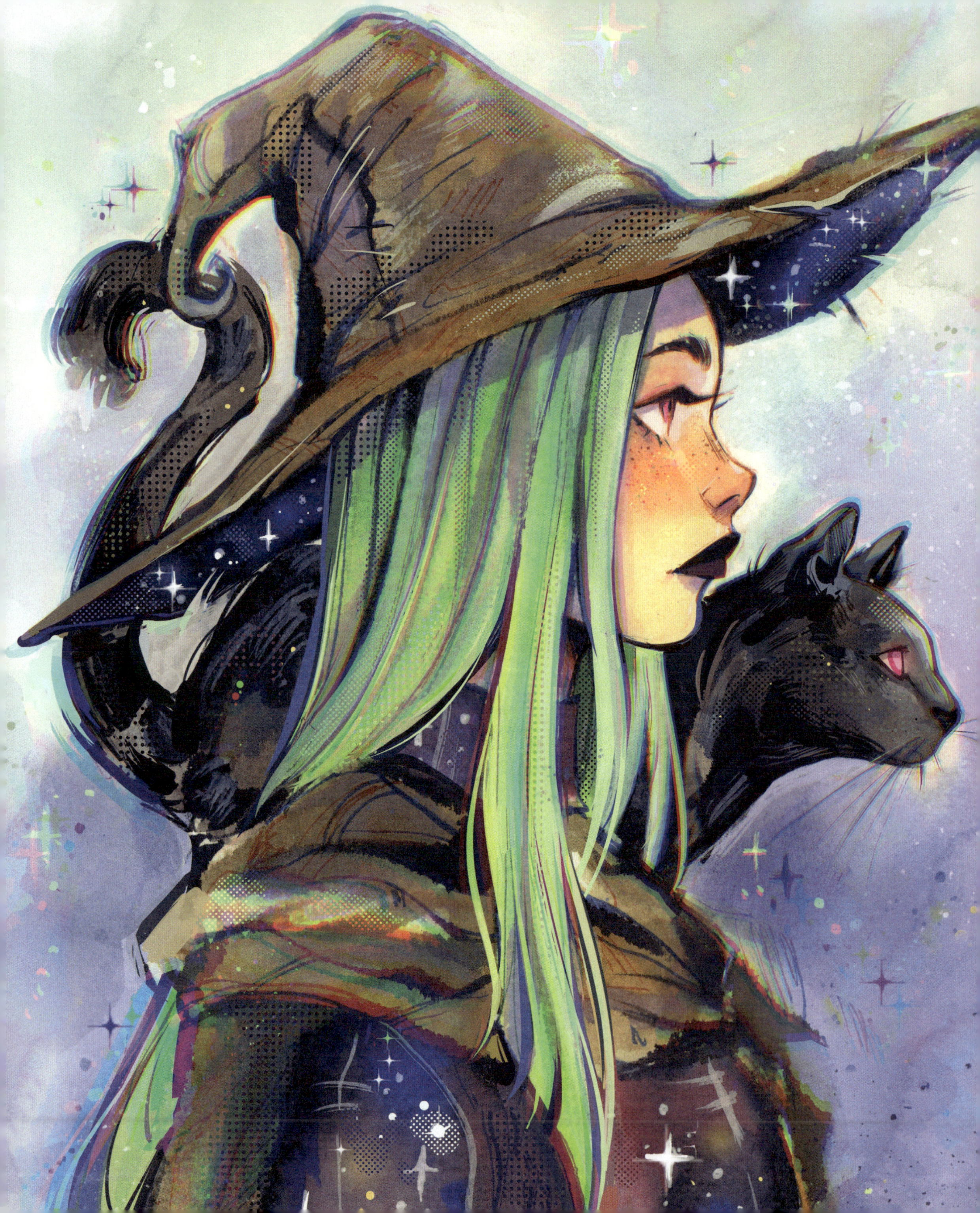

CREATIVE PROCESS

INFLUENCES & ART STYLE

There's been a few times where I've been asked what my art style is called, or how I'd describe it, and I'm never sure how to answer. It's not anime, or cartoon-like, or in the Western-comic style, but it's clearly been influenced by them all. However, if I had to list the inherent parts of my art style, I'd include dynamic shapes, loose lines, and vibrant colours as elements I try to elevate in each piece.

Developing an art style is such a personal journey. It's a combination of all the things we love, our identities, and our perception of the world around us. It's also the external influences we incorporate into our work over a long period of time. Understanding the kind of art we want to create, while focusing on the things that spark our interest, can be really helpful in setting our feet in the right direction.

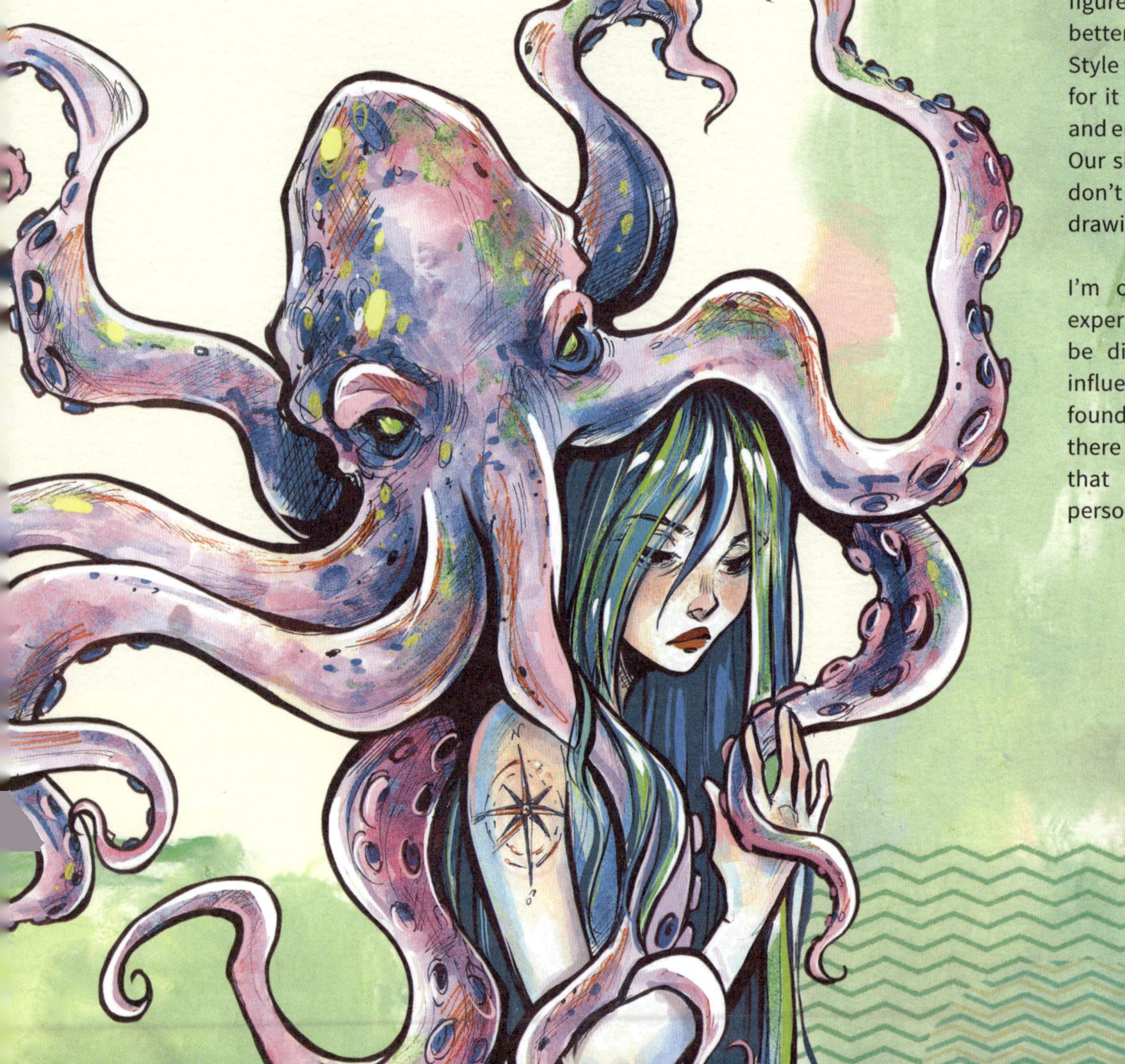

Having a recognizable way of drawing is a big deal for artists who are just starting out and I completely understand why. Social media has made it so easy and addictive to compare yourself to the best version of others. This means we sometimes forget to focus on our own growth. When I was starting out, I didn't really care about how my art looked – making it was enough for me and that made the process so much simpler. I'd love for young artists to embrace the process more instead of rushing towards the destination. In art (and in life), more time is spent trying to figure things out than otherwise, so you'd better feel comfortable in the meantime. Style will find you when you're not looking for it anymore, when you shift your focus and energy into practice and improvement. Our skills and tastes evolve constantly, so don't stress too much about it. Just keep drawing and stay curious!

I'm often inspired by new artists and experimenting with new things. It would be disingenuous to say that all of my influences come from TV shows or artists found in history books. That being said, there are some very specific influences that have been crucial in shaping my personal style.

Teen Titans

Teen Titans was the first show I watched daily. I was fascinated by both the stylization (a mix of American animation and anime) and the characters' expressiveness. It really made the show stand out from the others. I have a massive amount of *Teen Titans* fan art. I used to spend all my evenings obsessively copying images from the internet. I didn't know back then, but the artist responsible for this unique show was Glen Murakami. I had the chance to meet him a few years ago and he continues to be an inspiration to me.

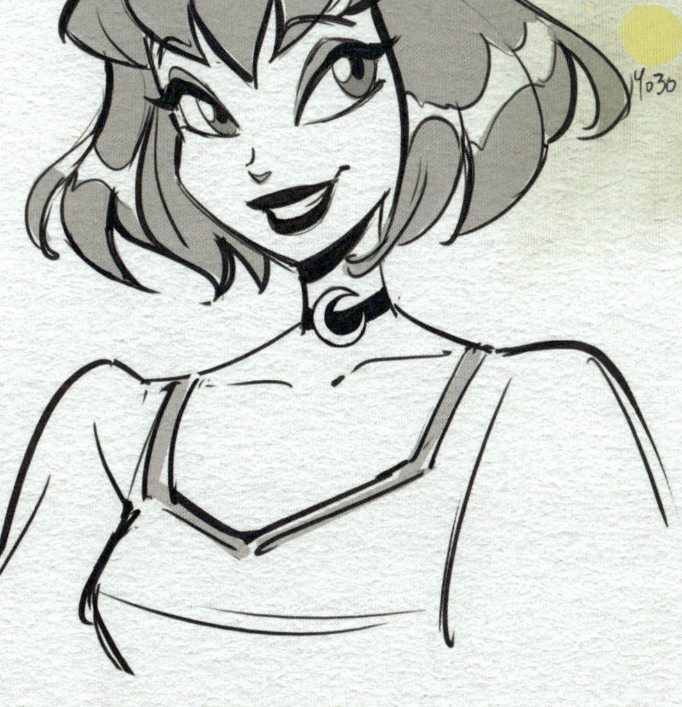

Winx Club

No matter how cheesy it sounds, it's important to mention the cartoons I admired and learned from when I was a kid. *Winx Club* was another show I'd copy, repeatedly and tirelessly. I was obsessed with the characters, clothes, and hair styling. One day, I sat down and copied hundreds of hands while watching an episode, and that was literally how I learned to draw hands. Of course, the magical, more colourful, and feminine themes definitely stuck with me throughout the years too.

Alessandro Barbucci

People often say that they see a lot of Barbucci's style in my work and that's because the *W.I.T.C.H.* comics were a significant part of my childhood. They moulded my art style into what it is today, topping every other influence. I love it when people can recognize some vestiges of their own childhood in my art because it reminds me how much our roots shape us.

My pull towards these three creative mediums (*Teen Titans*, *Winx Club*, and *W.I.T.C.H.* comics) was completely unconscious. I took what I liked from each one and left the rest. I like to think they were kind of the initial recipe; the perfect springboard for me to develop my own artistic style.

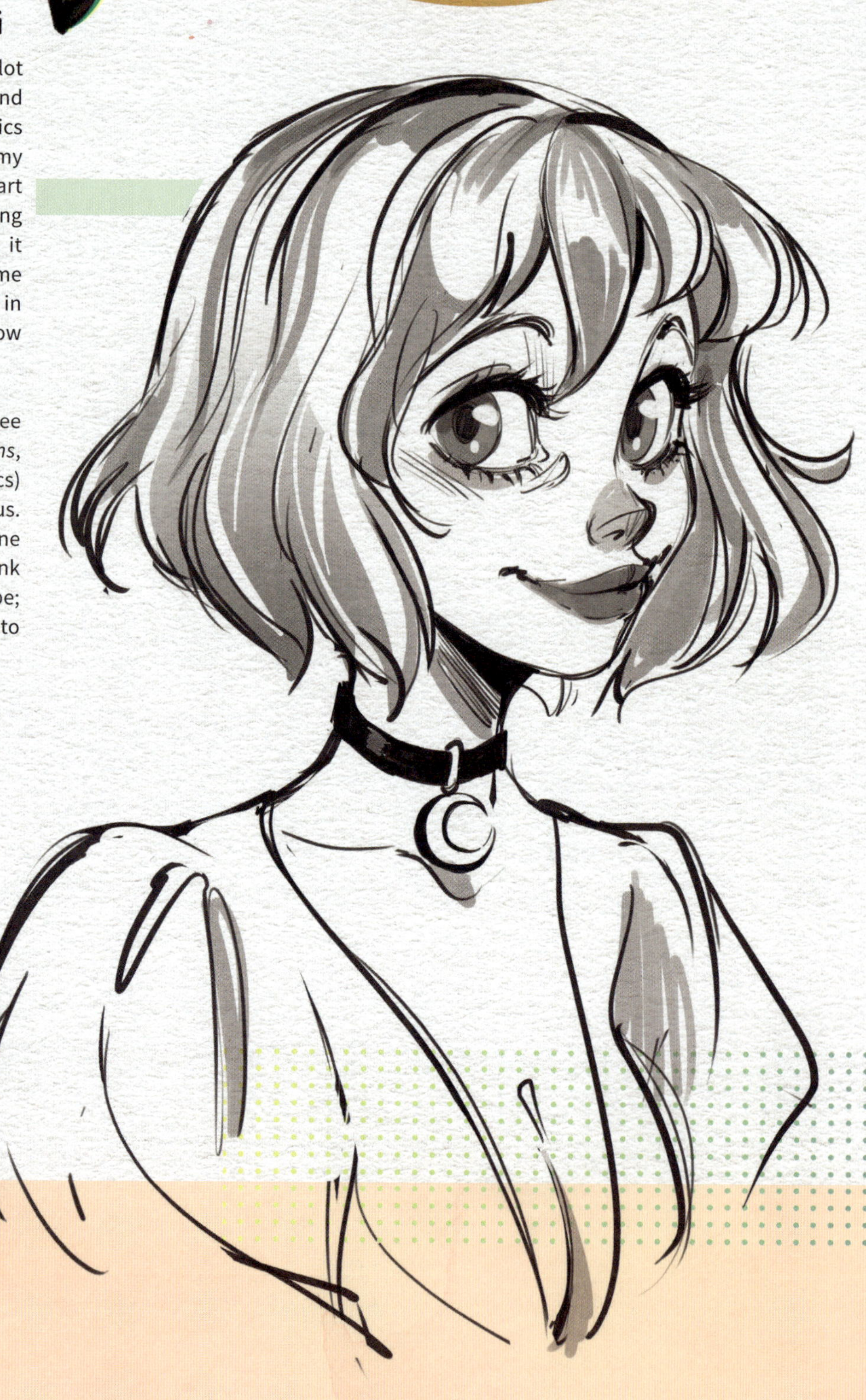

Andrew Loomis

I learned all the basics, fundamentals of anatomy, and composition from Andrew Loomis's exhaustive body of work. I've collected many of his books throughout the years and whenever I feel lost, I find myself reaching for them on my shelves.

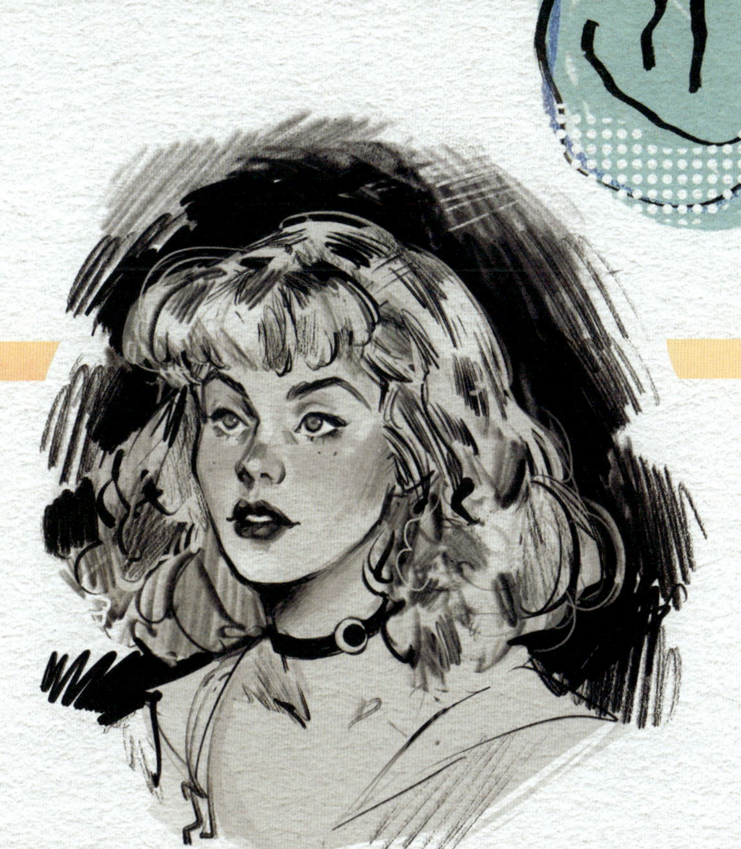

Chiara Bautista

Chiara's artwork spoke to me on a very different level. She put me in contact with my most sensitive side and pushed my art forwards in terms of storytelling. Her work was a missing puzzle piece that helped me to canalize my voice in a compelling and powerful way.

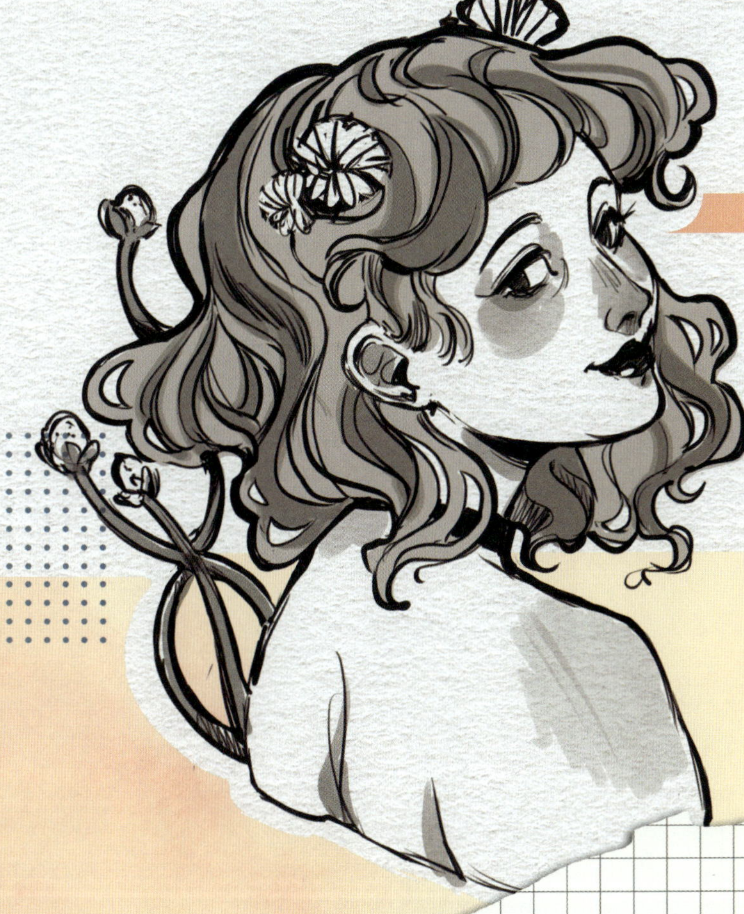

Art Nouveau

Although I'm not great with history, art nouveau was one of the movements that really resonated with me back in college. There was something so refreshing about letting go of the classical styles for more modern, revitalizing masters such as Gustav Klimt, Henri de Toulouse-Lautrec, and Alphonse Mucha.

The natural elements, flowing organic lines, ornaments, geometric shapes, and use of symbolic figures really inspired me to incorporate new things into my art.

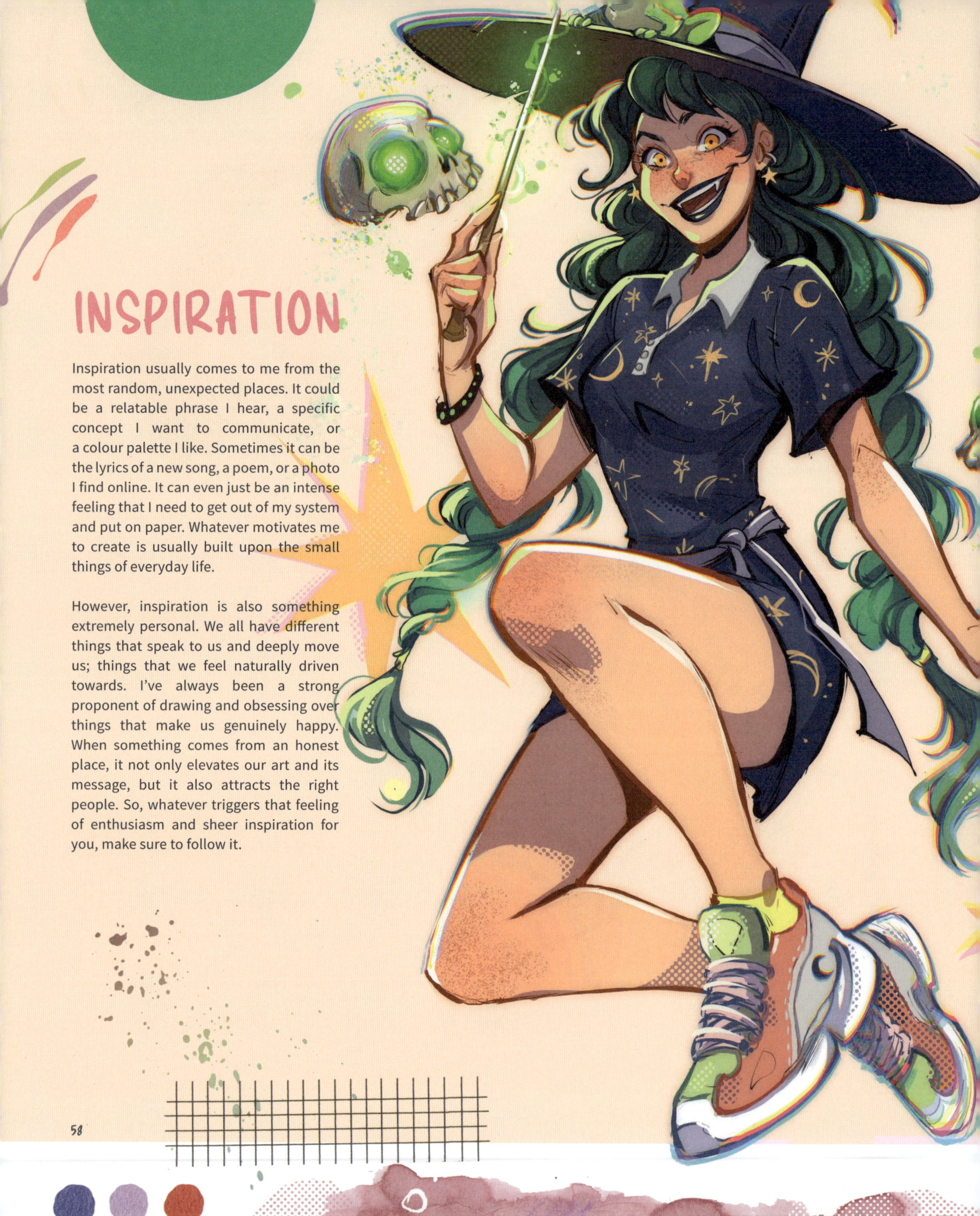

INSPIRATION

Inspiration usually comes to me from the most random, unexpected places. It could be a relatable phrase I hear, a specific concept I want to communicate, or a colour palette I like. Sometimes it can be the lyrics of a new song, a poem, or a photo I find online. It can even just be an intense feeling that I need to get out of my system and put on paper. Whatever motivates me to create is usually built upon the small things of everyday life.

However, inspiration is also something extremely personal. We all have different things that speak to us and deeply move us; things that we feel naturally driven towards. I've always been a strong proponent of drawing and obsessing over things that make us genuinely happy. When something comes from an honest place, it not only elevates our art and its message, but it also attracts the right people. So, whatever triggers that feeling of enthusiasm and sheer inspiration for you, make sure to follow it.

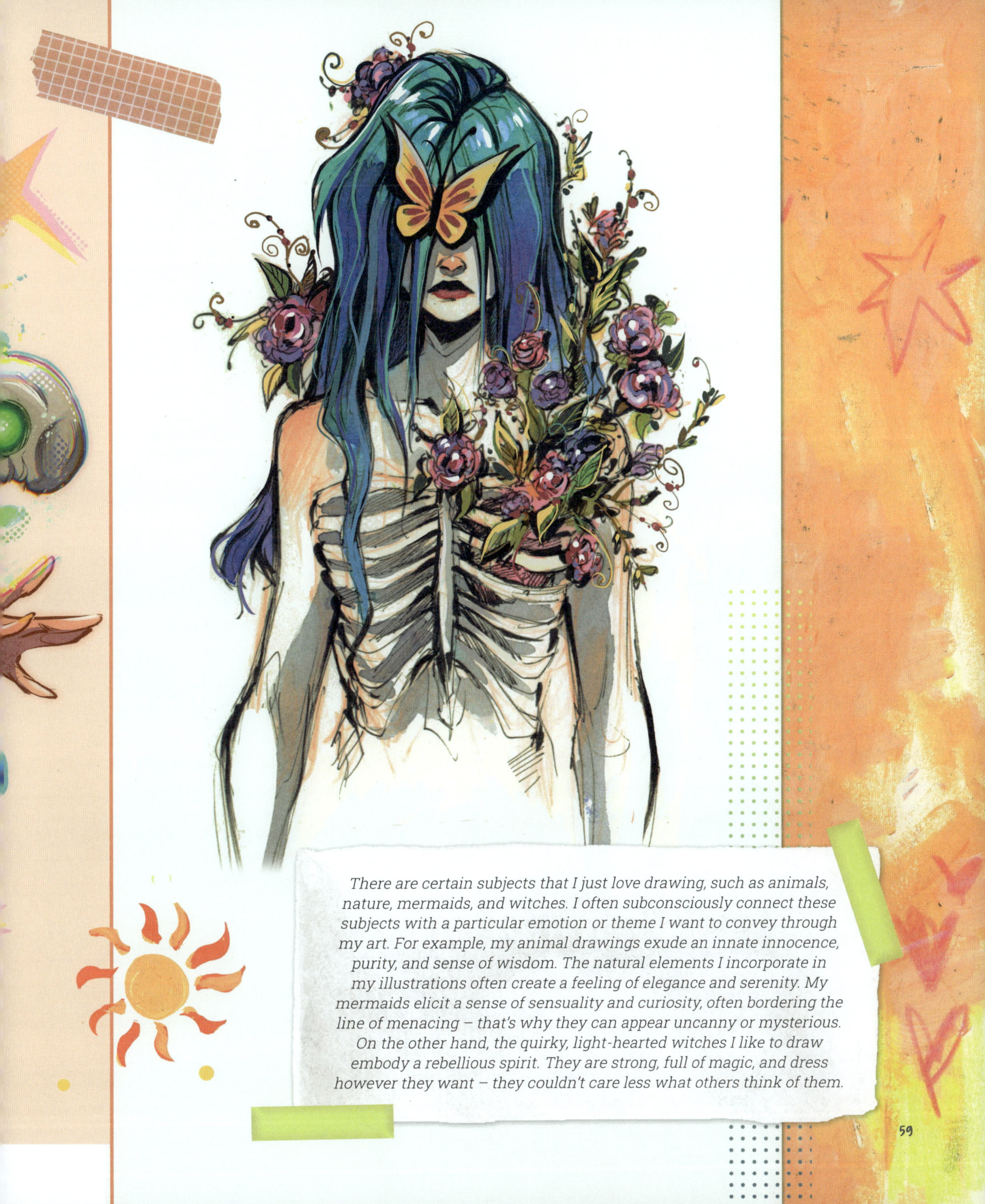

There are certain subjects that I just love drawing, such as animals, nature, mermaids, and witches. I often subconsciously connect these subjects with a particular emotion or theme I want to convey through my art. For example, my animal drawings exude an innate innocence, purity, and sense of wisdom. The natural elements I incorporate in my illustrations often create a feeling of elegance and serenity. My mermaids elicit a sense of sensuality and curiosity, often bordering the line of menacing – that's why they can appear uncanny or mysterious. On the other hand, the quirky, light-hearted witches I like to draw embody a rebellious spirit. They are strong, full of magic, and dress however they want – they couldn't care less what others think of them.

I guess in some sort of way, those are all aspects of who I am and what I find inspiring.

Some other topics that make me excited to grab a pencil are adventurous love stories, women in armour, celestial themes, fashion with bold colours, and fun patterns. I could go on!

As the years passed and adult life got in the way, I noticed how those magical bursts of inspiration became a bit less regular than normal. To make the process of getting into that creative mood as smooth as possible, I try to do things that keep me mentally stimulated. Below is a list of ways I keep my creative muscle strong:

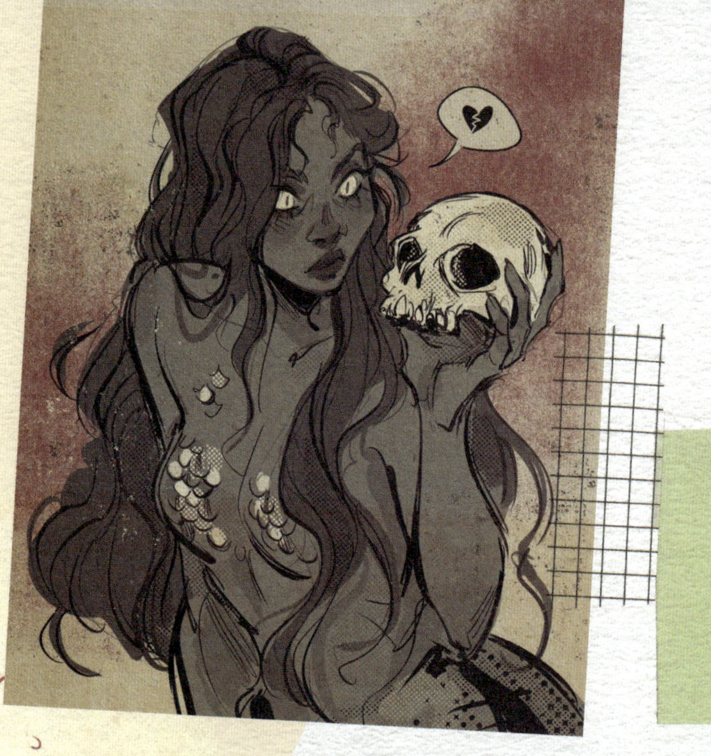

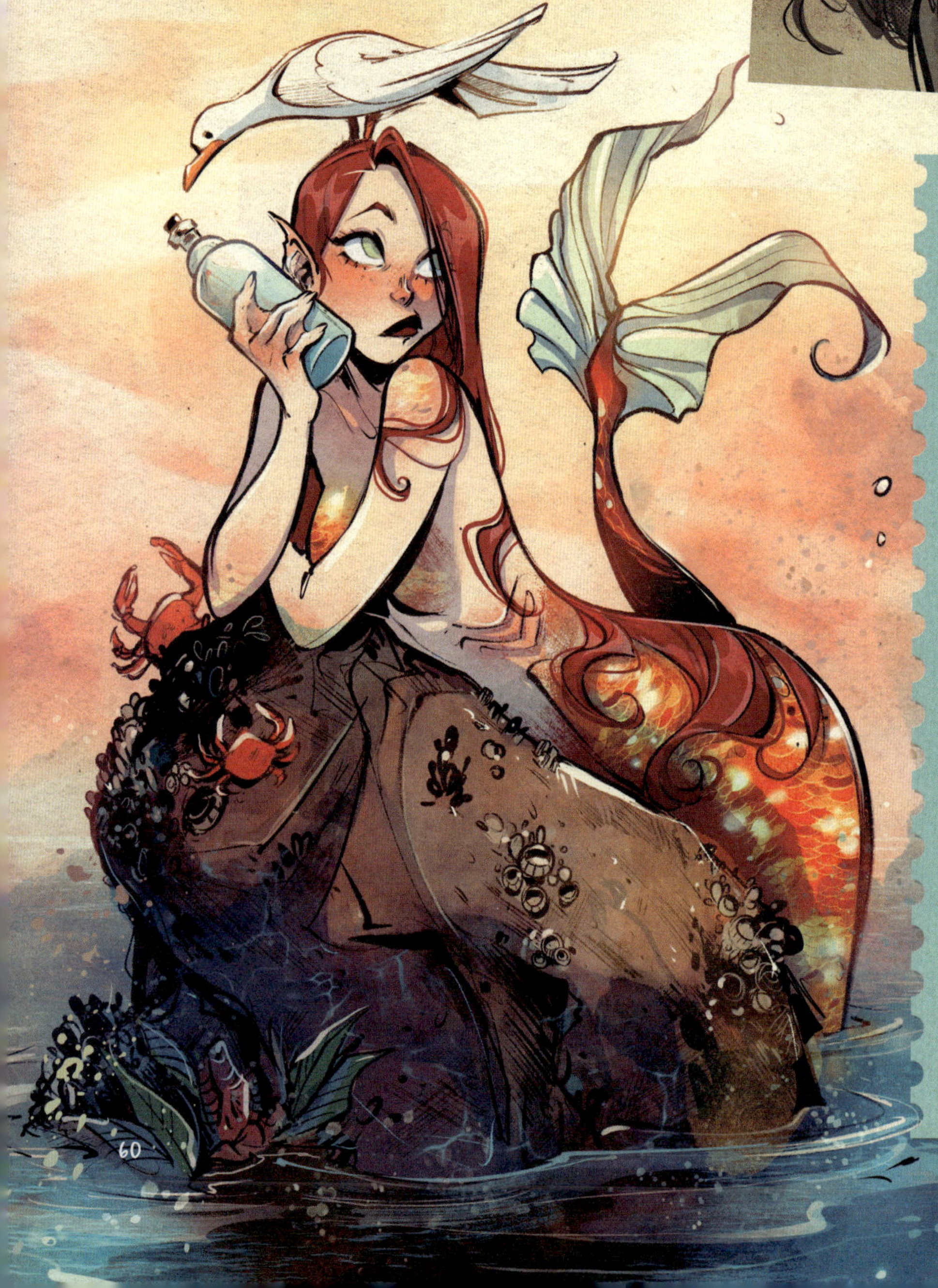

- Looking at art and photography daily
- Quick studies
- Writing down all my ideas for future drawings
- Keeping a list of colour palettes I want to use in my art
- Playing around with art supplies and trying new techniques
- Collecting books and comics of my favourite artists and studying my favourite pages
- Taking a walk/surrounding myself with nature whenever it's possible
- Sketching whatever comes to my mind (even if it's just the smallest doodle ever!)
- Disconnecting from social media from time to time

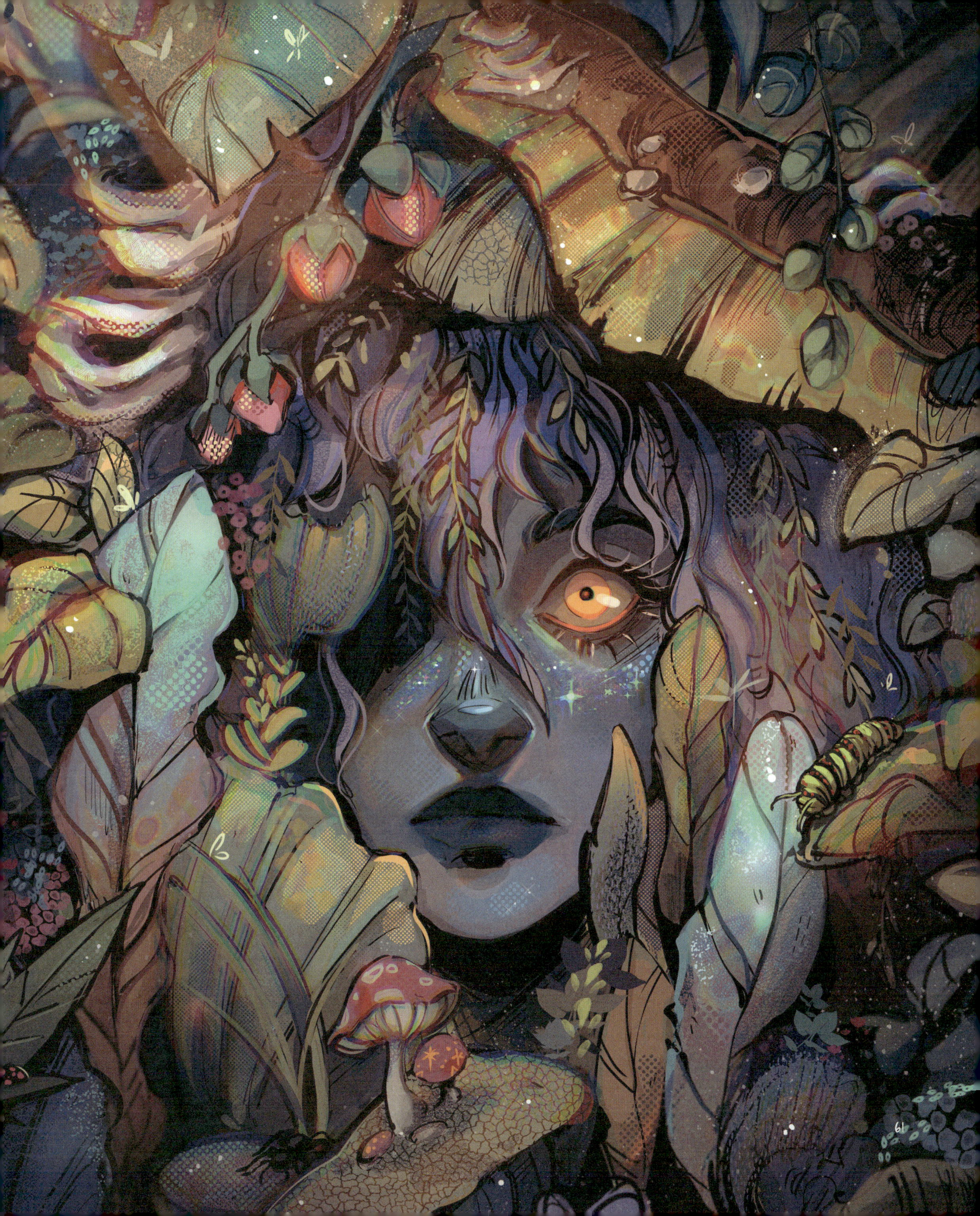

TELLING A STORY

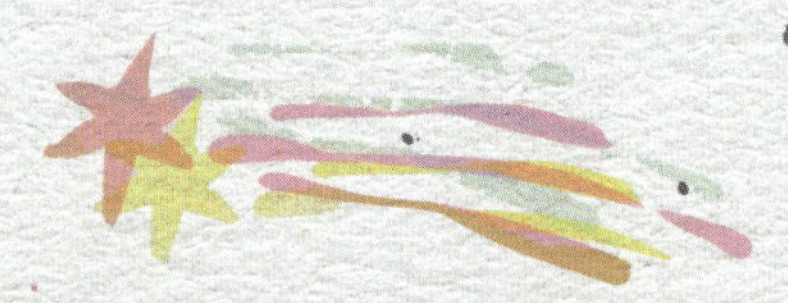

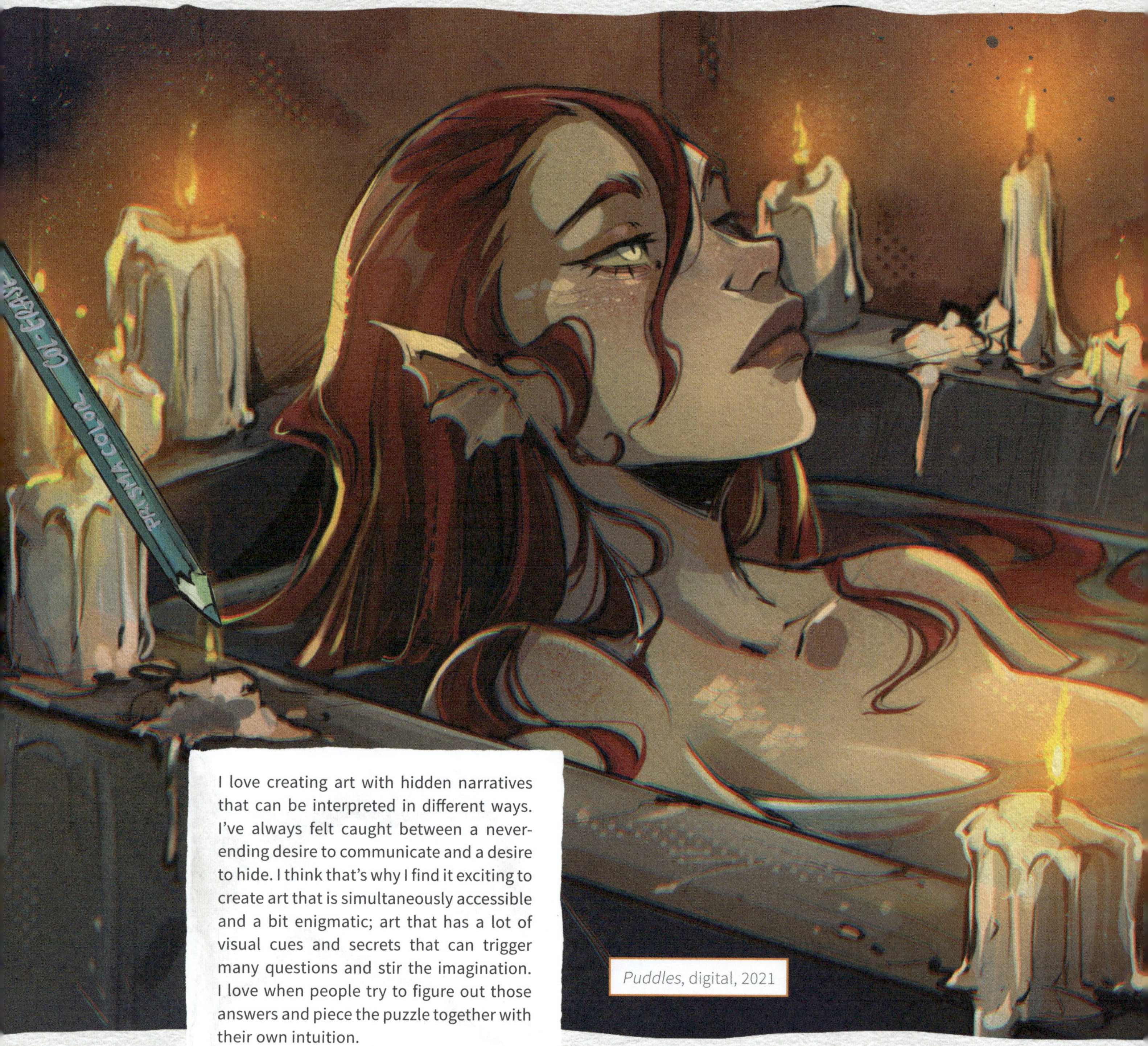

I love creating art with hidden narratives that can be interpreted in different ways. I've always felt caught between a never-ending desire to communicate and a desire to hide. I think that's why I find it exciting to create art that is simultaneously accessible and a bit enigmatic; art that has a lot of visual cues and secrets that can trigger many questions and stir the imagination. I love when people try to figure out those answers and piece the puzzle together with their own intuition.

Puddles, digital, 2021

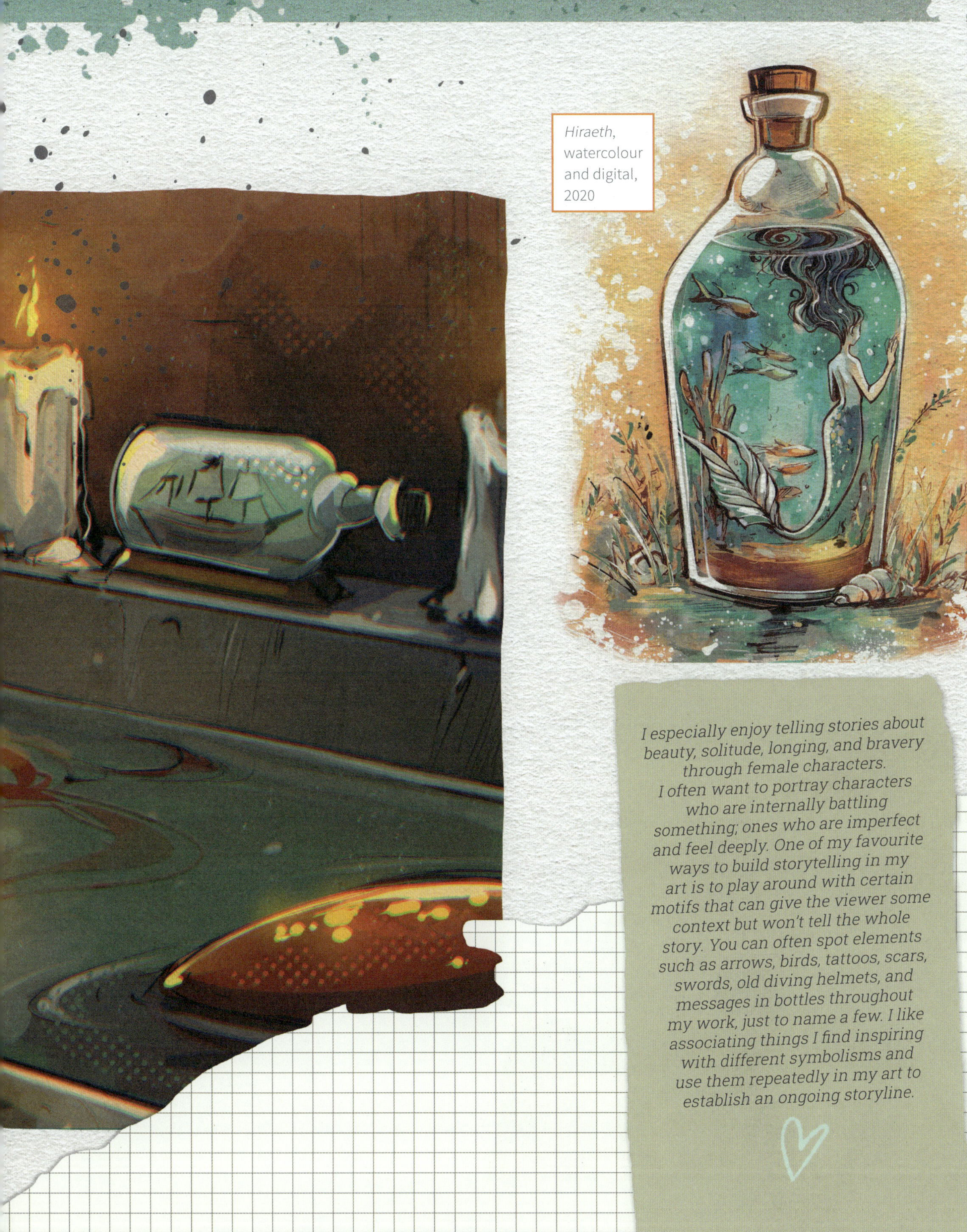

Hiraeth, watercolour and digital, 2020

I especially enjoy telling stories about beauty, solitude, longing, and bravery through female characters. I often want to portray characters who are internally battling something; ones who are imperfect and feel deeply. One of my favourite ways to build storytelling in my art is to play around with certain motifs that can give the viewer some context but won't tell the whole story. You can often spot elements such as arrows, birds, tattoos, scars, swords, old diving helmets, and messages in bottles throughout my work, just to name a few. I like associating things I find inspiring with different symbolisms and use them repeatedly in my art to establish an ongoing storyline.

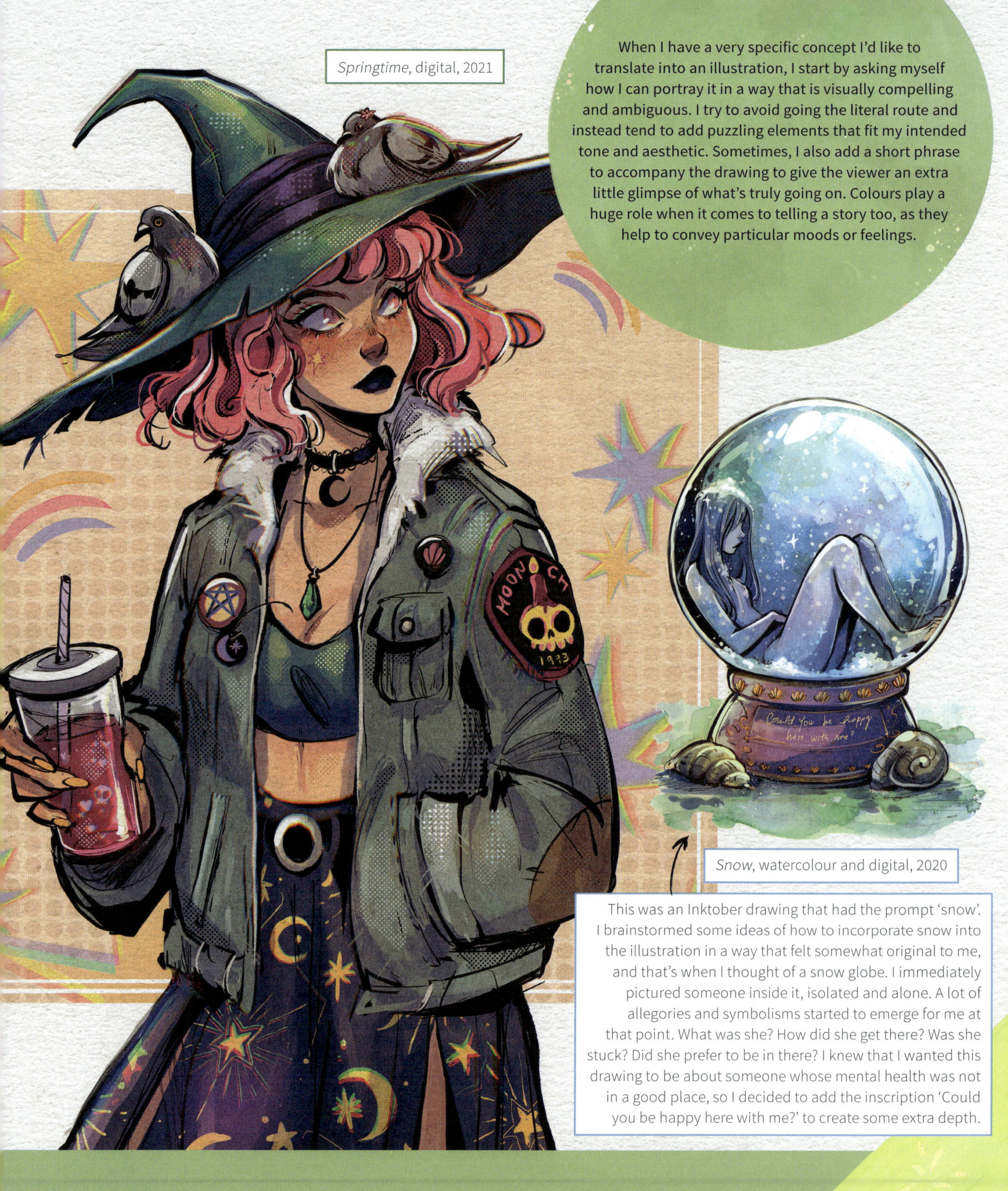

Springtime, digital, 2021

When I have a very specific concept I'd like to translate into an illustration, I start by asking myself how I can portray it in a way that is visually compelling and ambiguous. I try to avoid going the literal route and instead tend to add puzzling elements that fit my intended tone and aesthetic. Sometimes, I also add a short phrase to accompany the drawing to give the viewer an extra little glimpse of what's truly going on. Colours play a huge role when it comes to telling a story too, as they help to convey particular moods or feelings.

Snow, watercolour and digital, 2020

This was an Inktober drawing that had the prompt 'snow'. I brainstormed some ideas of how to incorporate snow into the illustration in a way that felt somewhat original to me, and that's when I thought of a snow globe. I immediately pictured someone inside it, isolated and alone. A lot of allegories and symbolisms started to emerge for me at that point. What was she? How did she get there? Was she stuck? Did she prefer to be in there? I knew that I wanted this drawing to be about someone whose mental health was not in a good place, so I decided to add the inscription 'Could you be happy here with me?' to create some extra depth.

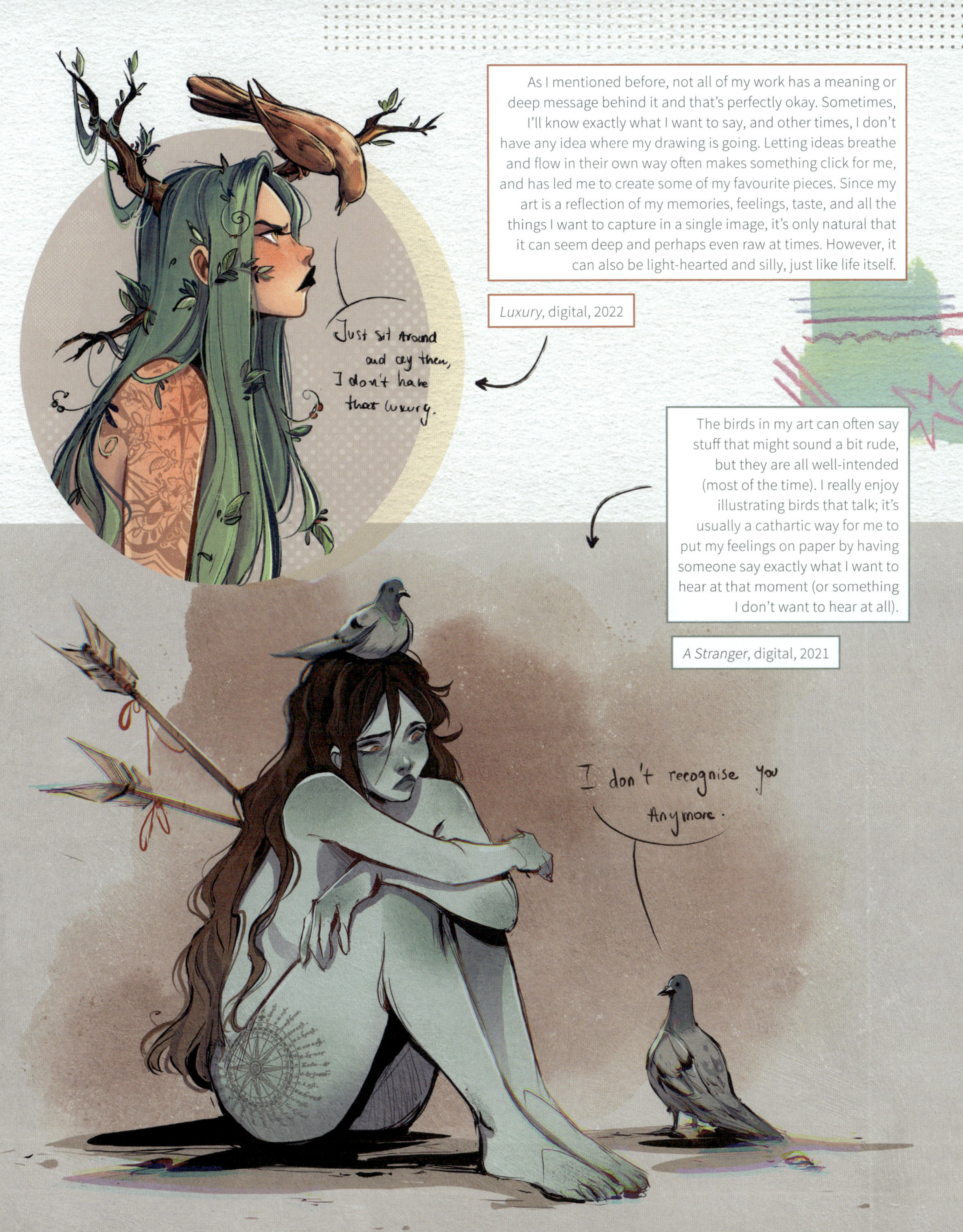

As I mentioned before, not all of my work has a meaning or deep message behind it and that's perfectly okay. Sometimes, I'll know exactly what I want to say, and other times, I don't have any idea where my drawing is going. Letting ideas breathe and flow in their own way often makes something click for me, and has led me to create some of my favourite pieces. Since my art is a reflection of my memories, feelings, taste, and all the things I want to capture in a single image, it's only natural that it can seem deep and perhaps even raw at times. However, it can also be light-hearted and silly, just like life itself.

Luxury, digital, 2022

The birds in my art can often say stuff that might sound a bit rude, but they are all well-intended (most of the time). I really enjoy illustrating birds that talk; it's usually a cathartic way for me to put my feelings on paper by having someone say exactly what I want to hear at that moment (or something I don't want to hear at all).

A Stranger, digital, 2021

MIXING MEDIUMS

Mixing mediums is a very raw process for me. When it comes to the traditional medium, I rarely plan out how the illustration will look once it's finished. I usually begin with a very vague idea of the shapes and colour palette, and once that is decided, I jump right into it. There's a lot that can go wrong when you are not in total control of the outcome, but I personally prefer it that way. I'm hasty and a little chaotic when I draw, so instead of following a formula, I like getting lost in the workflow, following my gut until the results start unfolding in front of my eyes. Most of the time, I just decide which mediums I want to use as I go, depending on the piece.

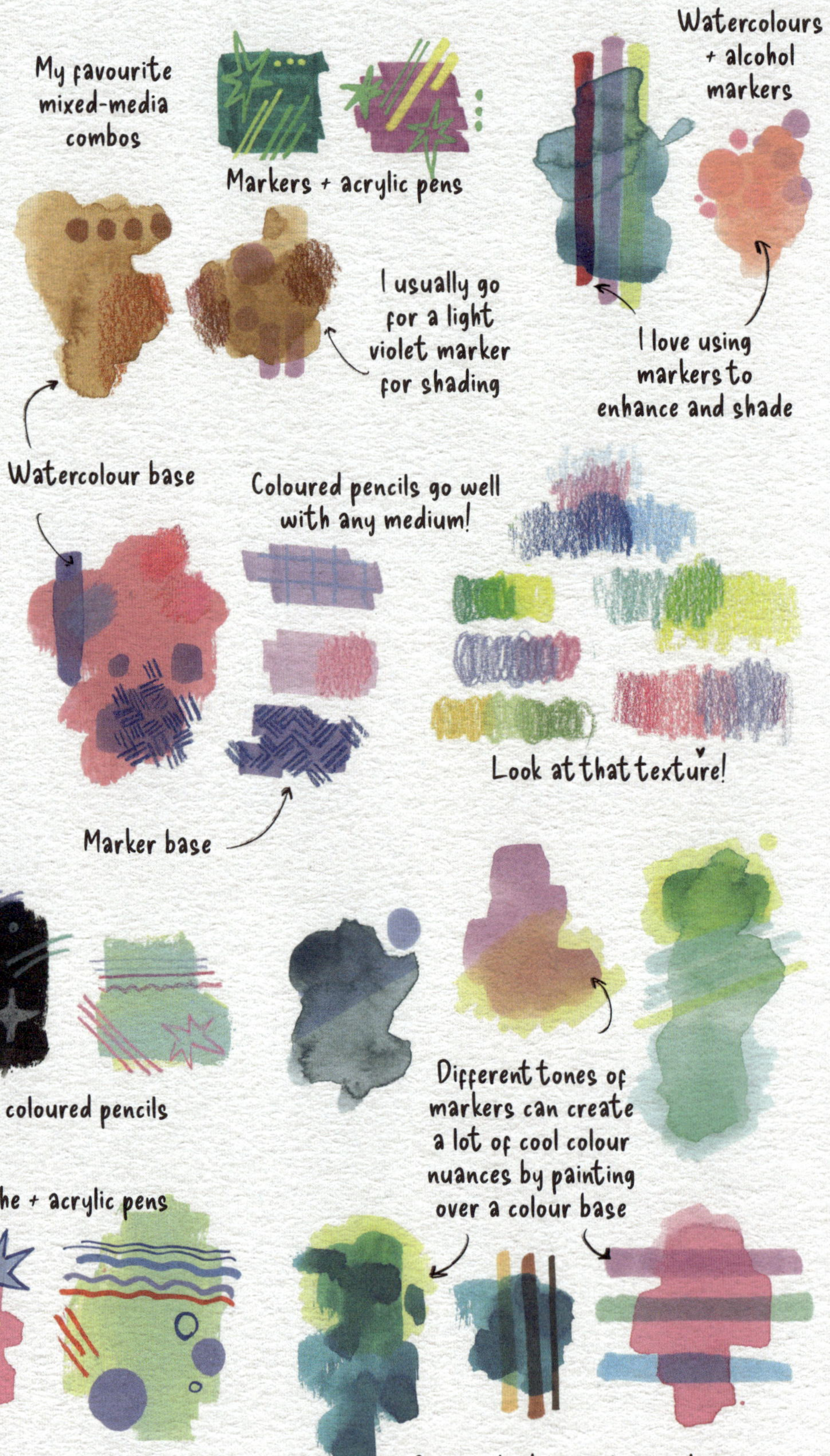

Watercolour + acryla gouache

Acryla gouache + coloured pencils

Gouache + acrylic pens

Gouache is perfect for details

Both are super opaque

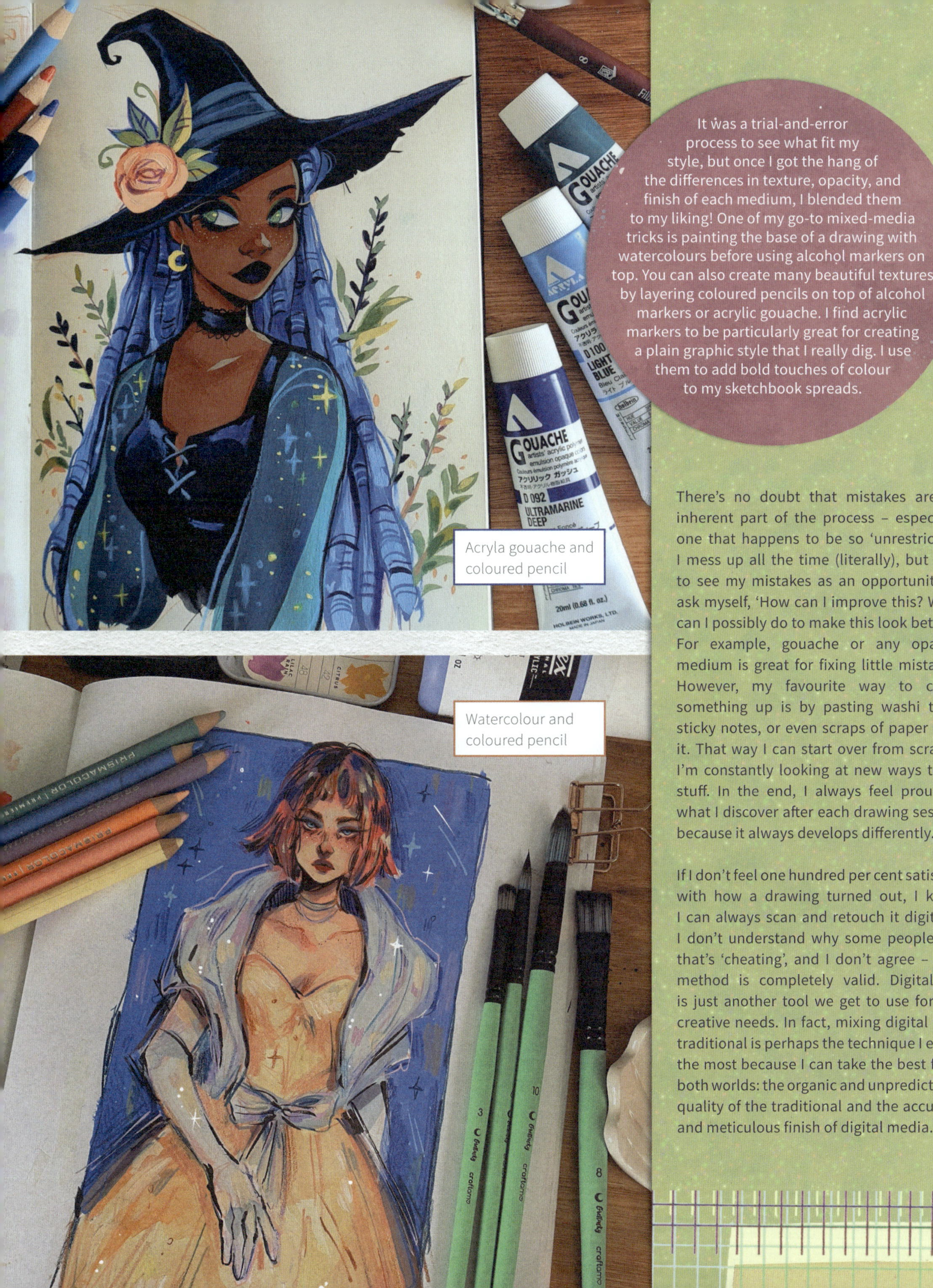

Acryla gouache and coloured pencil

Watercolour and coloured pencil

It was a trial-and-error process to see what fit my style, but once I got the hang of the differences in texture, opacity, and finish of each medium, I blended them to my liking! One of my go-to mixed-media tricks is painting the base of a drawing with watercolours before using alcohol markers on top. You can also create many beautiful textures by layering coloured pencils on top of alcohol markers or acrylic gouache. I find acrylic markers to be particularly great for creating a plain graphic style that I really dig. I use them to add bold touches of colour to my sketchbook spreads.

There's no doubt that mistakes are an inherent part of the process – especially one that happens to be so 'unrestricted'. I mess up all the time (literally), but I try to see my mistakes as an opportunity to ask myself, 'How can I improve this? What can I possibly do to make this look better?' For example, gouache or any opaque medium is great for fixing little mistakes. However, my favourite way to cover something up is by pasting washi tape, sticky notes, or even scraps of paper over it. That way I can start over from scratch. I'm constantly looking at new ways to fix stuff. In the end, I always feel proud of what I discover after each drawing session because it always develops differently.

If I don't feel one hundred per cent satisfied with how a drawing turned out, I know I can always scan and retouch it digitally. I don't understand why some people say that's 'cheating', and I don't agree – that method is completely valid. Digital art is just another tool we get to use for our creative needs. In fact, mixing digital with traditional is perhaps the technique I enjoy the most because I can take the best from both worlds: the organic and unpredictable quality of the traditional and the accuracy and meticulous finish of digital media.

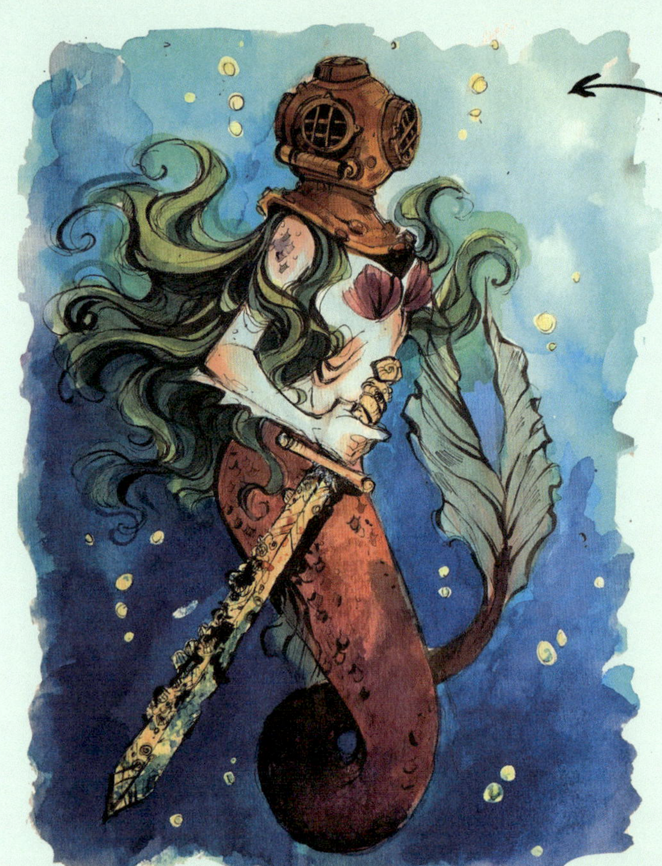

Watercolours are great for covering large areas and laying down a first layer of colour very quickly. They can be a little tricky to work with – I discovered that I love working on top of that first layer with other mediums that I find easier to control.

I love using alcohol markers for shading and creating colour variations to my watercolour base. Notice how the upper-right corner of the drawing goes from a light blue to a light green after doing a pass with a yellow marker. It's a great way for me to add volume in a fast and efficient way while having more control over the outcome. Yes, my marker tips usually get smudged by doing this, but fret not, they still work perfectly fine!

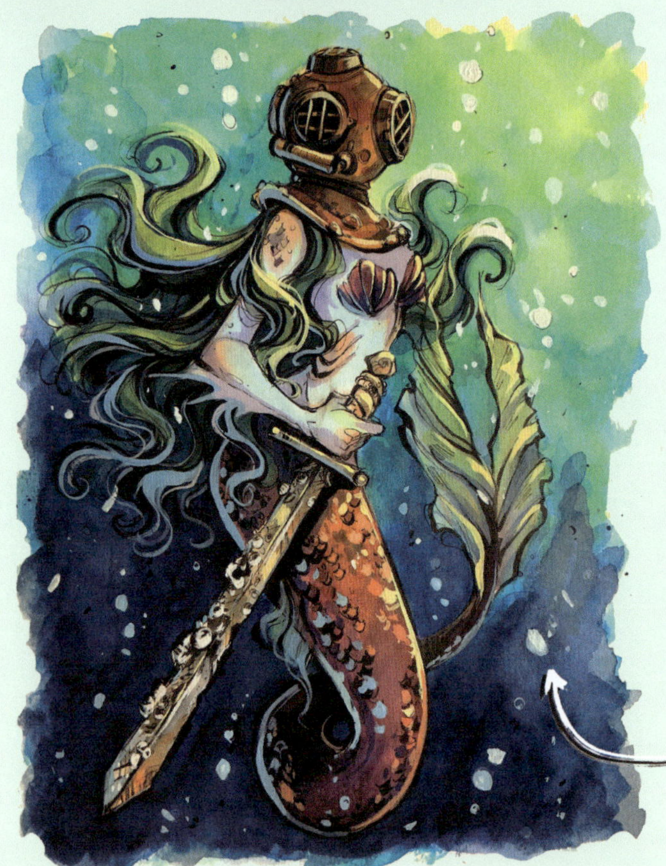

Gouache is very opaque and has a velvety matte finish when it dries. For me, it's the perfect medium for adding final touches and refining details that may have been lost along the way.

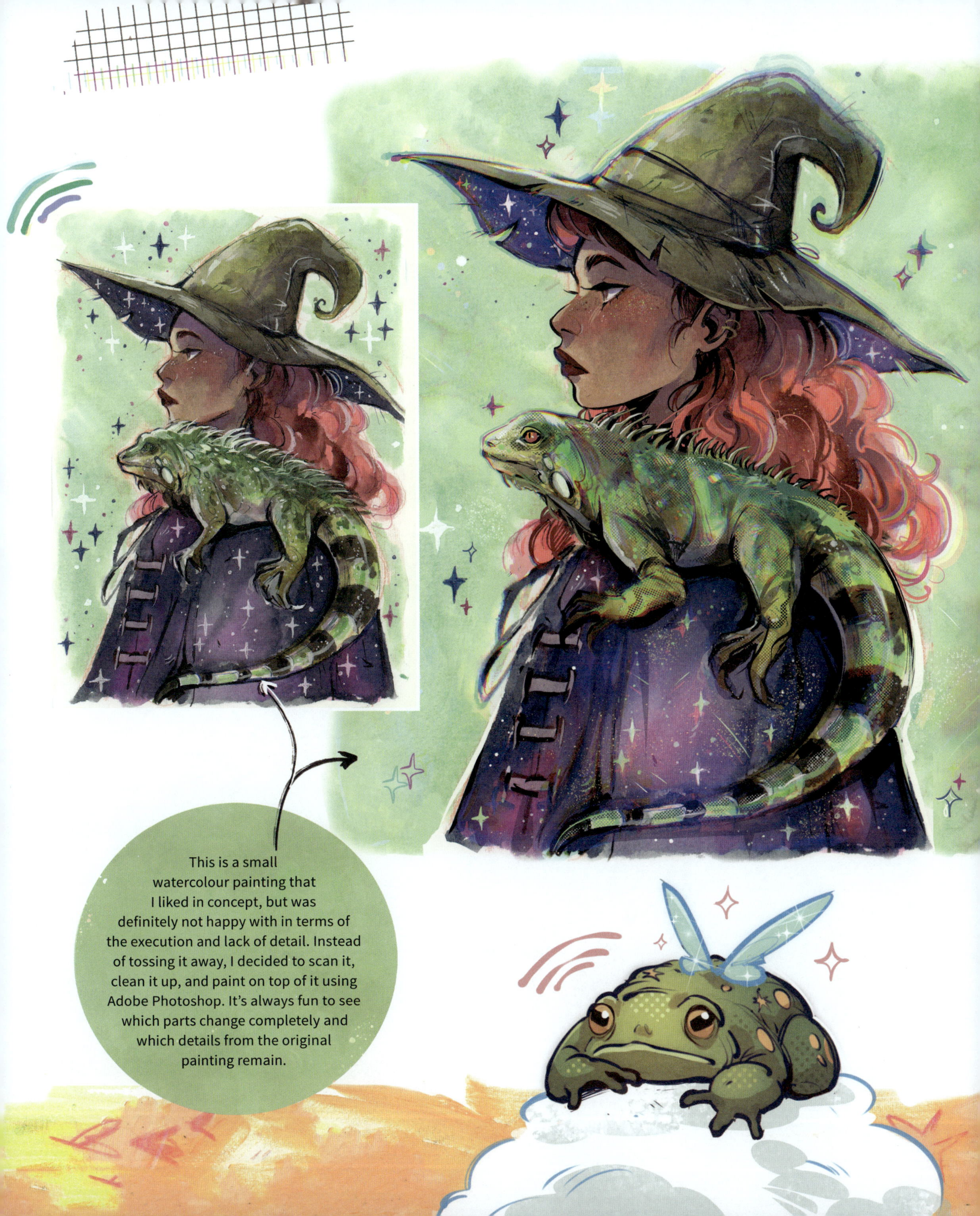

This is a small watercolour painting that I liked in concept, but was definitely not happy with in terms of the execution and lack of detail. Instead of tossing it away, I decided to scan it, clean it up, and paint on top of it using Adobe Photoshop. It's always fun to see which parts change completely and which details from the original painting remain.

STUDIES & REFERENCES

For many years, most of the stuff I drew emerged solely from my imagination. I just didn't have the patience to search for the perfect reference, so I always jumped straight into drawing. However, when I moved on to visual development for animation, I realized that I couldn't simply come up with everything. Instead of relying on my visual memory, I had to actually study the things I wanted to draw in order to create a stronger sense of believability. When I started working on comics, googling and searching for references became the norm.

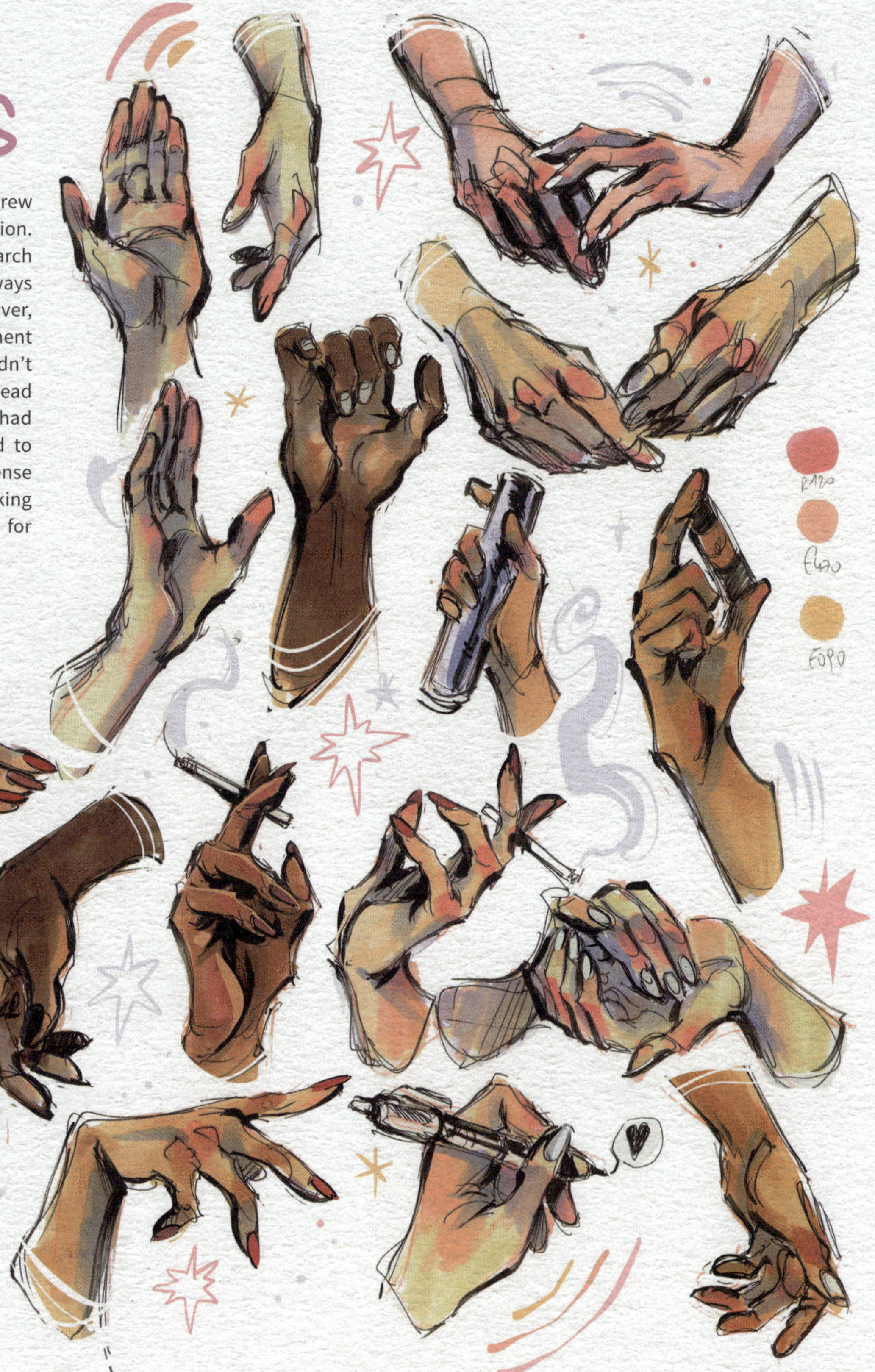

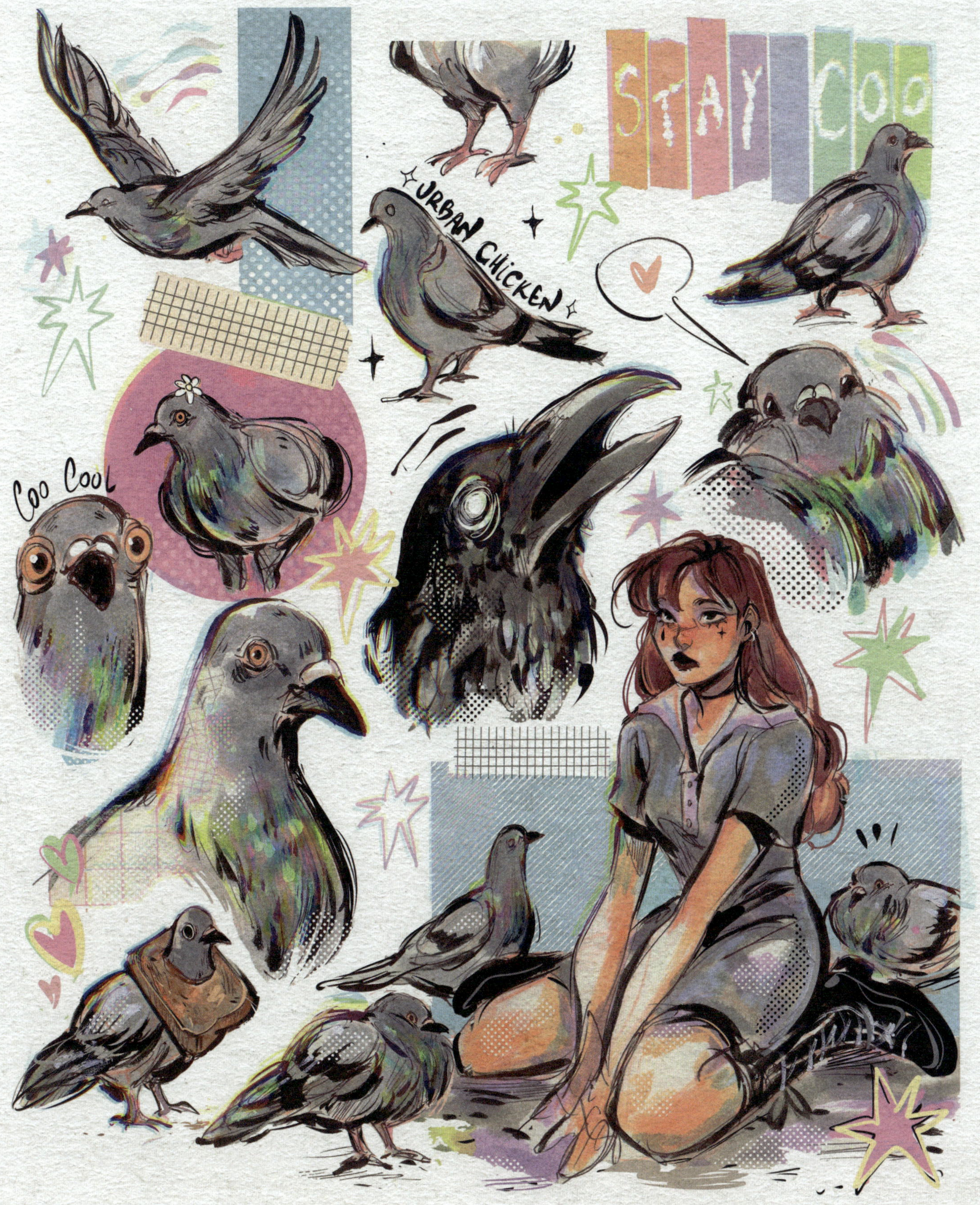
STAY COO
URBAN CHICKEN
Coo Cool

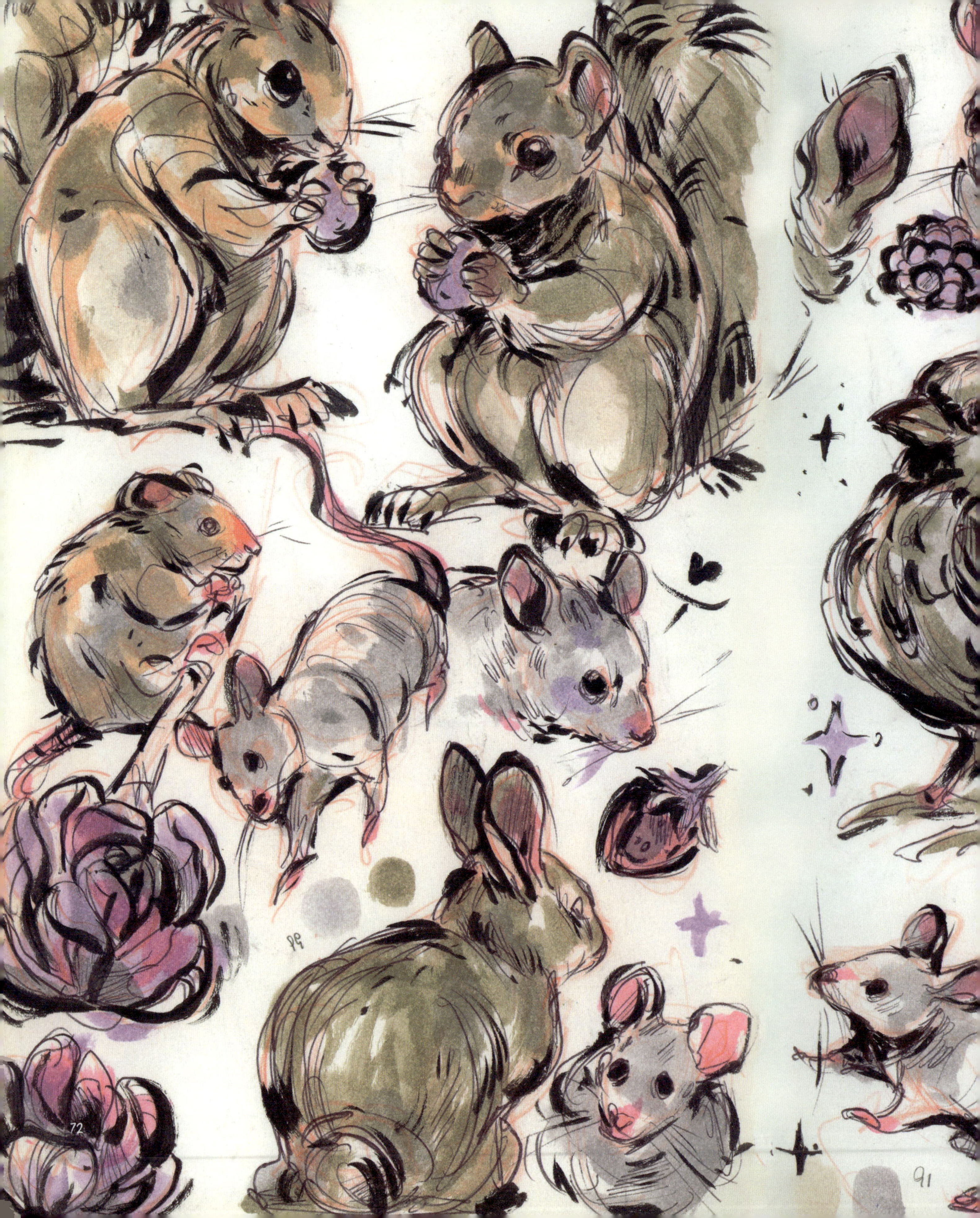

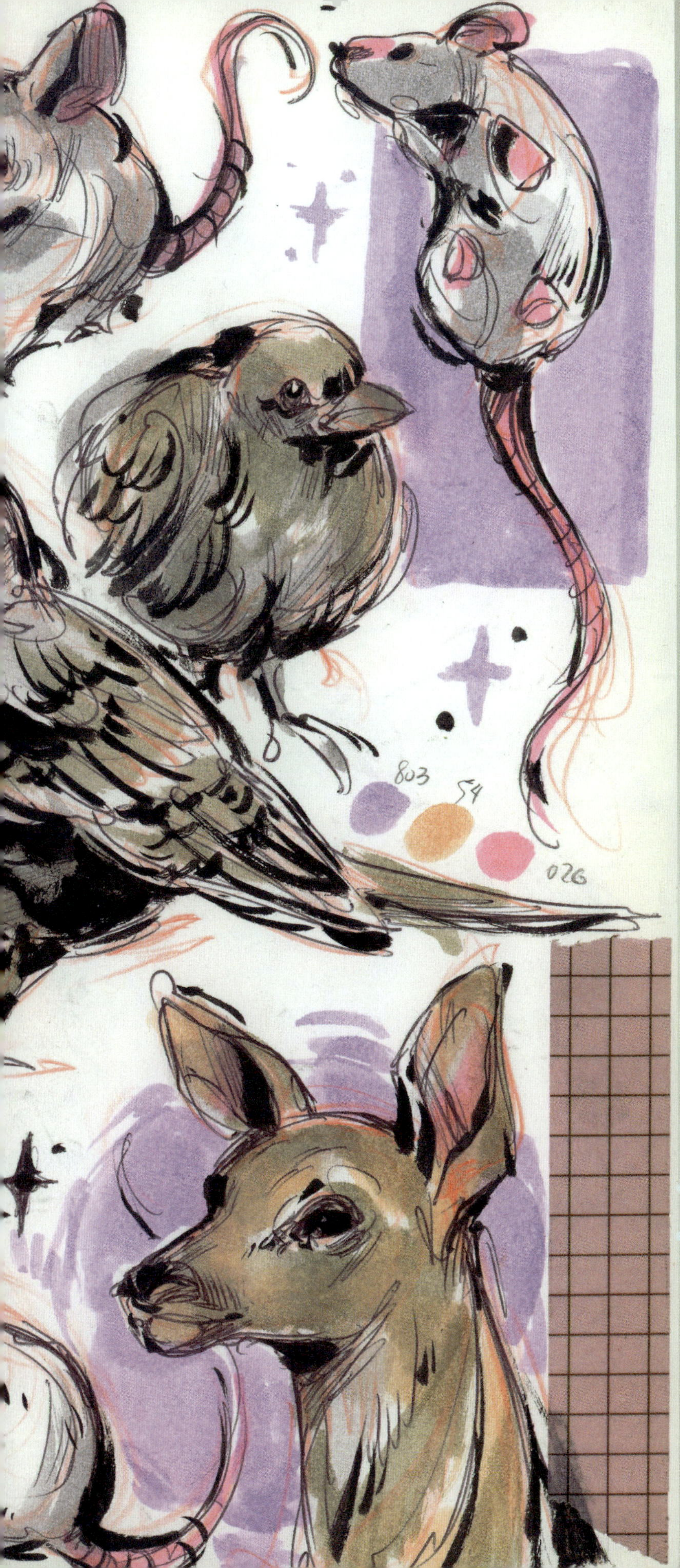

The use of references added much more depth to my art – my memory would never have been able to depict a certain attention to detail. Consequently, I noticed some major improvement and my art started to feel more solid. I love using references for studies, especially when I'm not sure what to draw. That way I can also extend my visual library, produce something new, and hopefully learn a few things along the way! I particularly like making spreads where I draw the same thing many times in order to really comprehend and internalize the shapes. It can be anything, too: faces, anatomy, animals, or painting techniques. Something always clicks along the process and it's as if I'm unlocking new knowledge. I also love making my studies look colourful and fun, so I play around with markers and watercolours, doing whatever I feel like doing to make the results more exciting.

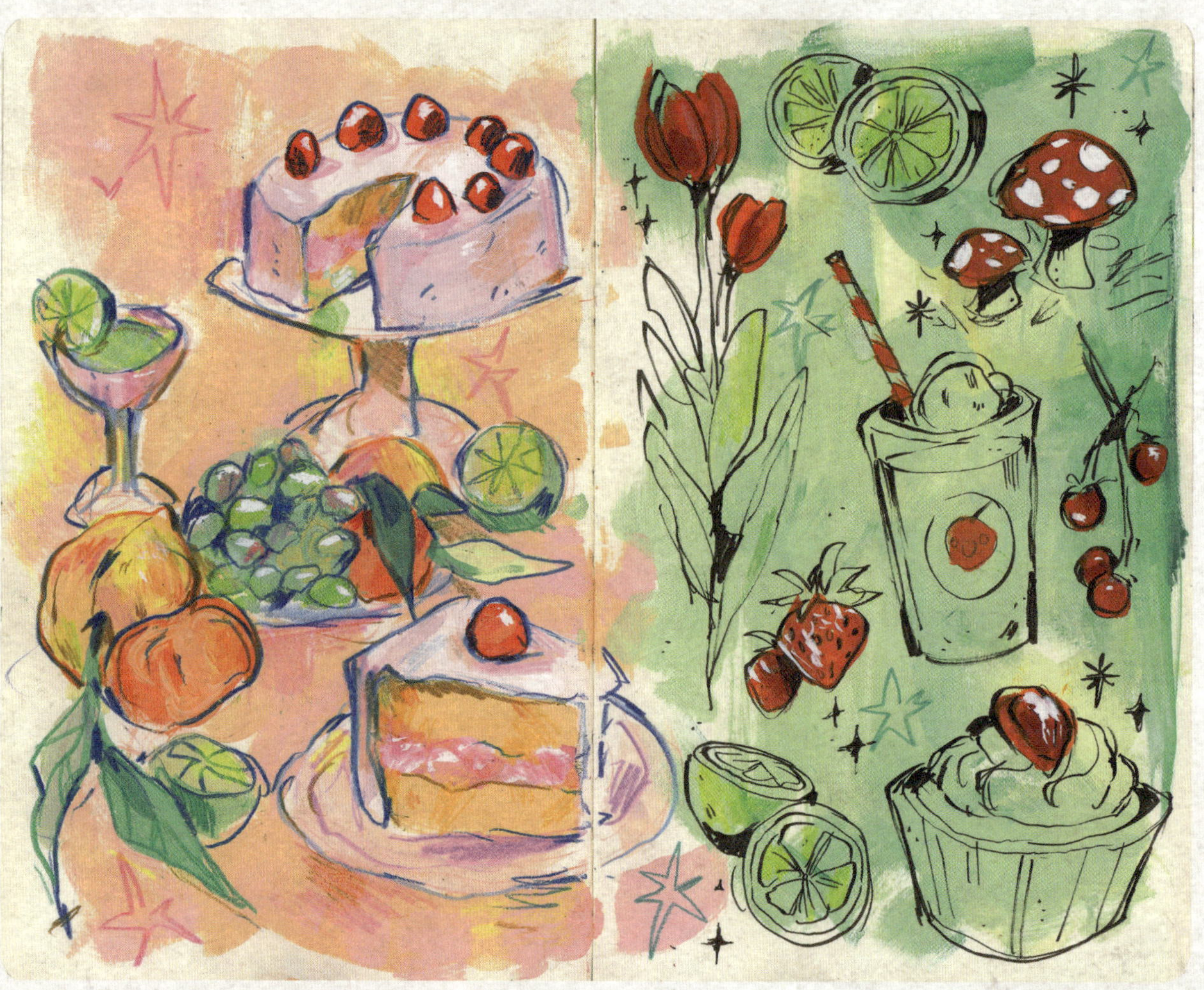

If we're not mindful of how to use references, there's sometimes a small risk of becoming dependent on them – and that's no fun! There have been a few times where I found myself staring at the blank page, incapable of sketching because I doubted my skills. I hated that feeling because it was like something inside was telling me that I could never make 'perfectly' accurate anatomy without relying on a reference, so I froze.

But I'm not interested in mastering a perfect level of anatomy or depicting reality exactly as it is. I took it as a sign to bring some boldness back into my practice, mixing it with a more balanced use of references. For me, that's the perfect recipe. Here are some tips I found useful:

- References are a source of information. It's not possible to know/remember everything. Use them to study and learn how certain things look, work, etc. But whenever you can, try to put the reference aside to sketch freely and train your memory muscle.
- Try to remain in control of the decision-making process. If you always let the reference determine the direction of your art, it's going to be really hard to try new things on your own.
- It's better to have a somewhat clear vision of what you want to draw before you start researching and collecting references to back up your initial idea. That way, you remain in charge of the creative direction.
- Creating your own references is such a time saver. I normally ask my partner to help me whenever I need a very specific pose. You can also have a small mirror on your desk or take quick photos of yourself!

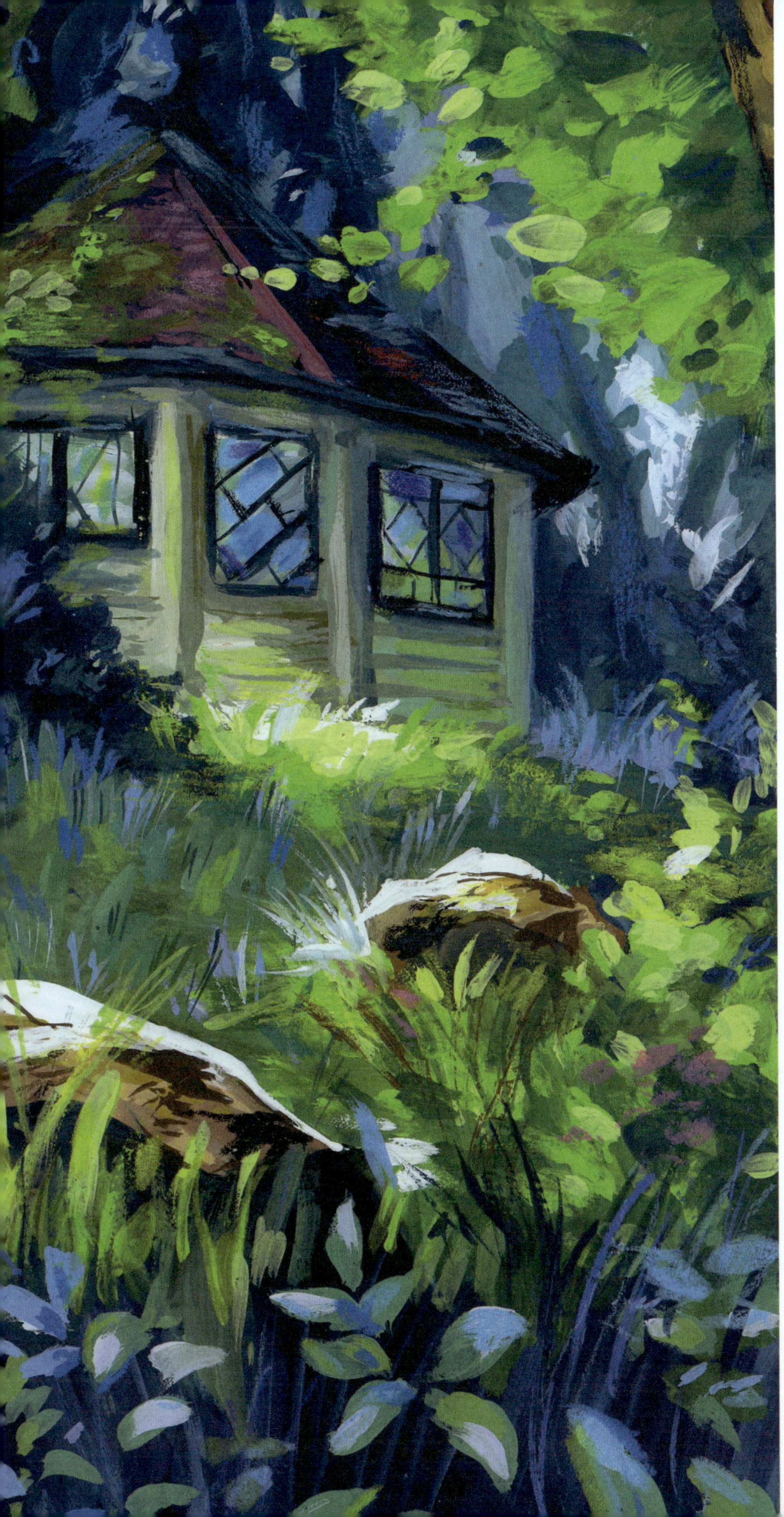

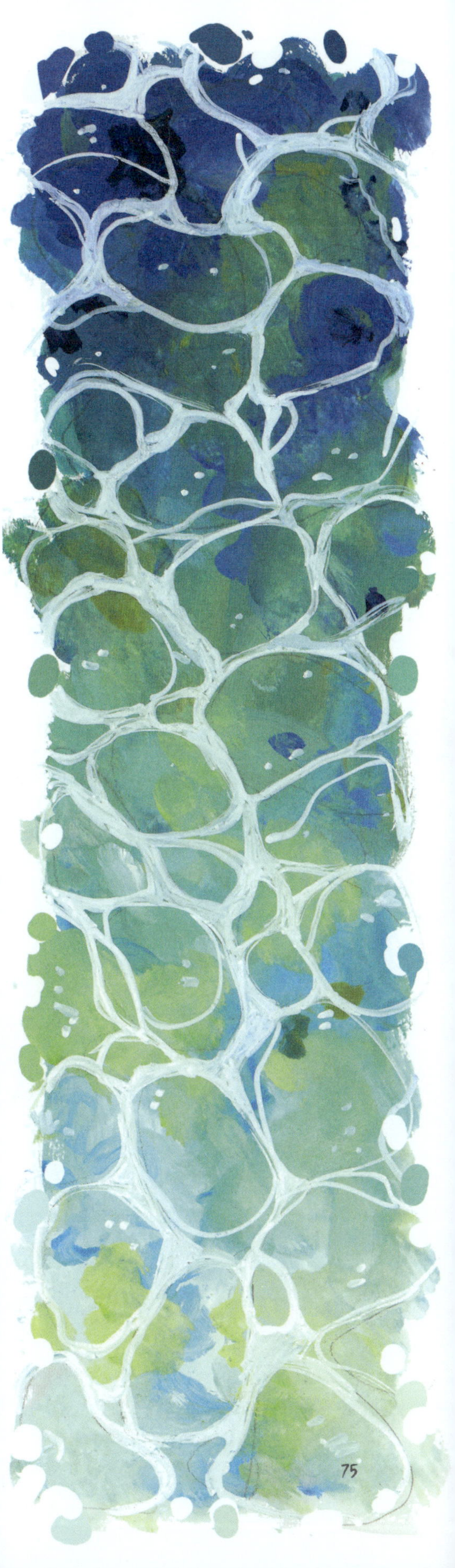

Perspective and technical drawing are not my strongest suits, so in order to draw this diorama, I had to collect hundreds of references. The fun part of gathering information from different sources is that you end up creating something entirely new out of them. I like to use PureRef to keep all my references organized for each project.

One of the best websites I found to practice gesture drawing is quickposes.com

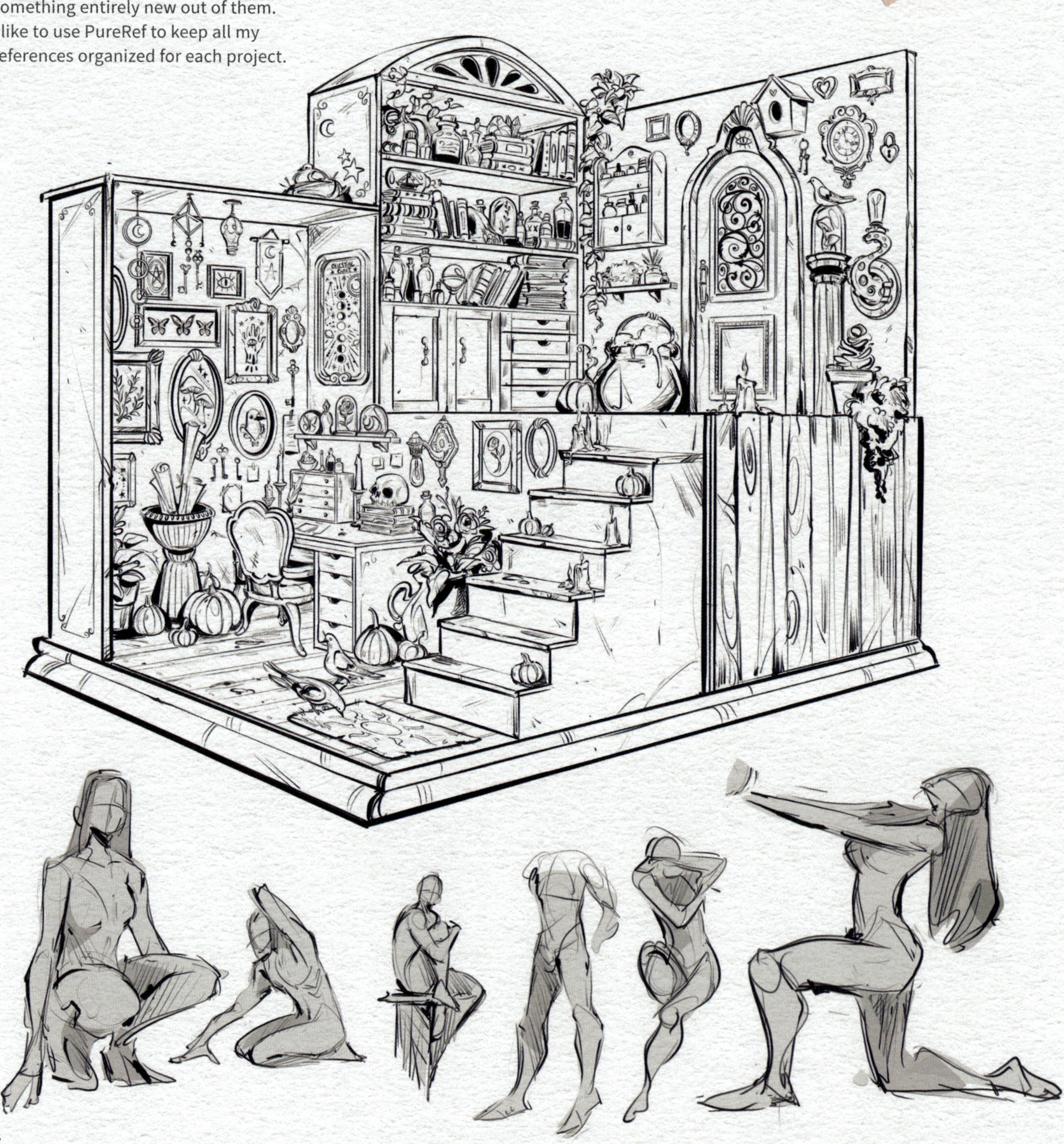

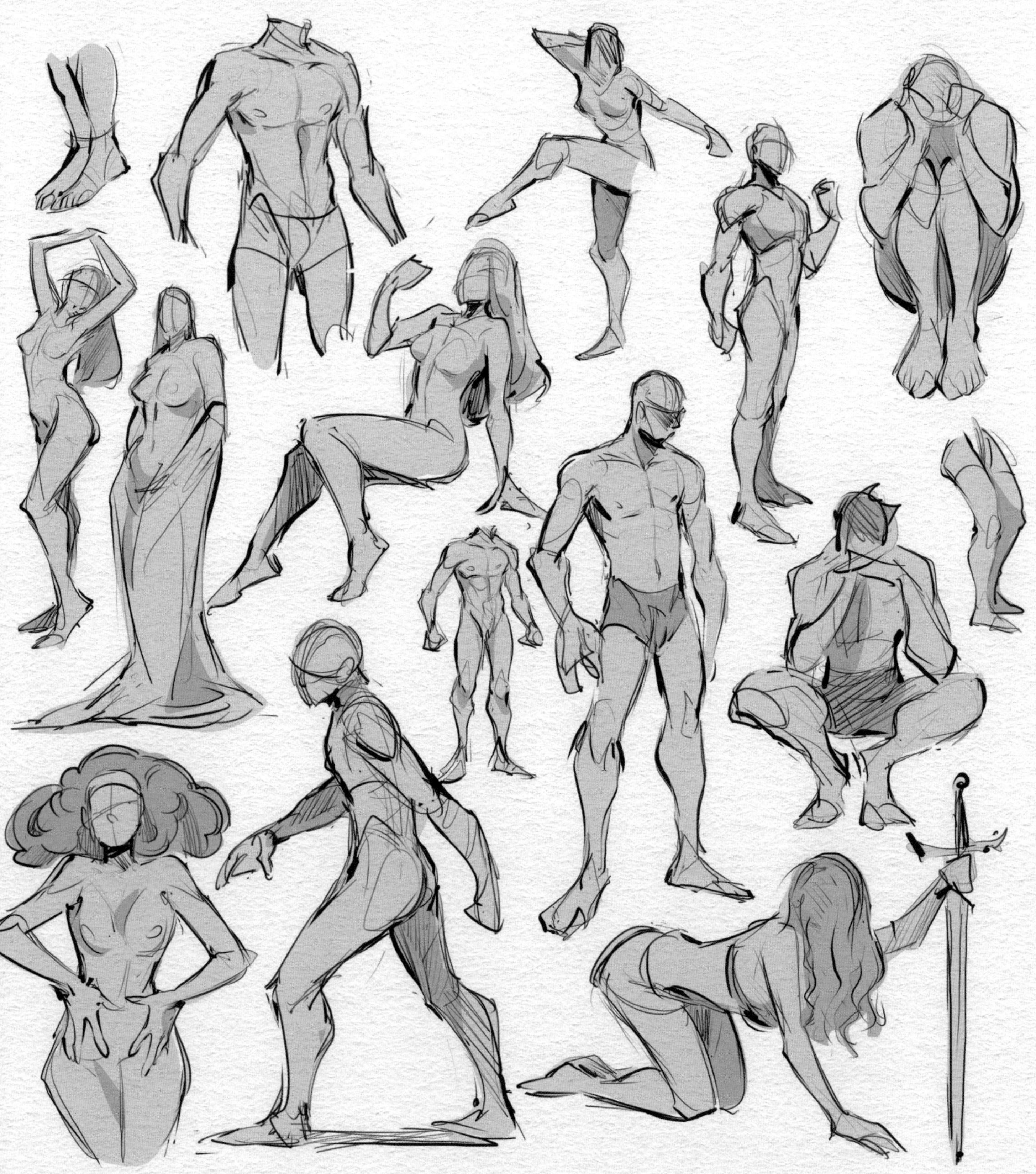

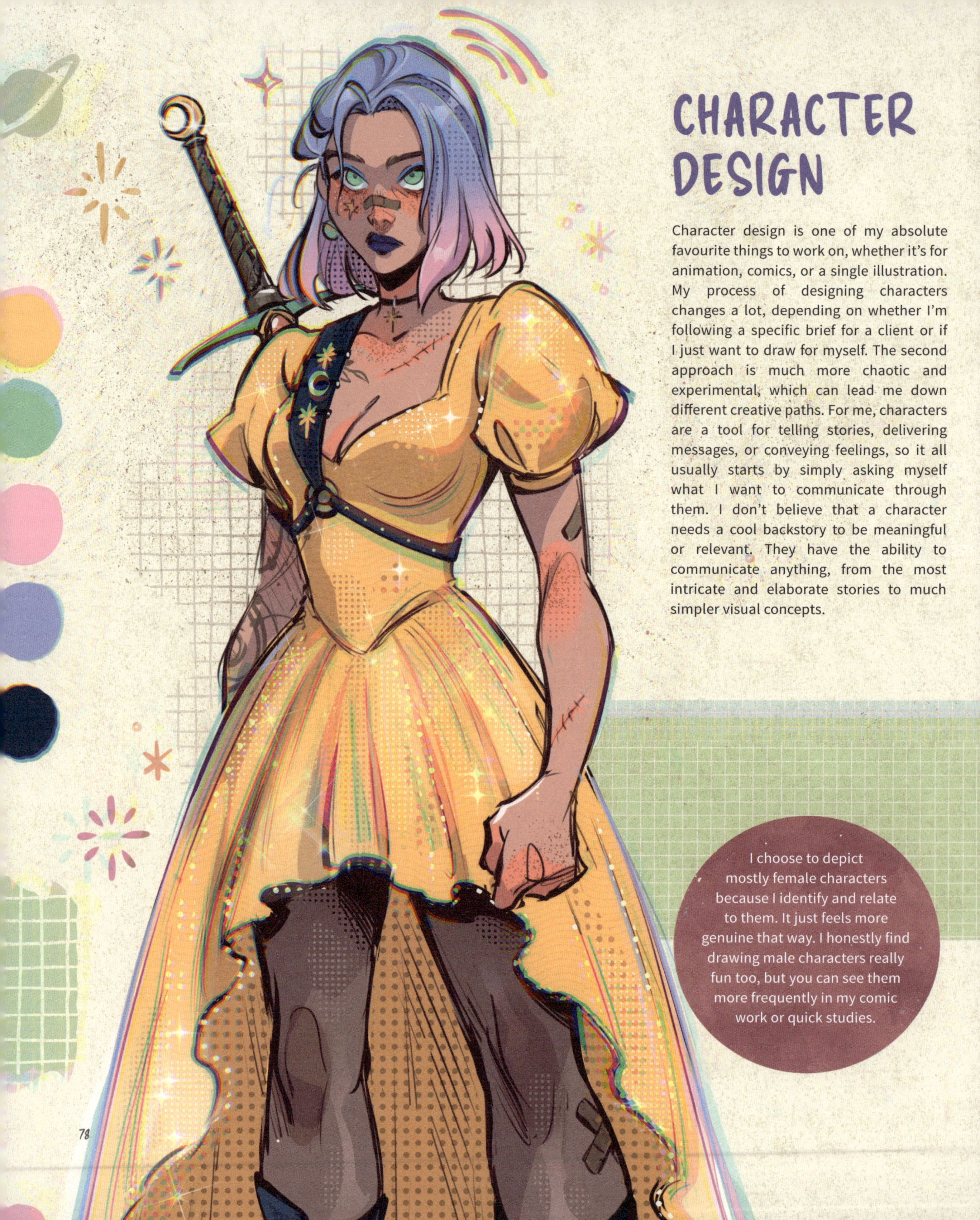

CHARACTER DESIGN

Character design is one of my absolute favourite things to work on, whether it's for animation, comics, or a single illustration. My process of designing characters changes a lot, depending on whether I'm following a specific brief for a client or if I just want to draw for myself. The second approach is much more chaotic and experimental, which can lead me down different creative paths. For me, characters are a tool for telling stories, delivering messages, or conveying feelings, so it all usually starts by simply asking myself what I want to communicate through them. I don't believe that a character needs a cool backstory to be meaningful or relevant. They have the ability to communicate anything, from the most intricate and elaborate stories to much simpler visual concepts.

I choose to depict mostly female characters because I identify and relate to them. It just feels more genuine that way. I honestly find drawing male characters really fun too, but you can see them more frequently in my comic work or quick studies.

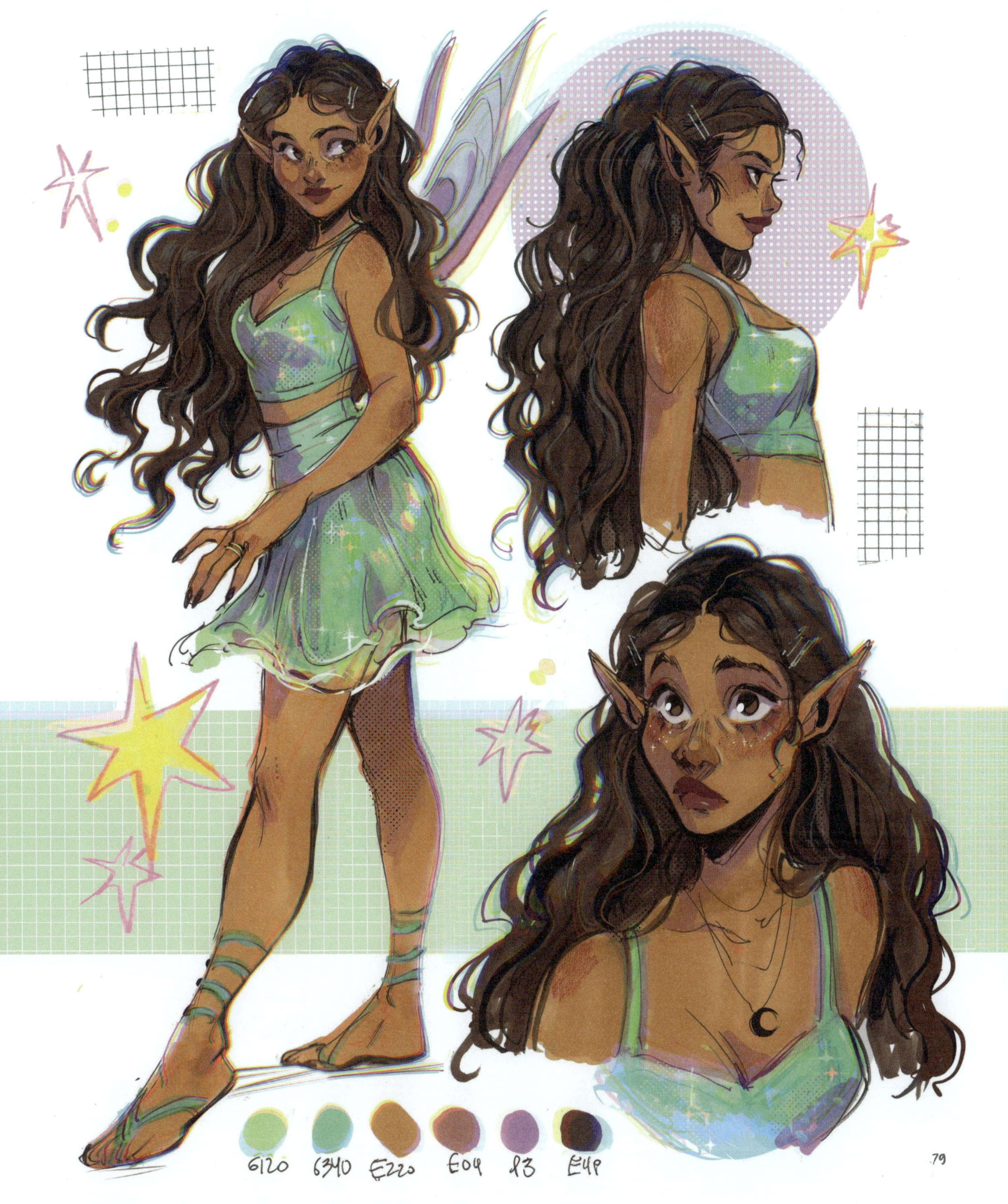
G120
G340
E220
E04
E49

Stylization

Stylization refers to the process of simplifying or exaggerating certain features in a character's design to make it more appealing or interesting. These aspects include proportions, facial features, line work, and rendering, among others. The stylization choices you make are completely tied to your personal preferences.

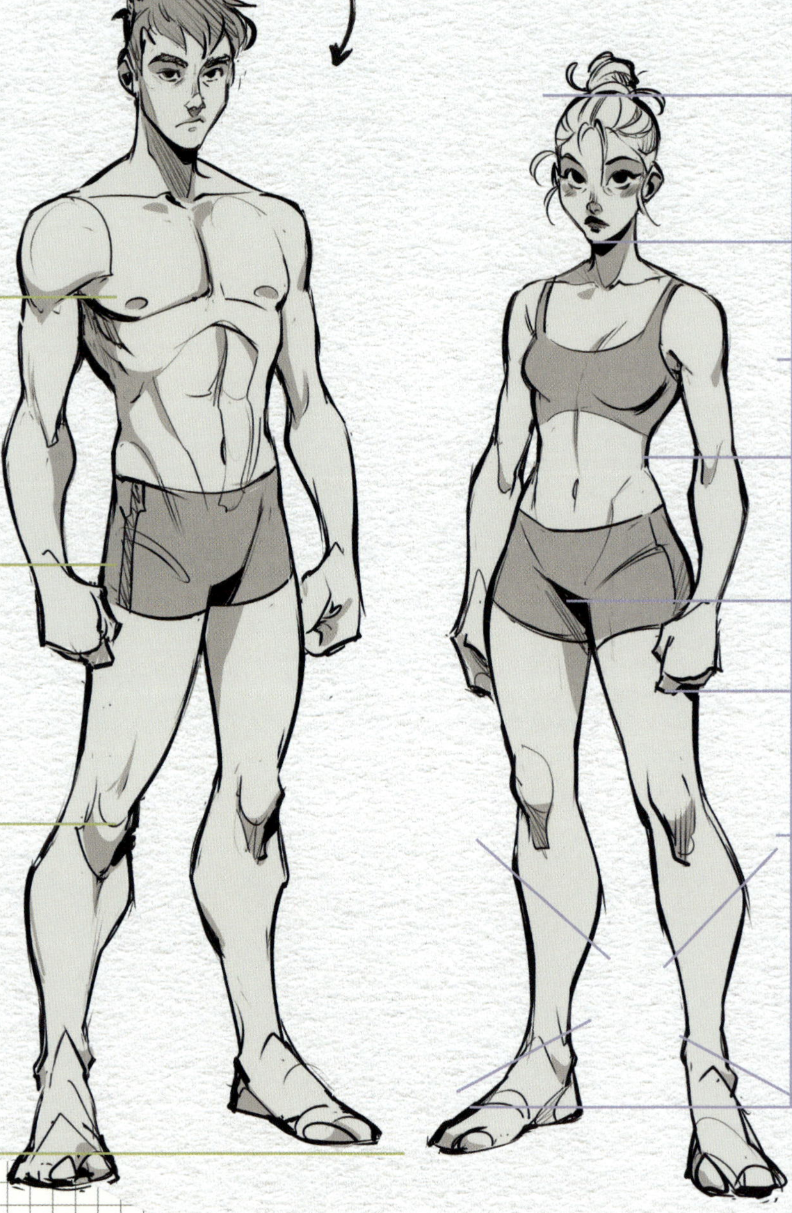

This is a simple example of my preferred stylization when it comes to character design; somewhere between realistic and cartoonish. Again, these stylization choices can be simplified, more detailed, or way more exaggerated depending on the body type I'm drawing and what I'm looking to achieve.

In order to bring strength to your designs and find the type of stylization you like, it's important to have a solid understanding of the fundamentals so that you can intentionally break the rules later on. Yes, anatomy is a complex subject that requires lots of practice to master, but it can be even more overwhelming if you're trying to learn everything all at once. Studying each part separately will help to break things down and make everything easier to tackle. Once you've filled dozens of pages with hand studies, feet from different angles, and you finally understand how anatomical torsos, arms, and legs work, you can begin to identify which aspects and shapes are essential. Everything else can be omitted.

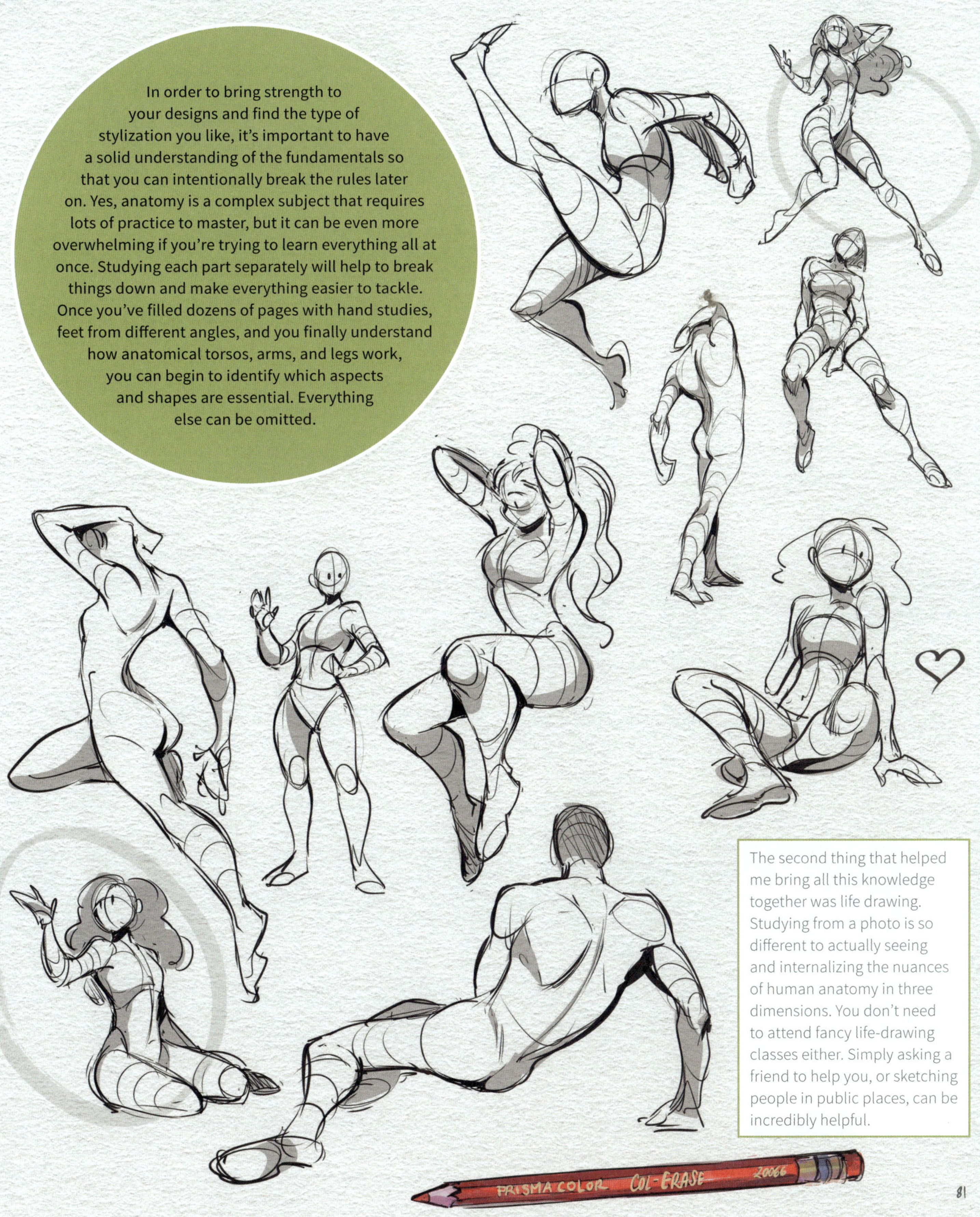

The second thing that helped me bring all this knowledge together was life drawing. Studying from a photo is so different to actually seeing and internalizing the nuances of human anatomy in three dimensions. You don't need to attend fancy life-drawing classes either. Simply asking a friend to help you, or sketching people in public places, can be incredibly helpful.

Attitude & personality

If I had to pick just one thing to draw for the rest of my life, it would have to be expressions. Not only do I find the process of capturing a range of different emotions to be really fun, but it also allows me to understand a character's personality and bring them to life. By drawing their reactions to different scenarios, I get a better sense of who they are, what they like/dislike, and what makes them tick. It's like stepping into their shoes and connecting with them on a deeper level, which no doubt helps to create a more compelling, lifelike character.

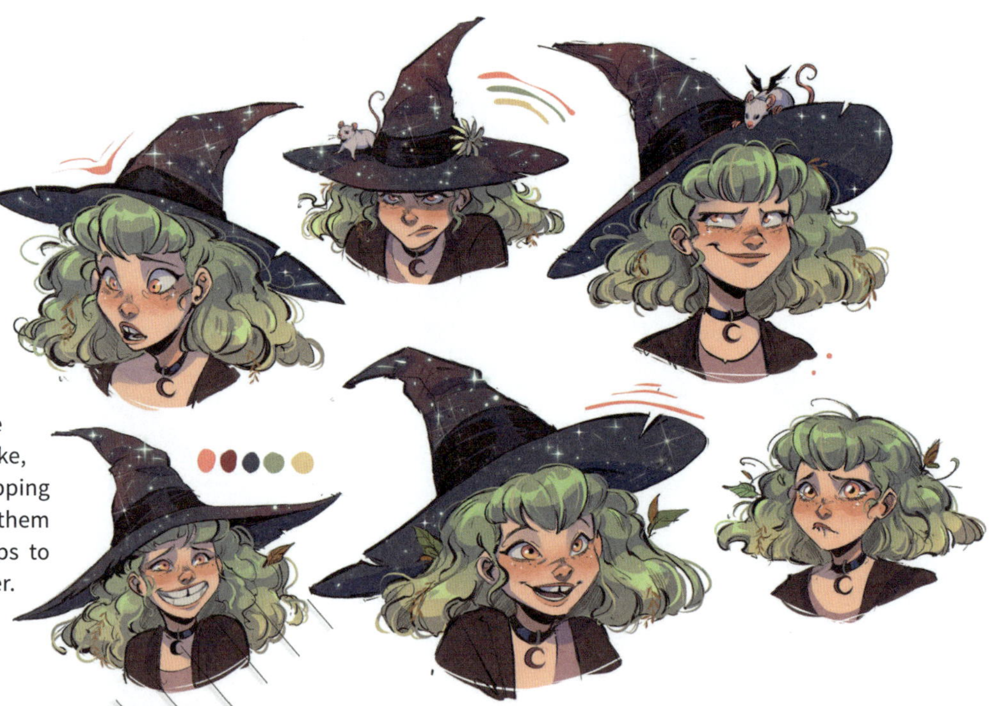

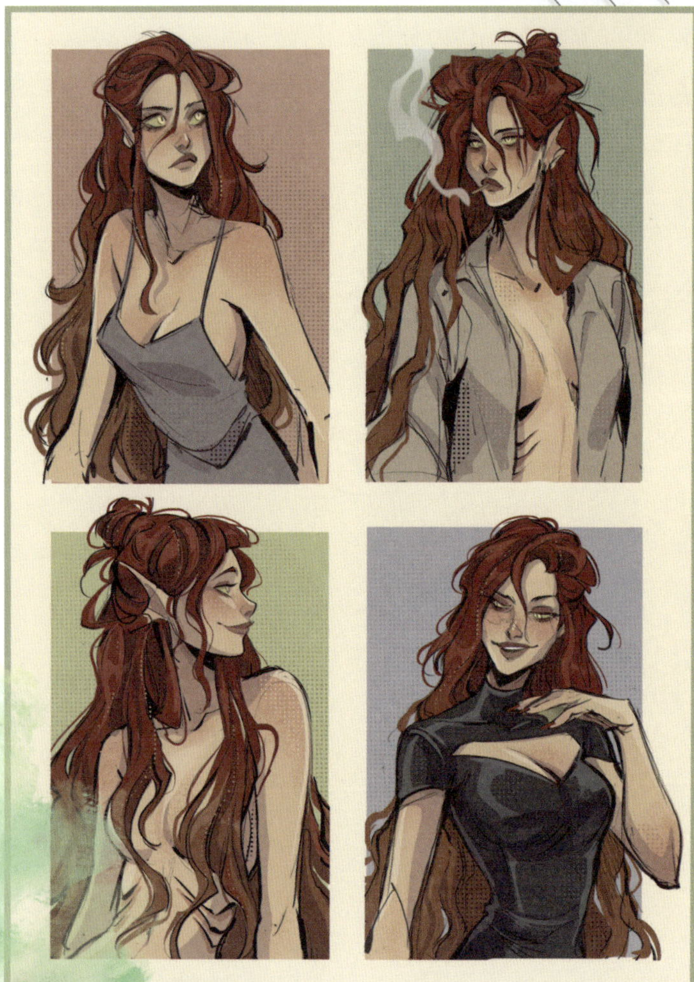

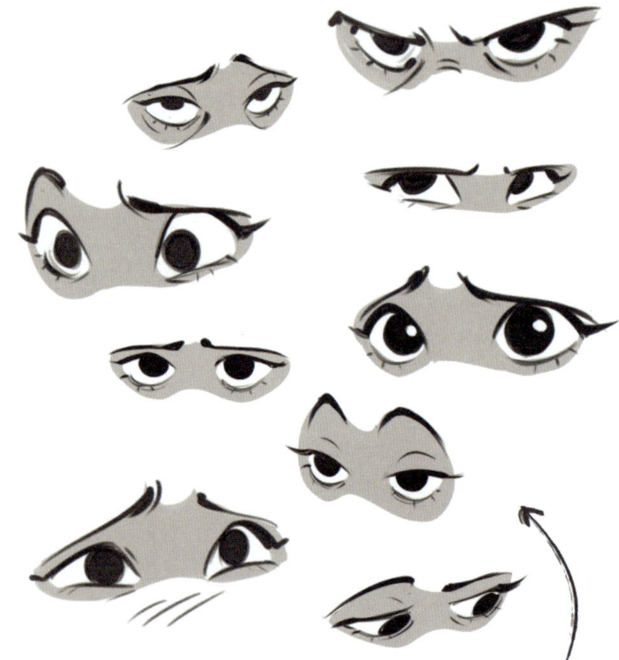

I know it can be difficult to draw the same character from different angles, and I still struggle with it from time to time! But I wouldn't worry too much, as it definitely gets easier with practice. Instead of striving for accuracy, try to focus on infusing raw emotion and attitude into your characters. Make them feel relatable and engaging by showing their intentions, who they are, and how they feel.

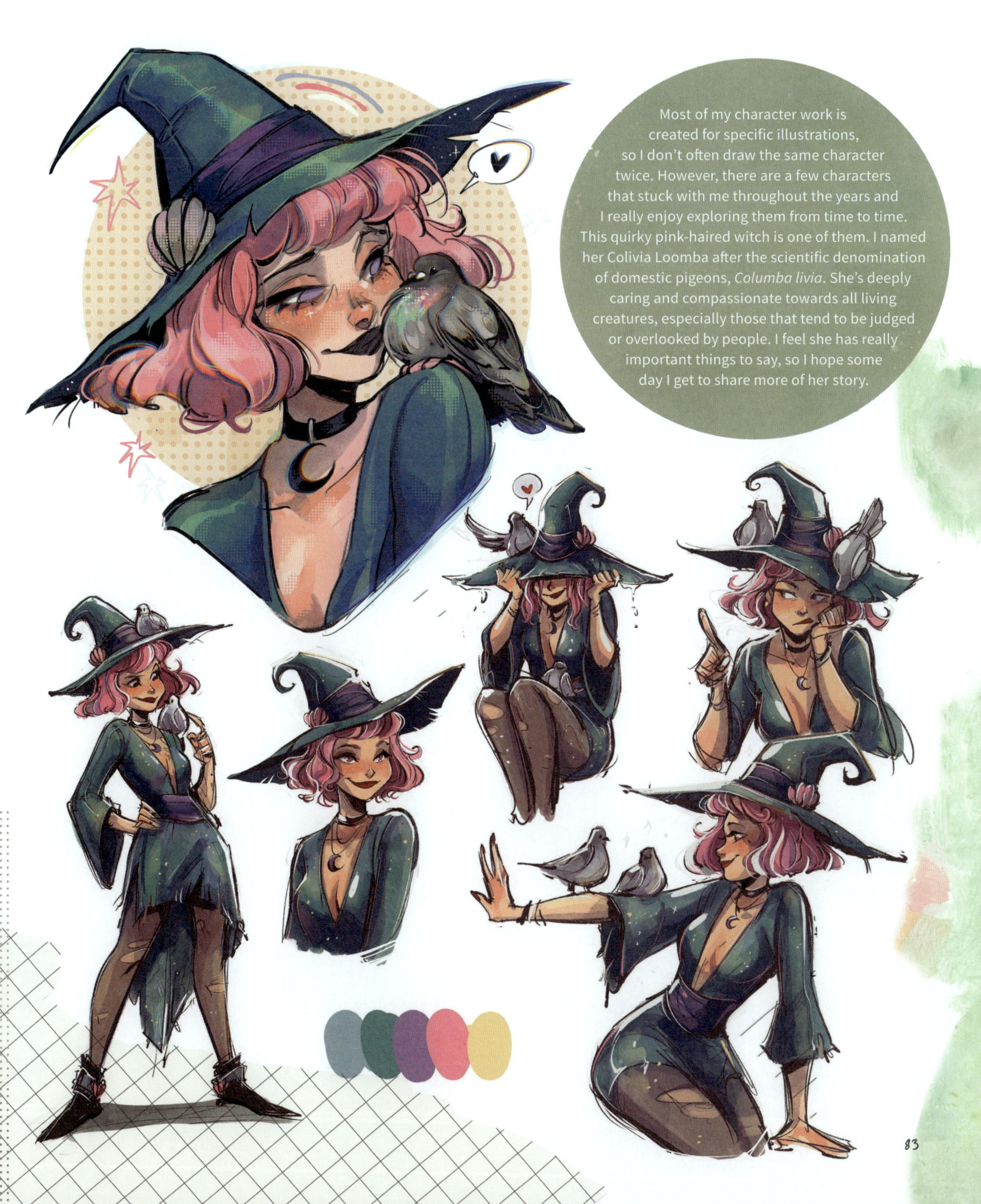

Most of my character work is created for specific illustrations, so I don't often draw the same character twice. However, there are a few characters that stuck with me throughout the years and I really enjoy exploring them from time to time. This quirky pink-haired witch is one of them. I named her Colivia Loomba after the scientific denomination of domestic pigeons, *Columba livia*. She's deeply caring and compassionate towards all living creatures, especially those that tend to be judged or overlooked by people. I feel she has really important things to say, so I hope some day I get to share more of her story.

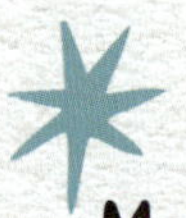

Make it stand out

Before I start drawing, I always try to have some sort of vision of how I want to portray a character, including key design elements such as visual traits, colour palettes, certain poses, or an interesting silhouette. This vision always starts out blurry but becomes clearer as I work on the character. It's really necessary for me to have that initial feel and motivation, no matter how much it can change and evolve along the way – it allows me to set a clear direction towards a specific idea.

You can also tell a lot about a character by the way they look. Ideally, you want the design to reflect the nature of the character and offer little visual clues of who they might be or where they come from. Rather than doing super busy, ornate costume designs, I prefer to focus on adding narrative in the form of simple details.

Atlante, watercolour and digital, 2019. Inspired by a bronze statue sculpted by Amaryllis Bataille, located in Cannes

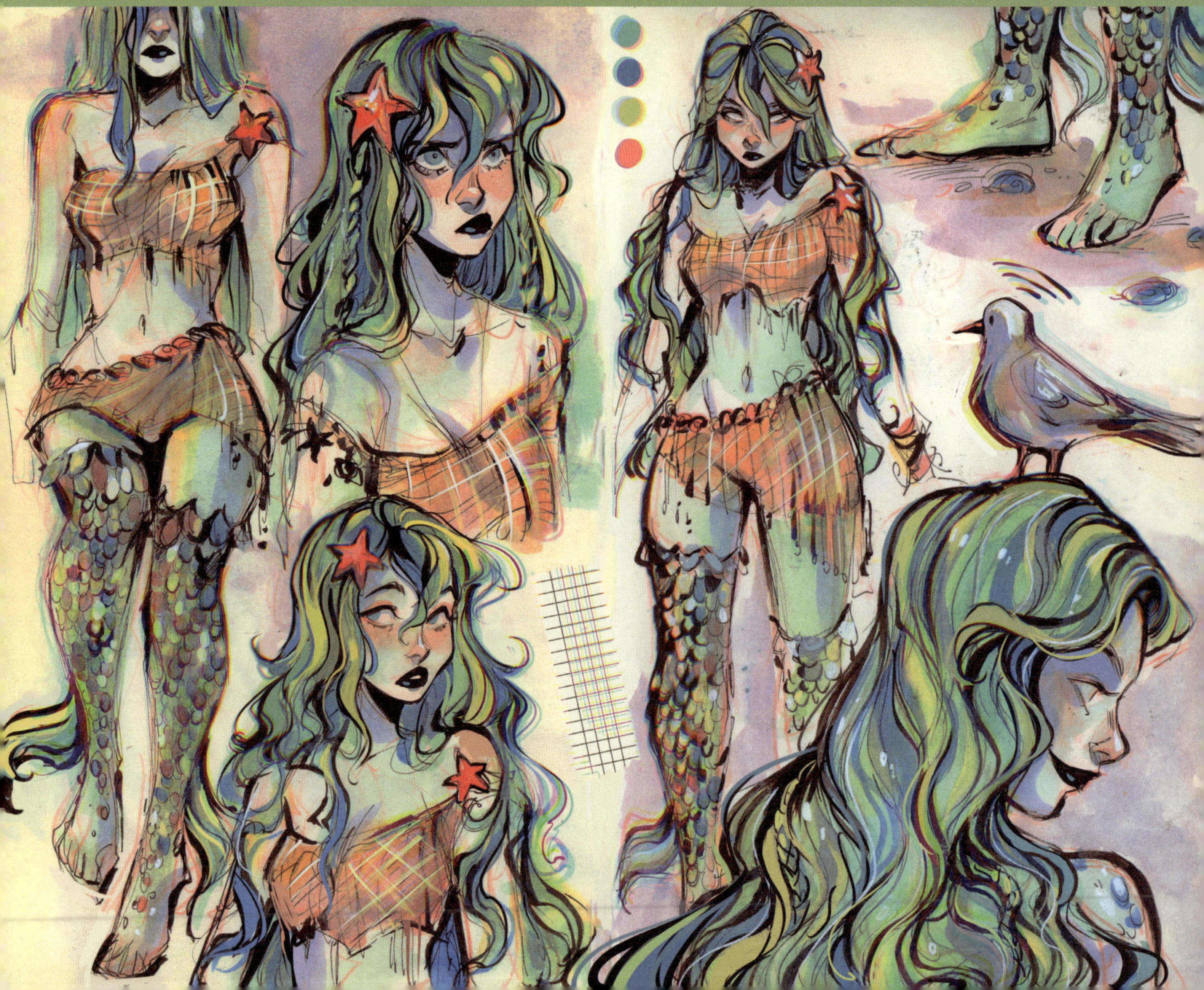

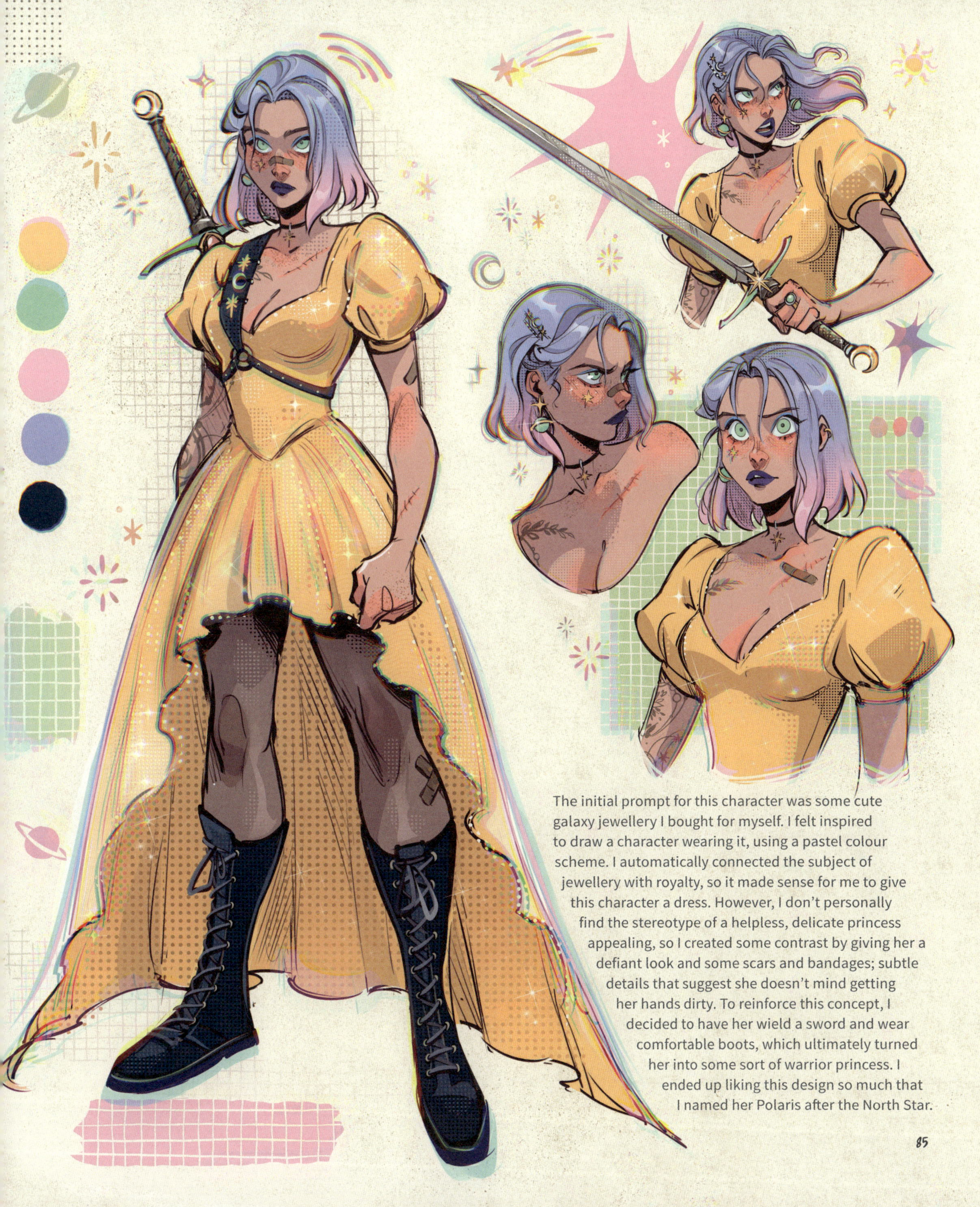

The initial prompt for this character was some cute galaxy jewellery I bought for myself. I felt inspired to draw a character wearing it, using a pastel colour scheme. I automatically connected the subject of jewellery with royalty, so it made sense for me to give this character a dress. However, I don't personally find the stereotype of a helpless, delicate princess appealing, so I created some contrast by giving her a defiant look and some scars and bandages; subtle details that suggest she doesn't mind getting her hands dirty. To reinforce this concept, I decided to have her wield a sword and wear comfortable boots, which ultimately turned her into some sort of warrior princess. I ended up liking this design so much that I named her Polaris after the North Star.

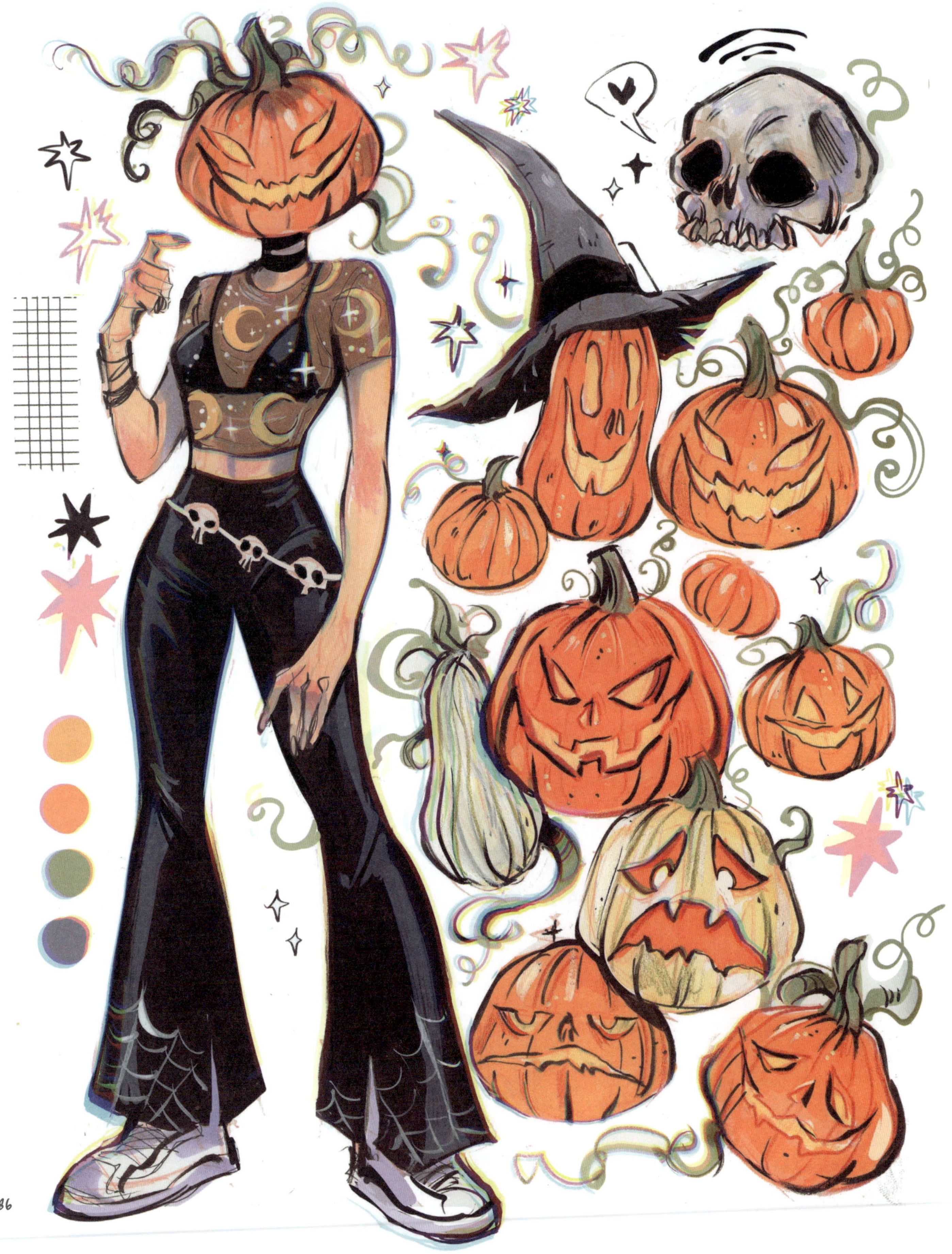

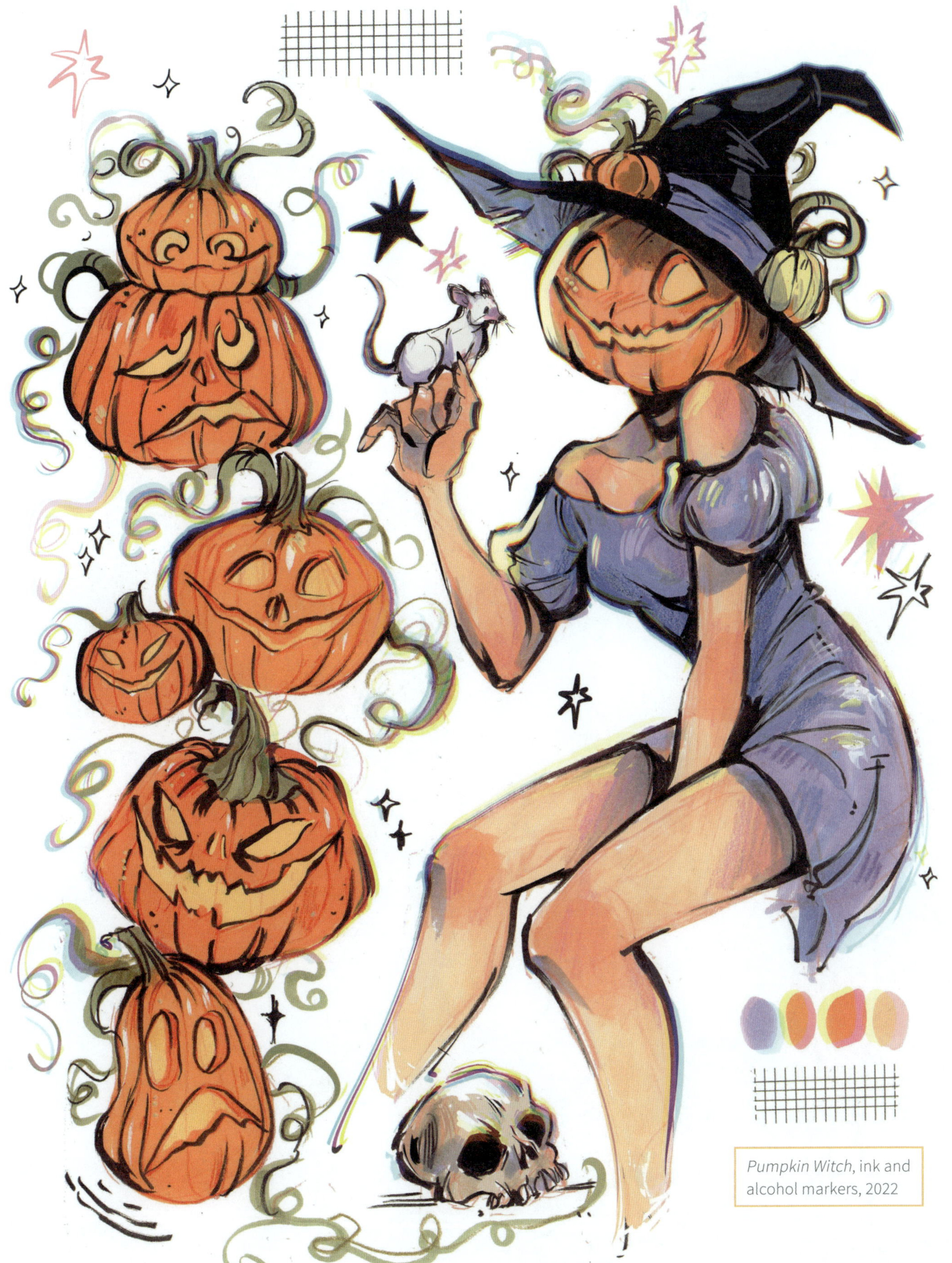

Pumpkin Witch, ink and alcohol markers, 2022

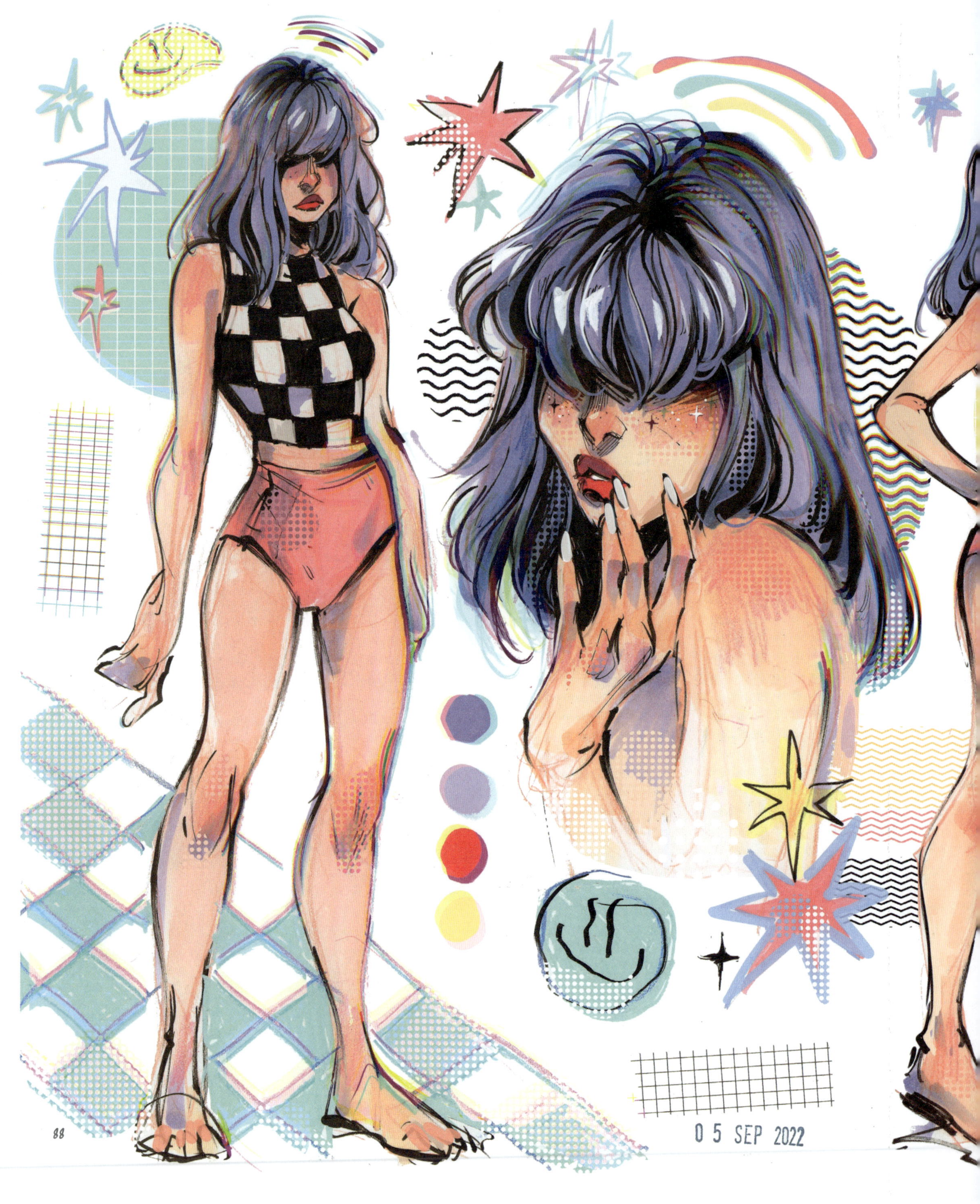

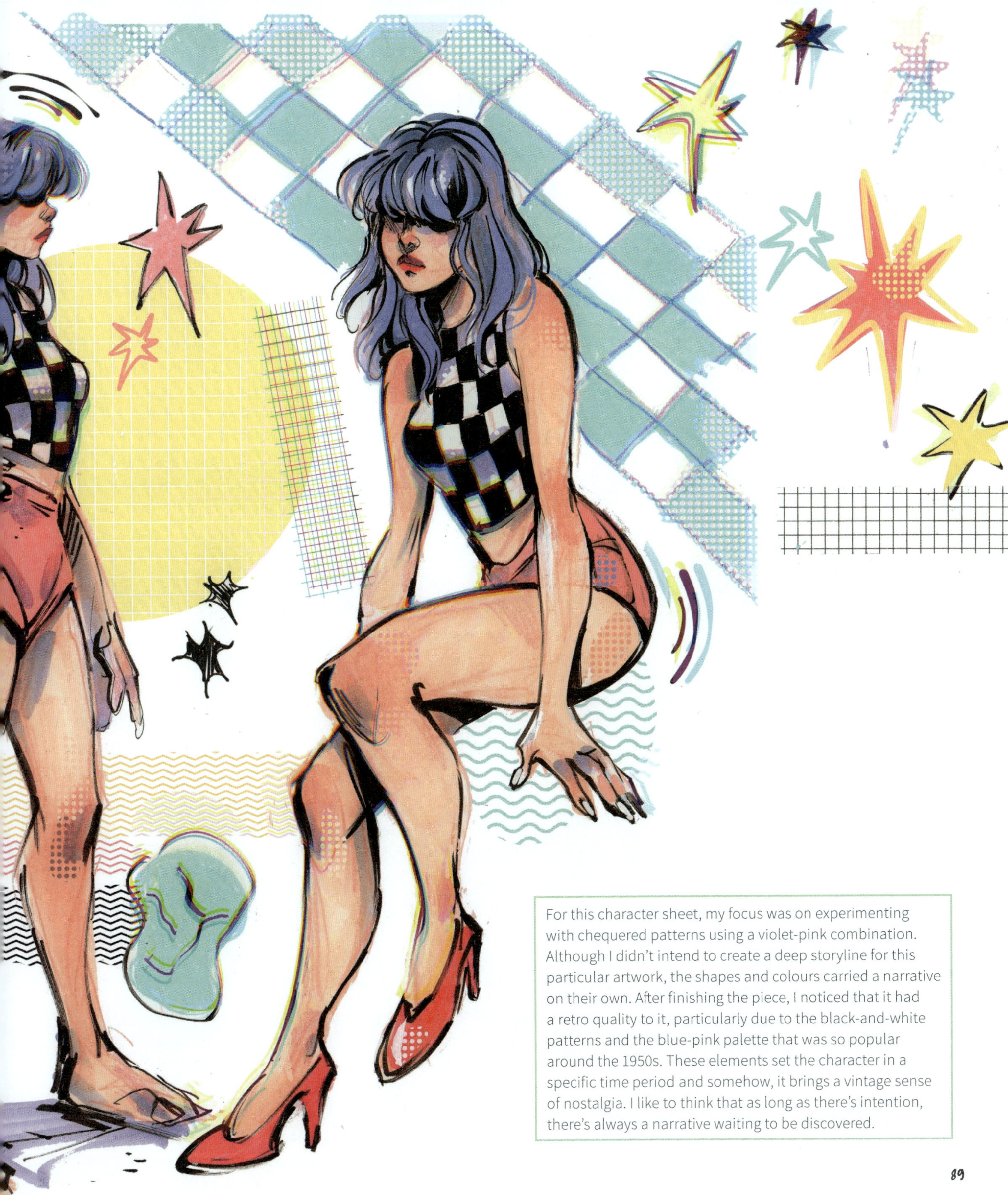

For this character sheet, my focus was on experimenting with chequered patterns using a violet-pink combination. Although I didn't intend to create a deep storyline for this particular artwork, the shapes and colours carried a narrative on their own. After finishing the piece, I noticed that it had a retro quality to it, particularly due to the black-and-white patterns and the blue-pink palette that was so popular around the 1950s. These elements set the character in a specific time period and somehow, it brings a vintage sense of nostalgia. I like to think that as long as there's intention, there's always a narrative waiting to be discovered.

BIRTHDAY

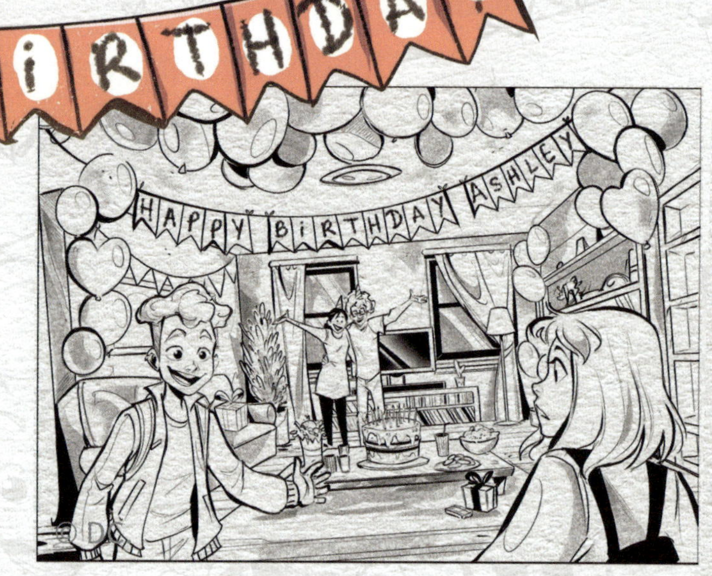

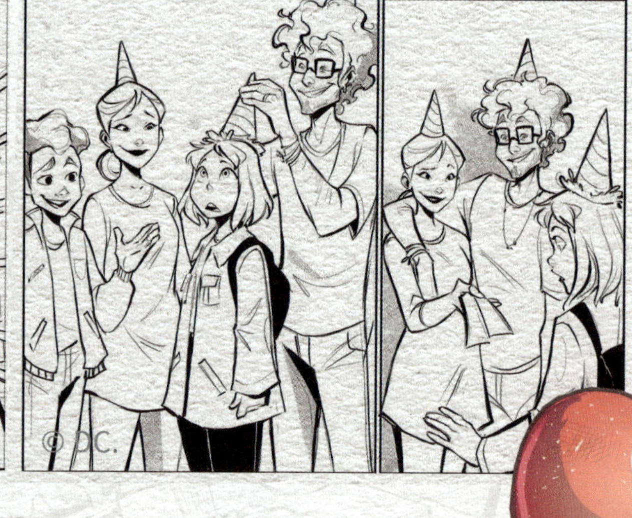

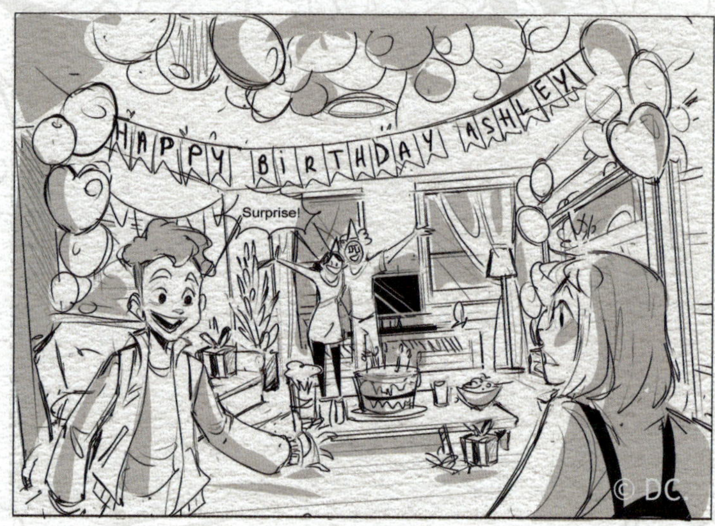

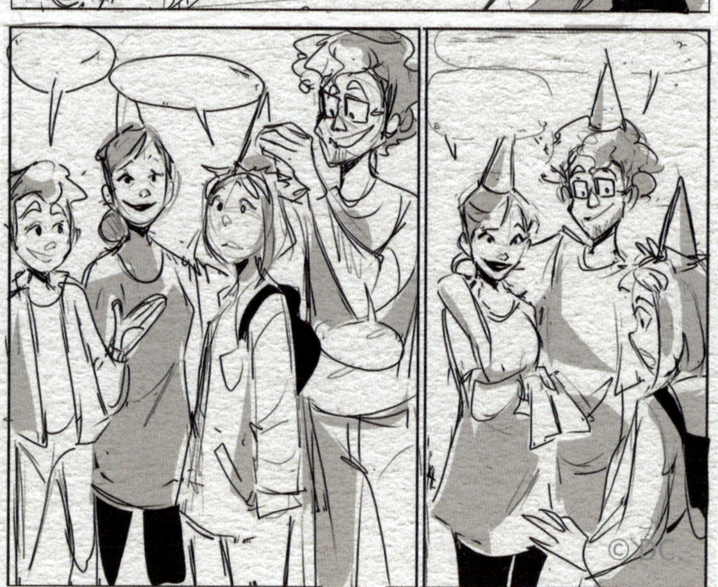

COMICS

Despite having worked on comics professionally for quite some time now, they still present a big challenge for me. I hadn't studied sequential art before I had the opportunity to work for DC, but I had consumed many, *many* comics throughout my life, so they felt very familiar to me. Sometimes, diving right in is the best way to fully learn something. I gathered a humble amount of knowledge by working on *Primer* (my very first graphic novel), considering editor feedback, and referencing artists I admired. One of the most daunting realizations I had when first starting out was the importance of trusting myself. Although there are countless different ways to communicate an idea, it took me some time to understand that no artist will tackle a script the same way. There's a lot of power in fully embracing your unique approach to storytelling.

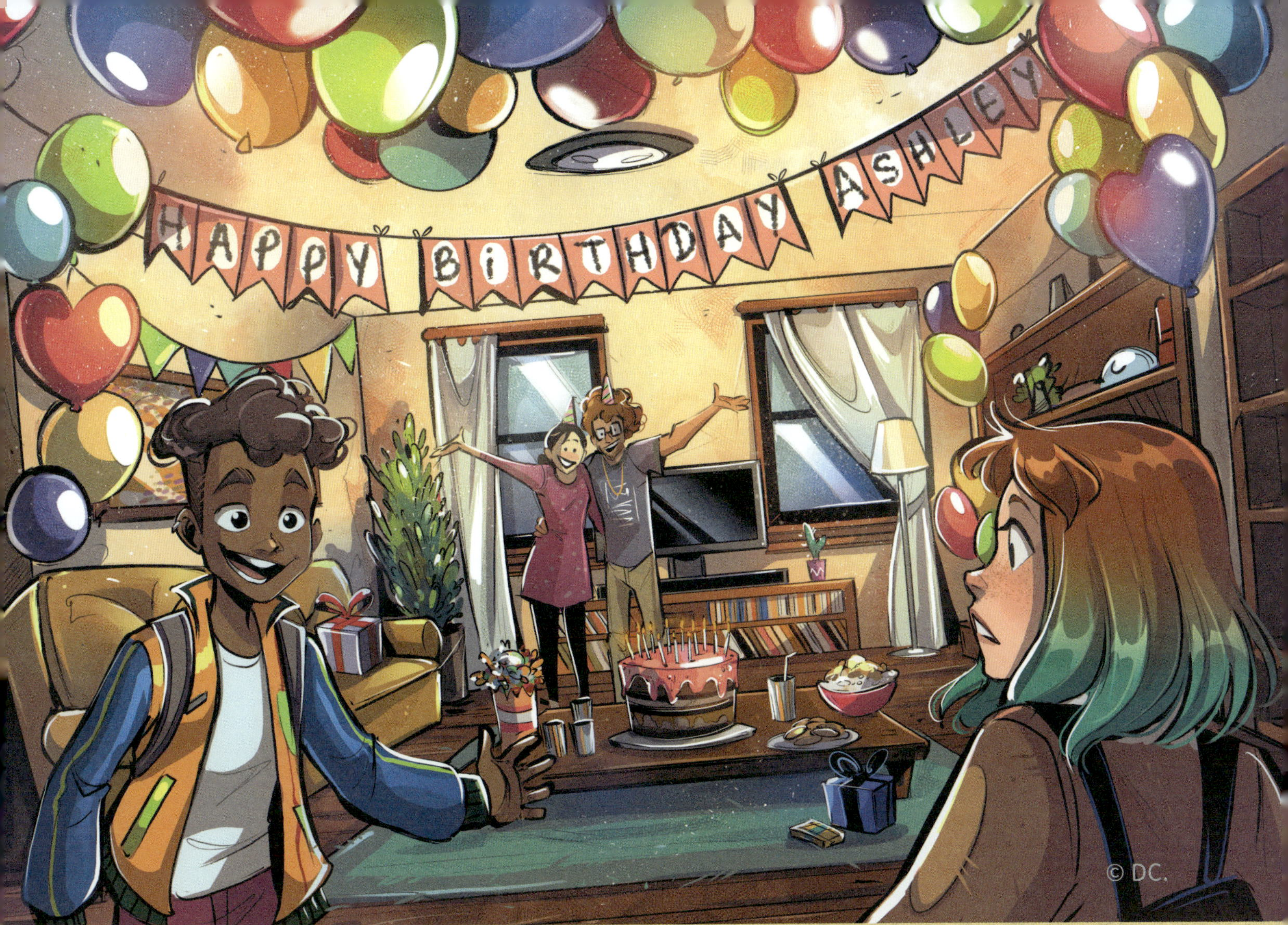

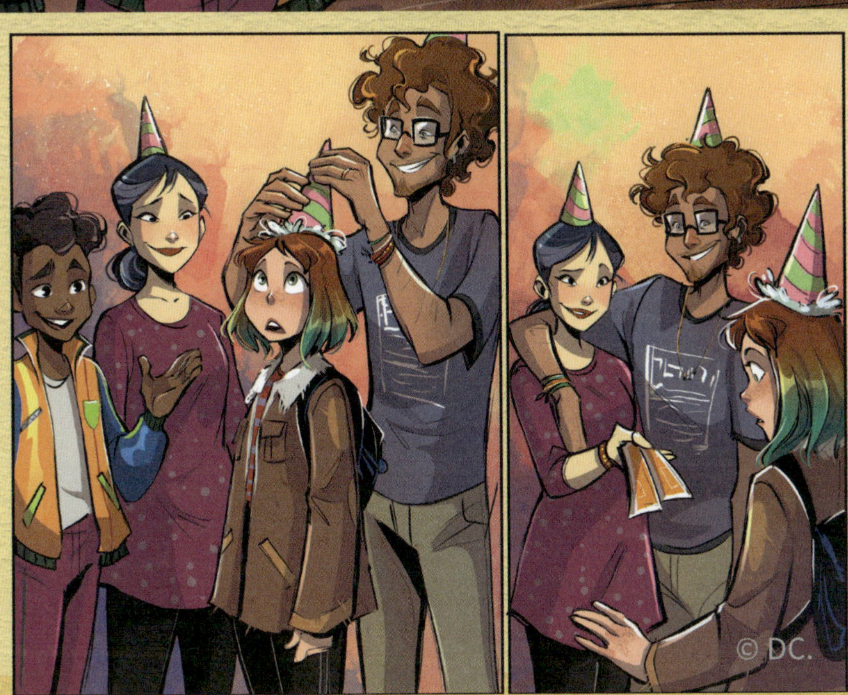

I think because I have read comics my entire life, my approach relies heavily on my intuition. I tend to pay more attention to how everything feels as a whole; how the panels interact with each other and how the action flows through the page, not rationalizing my choices too much. If something feels off, I can immediately tell. I'm not saying it's okay to neglect studying the technical aspects of storytelling, but I do believe that you should absolutely follow these feelings of intuition in order to build more confidence in your work!

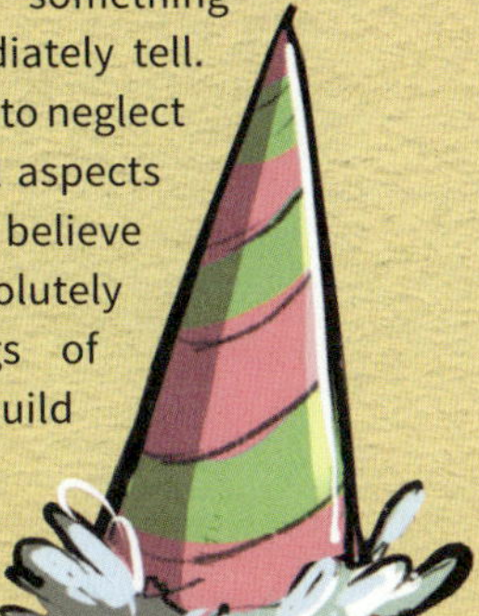

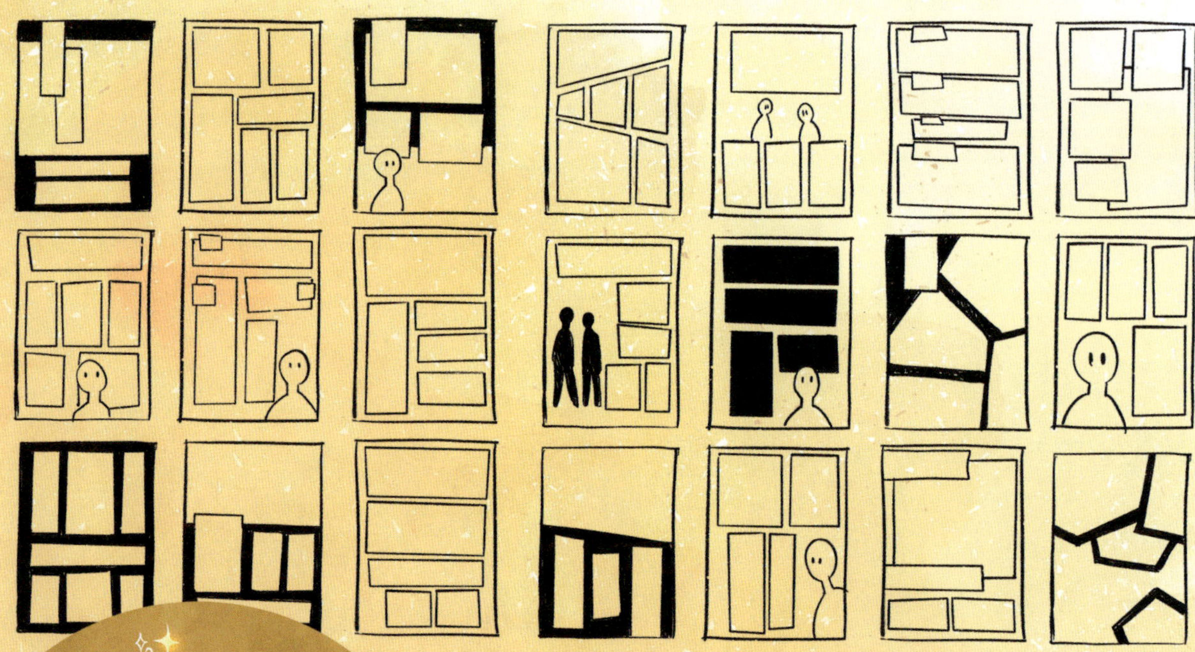

These are a few of the many layout ideas I roughly scribble down each time I flip through a comic and find a page I like. Doing these tiny studies gives me a lot of insight into the creative choices of other artists and helps me understand the endless possibilities when it comes to page composition. They are also a great way to figure out what kind of narrative tools I prefer for my comics.

Normally, my comic work starts as small, incomprehensible pencil thumbnails. I find it easier to work traditionally when tackling a bunch of new pages in order to quickly establish the panels and character placement. Once I'm happy with a batch of thumbnails, I scan them or take a picture and open them in Adobe Photoshop. I then proceed to do a more detailed pass, ensuring the characters' expressions are clear and the action unfolds smoothly across the page. I also make sure to search for any references if I need them, so it's usually the most time-consuming step.

These kinds of digital layouts are the ones I send to my editor for feedback. Once a layout is approved, I move on to inking the page.

Layout

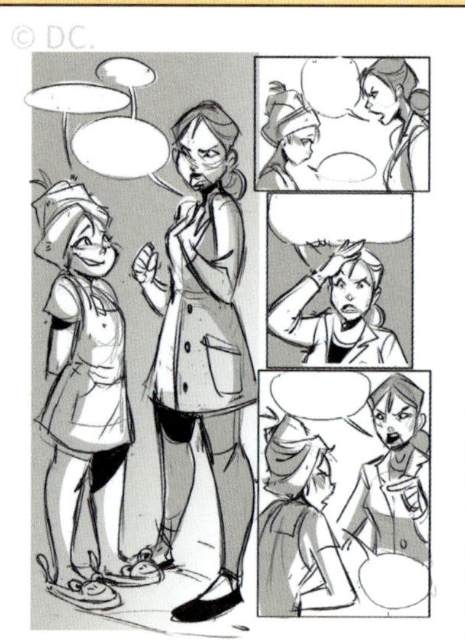

Inks

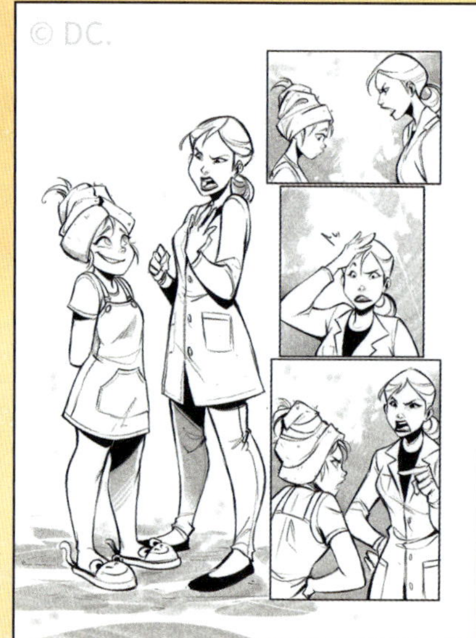

Colours

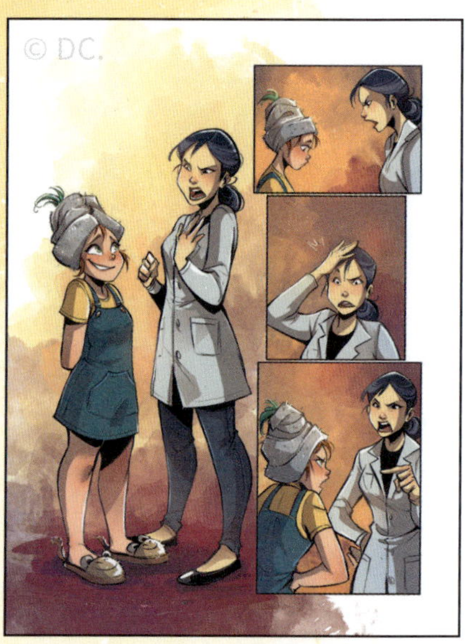

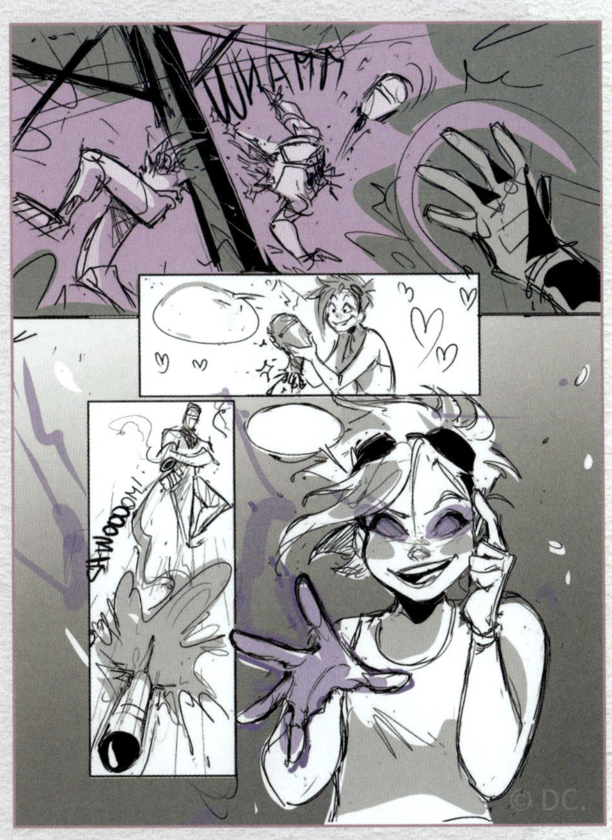

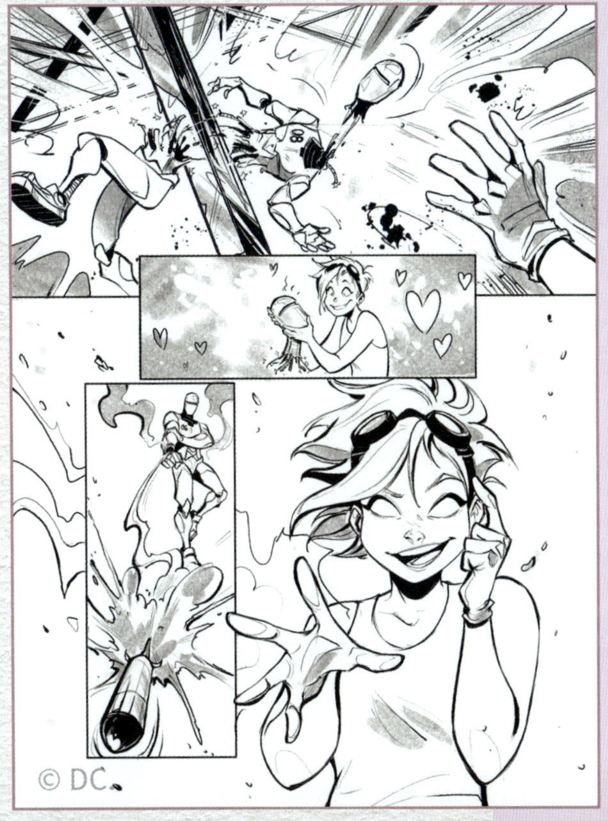

I really enjoy the inking process. When I do all the necessary prep work, inking can be very relaxing and fun. For *Primer* in particular, I inked around six pages a week and then coloured them in batches of ten. Drawing and colouring a whole graphic novel by yourself is a lot of work, so I found that switching between layouts, inking, and colouring, from time to time, made the process less repetitive and kept me engaged.

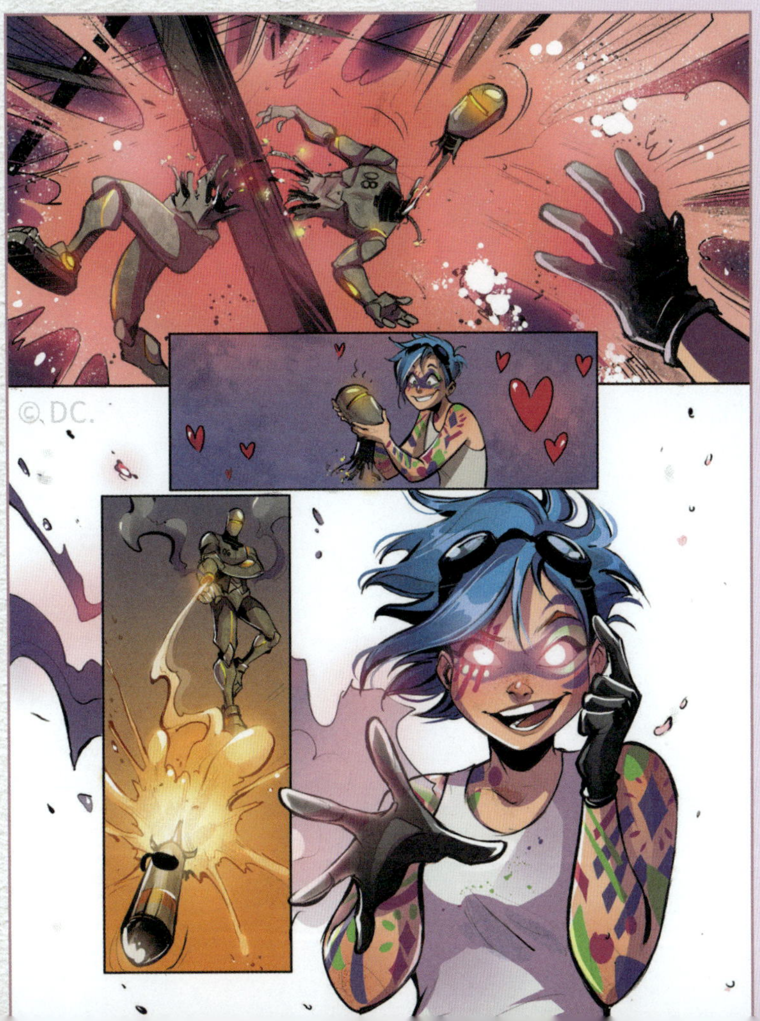

CLIENT WORK VS. PERSONAL WORK

Over the past few years, I've bounced a lot between client and personal work and have experienced the ups and downs of both worlds. I've often asked myself which path I want to take my career down. Does having a Patreon, doing my own merchandise, and running a shop truly make me happy, or does working on books and comics as a published artist make me feel more complete?

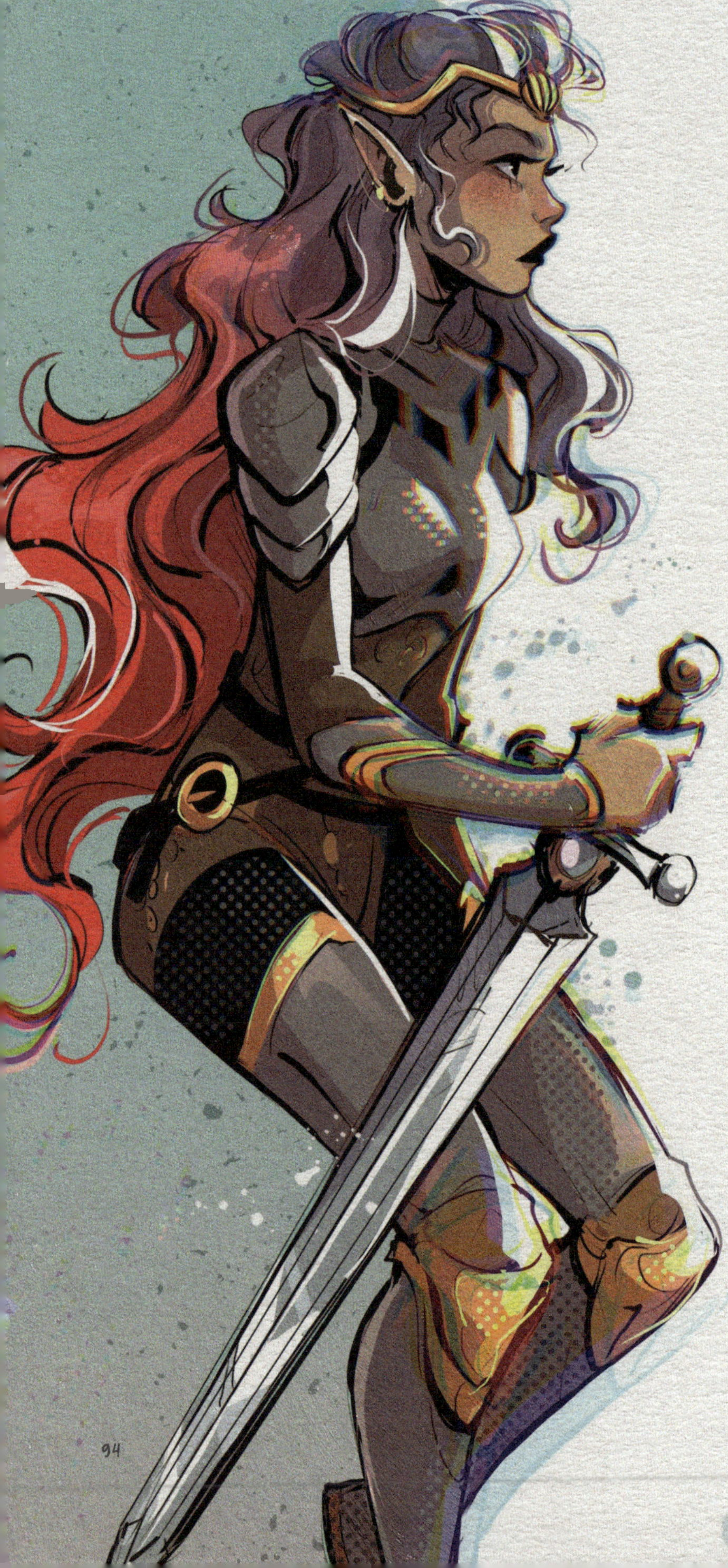

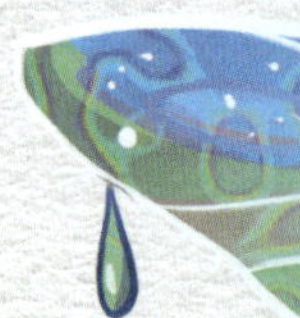

Personal art comes with a lot of uncertainty. It can be quite difficult to grow an audience and find people who are interested in your ideas, let alone generate an income from them. It requires a lot of patience from trial and error, but I believe it's completely worth the effort. Personal art is something I've been doing since I was a kid – it eases my mind and makes me feel good. I can get really anxious if I go too much time without drawing for myself, so I've learned to treat it as a priority, no matter how tough client work can get.

There's so much satisfaction in the challenges that come with working for others too. Not only is it great seeing your work published and circulating with editors, producers, and colleagues, but you also end up pushing yourself *a lot* and drawing stuff you normally wouldn't. It forces you to improve at a much faster pace. I'm always my most productive self when deadlines are looming, that's for sure.

Sea Knight, digital, 2020

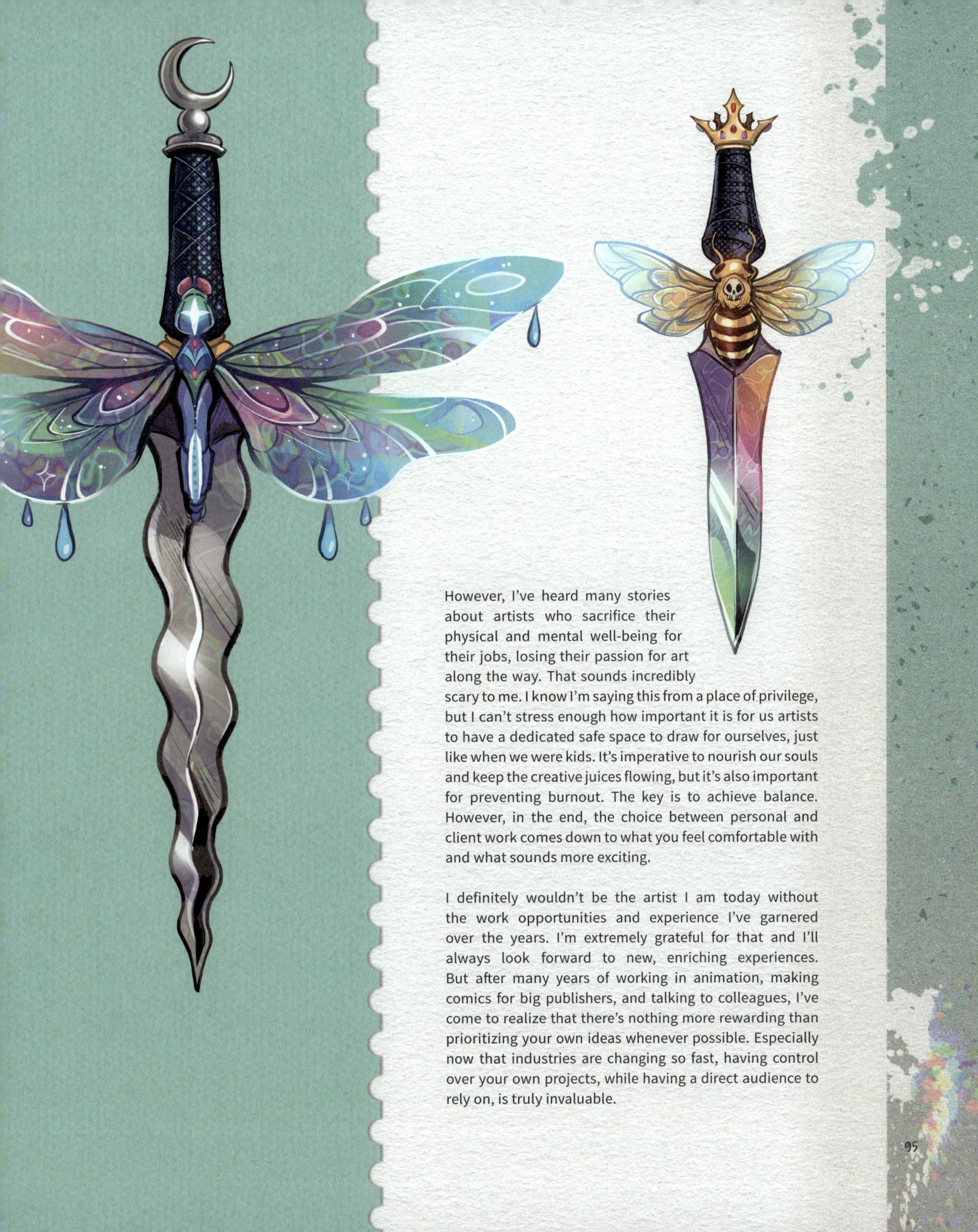

However, I've heard many stories about artists who sacrifice their physical and mental well-being for their jobs, losing their passion for art along the way. That sounds incredibly scary to me. I know I'm saying this from a place of privilege, but I can't stress enough how important it is for us artists to have a dedicated safe space to draw for ourselves, just like when we were kids. It's imperative to nourish our souls and keep the creative juices flowing, but it's also important for preventing burnout. The key is to achieve balance. However, in the end, the choice between personal and client work comes down to what you feel comfortable with and what sounds more exciting.

I definitely wouldn't be the artist I am today without the work opportunities and experience I've garnered over the years. I'm extremely grateful for that and I'll always look forward to new, enriching experiences. But after many years of working in animation, making comics for big publishers, and talking to colleagues, I've come to realize that there's nothing more rewarding than prioritizing your own ideas whenever possible. Especially now that industries are changing so fast, having control over your own projects, while having a direct audience to rely on, is truly invaluable.

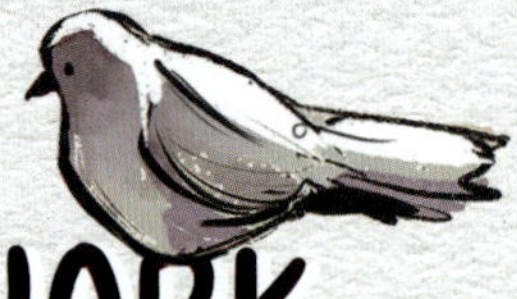

SHARING WORK

Posting my artwork online has been such an integral part of my journey. There's so much I was able to accomplish in the past few years that was only possible because of social media. I know tons of artists who don't rely on it, and their careers are absolutely thriving, but as a Latin artist who has lived her whole life far away from where things actually 'happen', social media allowed me to feel relevant and seen. Growing an audience that cared about my work, connecting with like-minded people, and receiving exciting job opportunities no doubt came as a result of having an online presence – ten consecutive years of posting art. Social media is an incredibly powerful tool that allows artists to make a living from their work and I don't think I could have come this far without it.

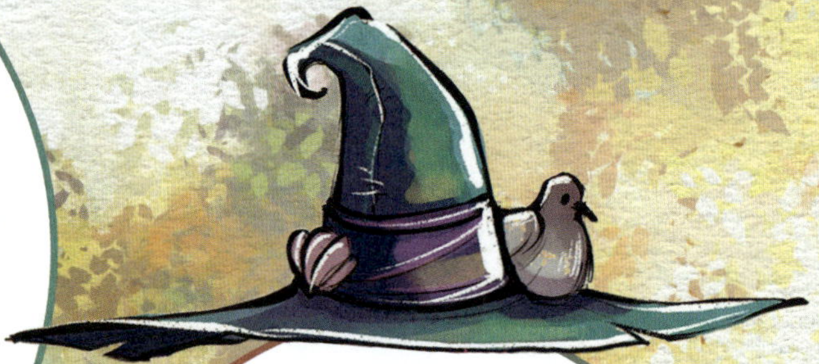

However, as much as social media has helped me, I'm also aware that it was the cause of much of my anxiety. I put a lot of pressure on myself to perform, produce more… to generally be better. Measuring your worth by your follower count, obsessing over 'likes', seeking popularity, and doing things just because they are trending are just a few of the many pitfalls that come with the social-media game and can be extremely damaging to your work.

Posting your art when you're too young can sometimes be prejudicial too. Before it even occurred to me to start posting my work online, I'd been drawing consistently for over two years and I can see now how important it is to navigate those first steps without the extra pressure and distraction that modern social media presents. If you're struggling to find your voice, try taking a step back from social media to practise and fall in love with the art you like – the art you want to create. Losing yourself to a world of comparisons and numbers can really stunt your improvement, so it's important to set clear boundaries and understand the place you let these platforms take you.

Once you have that clearly figured out, you can't go wrong. Take advantage of the good parts and enjoy the process of documenting and sharing your creativity with others. When you look back, you'll be extremely proud of all the effort you poured in! Just remember: algorithms constantly change and 'likes' and 'follows' come and go, but making art that's meaningful to you will stay forever.

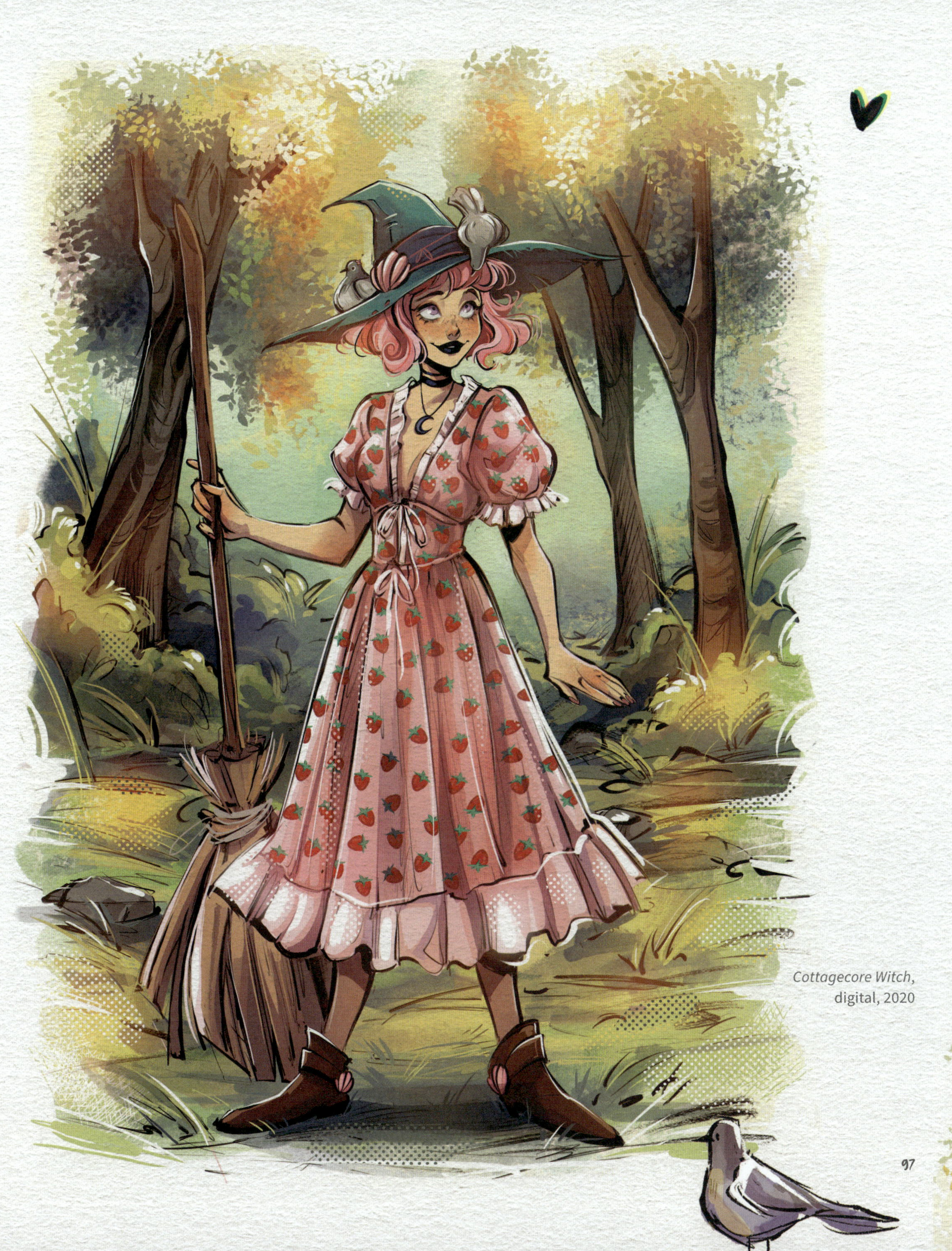

Cottagecore Witch,
digital, 2020

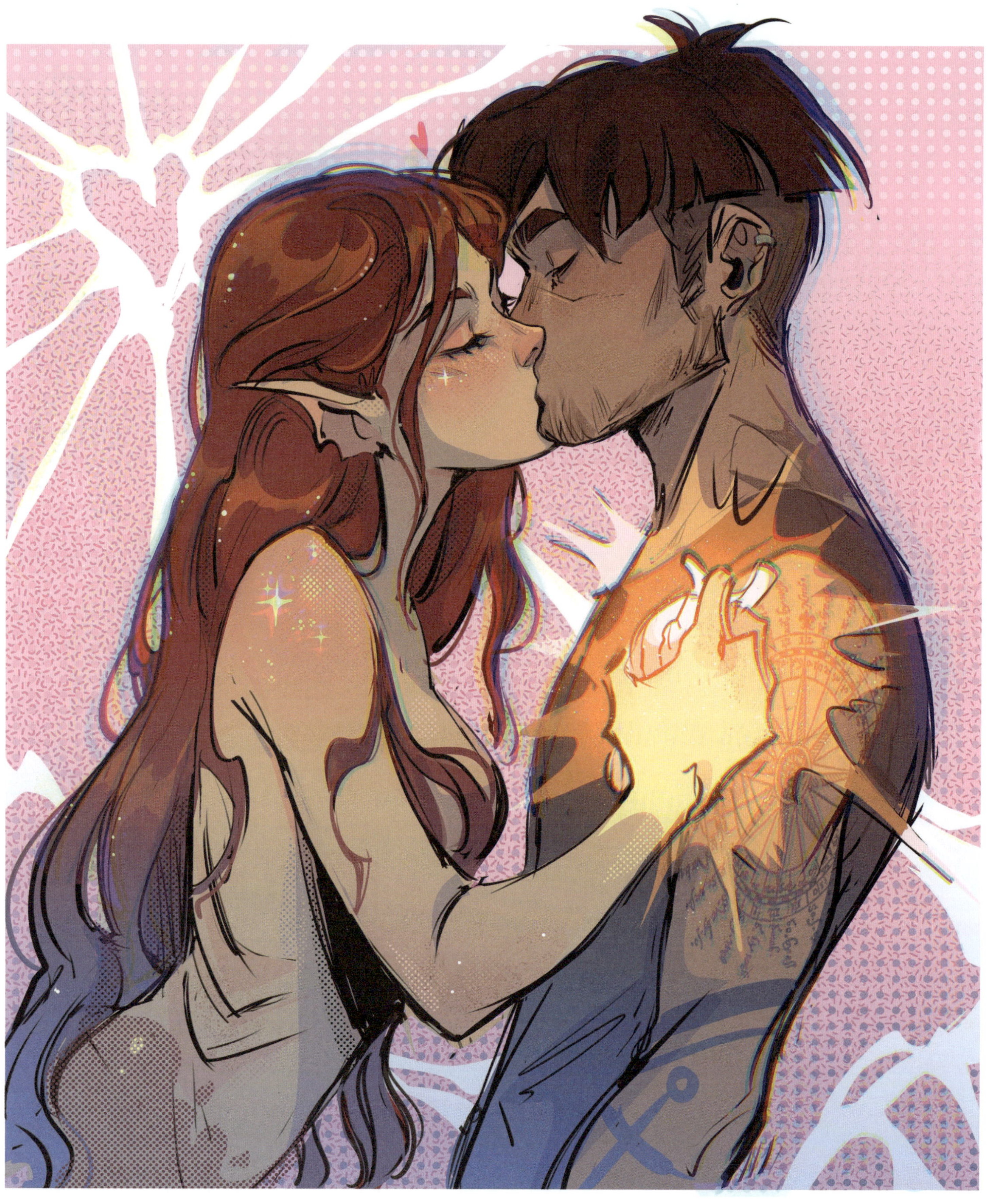

EMBRACING THE MESS

LETTING GO OF PERFECTIONISM & TRUSTING YOUR GUT

Clean work, particularly when it comes to line art, has always required a tremendous amount of mental and physical effort from me, and tires out my hand very quickly. I guess that's why my art has developed this sketchy quality over time. It wasn't until I started posting short videos of my art process on social media a few years ago that I began to truly appreciate this. I was surprised by how much people seemed to like the imperfection in my work – the roughness of the lines, the hasty sketches, and how something that started out looking bad could turn out pretty decent. These videos showed me how important it was to share my process as raw and unfiltered as possible, never skipping the 'ugly' stage. Not only did it inspire others, but it also became a valuable lesson for myself. I stopped resisting the messy nature of my art and started seeing beauty in my unrefined colours and crooked line work.

Since then, I've let go of the exhausting strive for perfection to refocus my mindset on creating artwork filled with dynamism, expressiveness, and life. Perfectionism usually hinders your ability to take risks or try new things and can even prevent you from starting something if you aren't certain it will lead to a masterpiece. So, it's important to understand that perfection is not only unreachable, but it's also fear in disguise that often leads to periods of stagnation and lack of growth.

To me, **embracing the mess** can go from the most literal interpretation to a wilder, much bigger picture. It means being open and accepting of all possible outcomes, whether good or bad. It's about trusting the creative process and allowing things to unfold into what they're meant to be.

Traditional art has personally been the perfect way to fully embrace the messiness of art in all its forms. Unlike digital tools that make it possible to retouch, erase, and polish (which can definitely bring out the perfectionist in me), traditional art is permanent and a little more of a risk. That's precisely why I love it so much. Working with traditional media allowed me to embrace unpredictability and accept mistakes more readily. It has pushed me to loosen up and show no fear towards mark-making. Traditional art is also a huge help when it comes to trusting your instincts. We all have this pulling energy inside that is a product of existing knowledge, and it tries to guide us towards our best interests. While this intuition cannot always be logically explained, it can certainly be trusted.

Getting back to the analogue tools from time to time is one of the best ways to get in touch with your intuitive side, gain confidence in your creative decisions, and rediscover what you love about making art. Let go of the notion that your work has to turn out perfect. Once you have embraced the mess, failure will be nothing more than a learning experience.

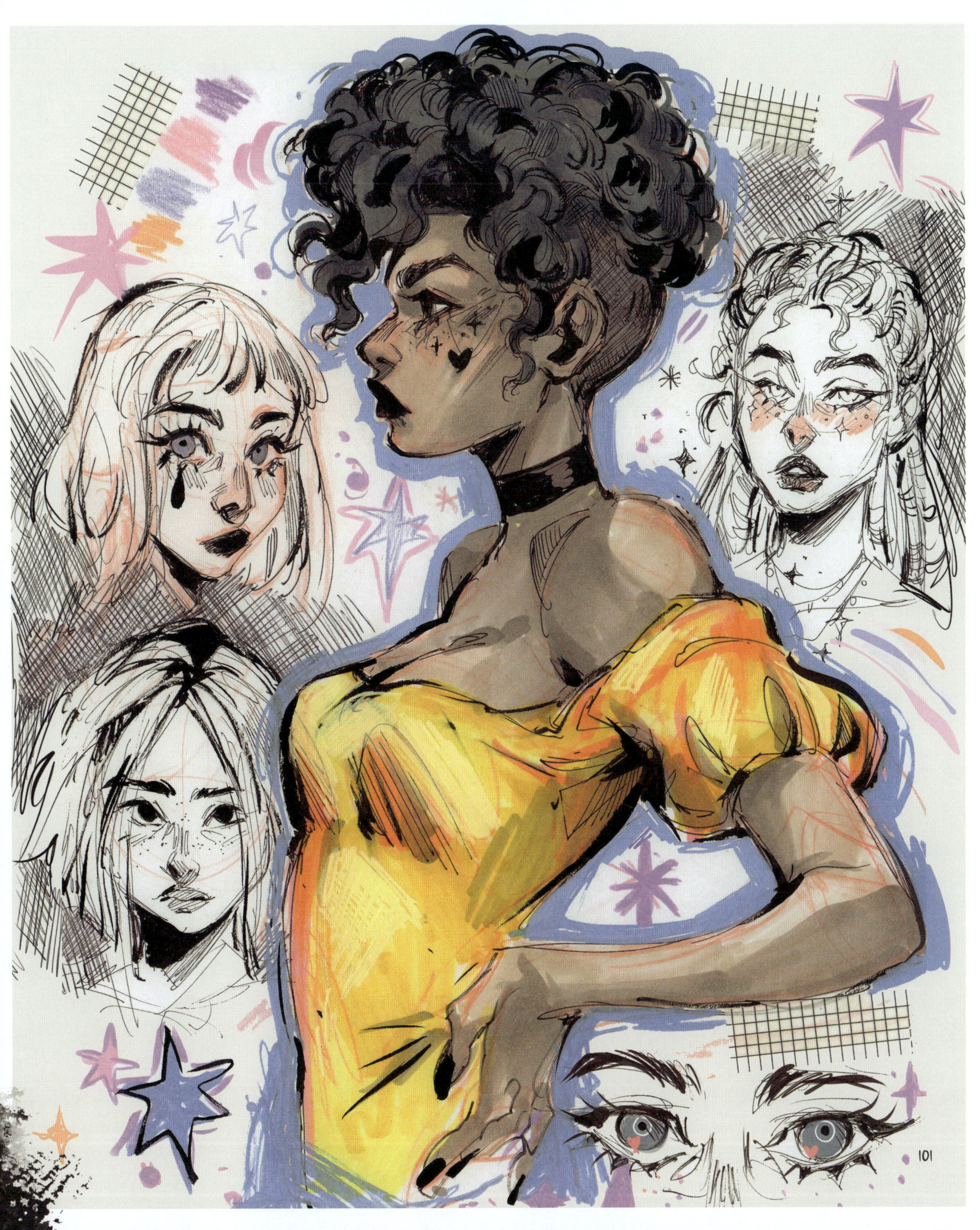

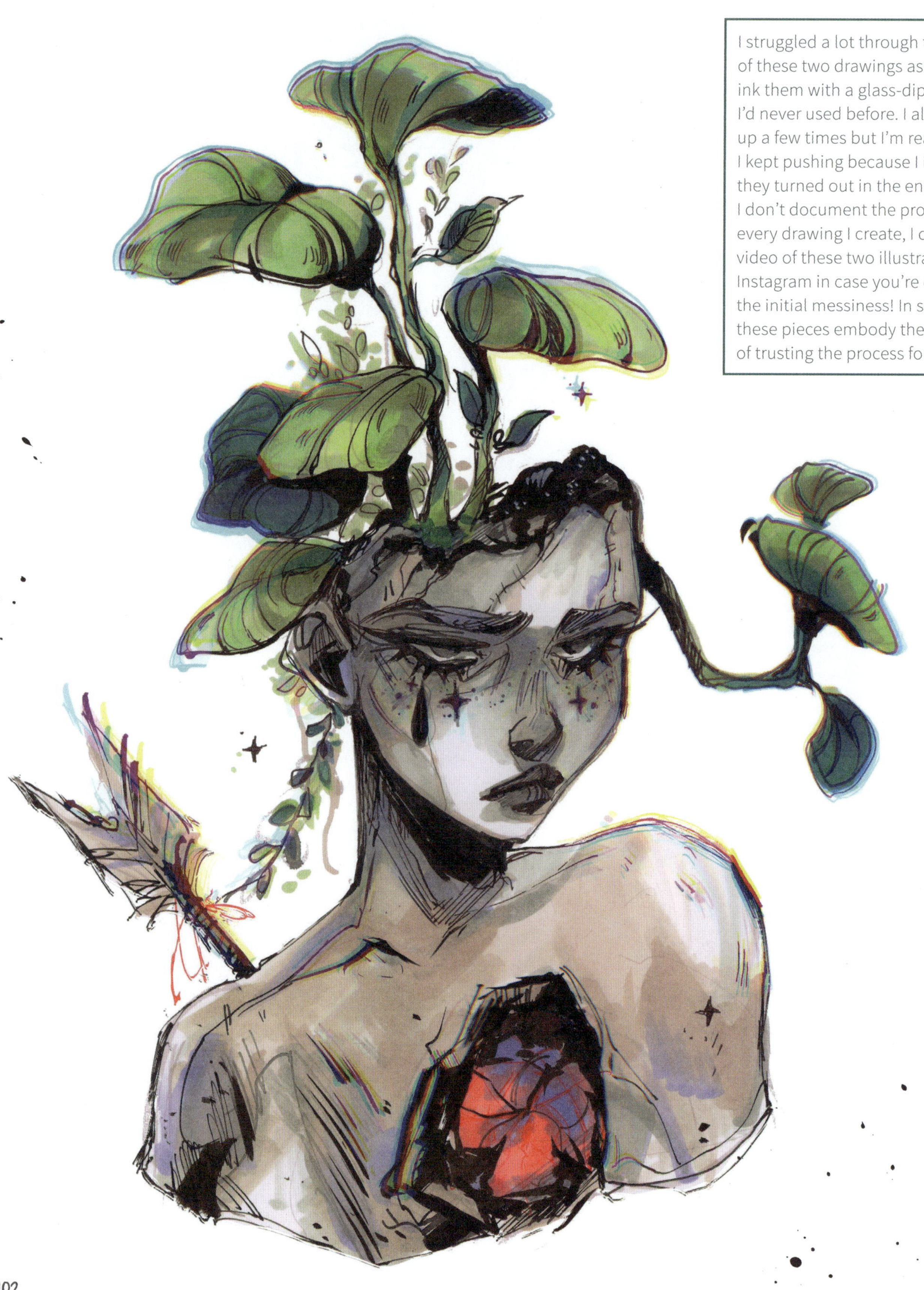

I struggled a lot through the making of these two drawings as I chose to ink them with a glass-dip pen – a tool I'd never used before. I almost gave up a few times but I'm really glad I kept pushing because I love how they turned out in the end. Although I don't document the process of every drawing I create, I do have the video of these two illustrations on my Instagram in case you're curious to see the initial messiness! In some ways, these pieces embody the true meaning of trusting the process for me.

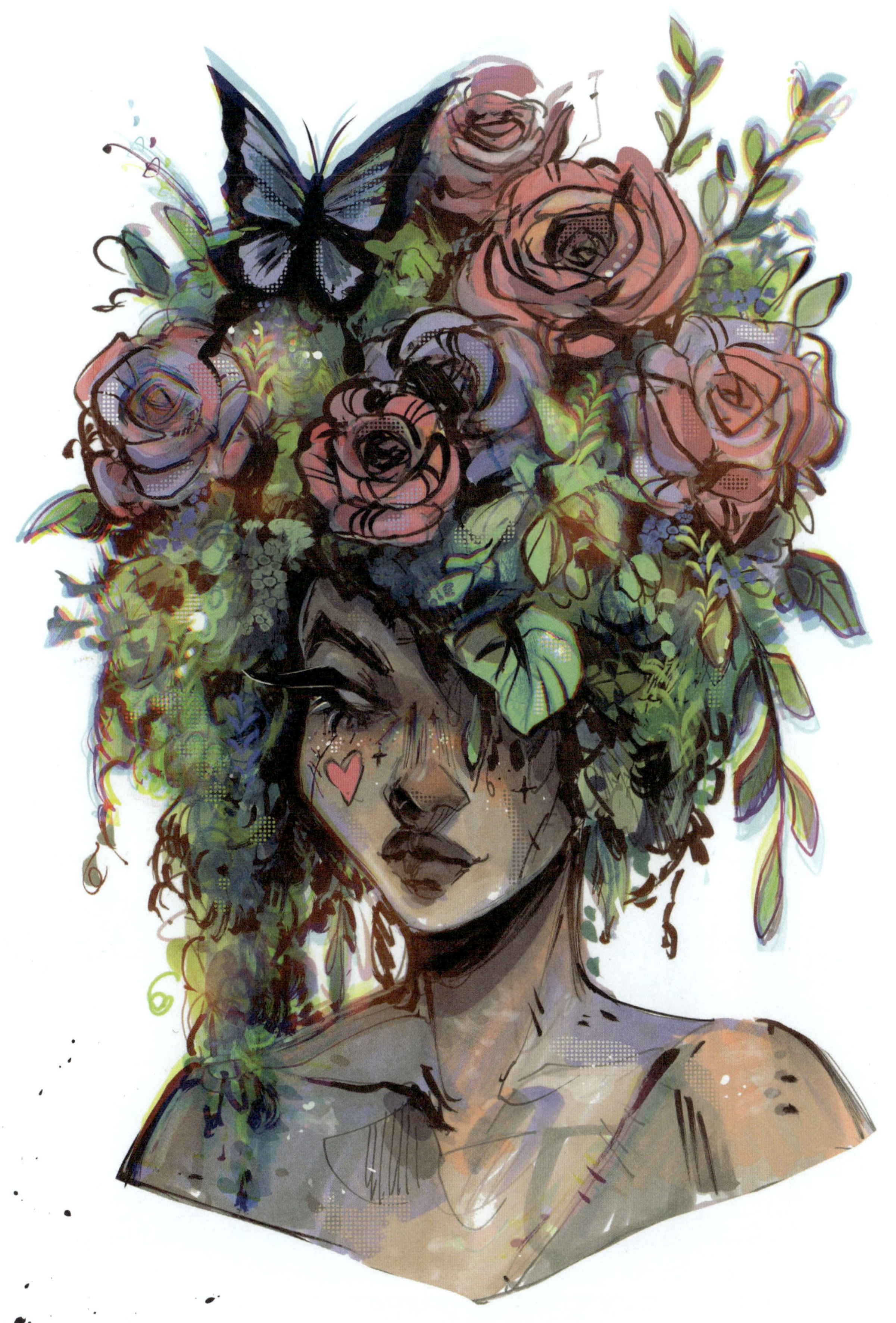

SKETCHING, LINE WORK & TEXTURE

I like sketching with large, loose movements and try to keep my lines as expressive as possible. When I'm quickly laying down all the basic shapes, I make sure to construct inside the forms instead of simply outlining them. This allows me to focus on the overall rhythm and flow of the piece without getting into too much detail at first.

FAVOURITE TOOLS

The Prismacolor Col-erase pencil in Scarlet Red is my favourite pencil to sketch out the basic shapes and construction lines of my traditional work. It doesn't smudge all over the place like graphite does. Also, since I don't usually get rid of the sketch lines once I add ink, I like the nice warm undertones.

Another favourite tool of mine for traditional sketching is fine-point ballpoint pens. I've been using pens instead of pencils for years, and the inability to erase has really helped me in terms of line confidence and precision.

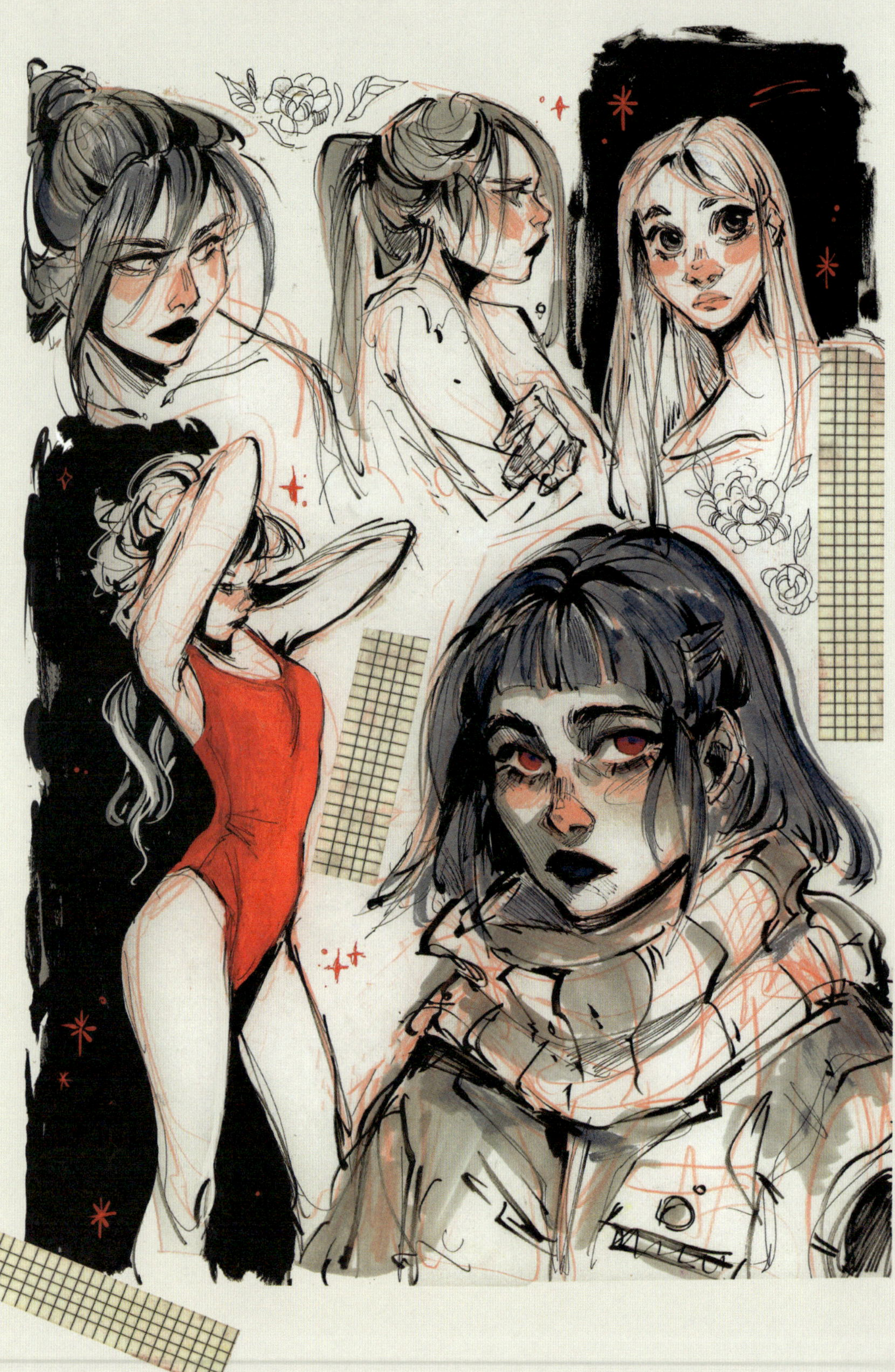

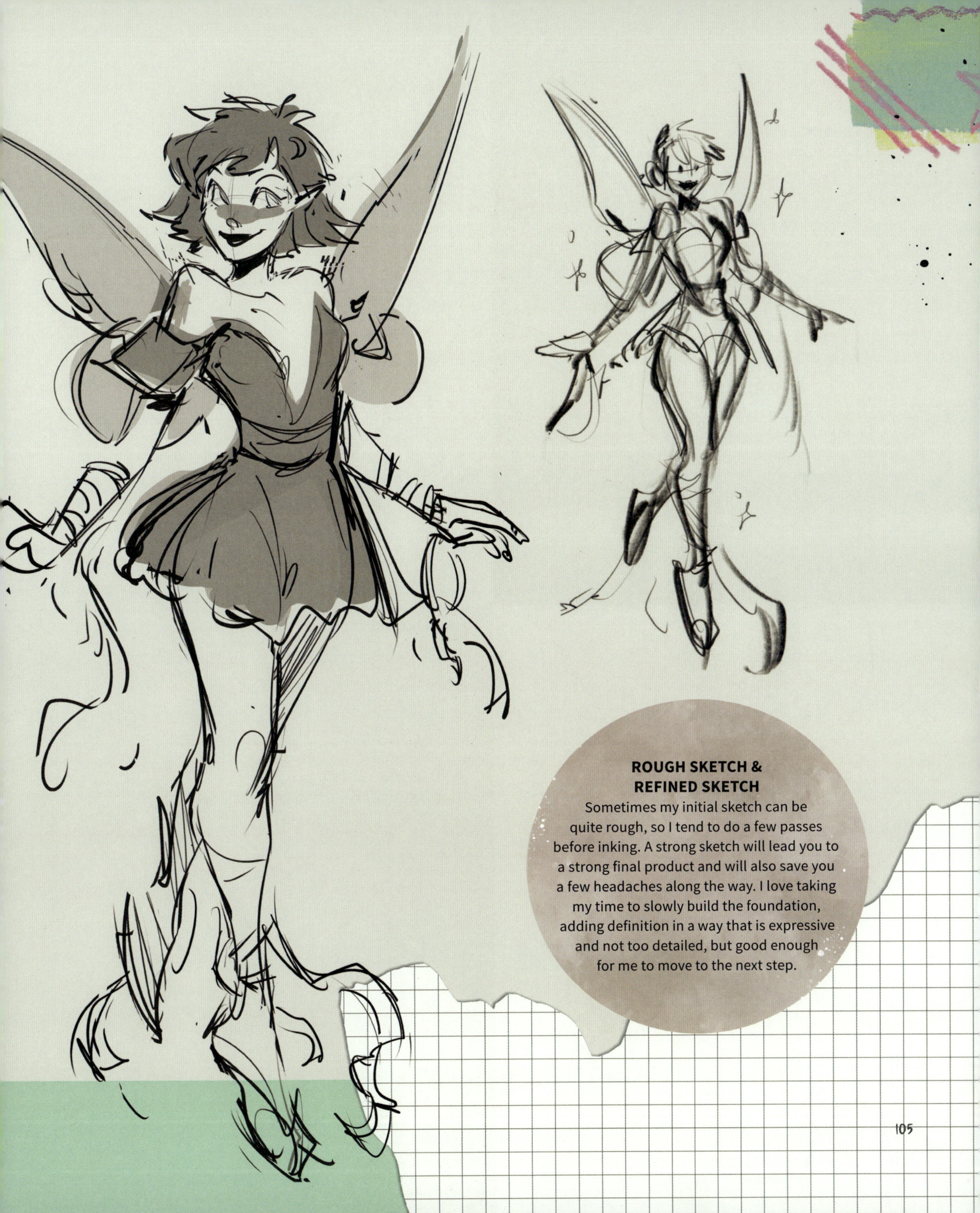

ROUGH SKETCH & REFINED SKETCH

Sometimes my initial sketch can be quite rough, so I tend to do a few passes before inking. A strong sketch will lead you to a strong final product and will also save you a few headaches along the way. I love taking my time to slowly build the foundation, adding definition in a way that is expressive and not too detailed, but good enough for me to move to the next step.

Line work

Line work is one of my favourite parts of the process. Given that lines are such an essential element in my art style, it's typically the part that takes up the most time. One common issue with inking is that it can turn out rather stiff compared to the sketch. To avoid this, I like to approach inking with the same exact mindset I have for sketching, keeping the strokes relaxed and dynamic – just a little more precise. While I don't necessarily strive for perfectly clean lines, I obsess a lot over keeping them expressive. When working digitally, I turn the layer on and off to constantly compare my inked lines to my sketch, ensuring that they reflect that initial strength/intention. The trick for line work is to understand that the sketch is just a guide that sets the bar. Ideally, you don't want to fall below it, but you absolutely want to push it as far as you can for the final outcome.

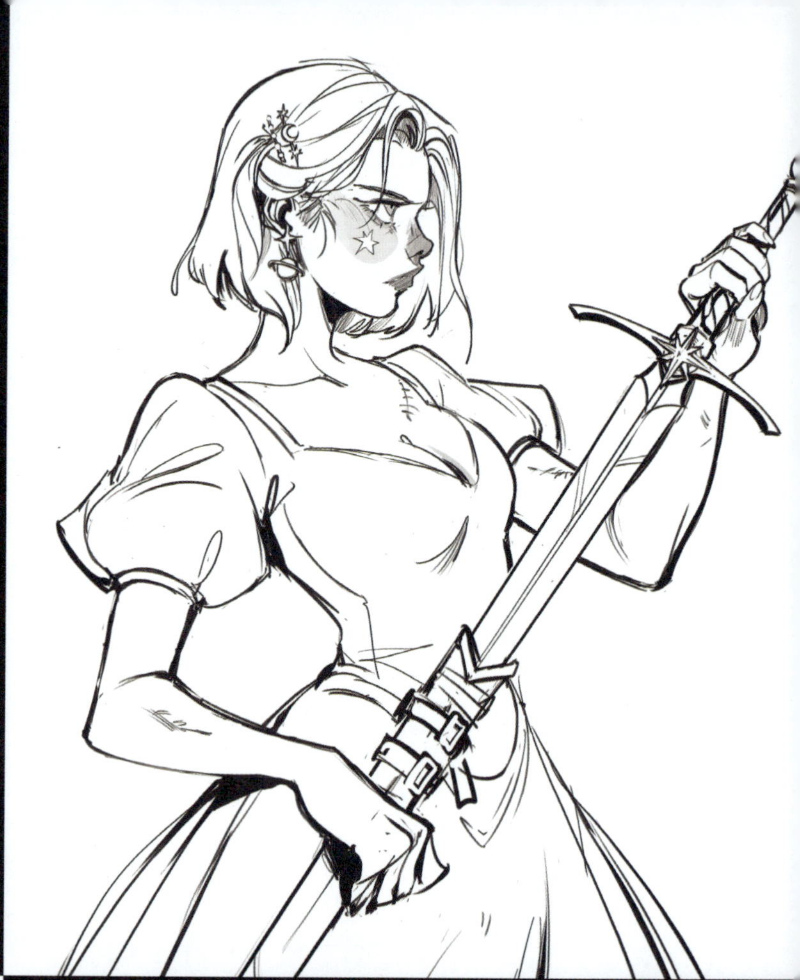

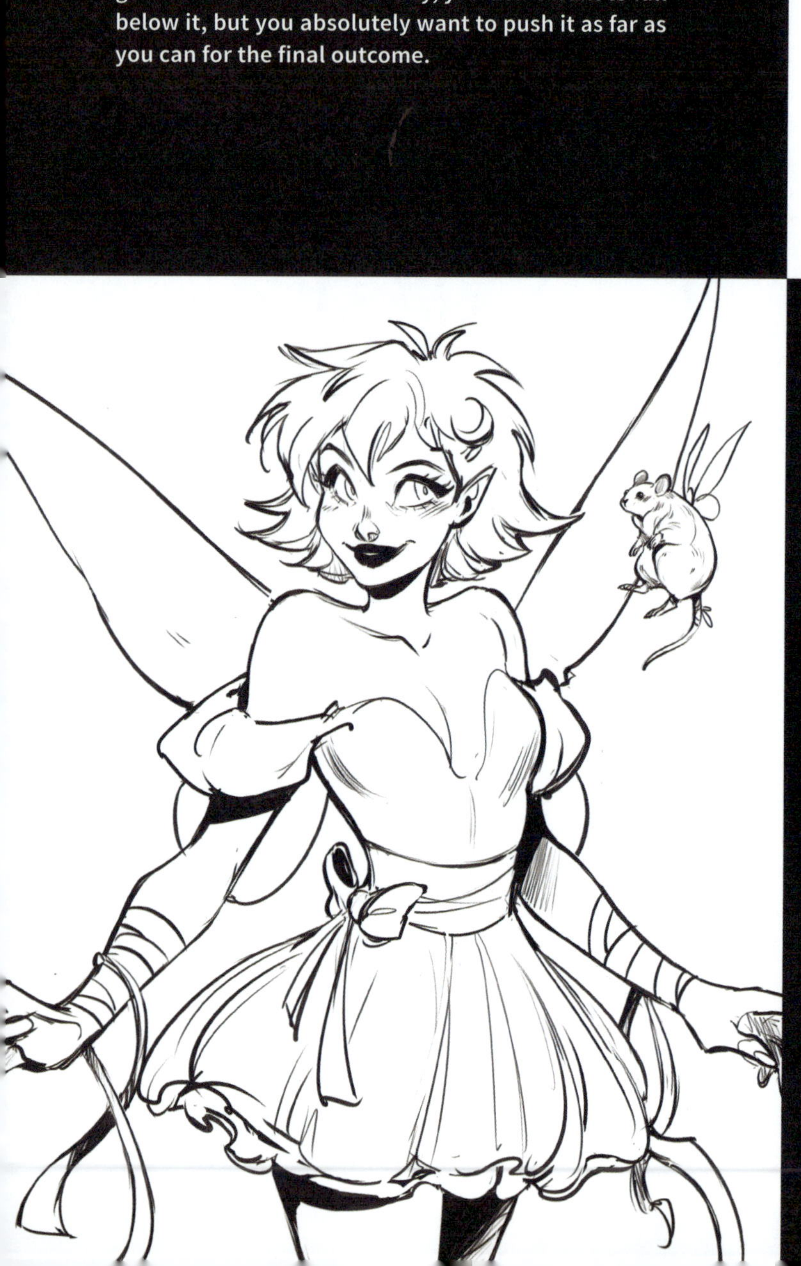

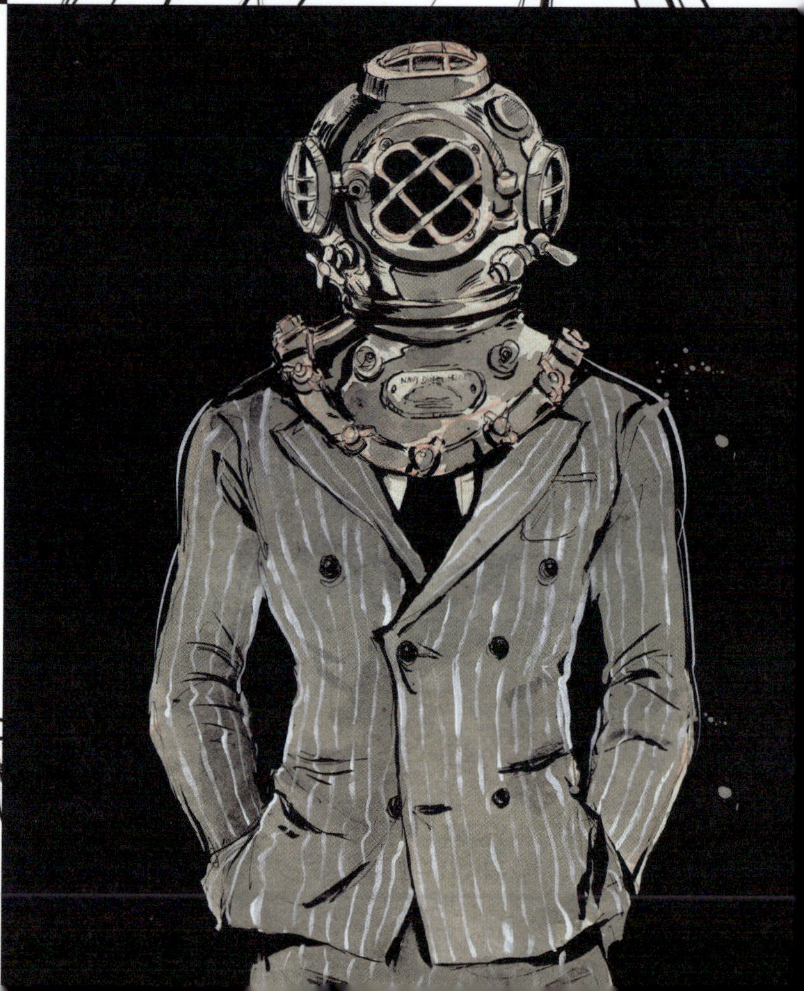

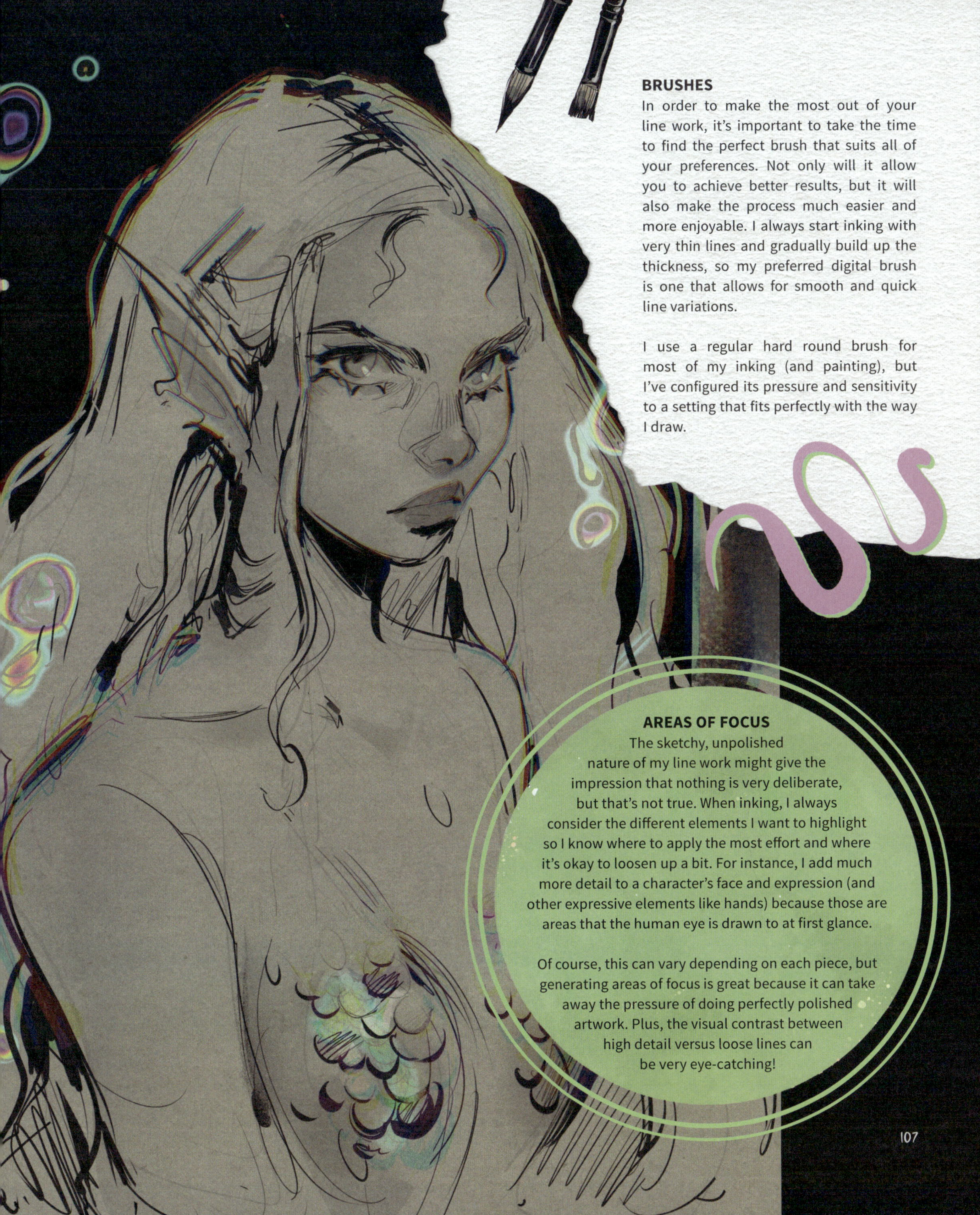

BRUSHES

In order to make the most out of your line work, it's important to take the time to find the perfect brush that suits all of your preferences. Not only will it allow you to achieve better results, but it will also make the process much easier and more enjoyable. I always start inking with very thin lines and gradually build up the thickness, so my preferred digital brush is one that allows for smooth and quick line variations.

I use a regular hard round brush for most of my inking (and painting), but I've configured its pressure and sensitivity to a setting that fits perfectly with the way I draw.

AREAS OF FOCUS

The sketchy, unpolished nature of my line work might give the impression that nothing is very deliberate, but that's not true. When inking, I always consider the different elements I want to highlight so I know where to apply the most effort and where it's okay to loosen up a bit. For instance, I add much more detail to a character's face and expression (and other expressive elements like hands) because those are areas that the human eye is drawn to at first glance.

Of course, this can vary depending on each piece, but generating areas of focus is great because it can take away the pressure of doing perfectly polished artwork. Plus, the visual contrast between high detail versus loose lines can be very eye-catching!

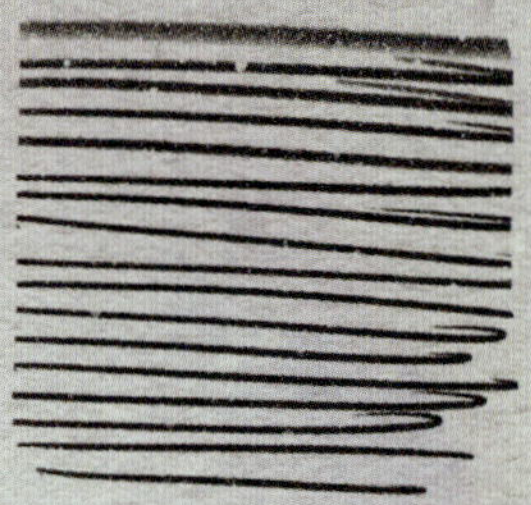

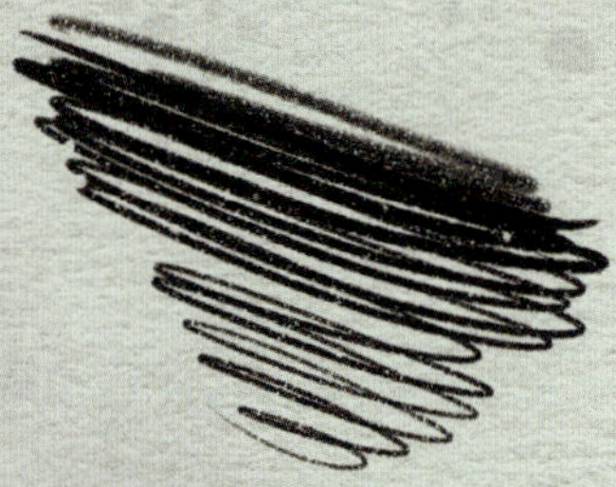

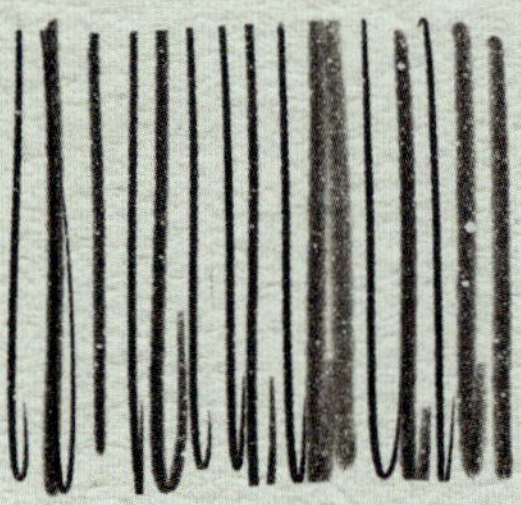

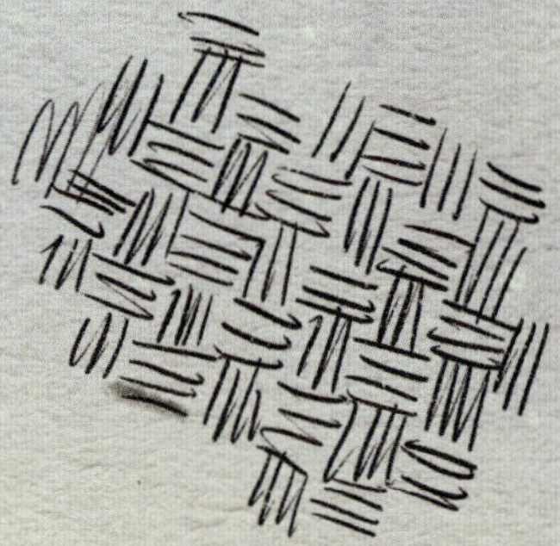

HATCHING

Hatching is a technique used to create shading effects by drawing parallel lines in the same direction to create the illusion of value and dimension. Although by no means am I an expert when it comes to hatching techniques, I do love incorporating lines and little scribbles to create subtle shading and texture to specific parts of my ink work.

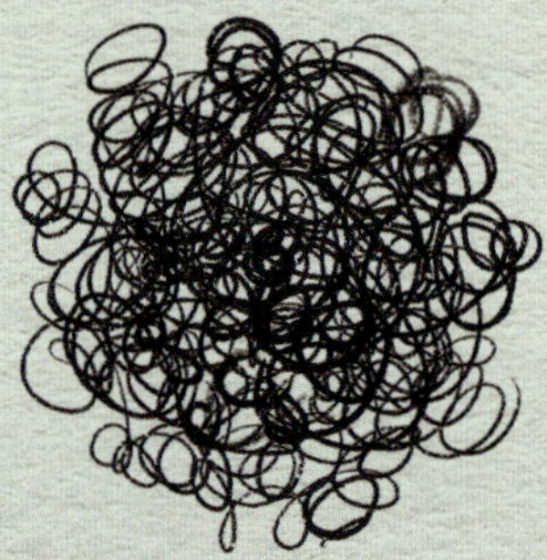

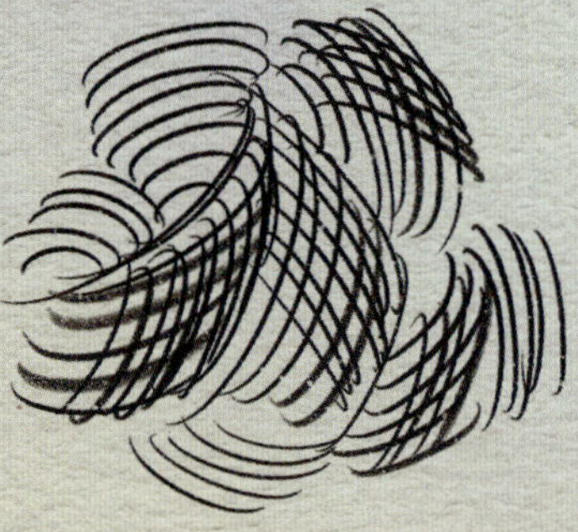

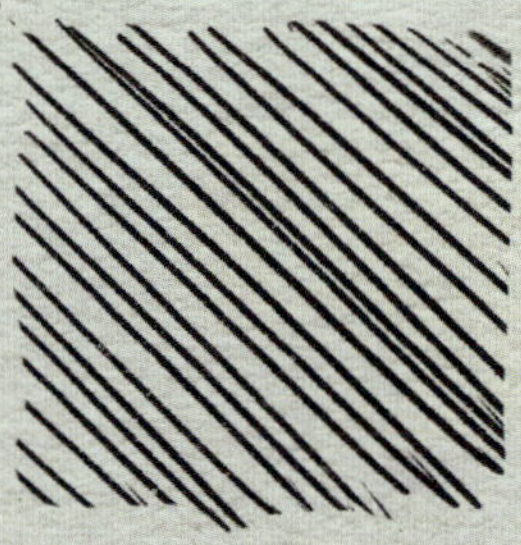

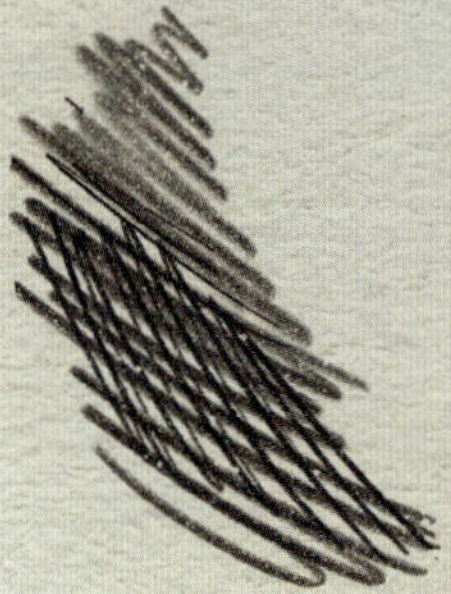

One of my favourite techniques to use is cross-hatching, which is pretty much the same thing. It involves multiple layers of parallel lines crossing each other, resulting in a fun criss-cross pattern. Here, you can see how varying the thickness and spacing of the lines can achieve different styles.

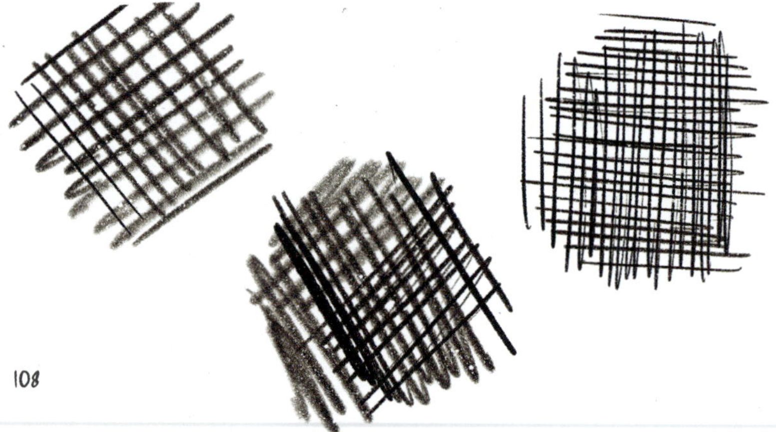

LINE WEIGHT

Line weight refers to the gradual thickness of a line and *I cannot stress enough* how important that is when it comes to inking. Varying the thickness or intensity of the lines helps to convey a sense of light, shadow, and movement, which can add so much depth and dimensionality to even the simplest doodle.

Line weight can also be achieved both with the natural tool pressure or by manually thickening certain areas – almost like sculpting. While I don't believe there are any strict rules when it comes to adding line variation, there are a few things you can do that may help you achieve better results. The most important thing to keep in mind is not to overdo it. Adding line weight everywhere can actually diminish the effect, so it's important to keep it contained and precise. Here are some tips to guide you:

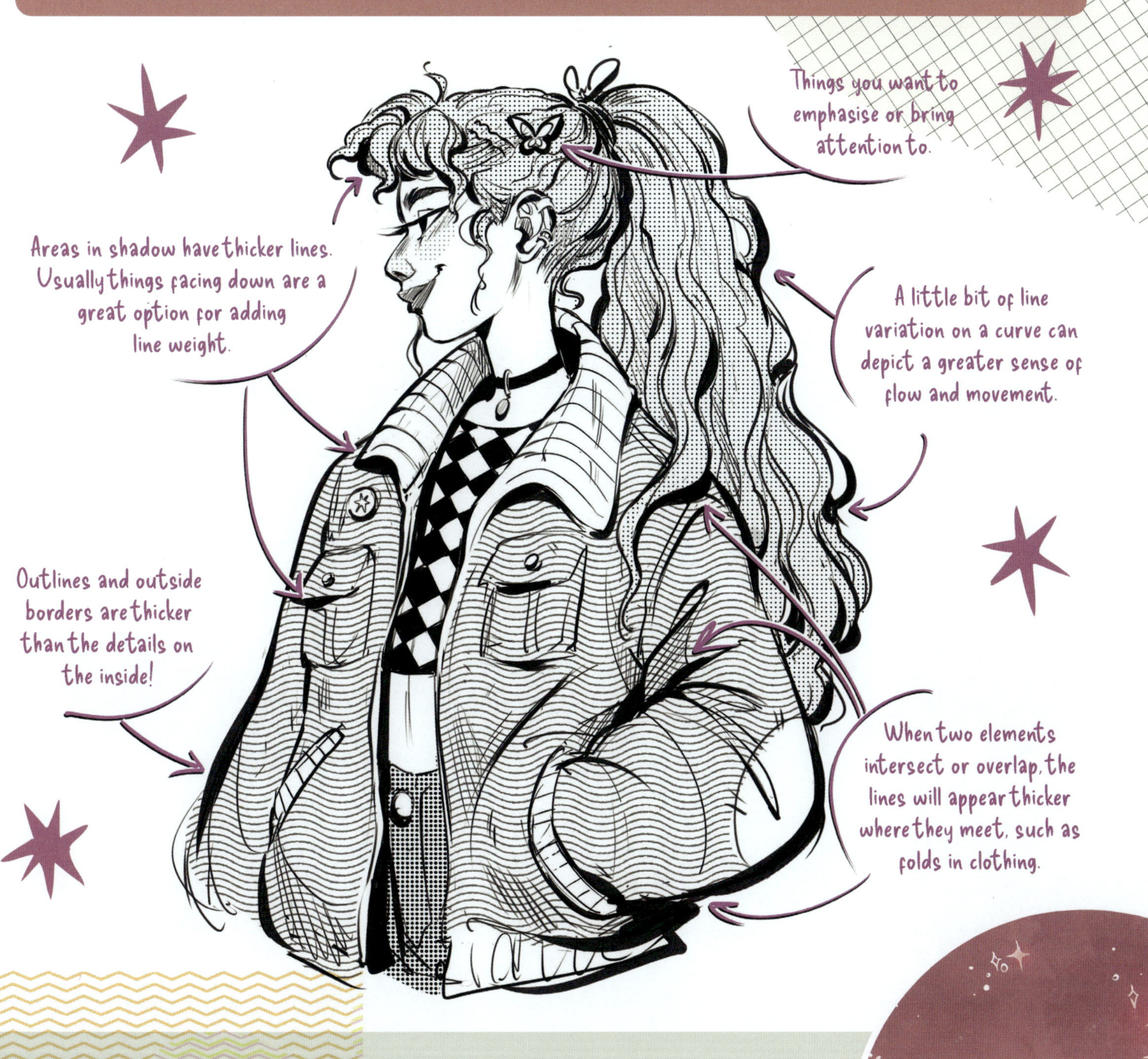

Texture

I love to play around with different ways of incorporating texture in my digital art. These are some of my favourite methods for adding depth and an overall organic feel:

TEXTURED BRUSHES

I really don't use many fancy brushes besides my super trusty hard round brush, but I do have a few brush types that are essential to my process: Grainy & Splattered, Painterly, and Speckled.

TRADITIONAL SCREEN TONES

Although I'm a newbie when it comes to traditional screen tones, I've fallen completely in love with the process. Essentially, they are sticky sheets of textured patterns – dots, lines, and gradients – printed in various densities to create different shades and tones. They have been widely used by manga artists for many years. The process consists of manually cutting and pasting the sheet onto specific areas of the drawing, which can be a little time-consuming but also surprisingly calming. I especially like to use them for details on a character's hair, or perhaps their clothing, to create interesting contrasts. There's something about the tactile experience of working with your hands to apply these intricate patterns that is so incredibly satisfying and visually appealing to me.

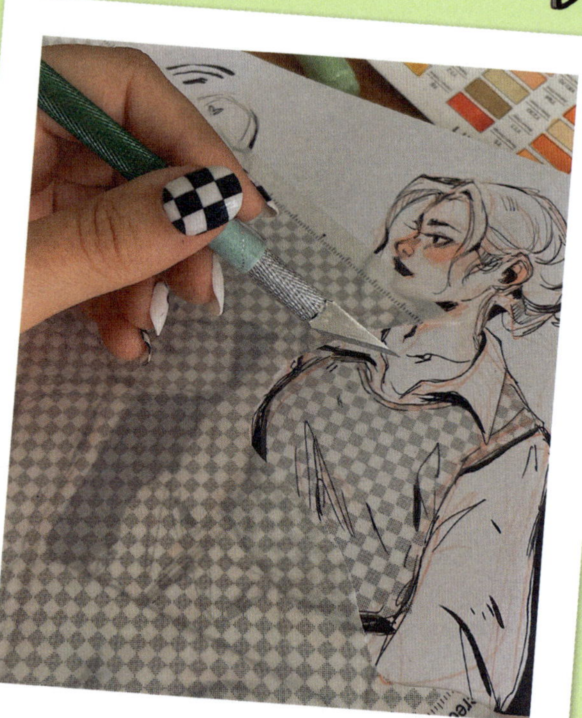

However, with the increasing popularity of digital art, the demand for traditional screen tones has decreased over the years, making them hard to find and quite expensive.

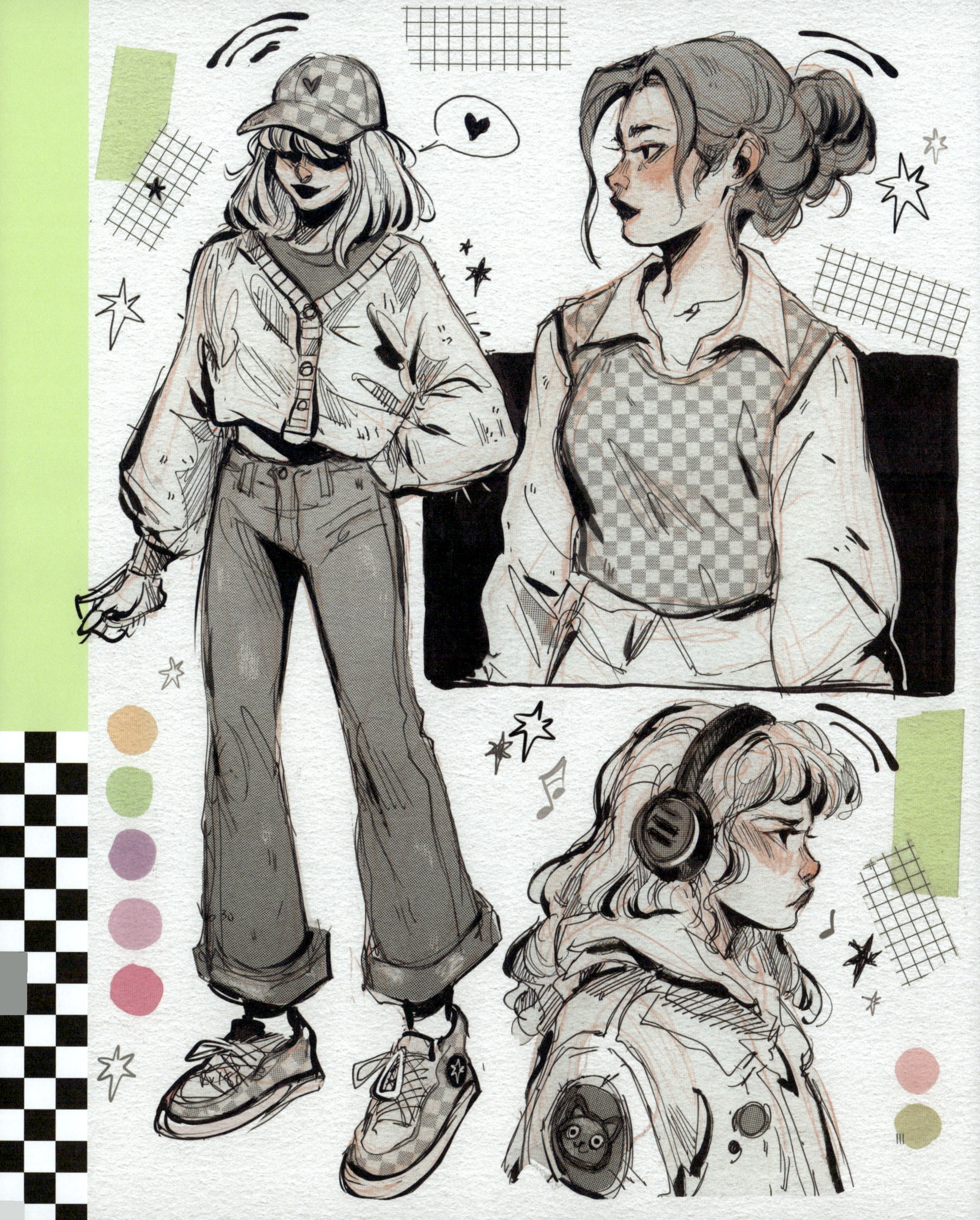

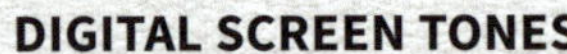

DIGITAL SCREEN TONES

Digital screen tones are incredibly fun and visually appealing too! I absolutely love the graphic, print-like personality they add to artworks. I'm a big fan of the Lithotone brush set from True Grit Texture Supply and the examples shown are patterns I use all the time. These can be applied much more quickly and are easier to manipulate than traditional screen tones, creating seamless, rich textures.

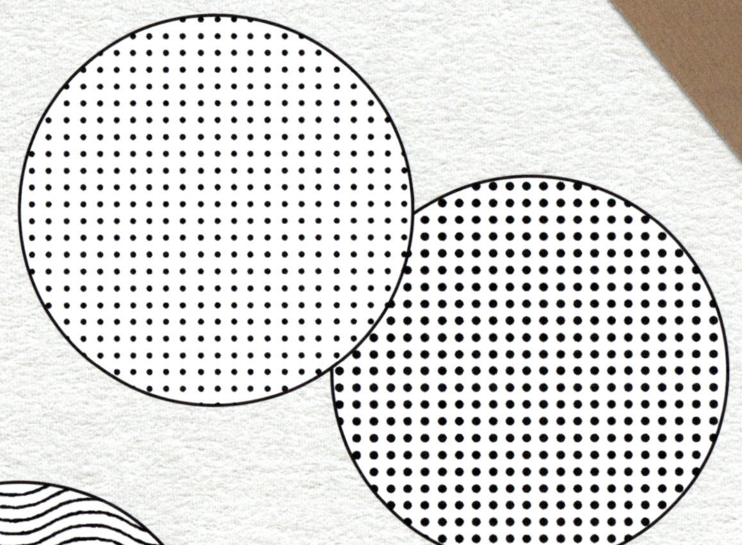

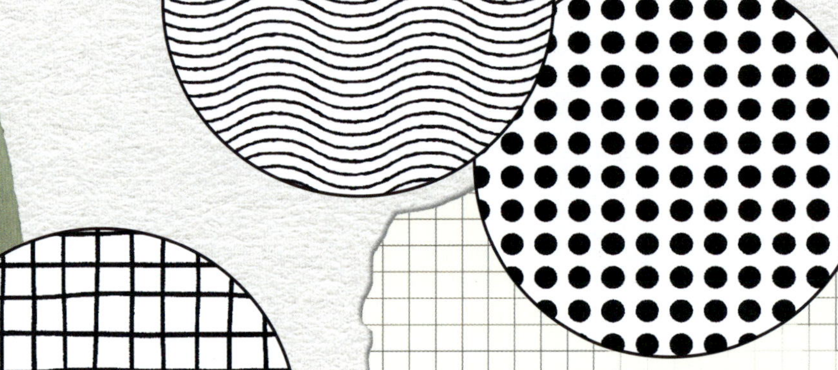

PAPER TEXTURES

This is a great way to add an organic feel to digital illustrations since creating visual and textural depth can be difficult to achieve with digital tools alone. There are many free paper packs available, or you could try creating them yourself using photos. I always apply these textures over the final artwork in a new layer, after setting the blending mode to Overlay or Soft Light. I also adjust the opacity to control how much texture shows through. This process can change depending on the piece, so I usually play around and see what works best.

NOISE

Noise is a versatile tool in Photoshop that adds a random pattern of dots or pixels to an image. It's the simplest way to quickly add texture when you don't want to think too much about it. The amount of noise can be adjusted, making it easy to achieve a variety of effects that range from a subtle film grain to a dramatic texture. I especially love using a small amount of noise to simulate vintage or retro effects while enhancing the mood of a piece.

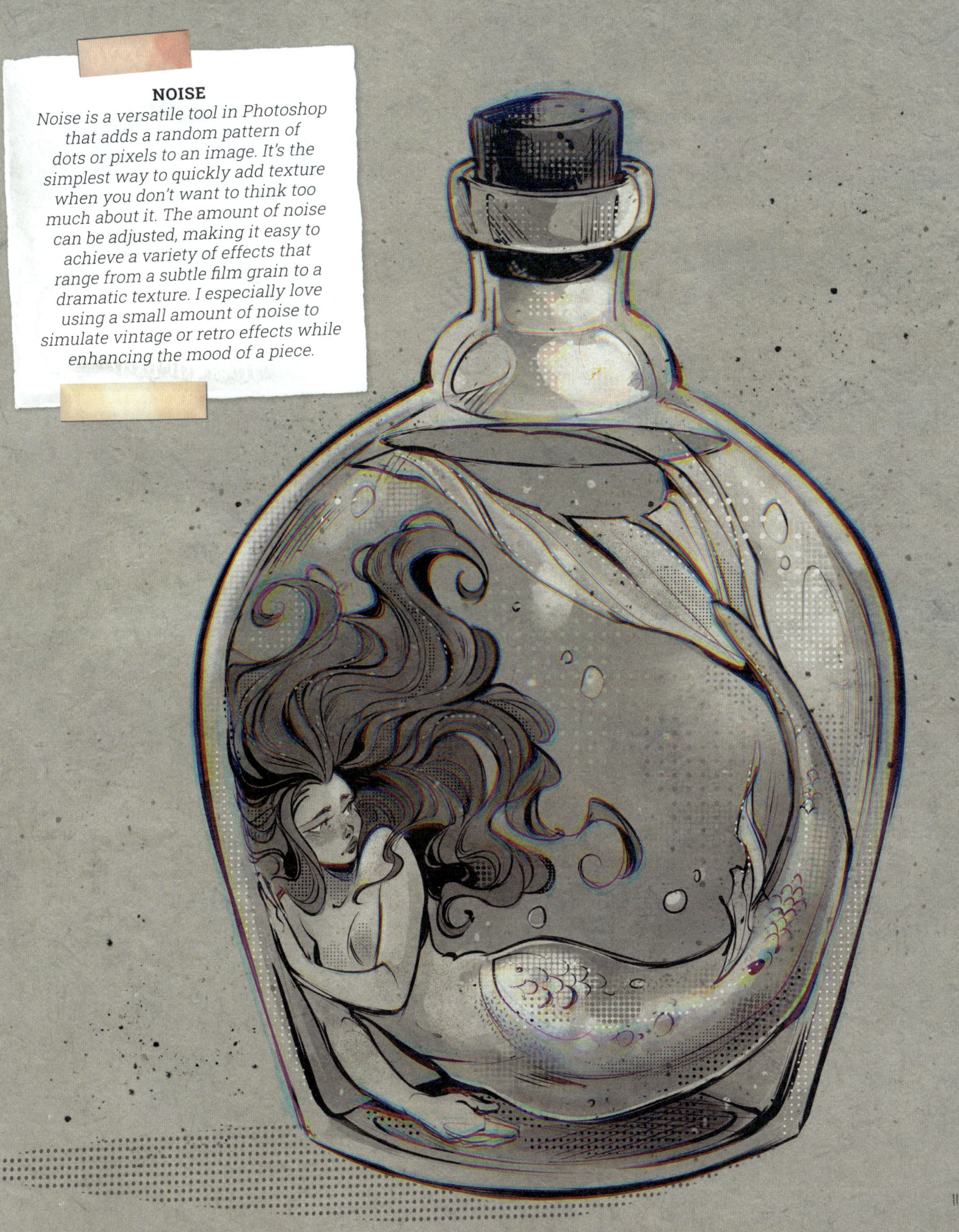

CHOOSING COLOURS

It's important to mention that I'm not an expert in colour theory whatsoever. My approach to colour is highly intuitive – my choices depend on what I'm seeking to communicate and how specific colour combinations make me feel. However, colours are a really important aspect of my work as it's genuinely one of the things that make me the most excited about creating! I find so much joy in observing colours in nature, daily life, art, photography, and fashion. I'm always on the lookout for fun combinations to incorporate into my work.

I won't go into the technicalities, but I'd like to share some basic tips that have helped me choose colours.

HUE
Refers to the pure colour itself, such as green, red, yellow, etc.

TEMPERATURE
Colour temperature refers to the warmth or coolness. It's usually determined by how much blue or yellow a colour contains.

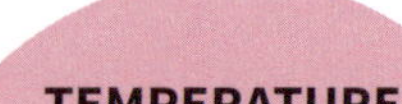

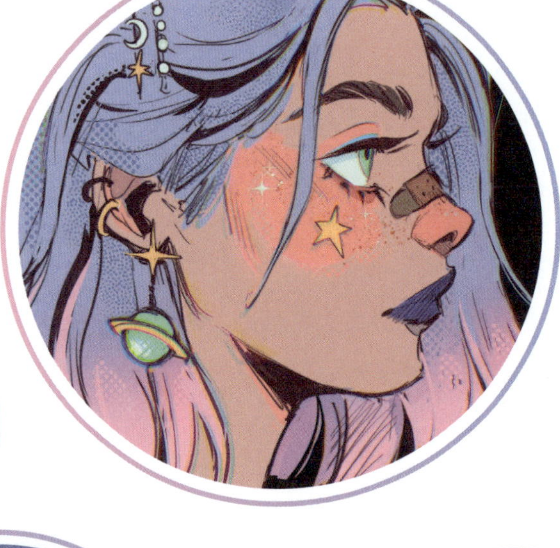

SATURATION
This is the intensity of a colour. A highly saturated colour is vivid, vibrant, and pure. A desaturated colour leans towards grey and appears muted or washed out.

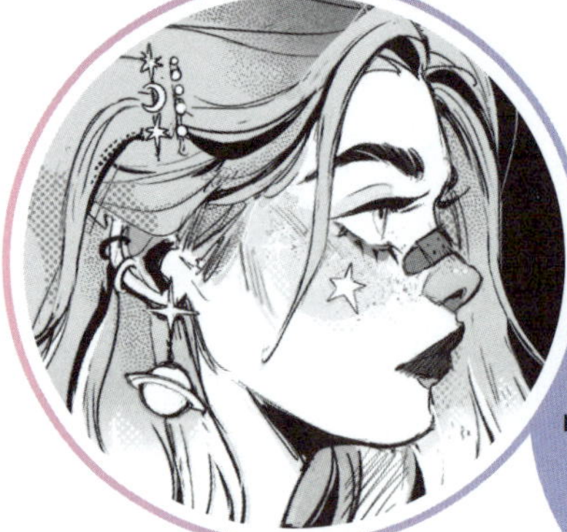

VALUE
Refers to the lightness or darkness of a colour. It is often represented on a greyscale, where white is the lightest value and black is the darkest value.

Understanding how colour works involves many factors and those are just a few examples. One of the things that completely changed the way I paint (especially how I incorporate volume and shading) was considering colours in terms of hue as well as value. Instead of relying solely on black for shading and white for highlighting, I incorporated different hues that resulted in much richer colour schemes.

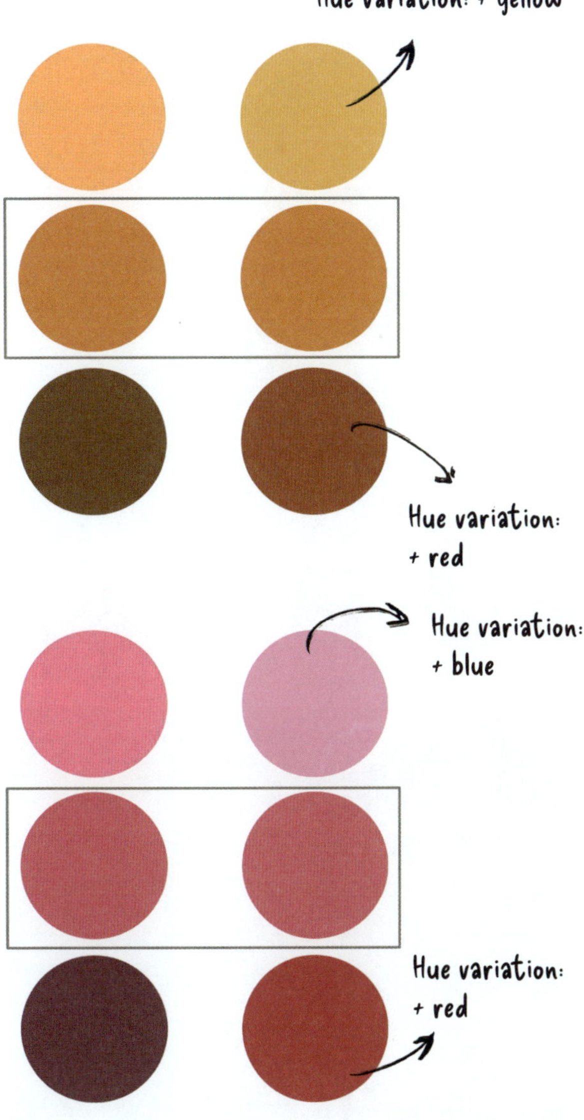

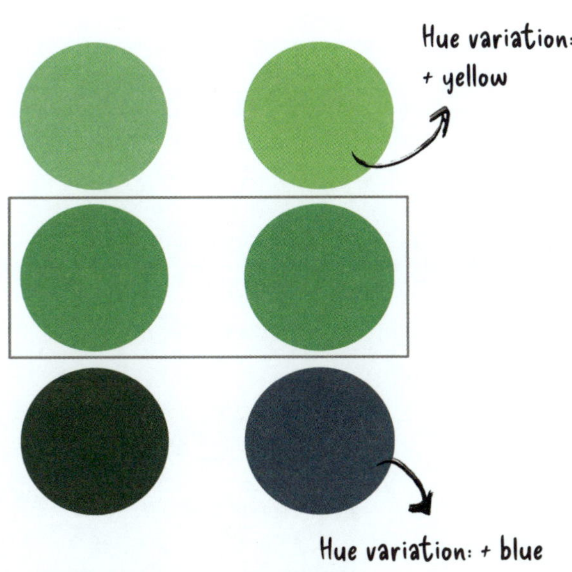

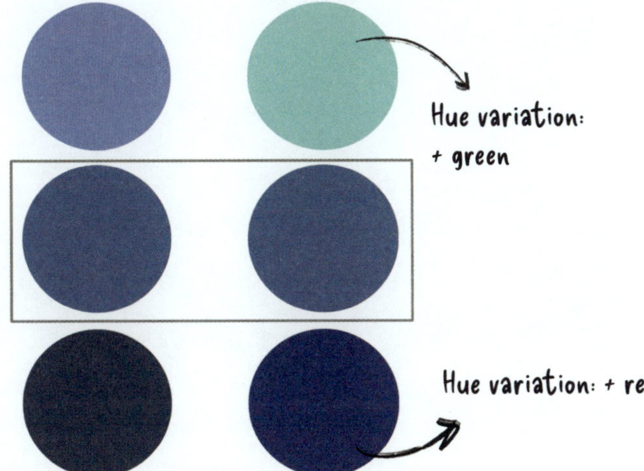

Here, the colours that are marked with rectangles are the same. In the first column, I adjusted each colour towards white for a lighter value and black for a darker value. In the second column, I considered value but pushed each colour towards a different hue. Notice how the colours in the second column appear more vivid and interesting compared to those in the first column. While shading with black is fine, it's good to consider the many shades and countless undertones in each colour in order to create dynamic outcomes.

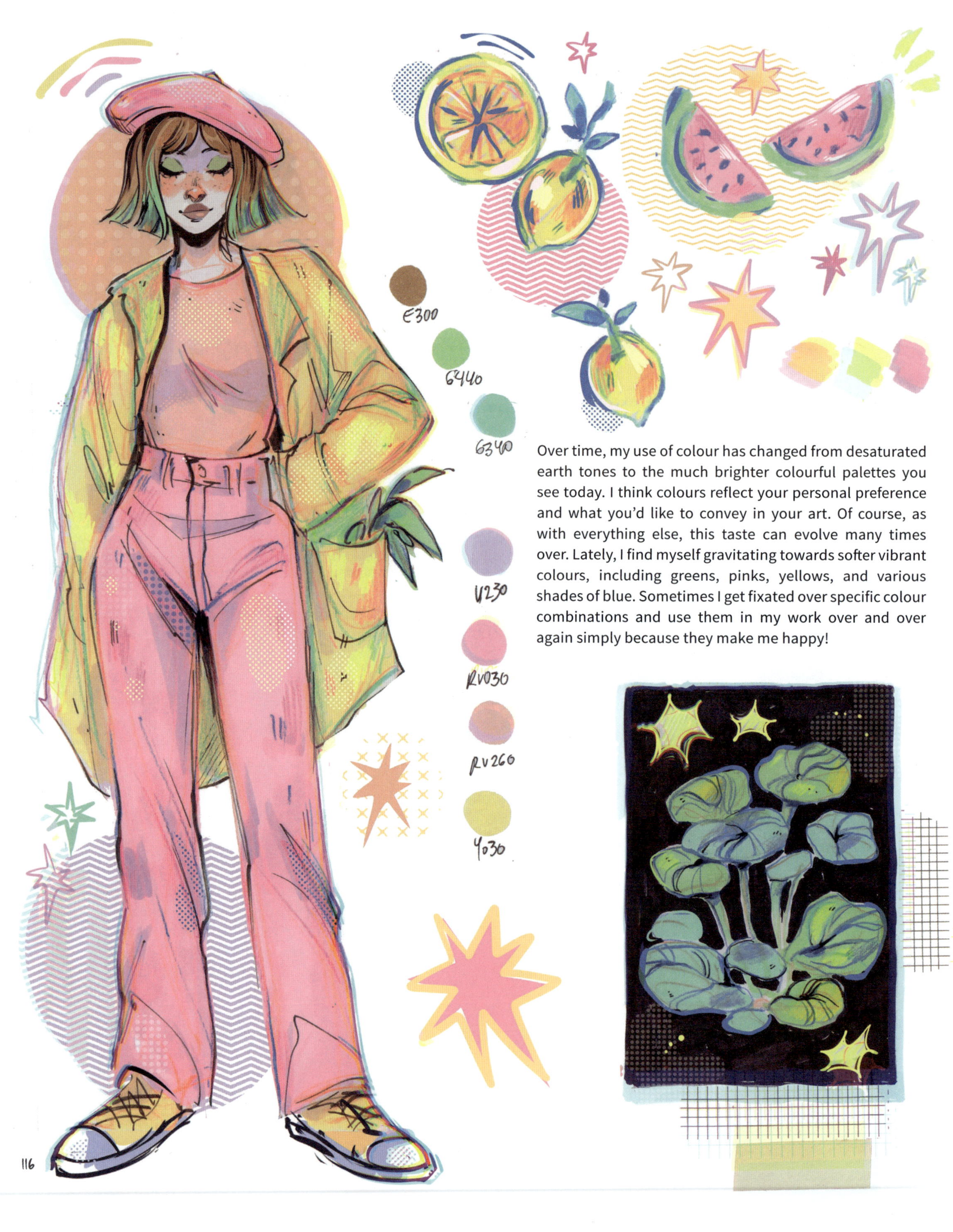

Over time, my use of colour has changed from desaturated earth tones to the much brighter colourful palettes you see today. I think colours reflect your personal preference and what you'd like to convey in your art. Of course, as with everything else, this taste can evolve many times over. Lately, I find myself gravitating towards softer vibrant colours, including greens, pinks, yellows, and various shades of blue. Sometimes I get fixated over specific colour combinations and use them in my work over and over again simply because they make me happy!

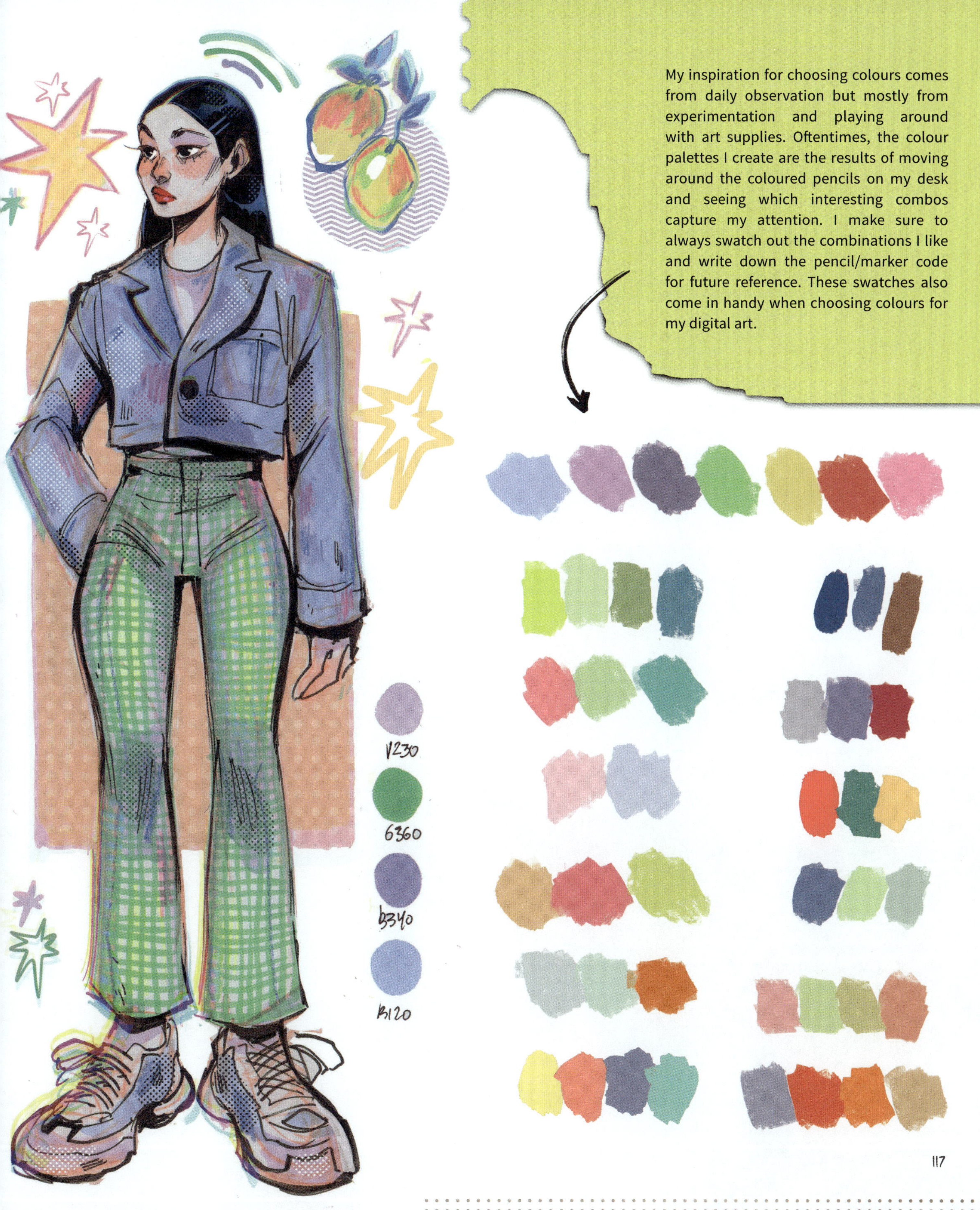

My inspiration for choosing colours comes from daily observation but mostly from experimentation and playing around with art supplies. Oftentimes, the colour palettes I create are the results of moving around the coloured pencils on my desk and seeing which interesting combos capture my attention. I make sure to always swatch out the combinations I like and write down the pencil/marker code for future reference. These swatches also come in handy when choosing colours for my digital art.

Colour harmony

I find that using limited colour palettes can be a great way to simplify the work *and* make it more impactful. By narrowing the range of colours, I'm able to create a cohesive, harmonious look by instilling a sense of balance. Typically, I choose one dominant colour as the base, a second to complement it, and a third for small accents. I use these as a starting point to create hue variations and a wider, consistent colour scheme.

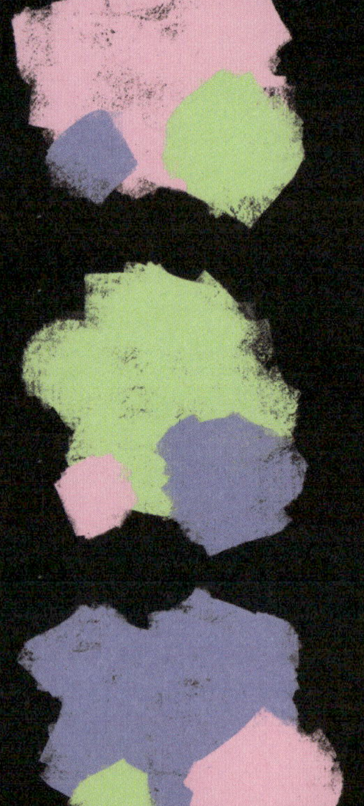

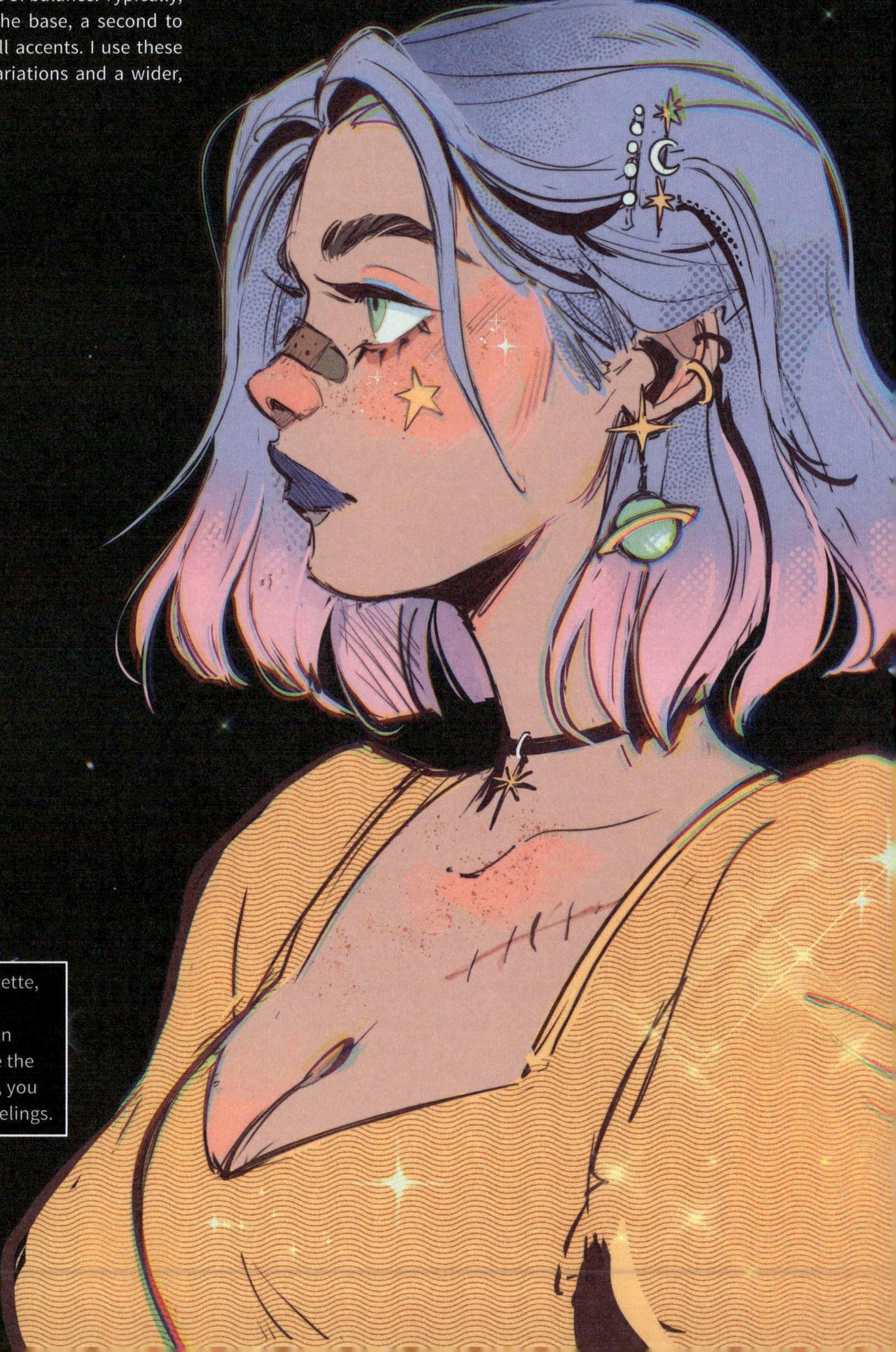

Once you have a chosen colour palette, proportionally varying how these colours interact with each other can create a visual hierarchy and guide the viewer's eye to specific areas. Plus, you can convey different moods and feelings.

I also love playing with combinations of cool and warm tones. For example, I might mix purples and blues with pops of orange, or yellow and reds with greens, etc. One of my favourite colour schemes are complementary colours. On the colour wheel, these colours are found opposite to one another. They have a natural contrast that enhances the other when used together, creating a striking, eye-catching effect. Another group of colours I love to use are pastels. Soft, muted shades can work perfectly fine alone or by complementing other colours. Honestly, they look so pretty together no matter how you mix them.

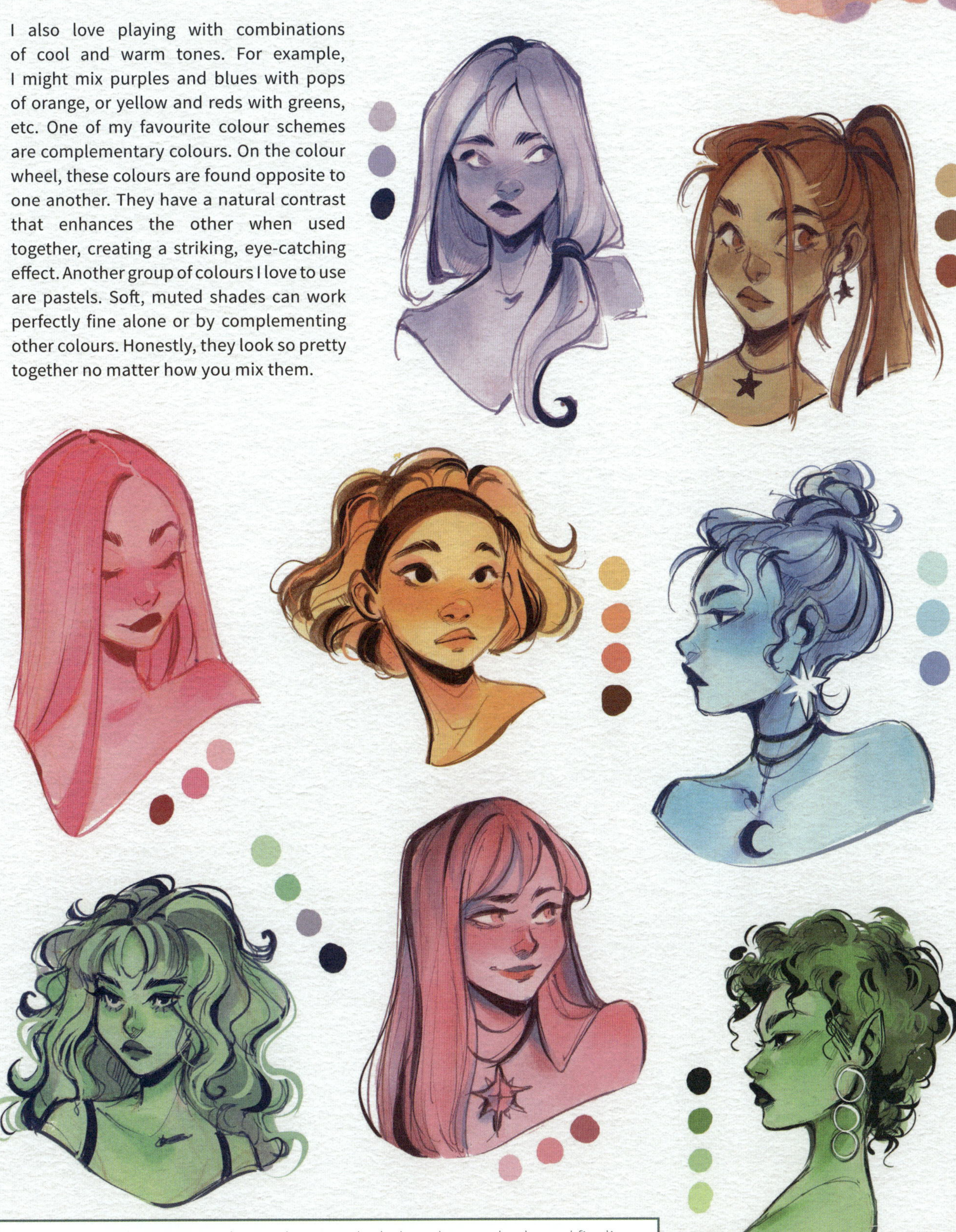

This is a monochromatic study I made using alcohol markers and coloured fineliners

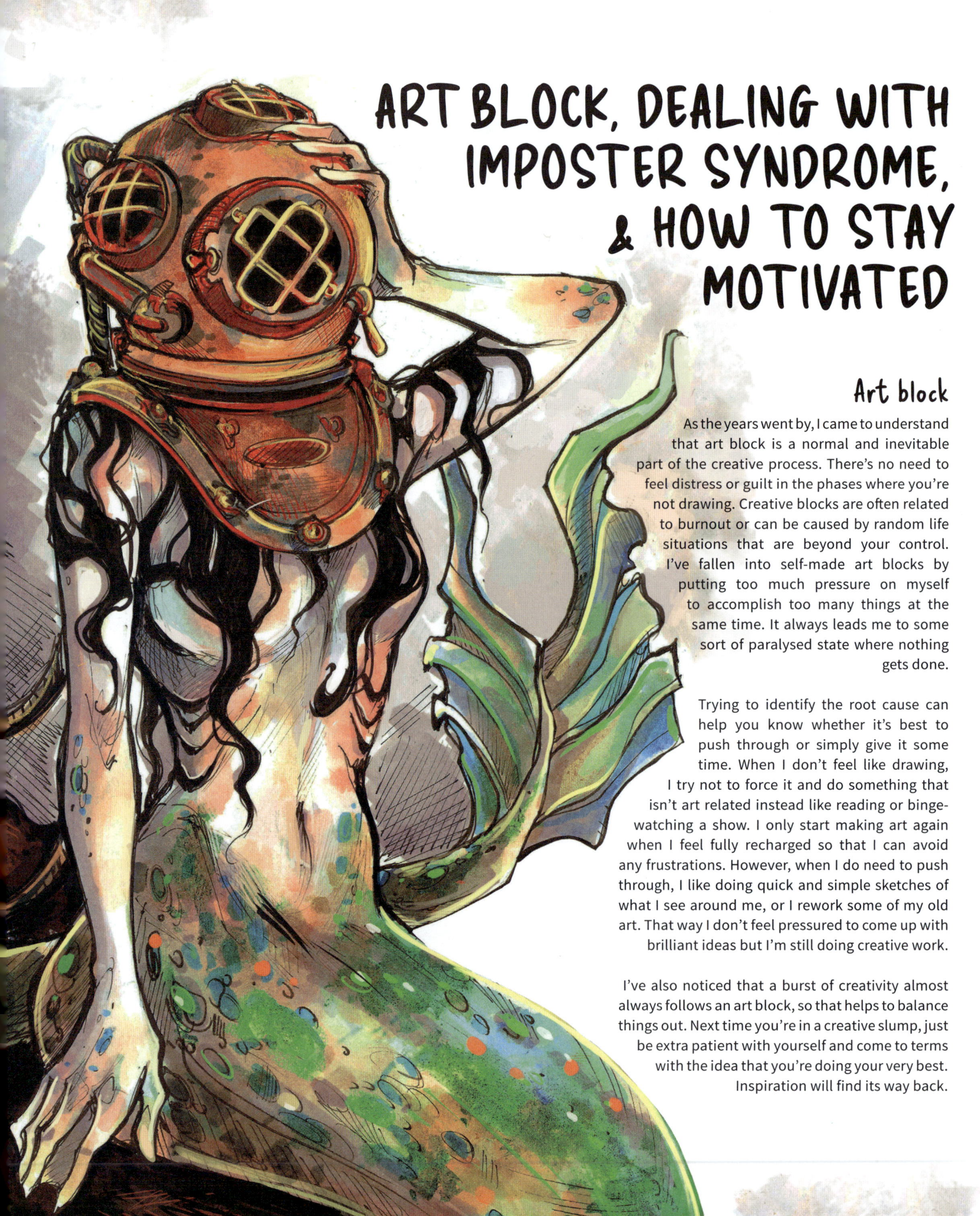

ART BLOCK, DEALING WITH IMPOSTER SYNDROME, & HOW TO STAY MOTIVATED

Art block

As the years went by, I came to understand that art block is a normal and inevitable part of the creative process. There's no need to feel distress or guilt in the phases where you're not drawing. Creative blocks are often related to burnout or can be caused by random life situations that are beyond your control. I've fallen into self-made art blocks by putting too much pressure on myself to accomplish too many things at the same time. It always leads me to some sort of paralysed state where nothing gets done.

Trying to identify the root cause can help you know whether it's best to push through or simply give it some time. When I don't feel like drawing, I try not to force it and do something that isn't art related instead like reading or binge-watching a show. I only start making art again when I feel fully recharged so that I can avoid any frustrations. However, when I do need to push through, I like doing quick and simple sketches of what I see around me, or I rework some of my old art. That way I don't feel pressured to come up with brilliant ideas but I'm still doing creative work.

I've also noticed that a burst of creativity almost always follows an art block, so that helps to balance things out. Next time you're in a creative slump, just be extra patient with yourself and come to terms with the idea that you're doing your very best. Inspiration will find its way back.

Dealing with imposter syndrome

I never knew what imposter syndrome was until I had to make a graphic novel for the first time without any previous experience in sequential art. Since then, it's never really gone away. Every new exciting job opportunity is always accompanied by the same anxious feelings: I'm not good enough, they made a mistake by giving me a chance, and it's only a matter of time before I disappoint everyone. Imposter syndrome is tricky because as the opportunities grow, so do the feelings of inadequacy. You forget what led you there in the first place and it makes you seek external validation. It dismisses the things you've done that deserve recognition, and instead of celebrating each new opportunity, you tend to panic and work harder than necessary.

I don't want to write about this like I have everything figured out because I certainly don't. But I came to understand that imposter syndrome is a common feeling that most artists endure at some point throughout their careers. It will always be there, to a greater or lesser extent, because you are constantly striving to improve your craft. Each time the syndrome kicks in, I try to reframe my thoughts and focus on what I know and what I've accomplished rather than what I don't know and haven't yet achieved. I focus on my own journey rather than comparing myself to others. I know – easier said than done! But once you take pride in your *own* abilities and the progress you're making as an artist, nothing else can take it away.

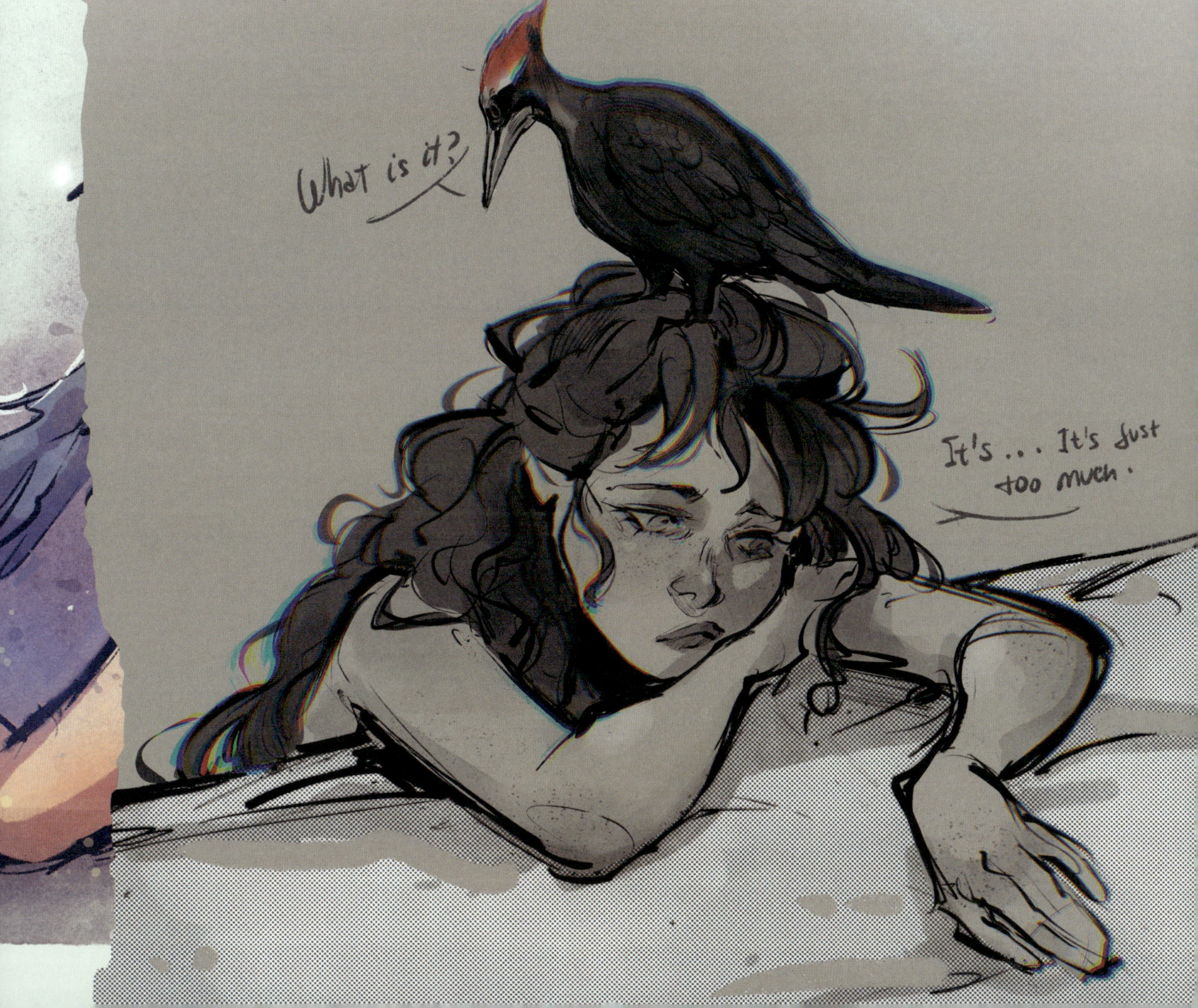

How to stay motivated

While inspiration can be a powerful trigger that can make you feel encouraged to do things, motivation is the driving force behind your actions. When paired with a little self-discipline, it makes you move forwards and keeps you accountable. I think the secret is to cultivate healthy habits by doing small things that can keep you motivated in the long run.

WORKSPACE

In order to produce your best work, try to create an environment that is quiet, free from distractions, and full of things that you find inspiring. It doesn't have to be big, it just needs to be functional and comfortable to you.

STAY CURIOUS

Explore a technique you haven't tried before, change your process entirely, learn to use a new tool, draw that thing that makes you nervous. Discovering new little things every day helps to expand your knowledge and keep your mind active and engaged.

TAKE IT EASY

If you're struggling with finding motivation, sometimes the best you can do is simply sit with that frustration for a moment. Allow yourself to do bad work without any judgement. See how fun and liberating it can be if you just let it follow its course!

RECOGNIZE YOUR ACHIEVEMENTS

It can be particularly difficult to maintain motivation in the long term it you fail to acknowledge your efforts and celebrate your small victories. When you recognize the progress you've made, you can feel a sense of accomplishment and satisfaction that will reinforce your efforts. Accept the fact that everyone is constantly learning and what you're doing is enough.

WORK ON A THEME

Coming up with new ideas can sometimes feel a bit overwhelming. When you're not sure what to draw, think of a few topics that sound interesting to you and brainstorm ideas around them (for example, fairies + flowers). Make sure to keep a list for future reference! Having a specific theme will give you a clear vision of what you're going to draw next so that it's easier to feel motivated to pick up a pencil.

KEEP SMALL GOALS

The thought of completing a large project can be daunting. Setting small, achievable goals can help to break down a big project into more manageable parts.

KEEP TRACK OF YOUR IMPROVEMENT

It always surprises me when I hear about artists throwing out their old art. I've kept the majority of my artwork, including all my doodles and terrible sketches from over the years, and they're some of the most precious things I own. I think it's important to show respect for the work done at all stages of an artist's journey, even if it's not at the level you'd like. Each little step contributes to the big picture. Next time you need a motivational booster, try revisiting some of your old art and see how far you've come!

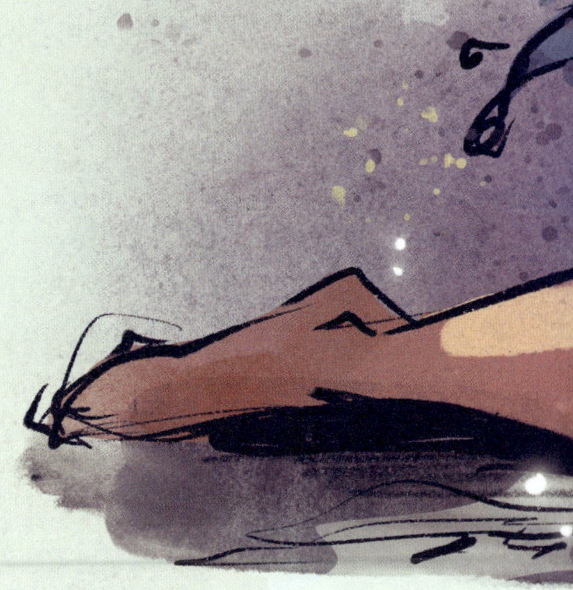

ENGAGE WITH THE ART COMMUNITY

I often think about how so many people across the world share the same love for drawing as me, and I find it fascinating. The exchange of a few words between artists, reading comments, asking for advice, and participating in art challenges can all yield immense inspiration and motivation. I believe creativity is a collaborative process and sharing your art with others can bring new ideas and perspectives to your work.

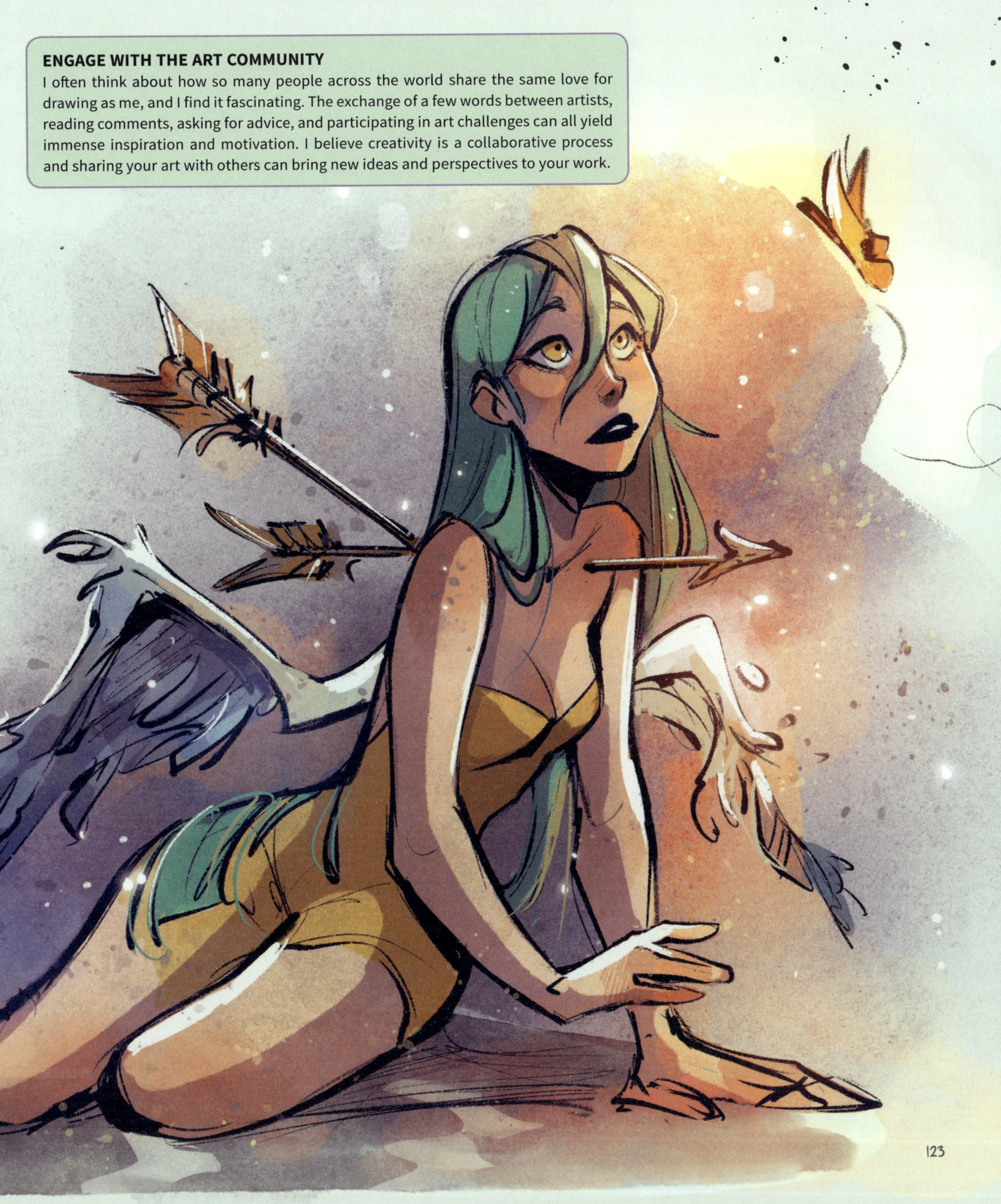

LISTENING TO YOUR BODY

I was never very conscious of taking care of my physical health and never cared much about my limitations. I've always been capable of working fairly quickly, so I was usually able to power through the most ridiculous deadlines. I loved saying yes to every project because I always found a way to be efficient and made room in my schedule to give more if it was required. We all know that overworking and lack of breaks can lead to burnout or even severe injuries, but you never believe it could *actually* happen until one day it does.

In 2021, while navigating a series of client projects, my hand started to hurt. Although I was anxious at first, I assumed the pain would go away as it had done in the past. However, this time it didn't. I didn't stop either because I had work to do. I ended up being diagnosed with tenosynovitis, a painful inflammation of the tendon and its sheath caused by overuse. It extended from my wrist to my elbow, and on really bad days, it reached my shoulder. I knew I needed to take a long break from drawing in order to recover, but instead, I only took two weeks off and convinced myself that was enough. I kept working and attended kinesiology sessions. The exercises and stretching helped loads, but it didn't fully get rid of the pain. It was depressing to see that my recovery was not straightforward and that my arm wasn't responding how I expected – even after thirty sessions.

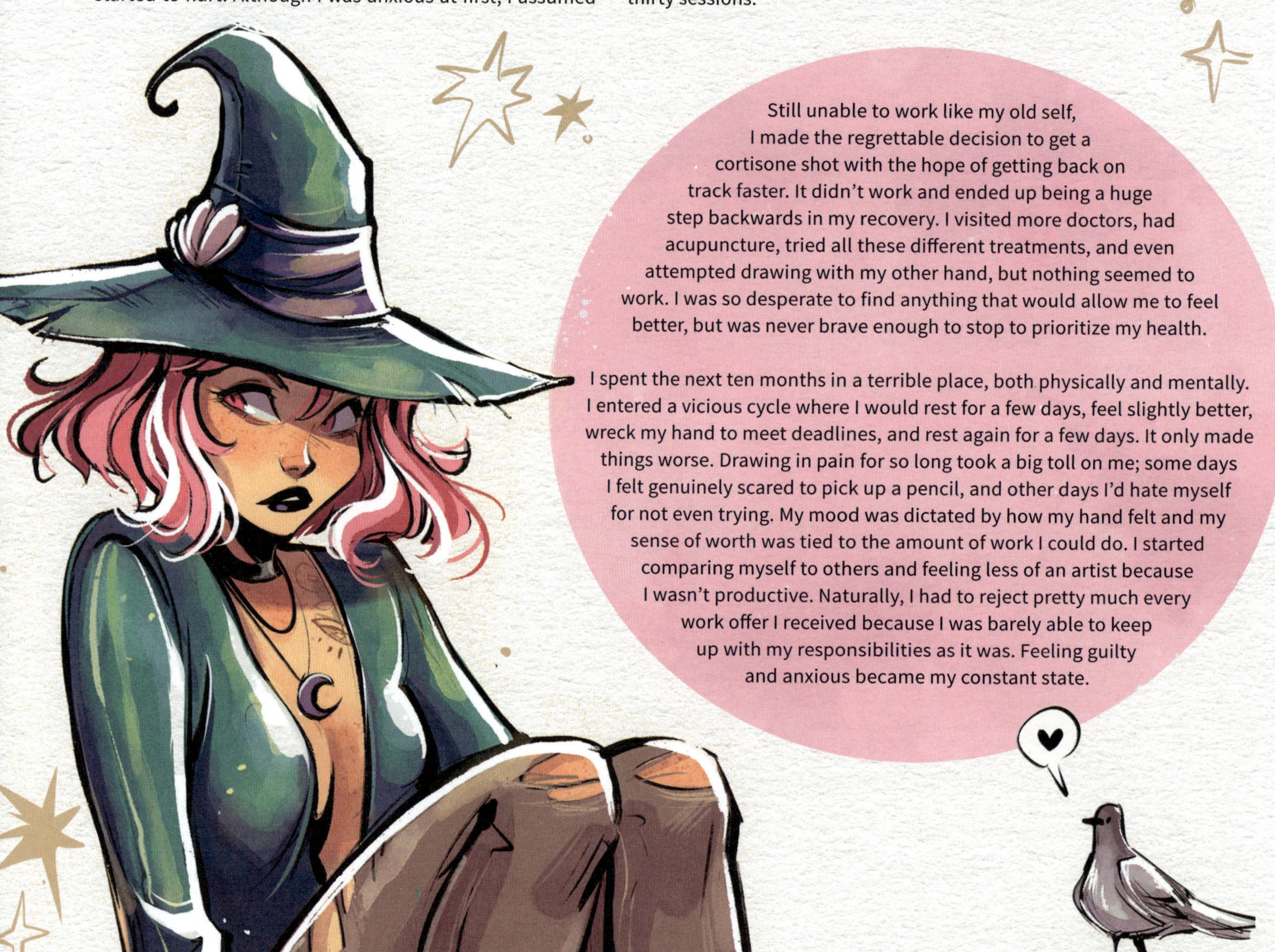

Still unable to work like my old self, I made the regrettable decision to get a cortisone shot with the hope of getting back on track faster. It didn't work and ended up being a huge step backwards in my recovery. I visited more doctors, had acupuncture, tried all these different treatments, and even attempted drawing with my other hand, but nothing seemed to work. I was so desperate to find anything that would allow me to feel better, but was never brave enough to stop to prioritize my health.

I spent the next ten months in a terrible place, both physically and mentally. I entered a vicious cycle where I would rest for a few days, feel slightly better, wreck my hand to meet deadlines, and rest again for a few days. It only made things worse. Drawing in pain for so long took a big toll on me; some days I felt genuinely scared to pick up a pencil, and other days I'd hate myself for not even trying. My mood was dictated by how my hand felt and my sense of worth was tied to the amount of work I could do. I started comparing myself to others and feeling less of an artist because I wasn't productive. Naturally, I had to reject pretty much every work offer I received because I was barely able to keep up with my responsibilities as it was. Feeling guilty and anxious became my constant state.

The thought of spending another year in the same condition terrified me, so I knew something had to change. I had to get out of the hole I'd dug myself into. After much thought, I decided to quit a long-term project that was very close to my heart. Lifting that heavy weight off my shoulders allowed me to breathe again and I regained some control I thought I'd lost. I understood that negative emotions and persistent stress could find physical outlets, worsening your condition. I decided to give therapy a go and started swimming regularly, which was a huge step towards my physical and mental well-being.

Determined to learn from my mistakes, I have since adopted new habits that have completely transformed the way I work. These include a good sitting posture, contrast therapy every time my wrist feels stiff, and holding the pencil in a way that is less taxing for my arm. I learned to draw without exerting too much pressure, changed all my brush settings, and upgraded my set-up to make it as ergonomic as possible. Most importantly, I started taking mandatory breaks every hour or so, which include a series of stretching exercises in the morning, evening, and after each heavy work session.

I wish that I could say that upon writing this my arm has fully healed, but that wouldn't be true. I still deal with pain from time to time and get frustrated when I can't draw for long periods. Neglecting my body's signals for an entire year has left me with a sense that I've broken something within me, and that fixing it entirely will take some time and a lot of care. But I think I've come to terms with that. I'm nowhere near where I used to be and I know the worst is behind me. There's only room for improvement.

I used to torture myself wondering if I'd ever be my old self again, or if I'd be able to draw without restraints. I understand now that there's no older version to go back to, especially if that means compromising my health again.

Life is about moving forward with the lessons you've learned, embracing change and growth as it comes. It took me a while, but I think I've finally learned that health is not worth sacrificing for anything.

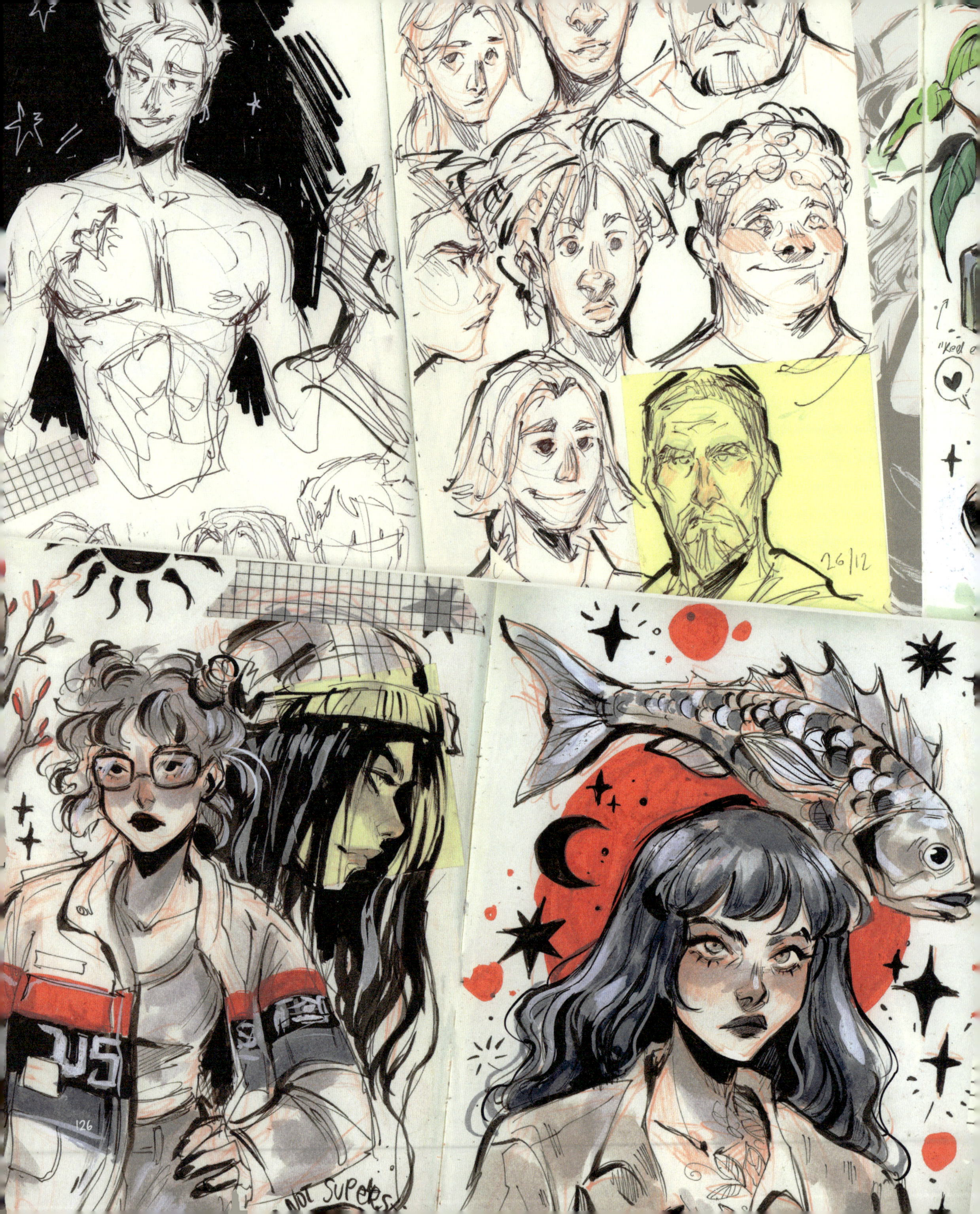
26/12

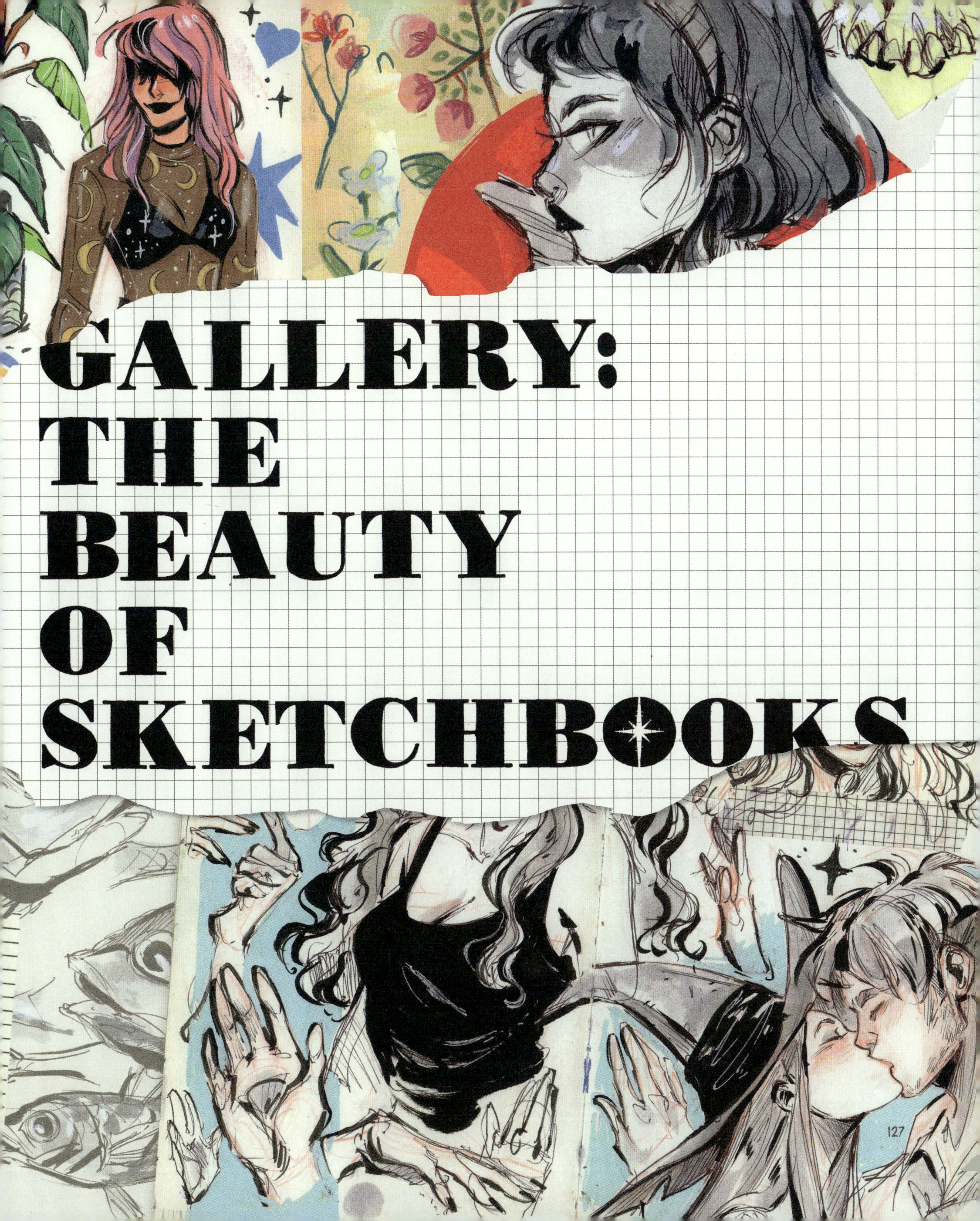

GALLERY: THE BEAUTY OF SKETCHBOOKS

Sketchbooks have become my favourite place to embrace the messy, unpredictable nature of my art. They've completely transformed my creative process over time. I like to think of my sketchbooks as a space free from the pressures of client work and the meticulosity of digital art. It's a space where I can draw just for the pure joy of it. I pour anything I want into these pages: quick studies, colour palettes, collages, mindless doodles, tool testing, swatches, ugly sketches, quotes, and lots and lots of experimentation. They often become a sort of scrapbook too, as I love mixing my art with stickers, clippings, tickets, and anything that has sentimental value. They are my visual journals.

I usually have a couple of sketchbooks going at the same time: one for more polished, colourful work that I feel comfortable sharing on social media, and a smaller, cheaper one that I take everywhere with me to fill with ballpoint-pen doodles and random stuff. Whenever I'm happy with how a batch of pages turn out, I scan them and fix little mistakes, make touch-ups, and tweak colours using Adobe Photoshop. I really enjoy the simpler quality of my traditional art compared to my fully digital illustrations. I love how the main focus of these sketchbook experiments is to play around with shapes and colours, seeing how they interact with each other to create fun and striking compositions!

In this chapter, you'll find artwork from the sketchbooks I've collected over the years.

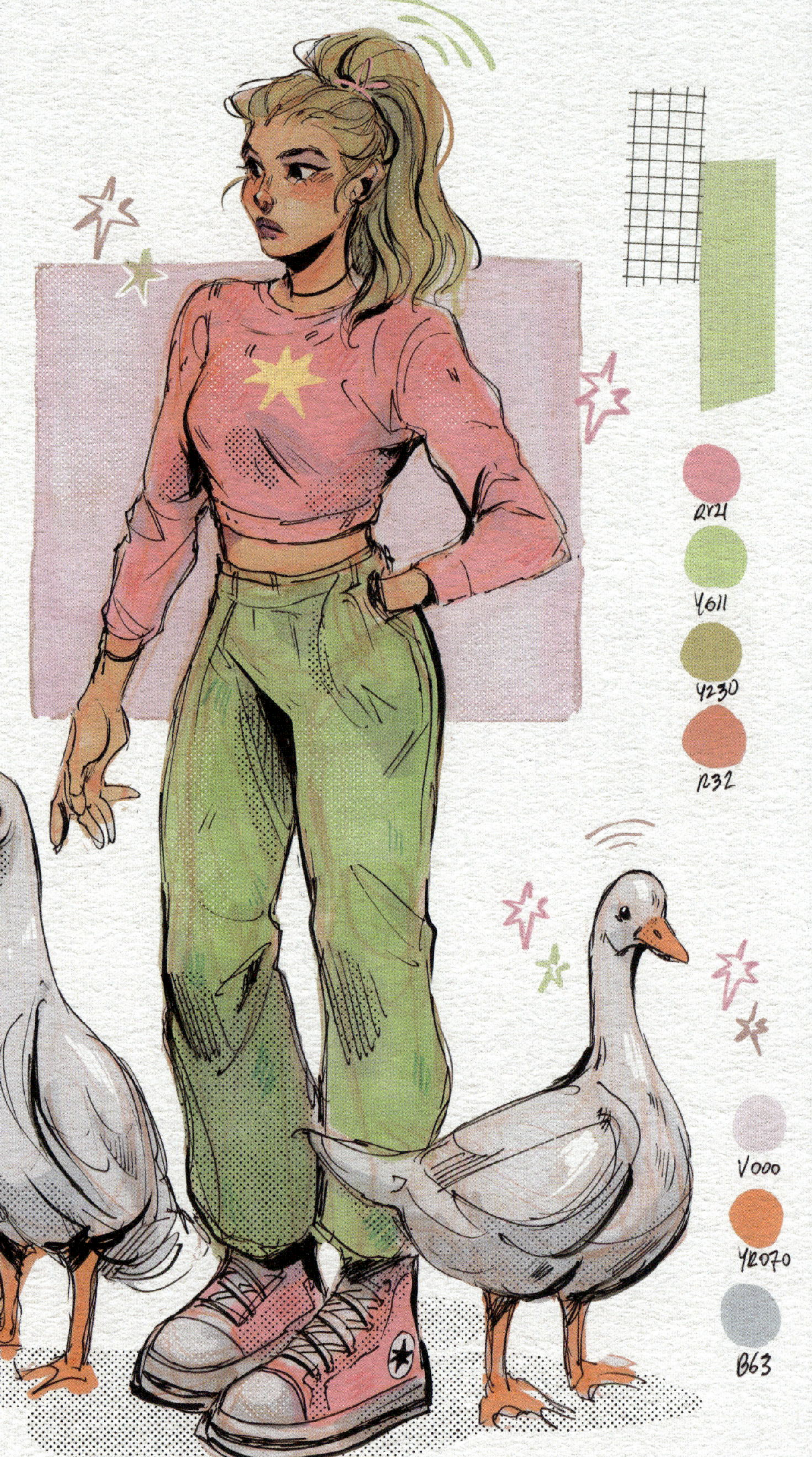

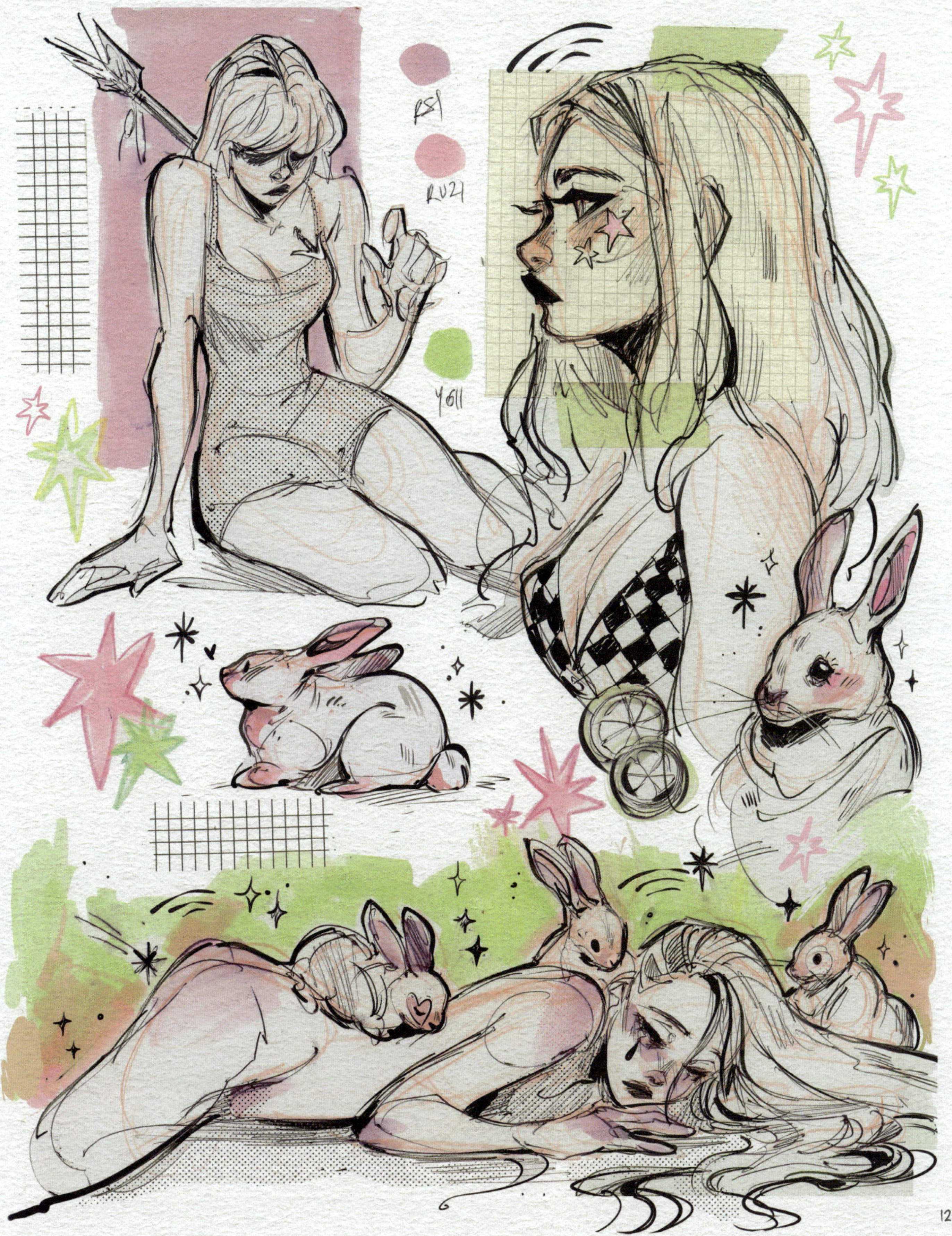
R81
RV21
YG11

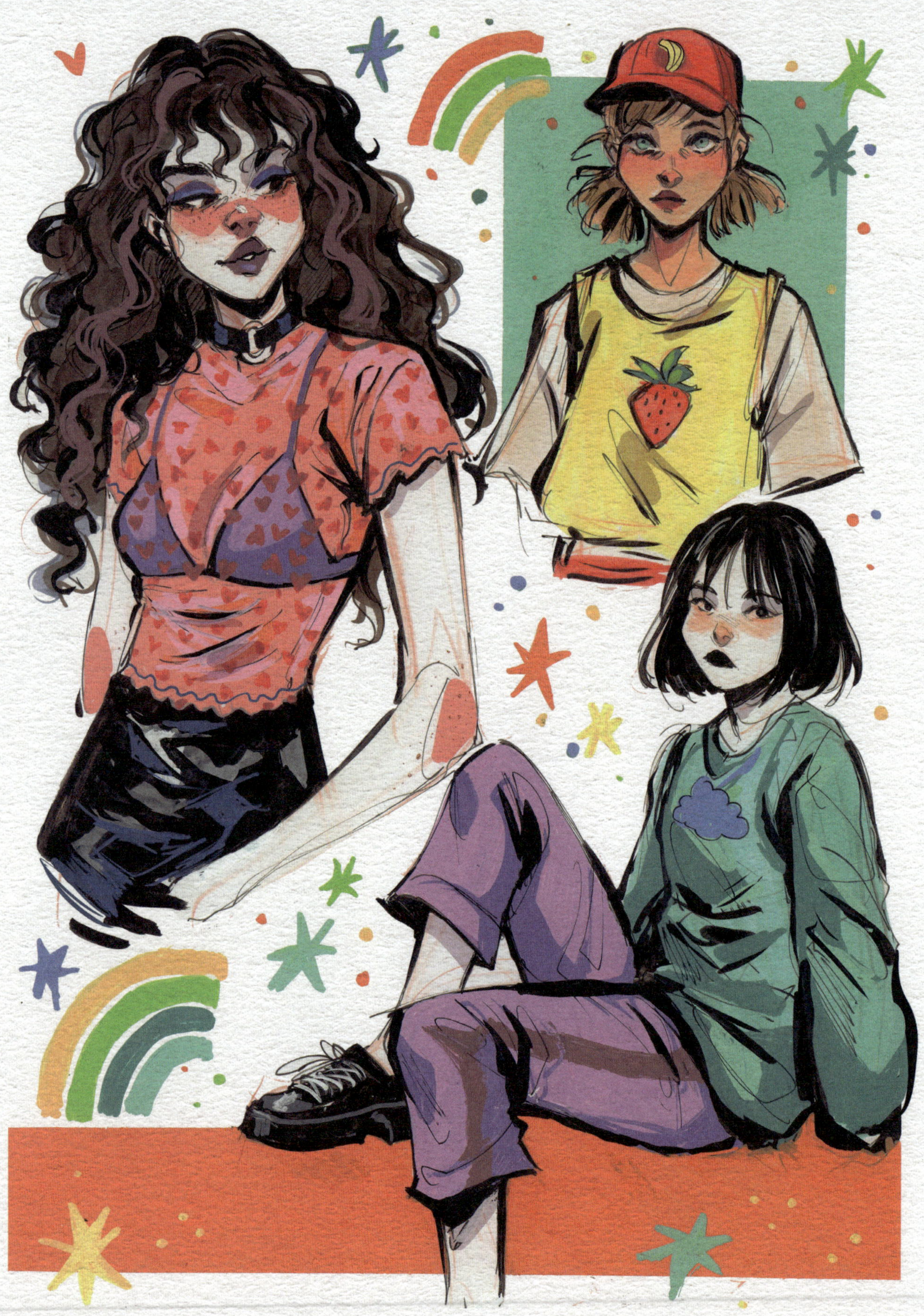

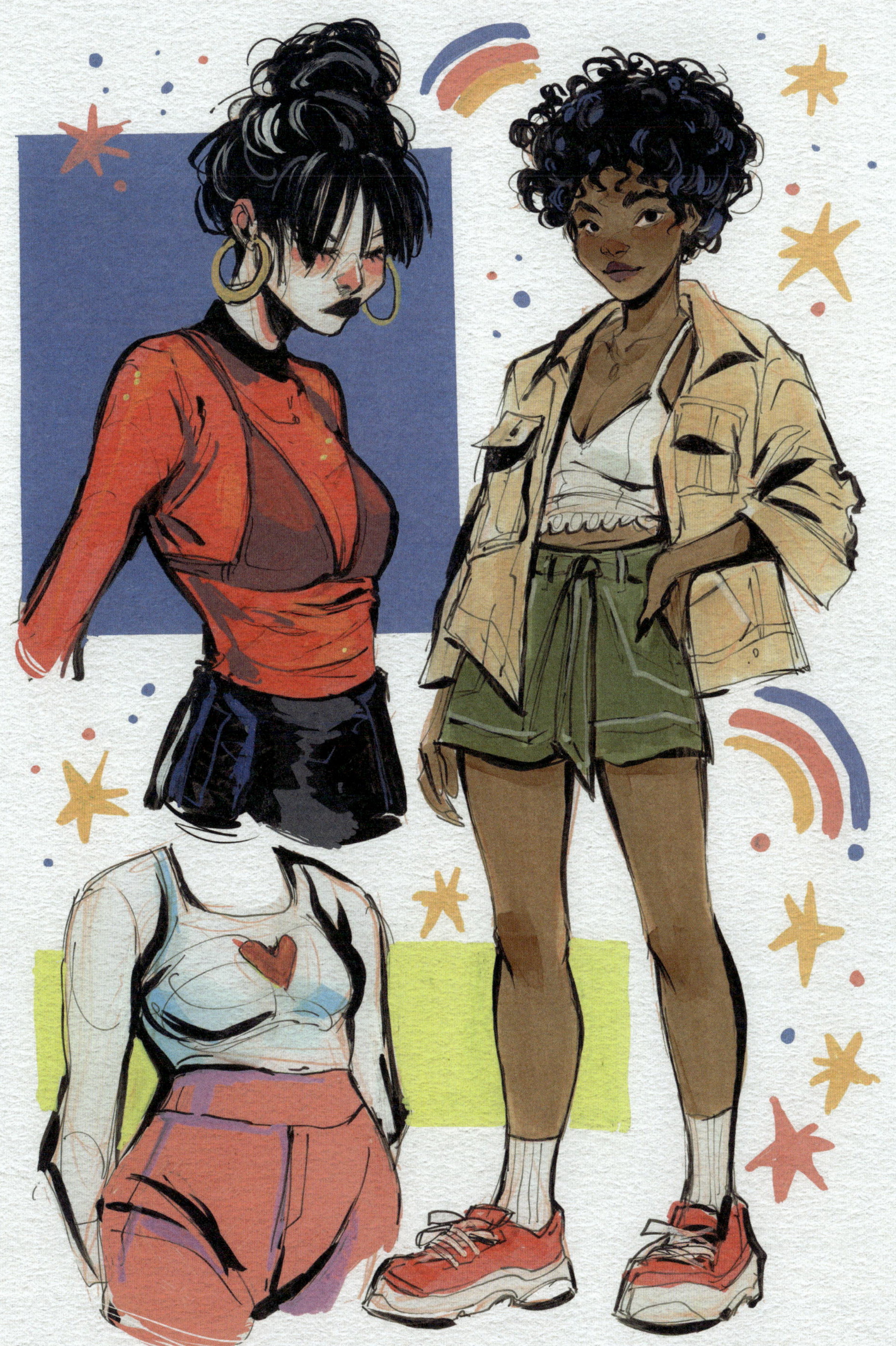

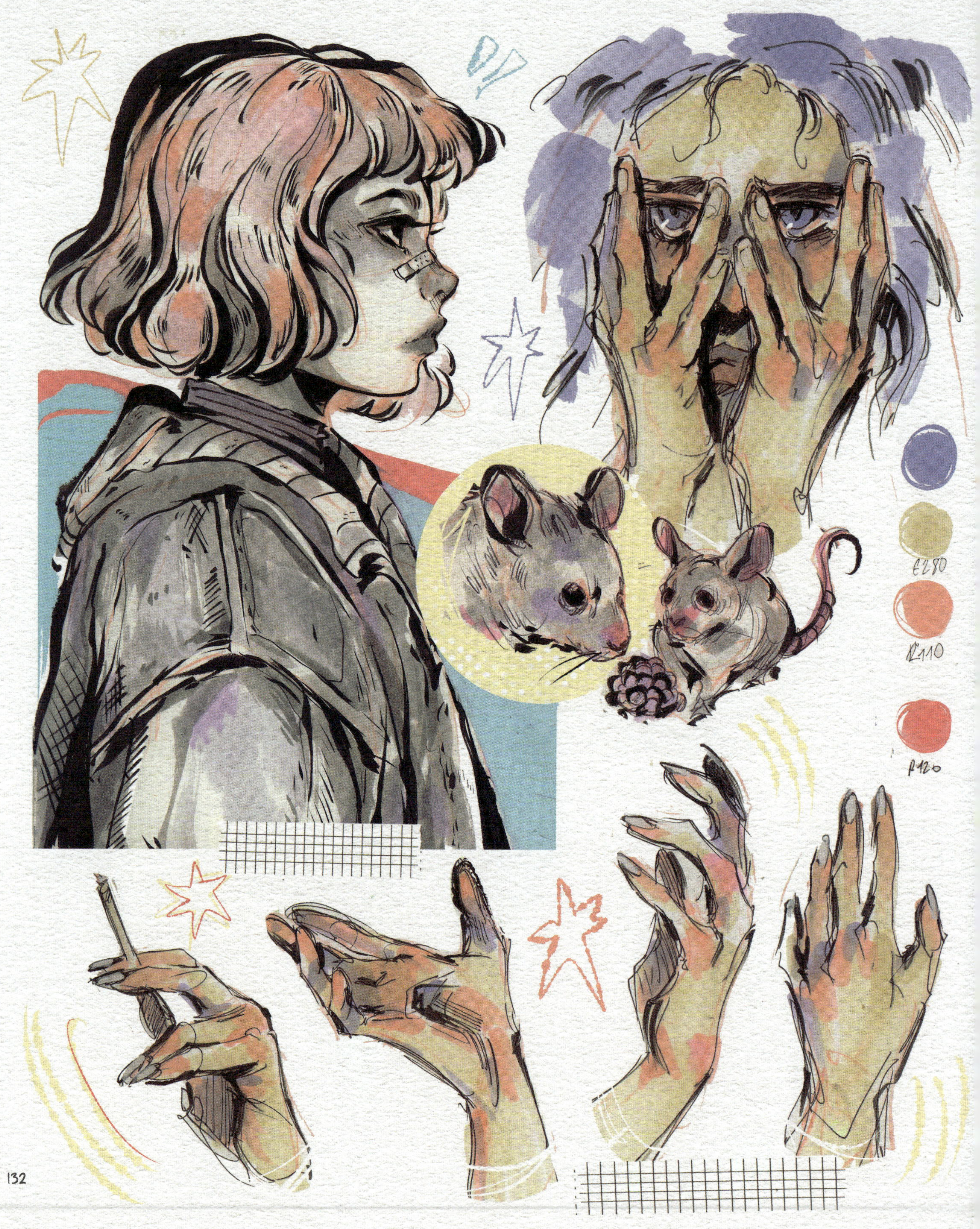
E280
R110
R120

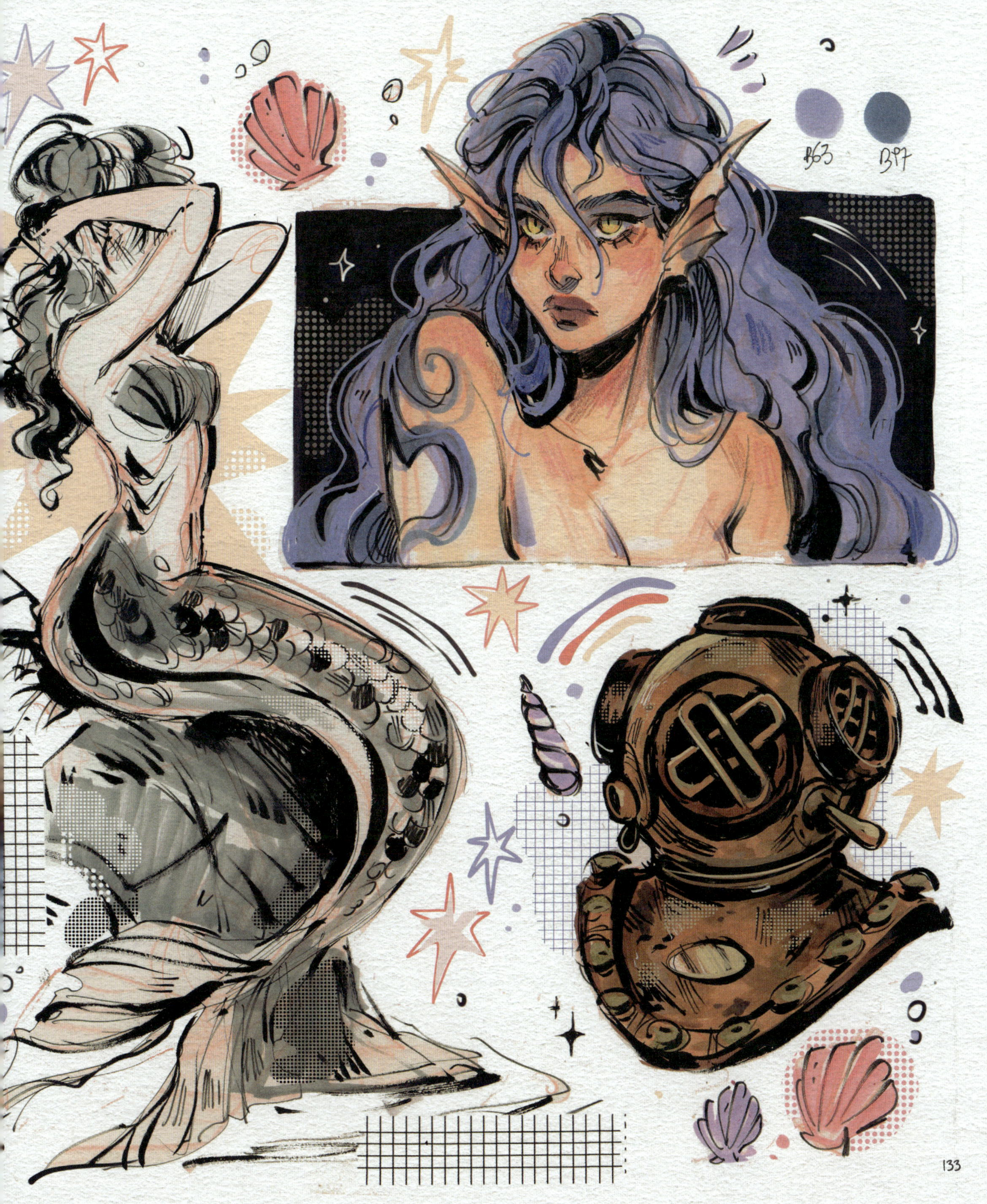

B63
B97

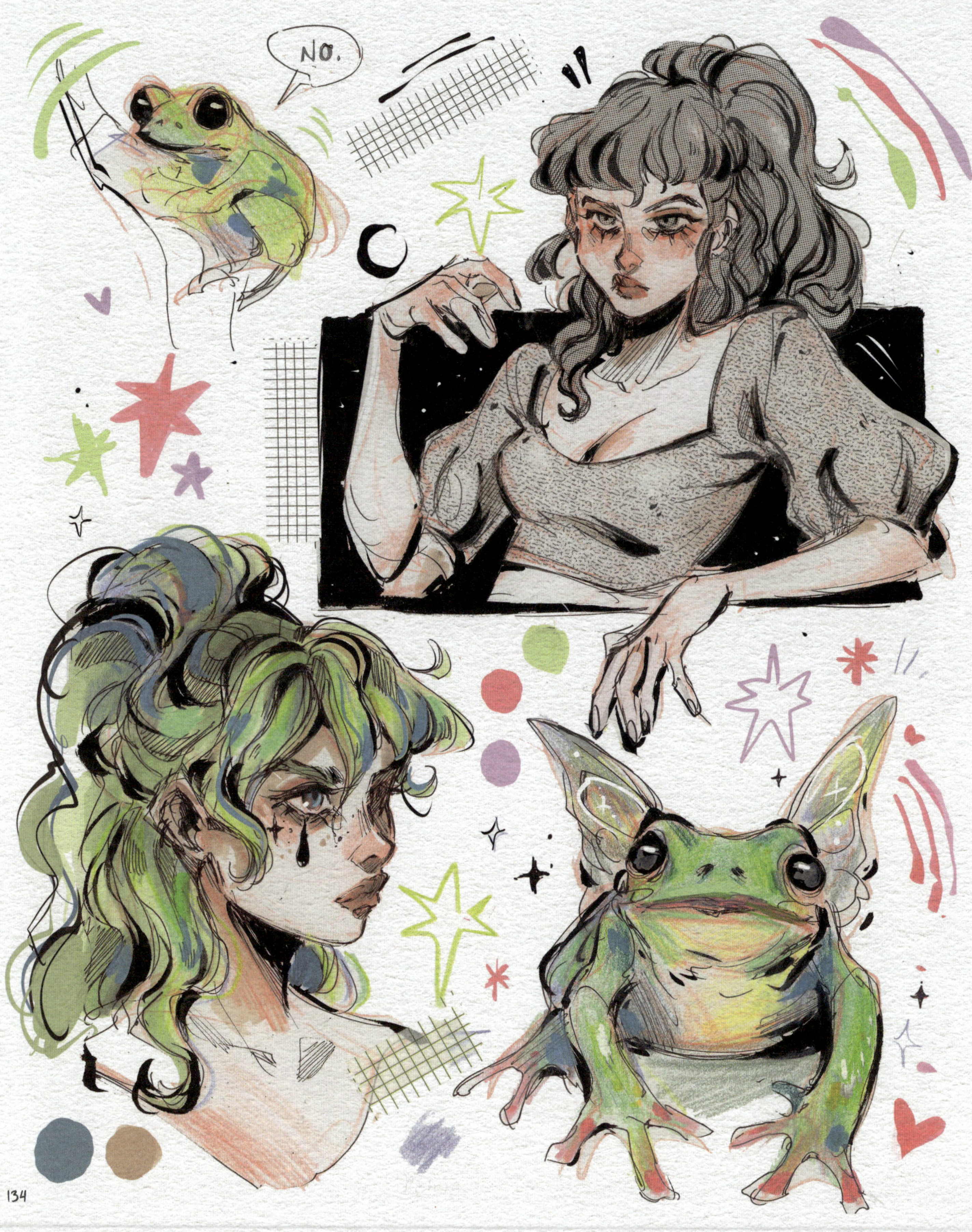
NO.

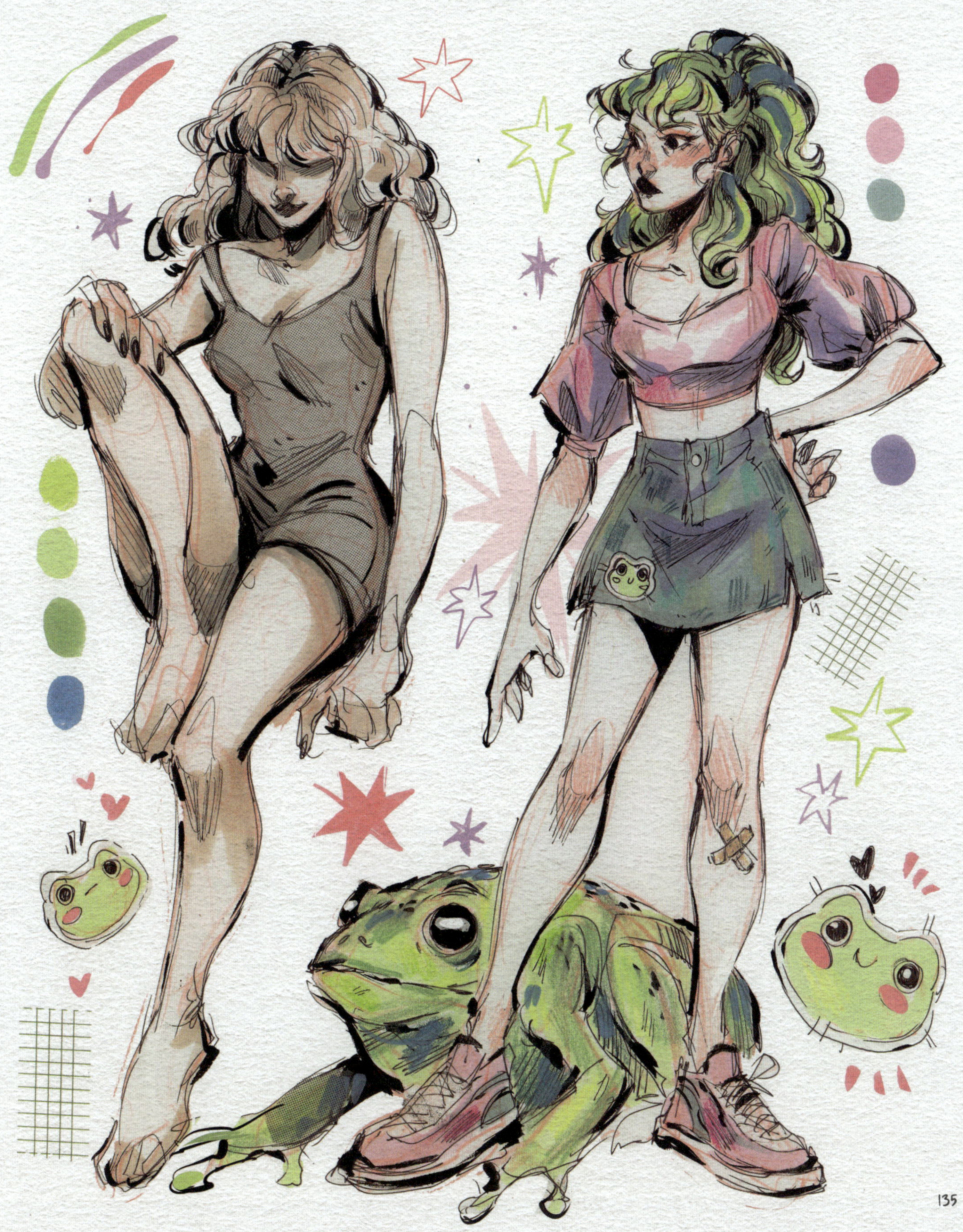

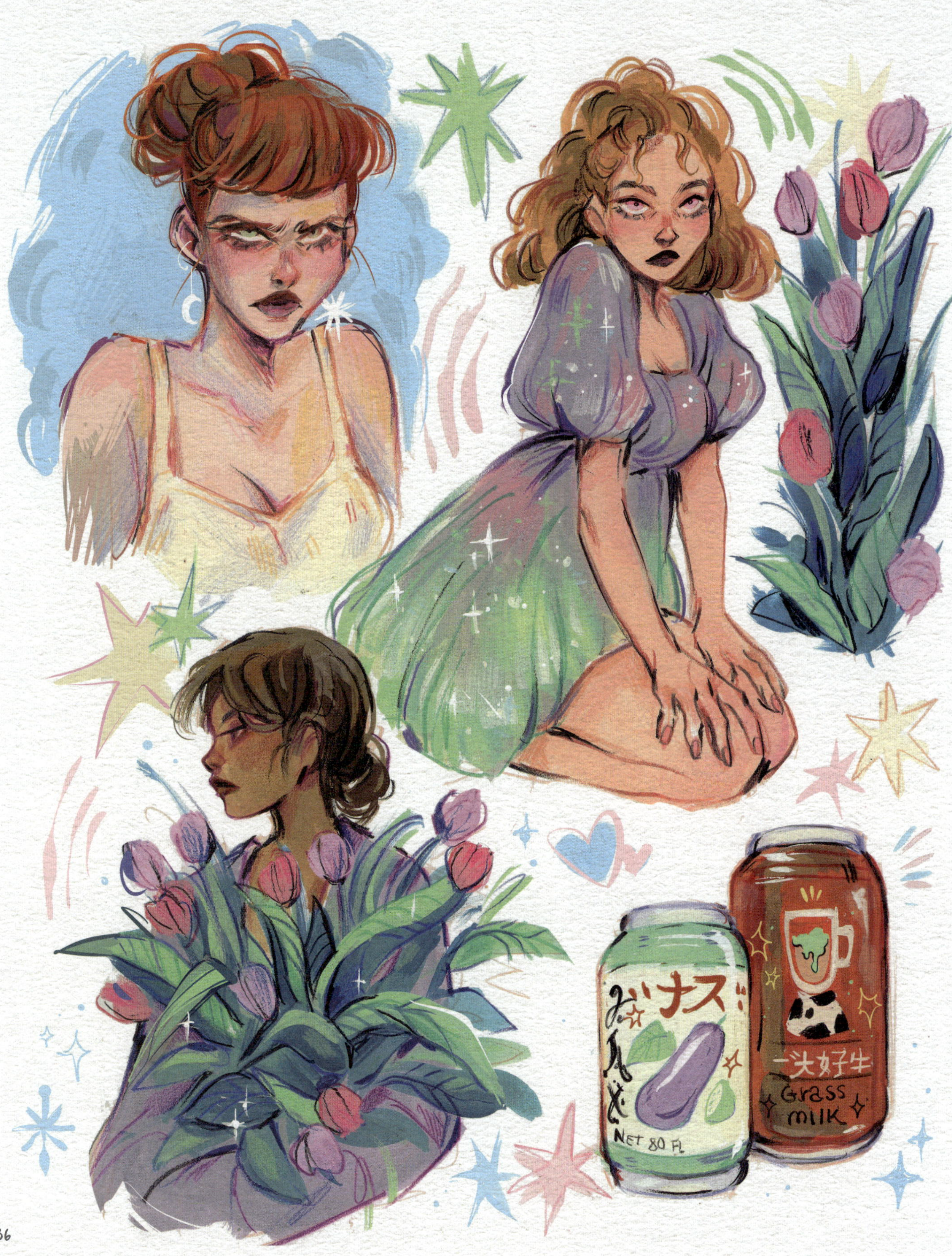
いナス
NET 80 FL
一头好牛
Grass milk

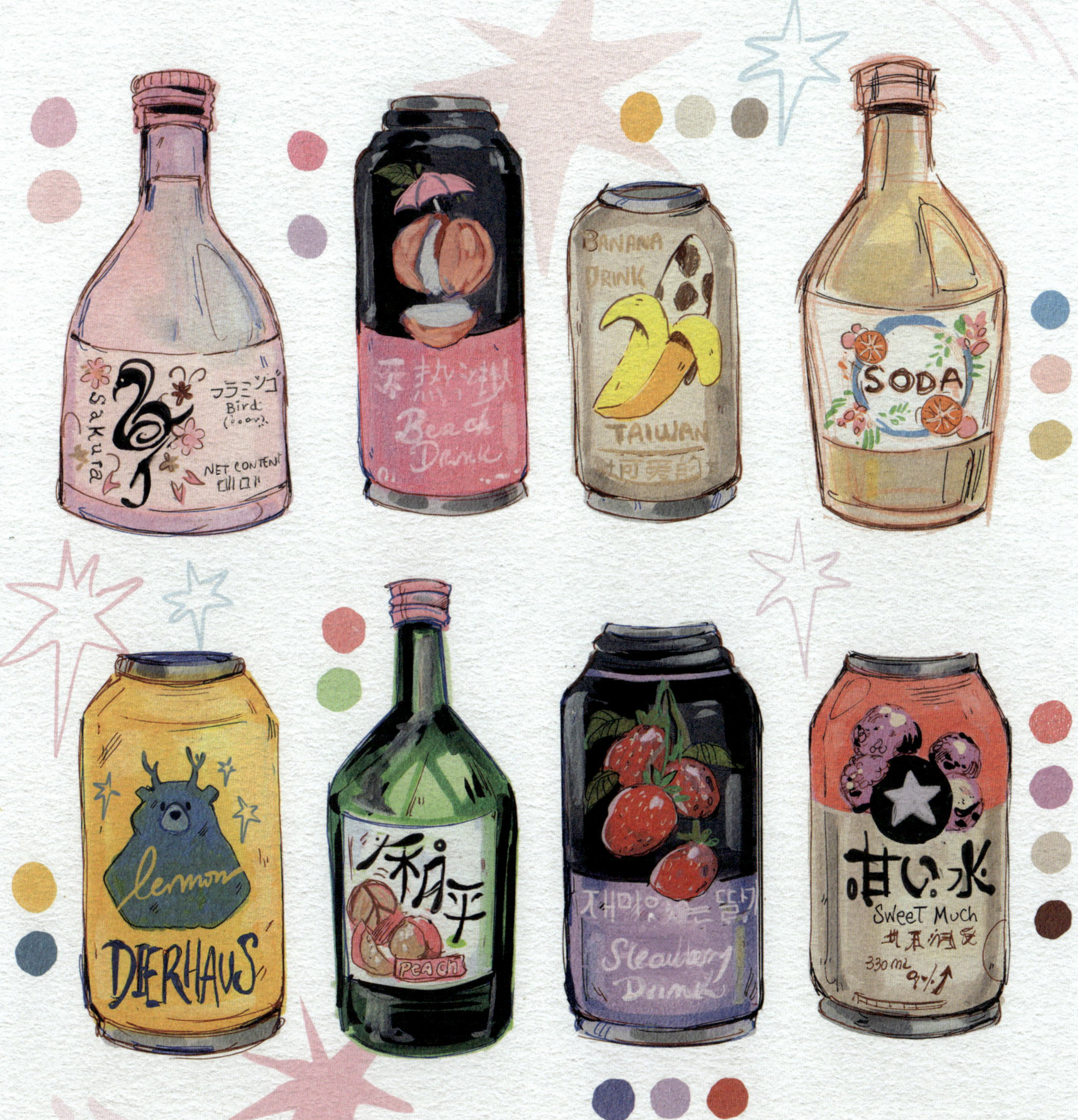

Sakura
フラミンゴ
Bird
NET CONTENT
Beach Drink
BANANA DRINK
TAIWAN
SODA
lemon
DIERHAUS
PEACH
甘い水
SWEET MUCH
330 mL

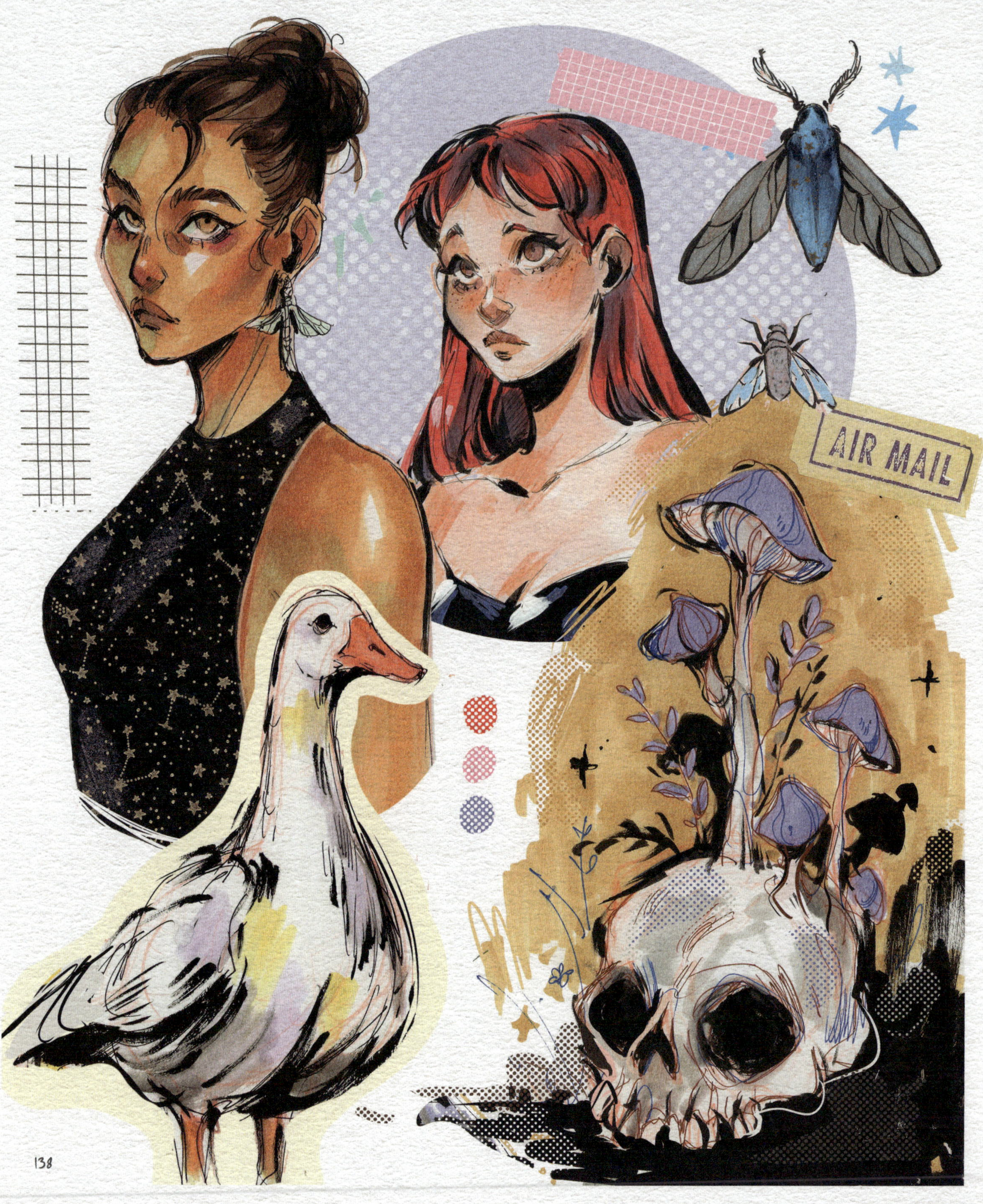
AIR MAIL

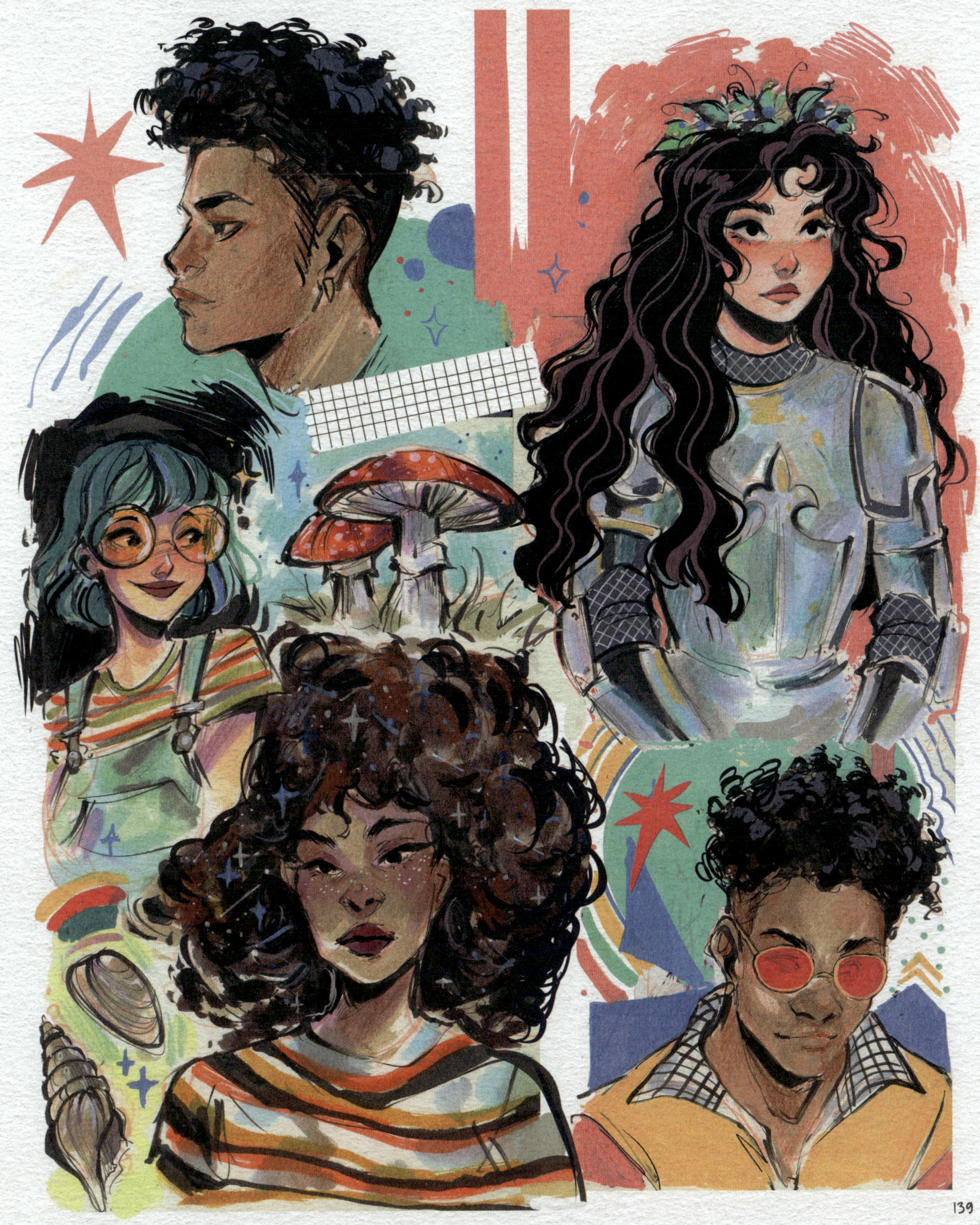

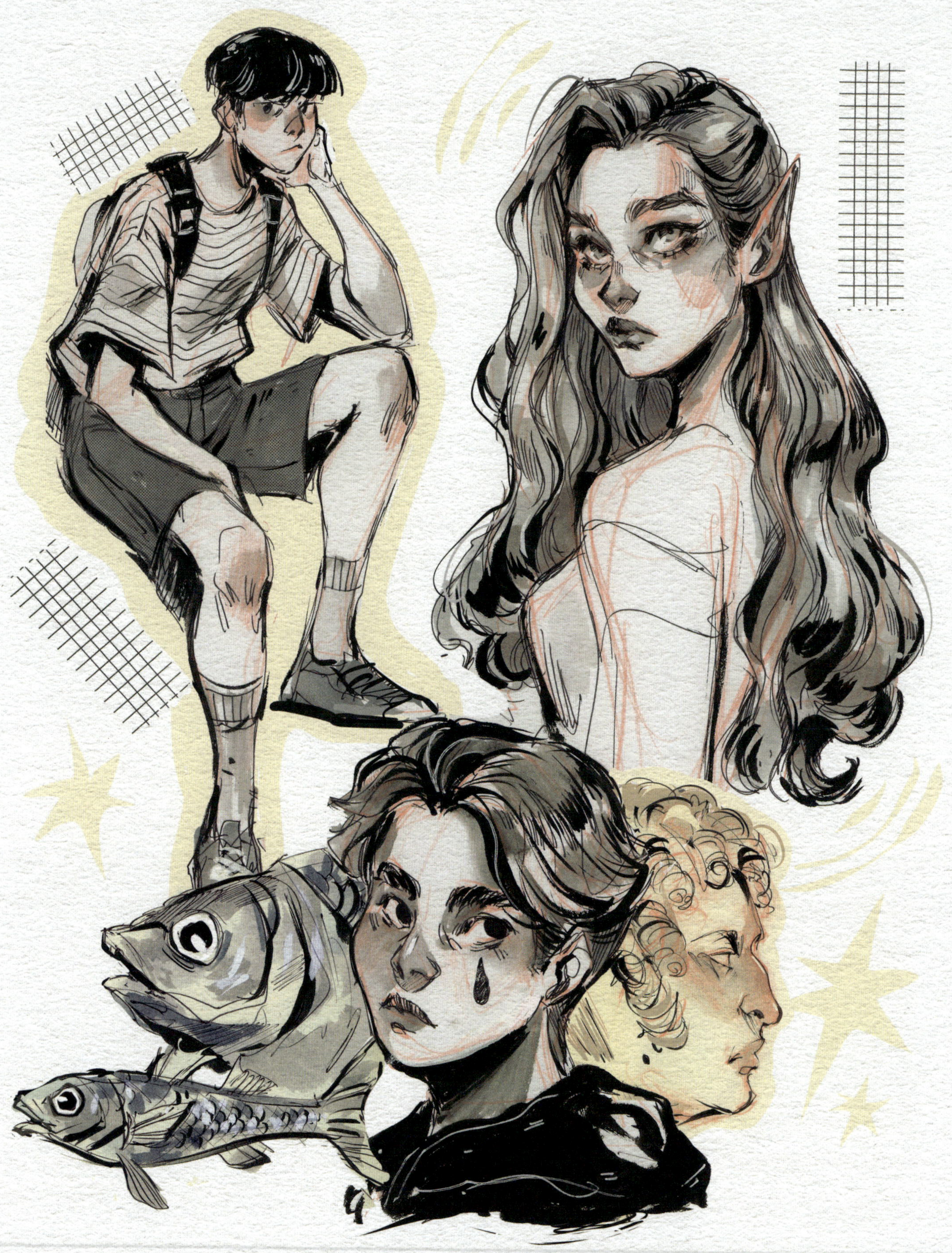

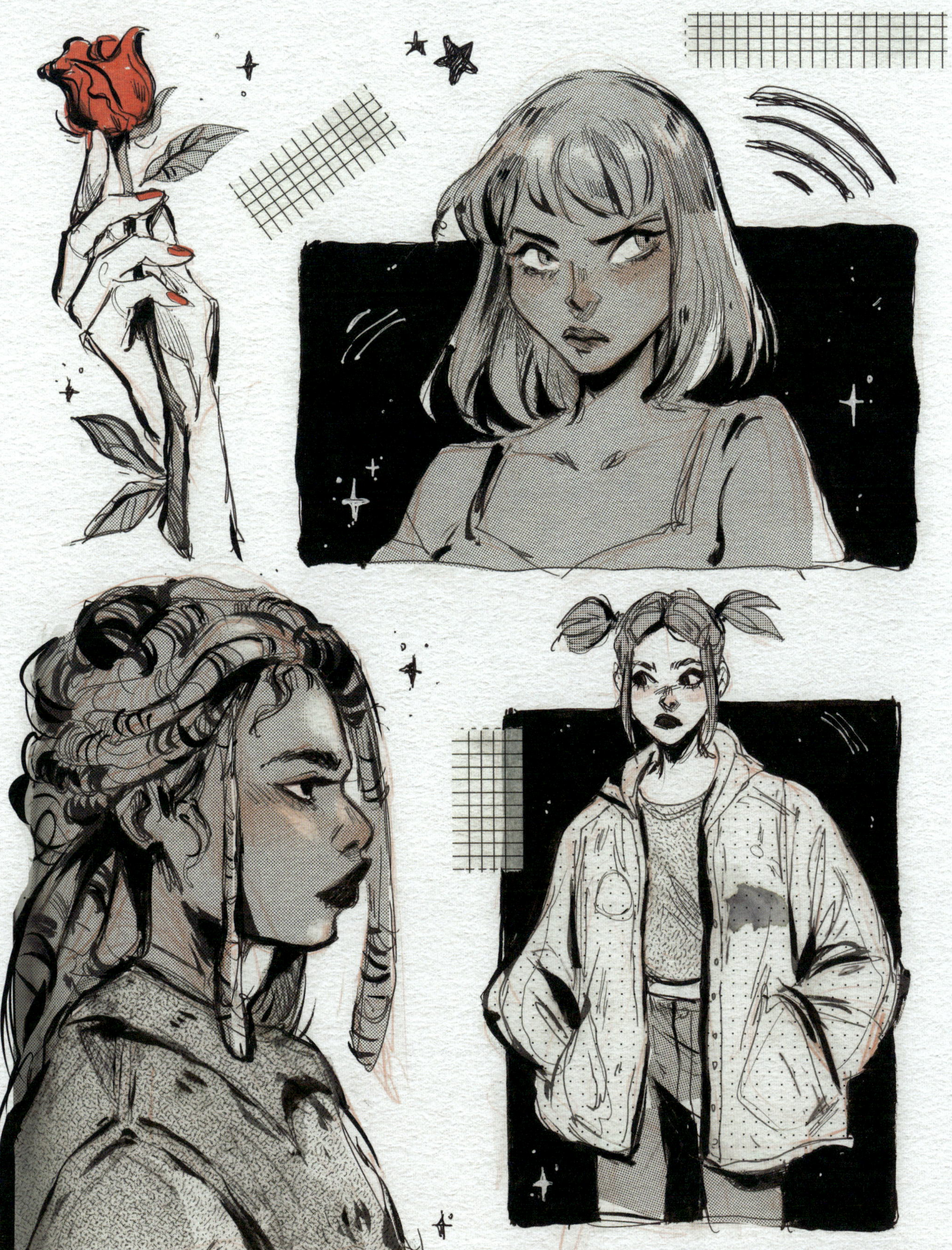

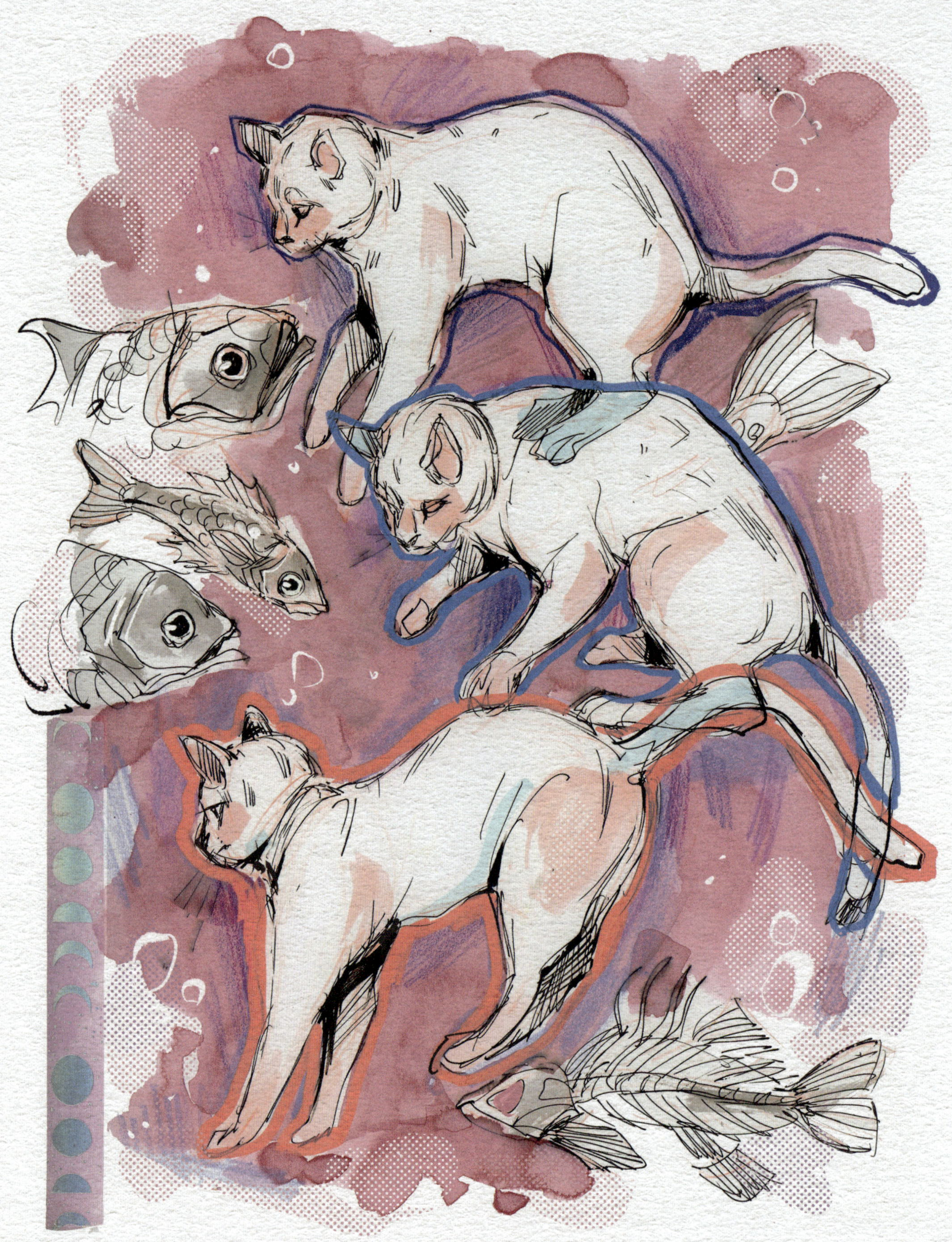

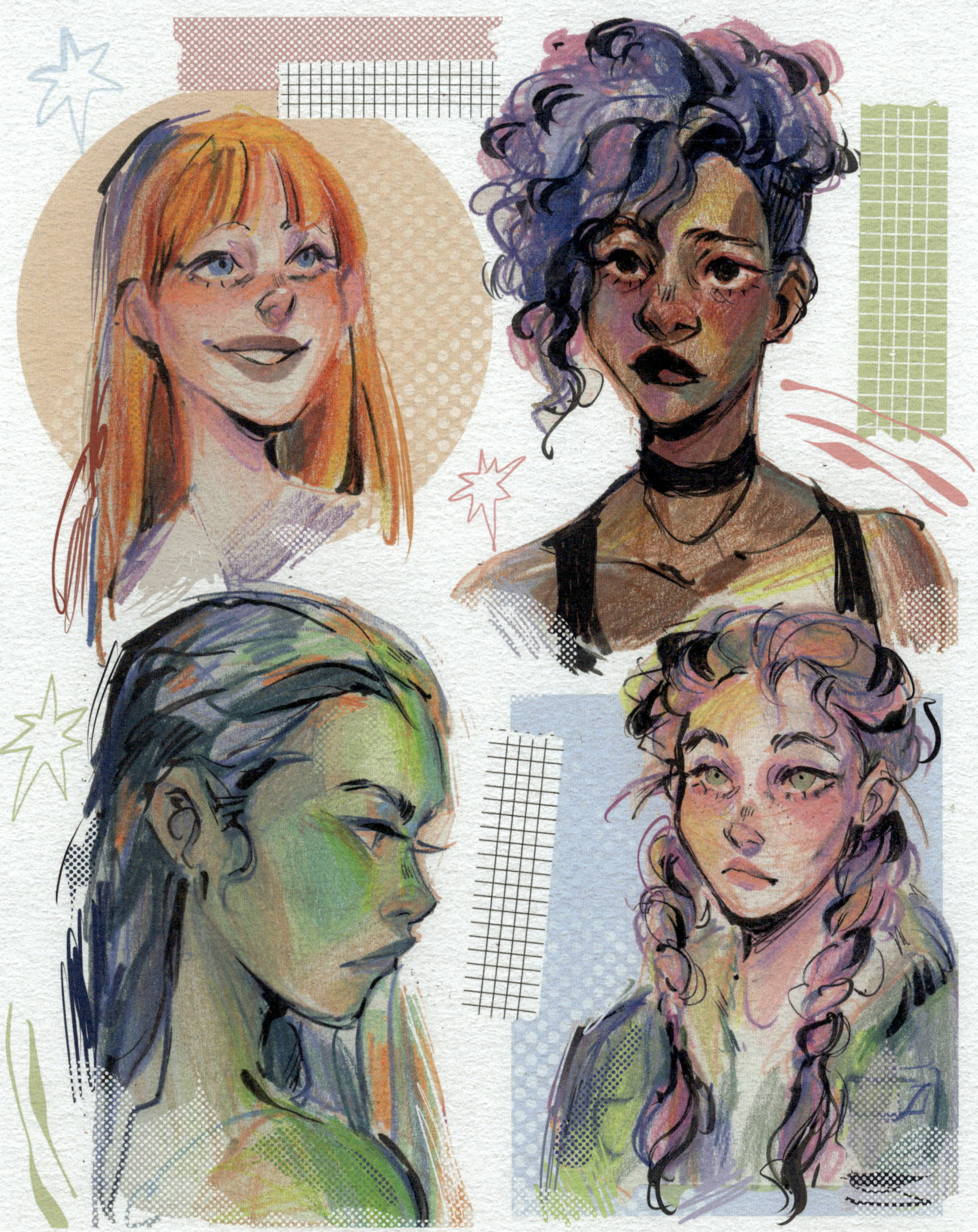

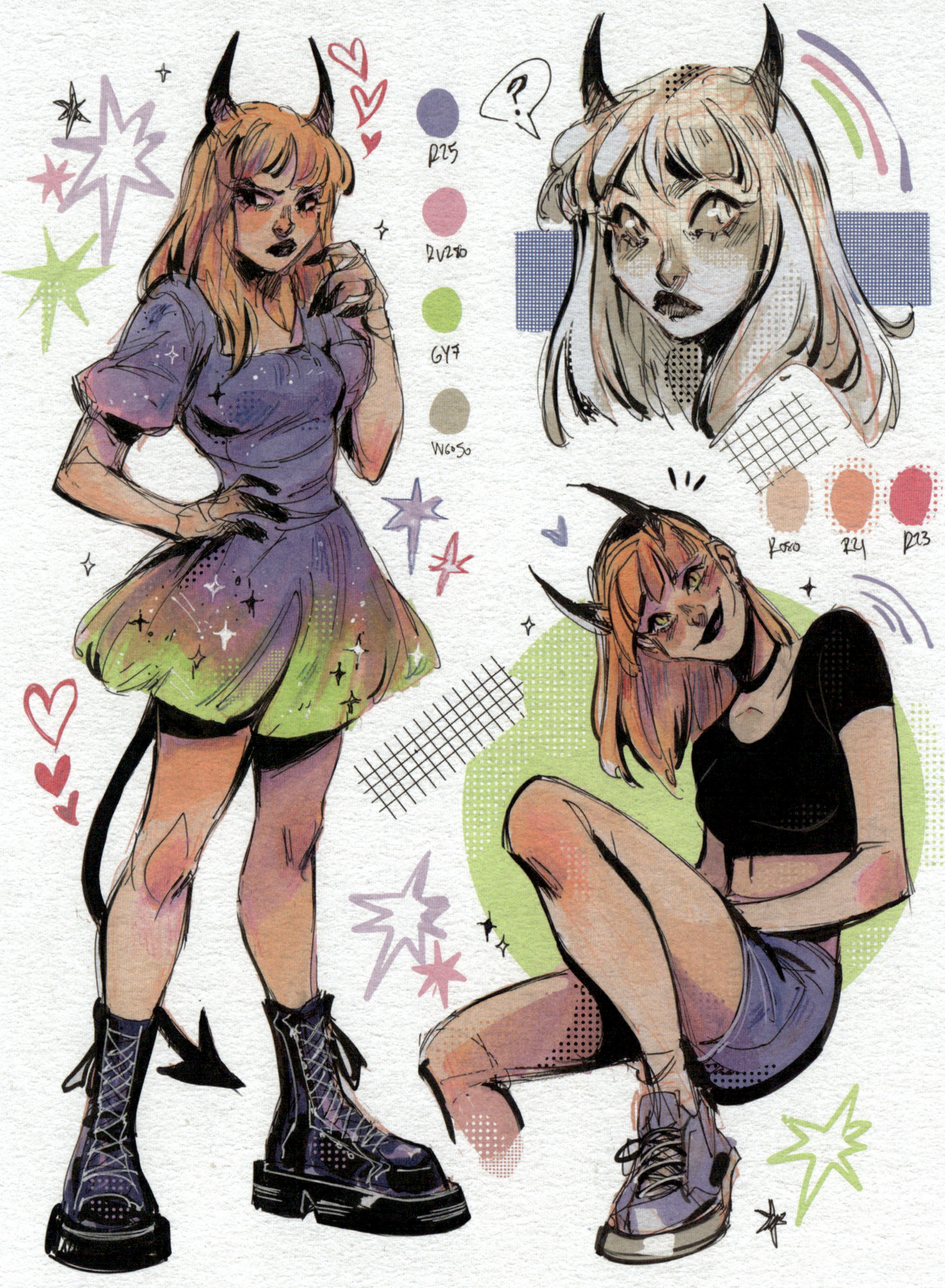
R25
GY7
?
R24
R13

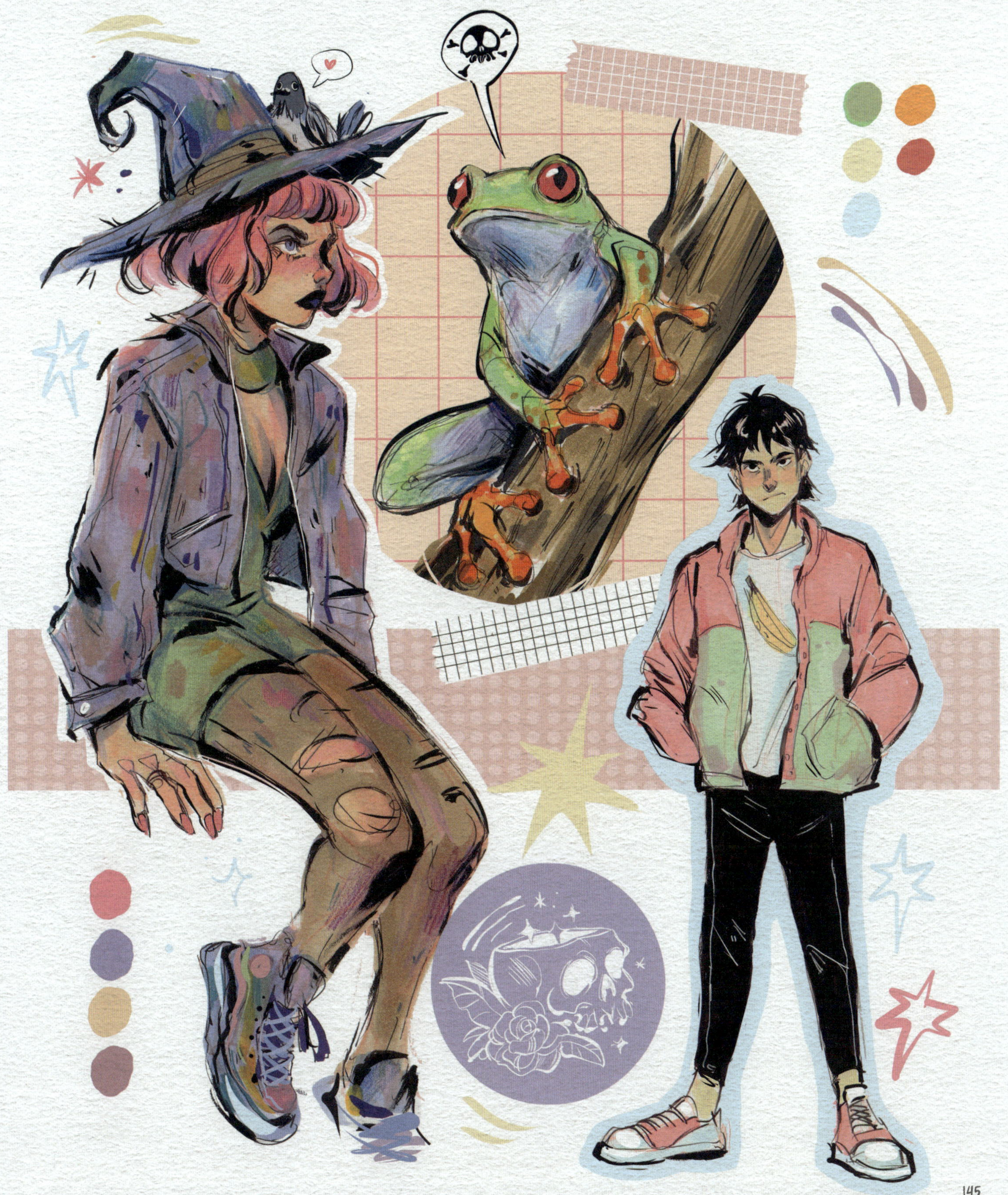

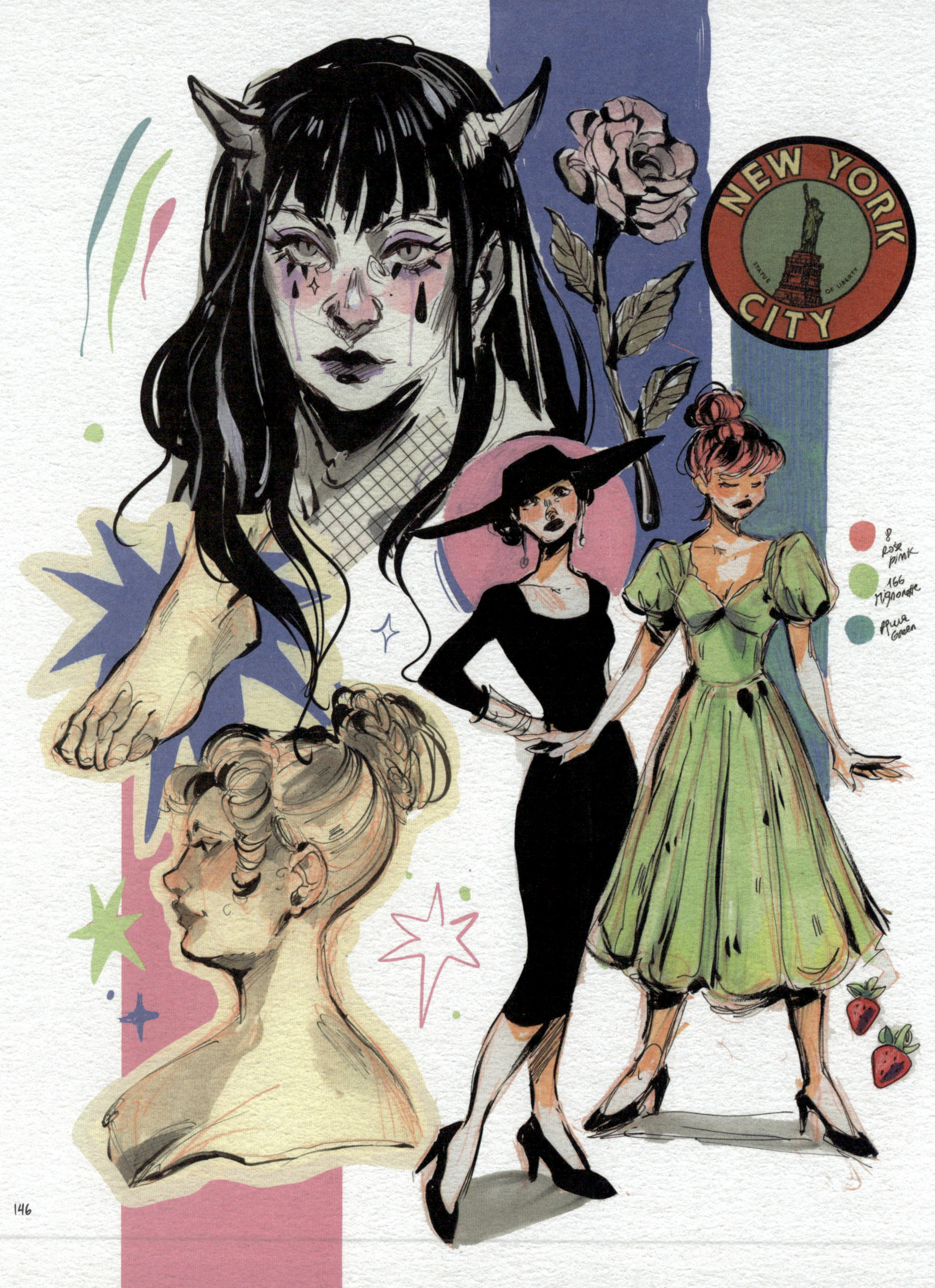
NEW YORK CITY
STATUE OF LIBERTY
8
Rose pink
166
Mignonette
Aqua Green

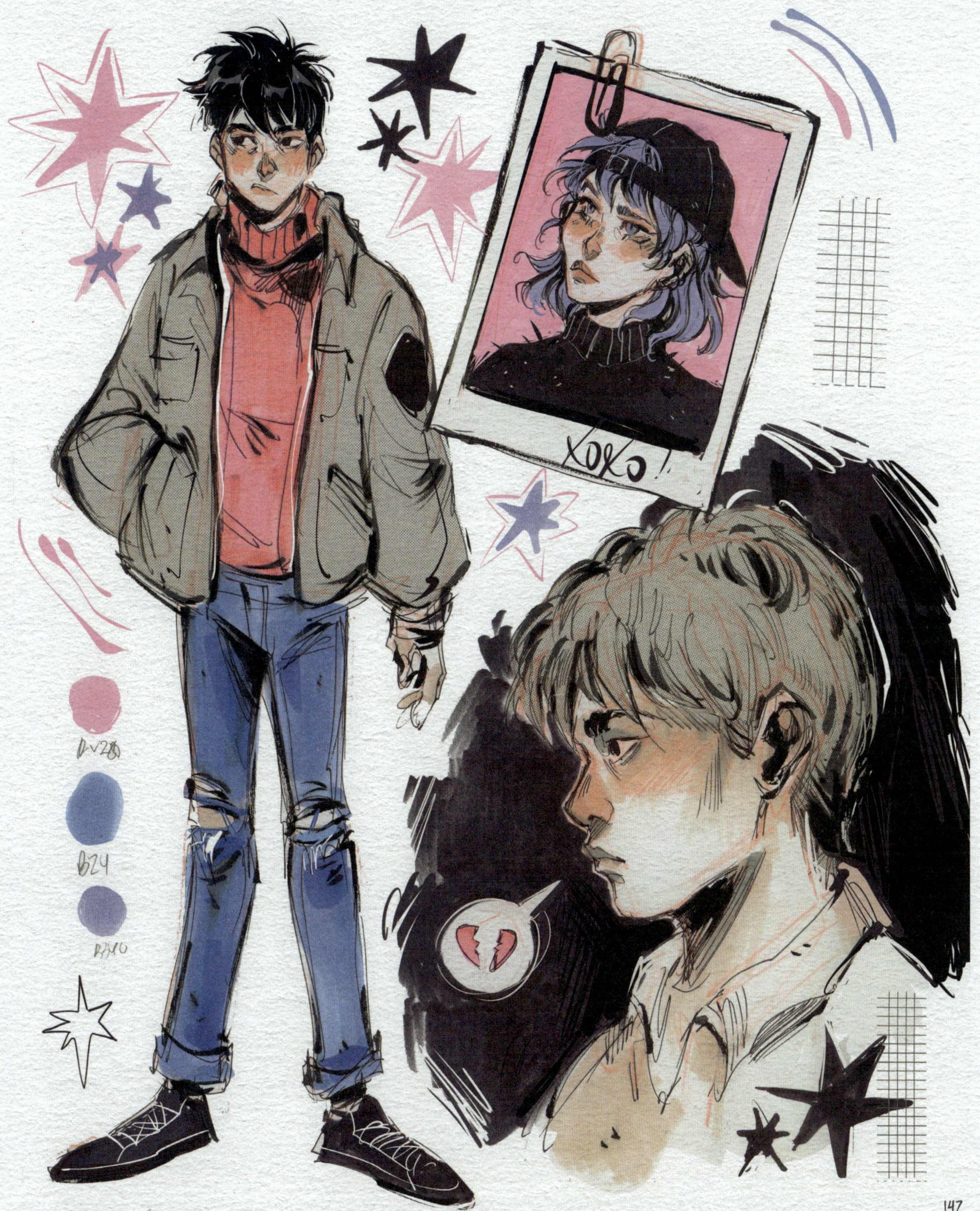
XOXO!
B24

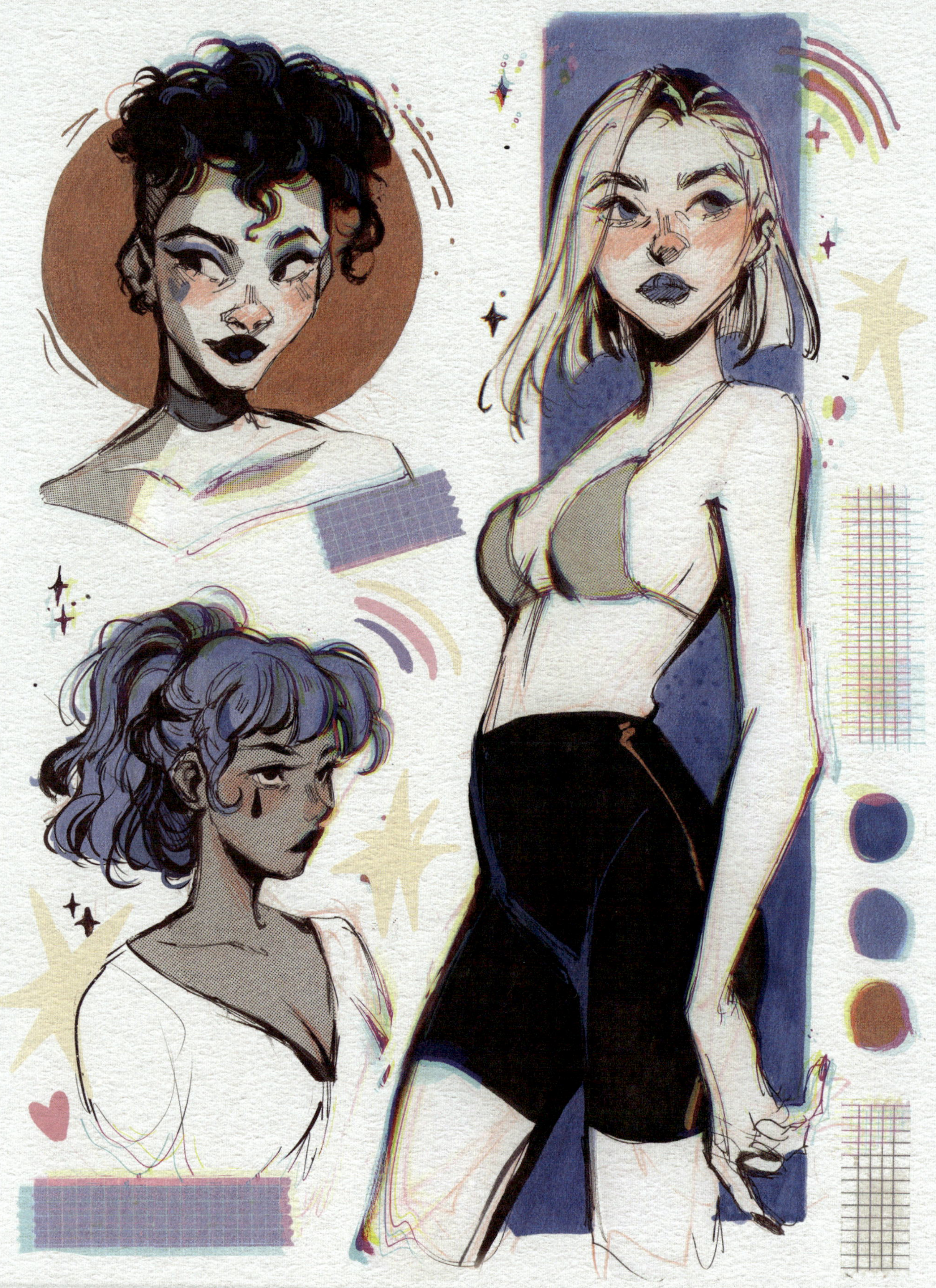

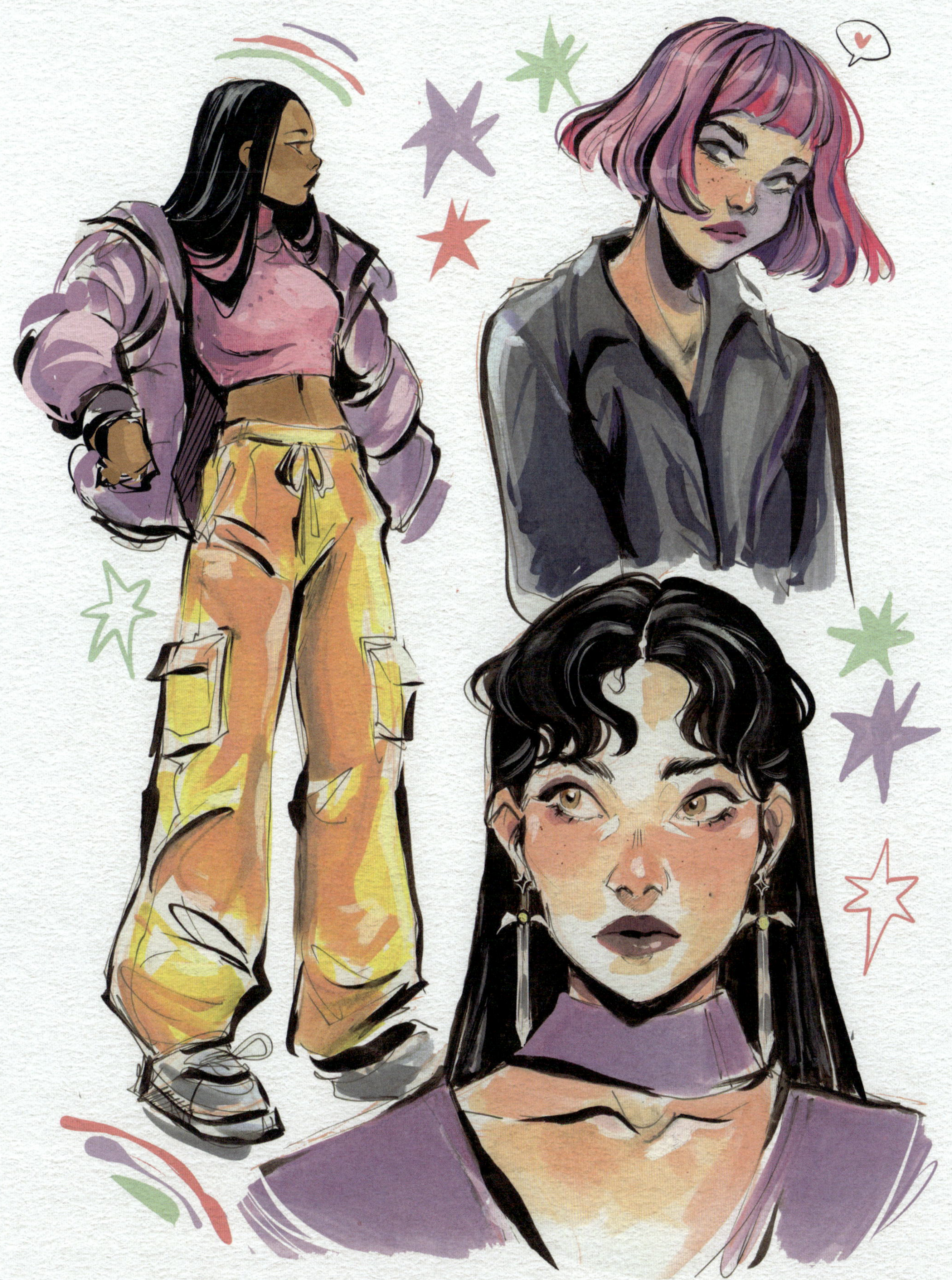

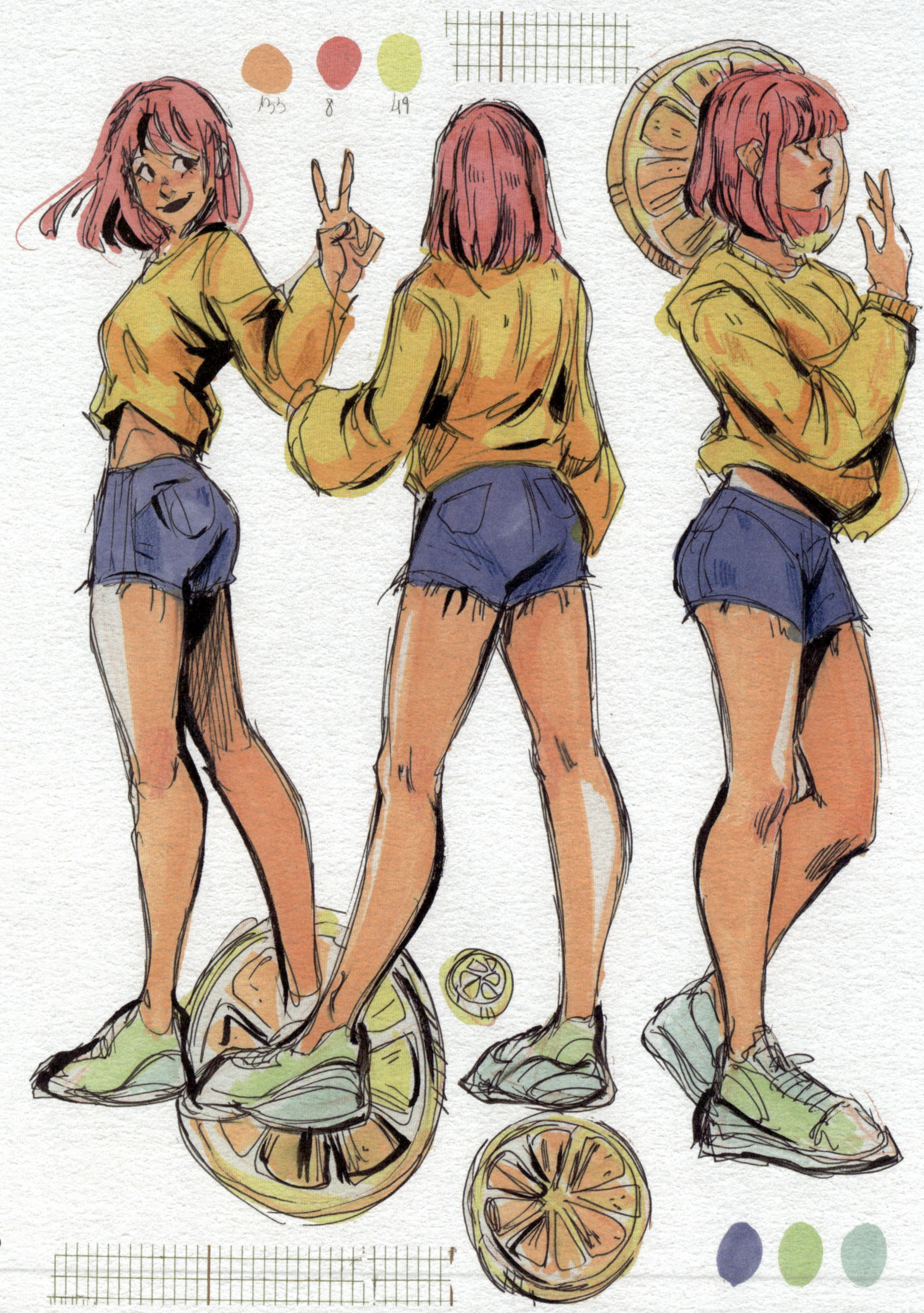
133
8
49

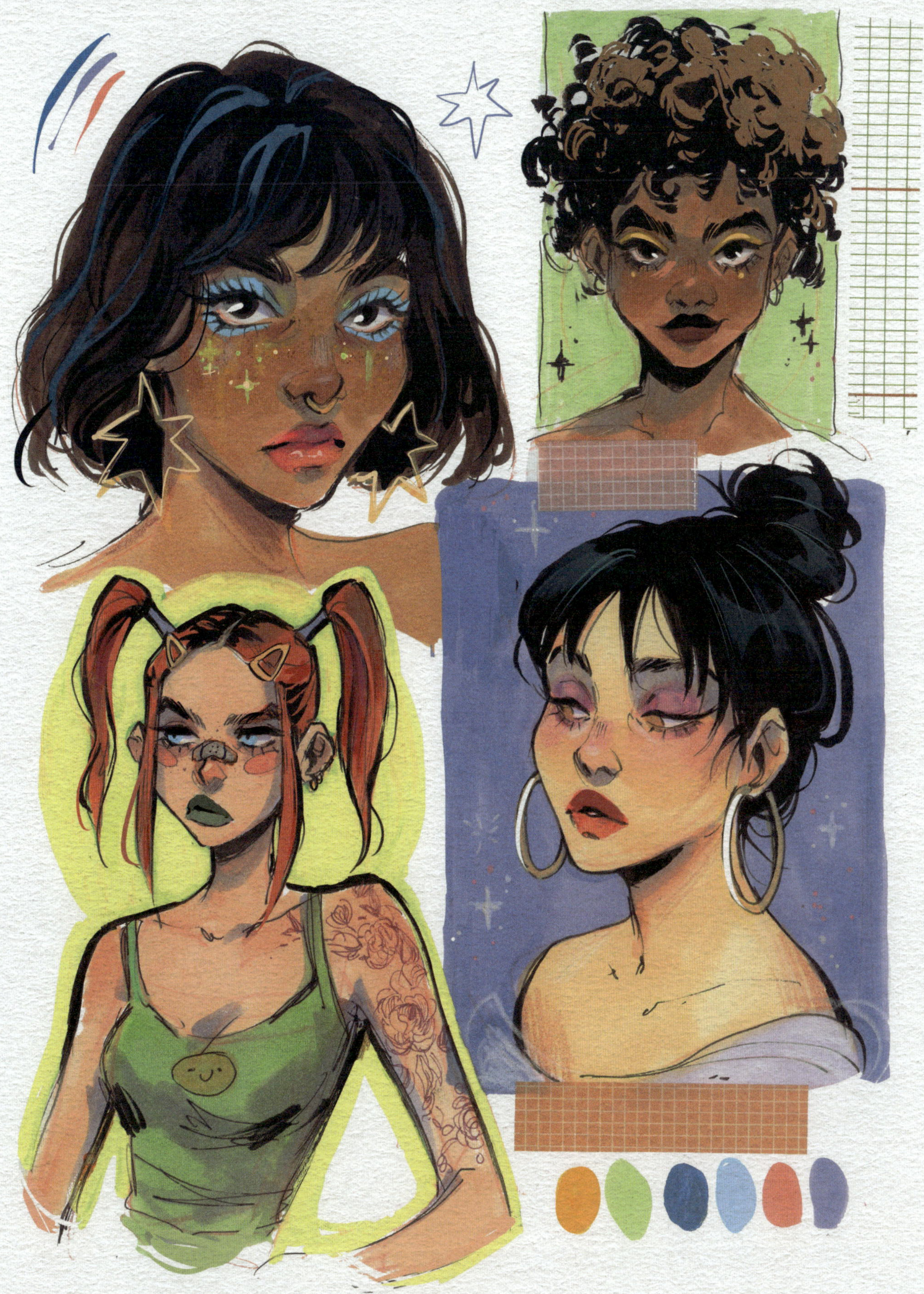

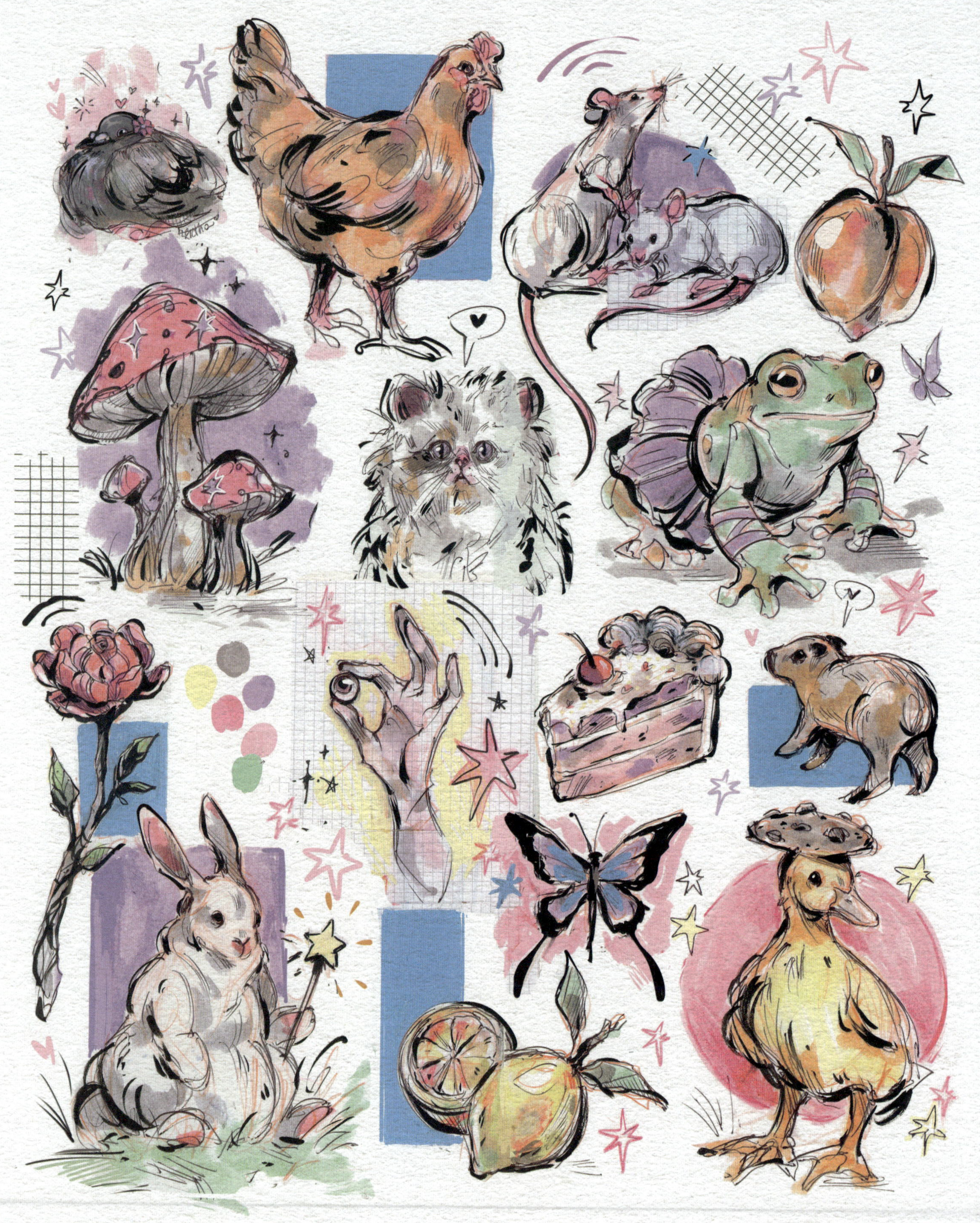

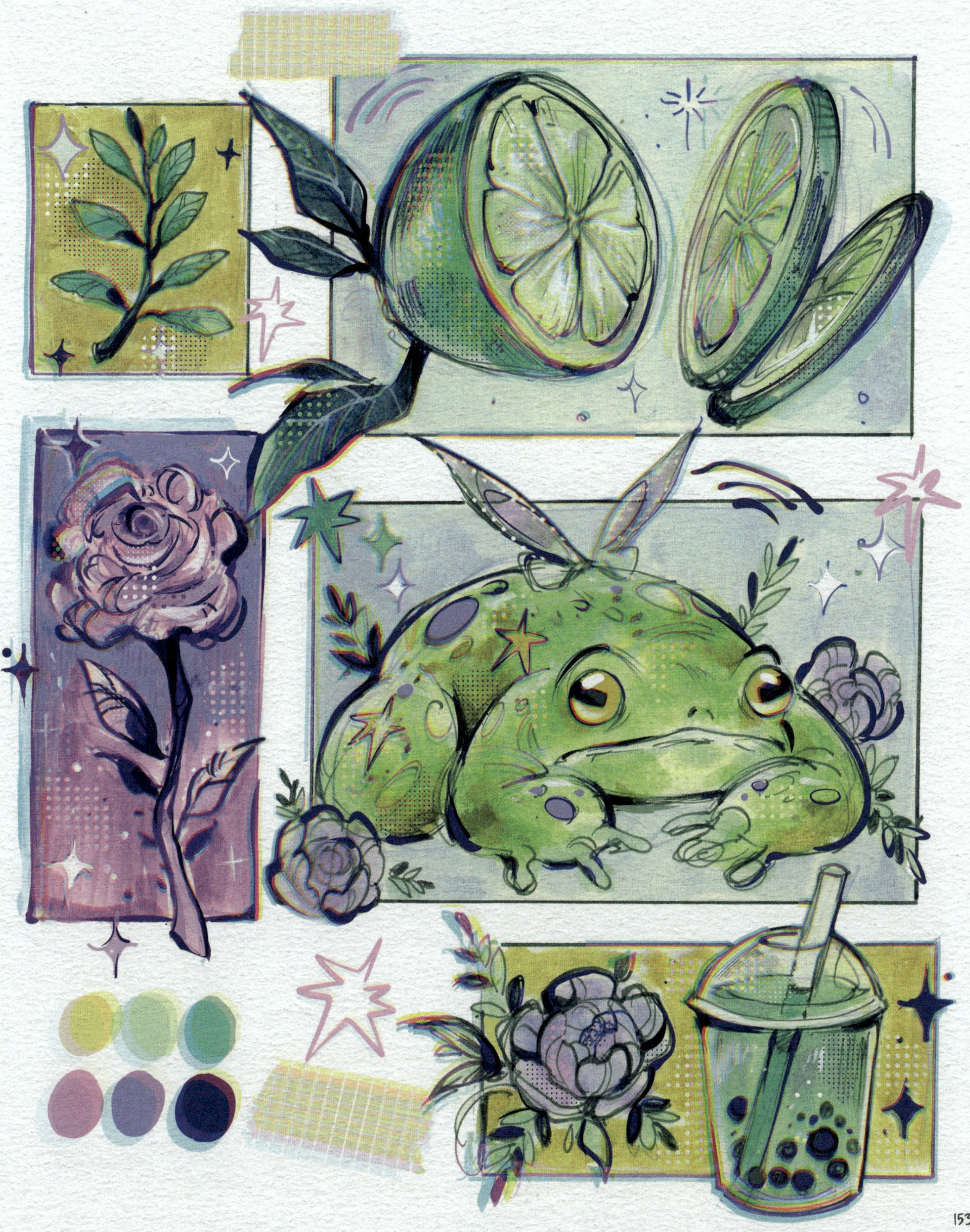

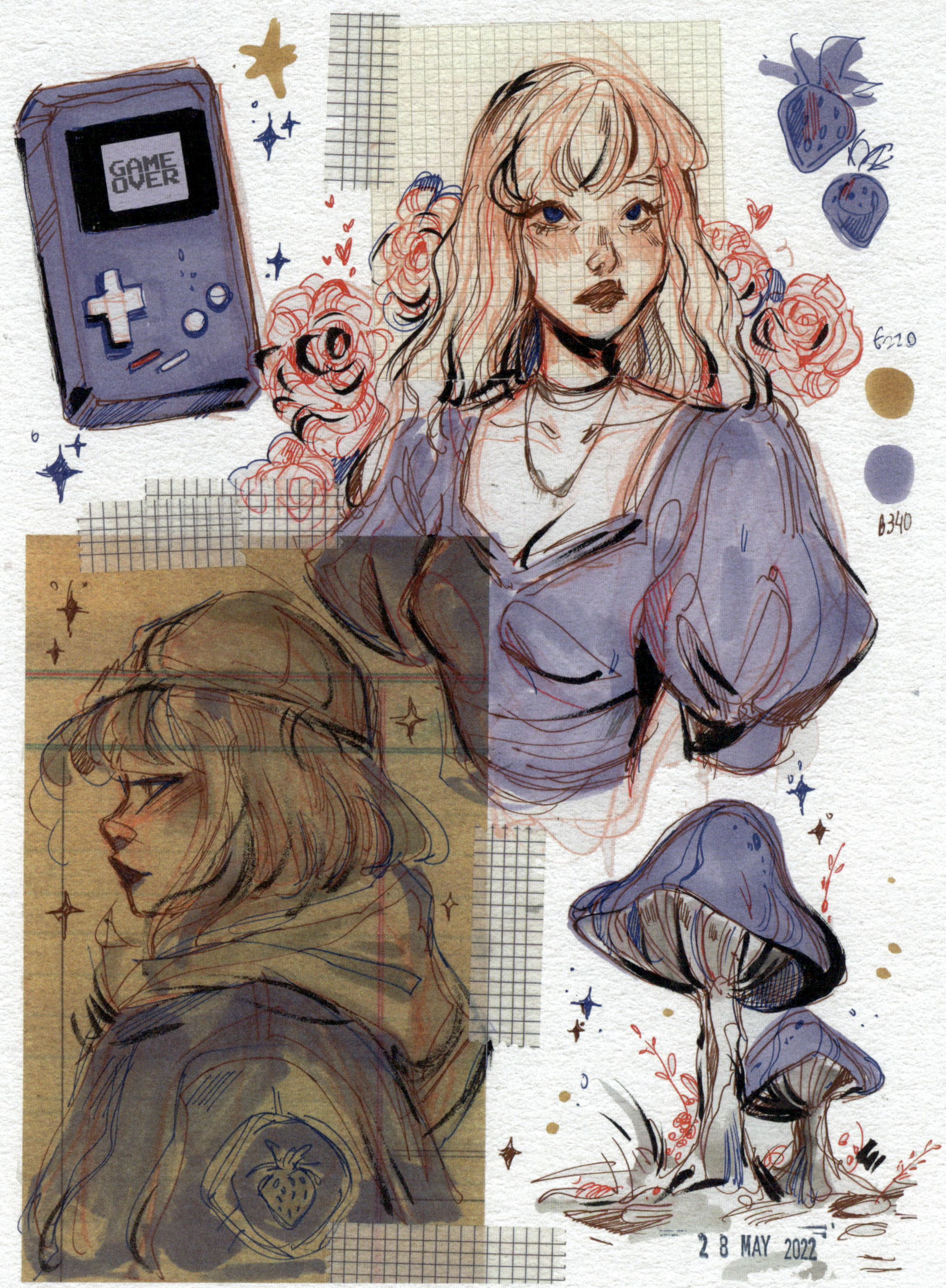
GAME OVER
E020
B340
28 MAY 2022

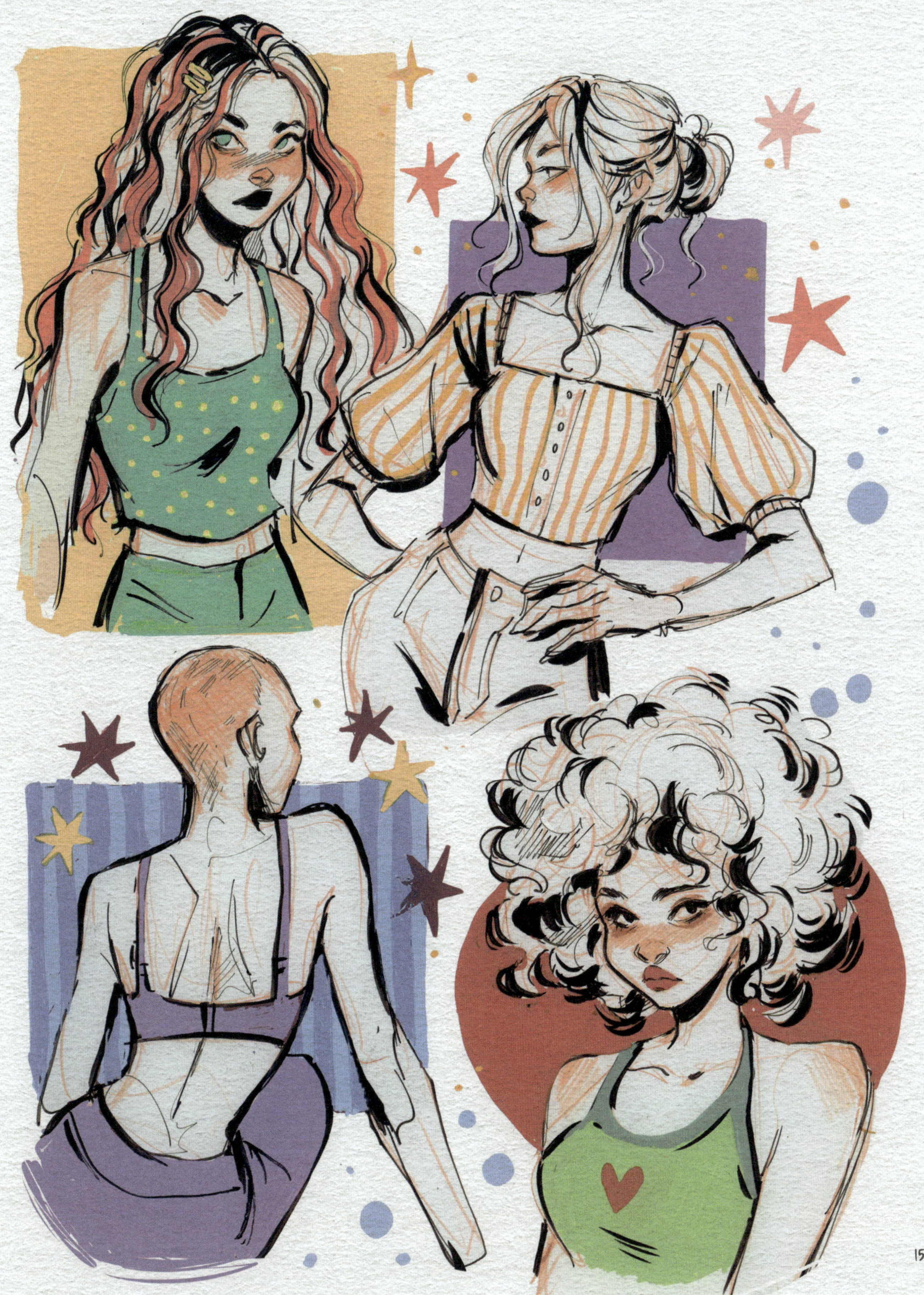

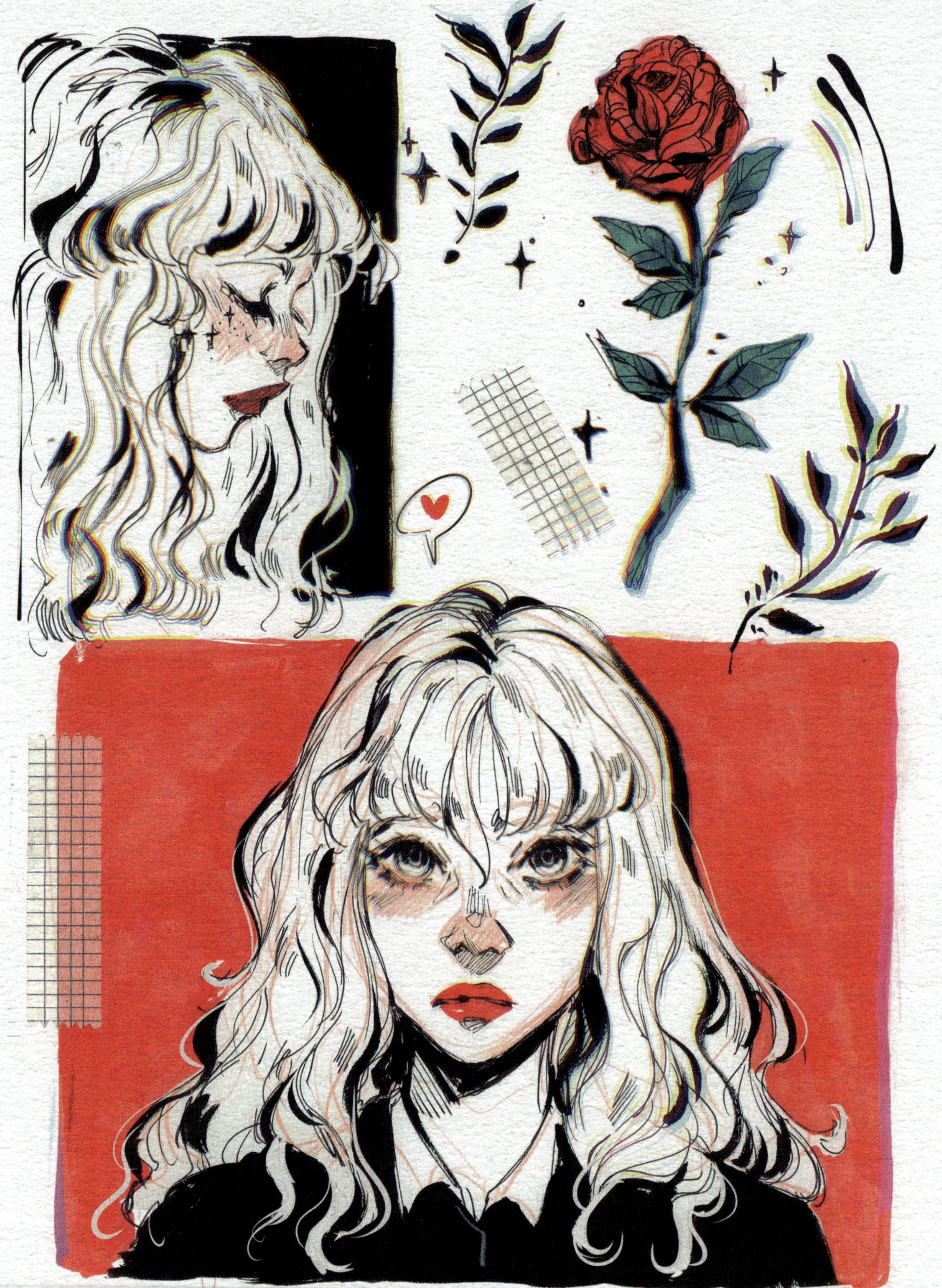

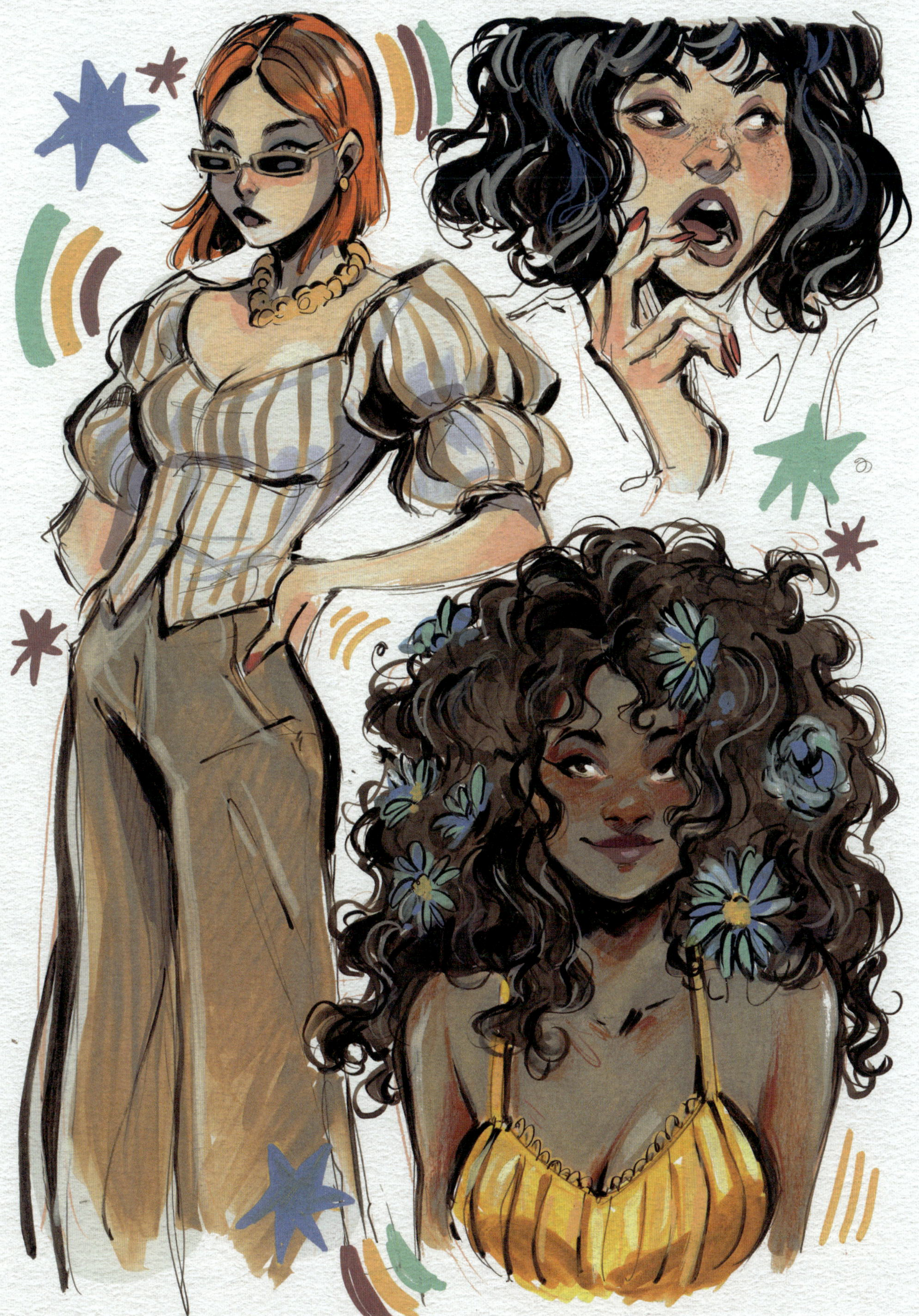

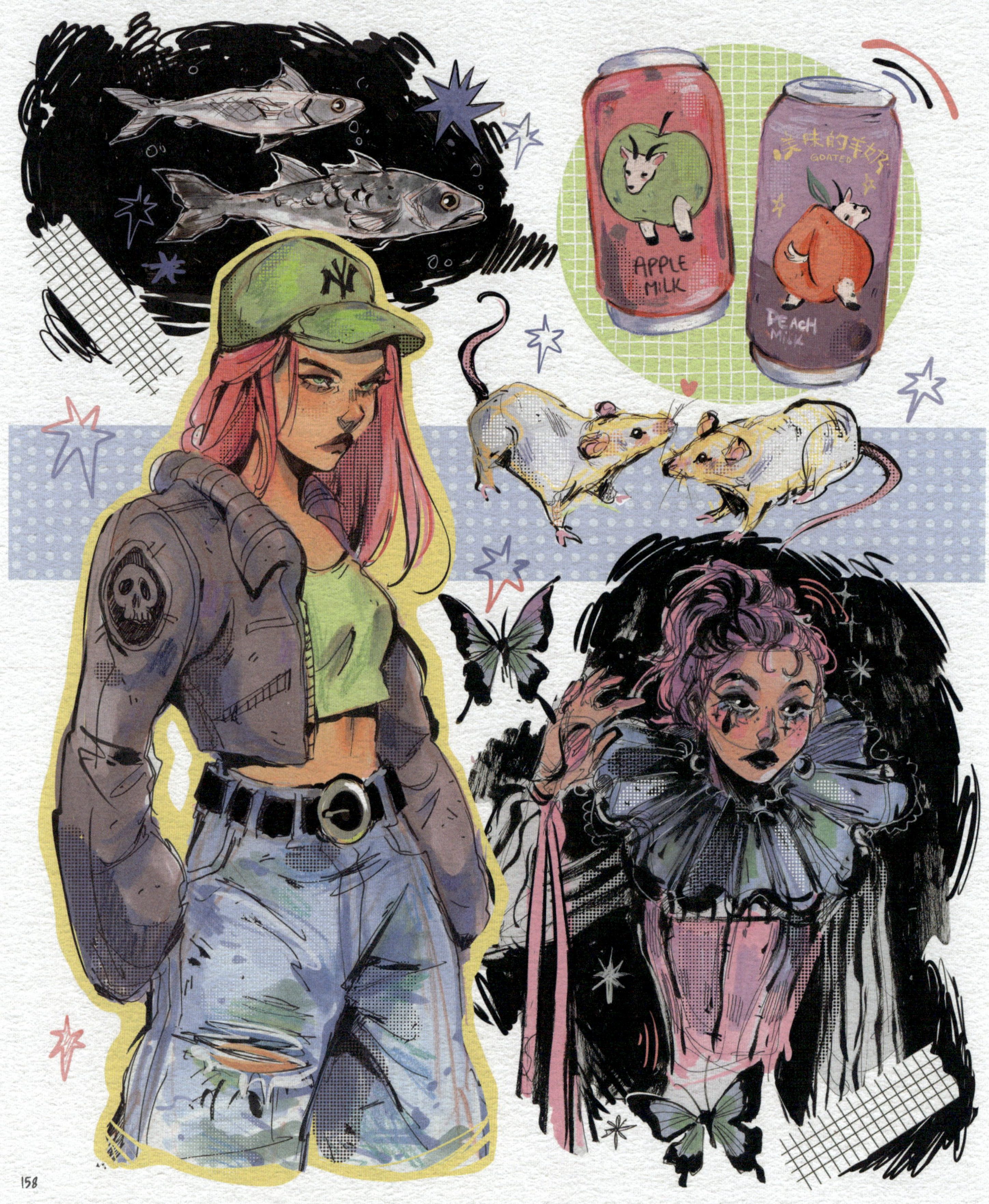

APPLE
MILK
美味的羊奶
GOATED
PEACH
MILK

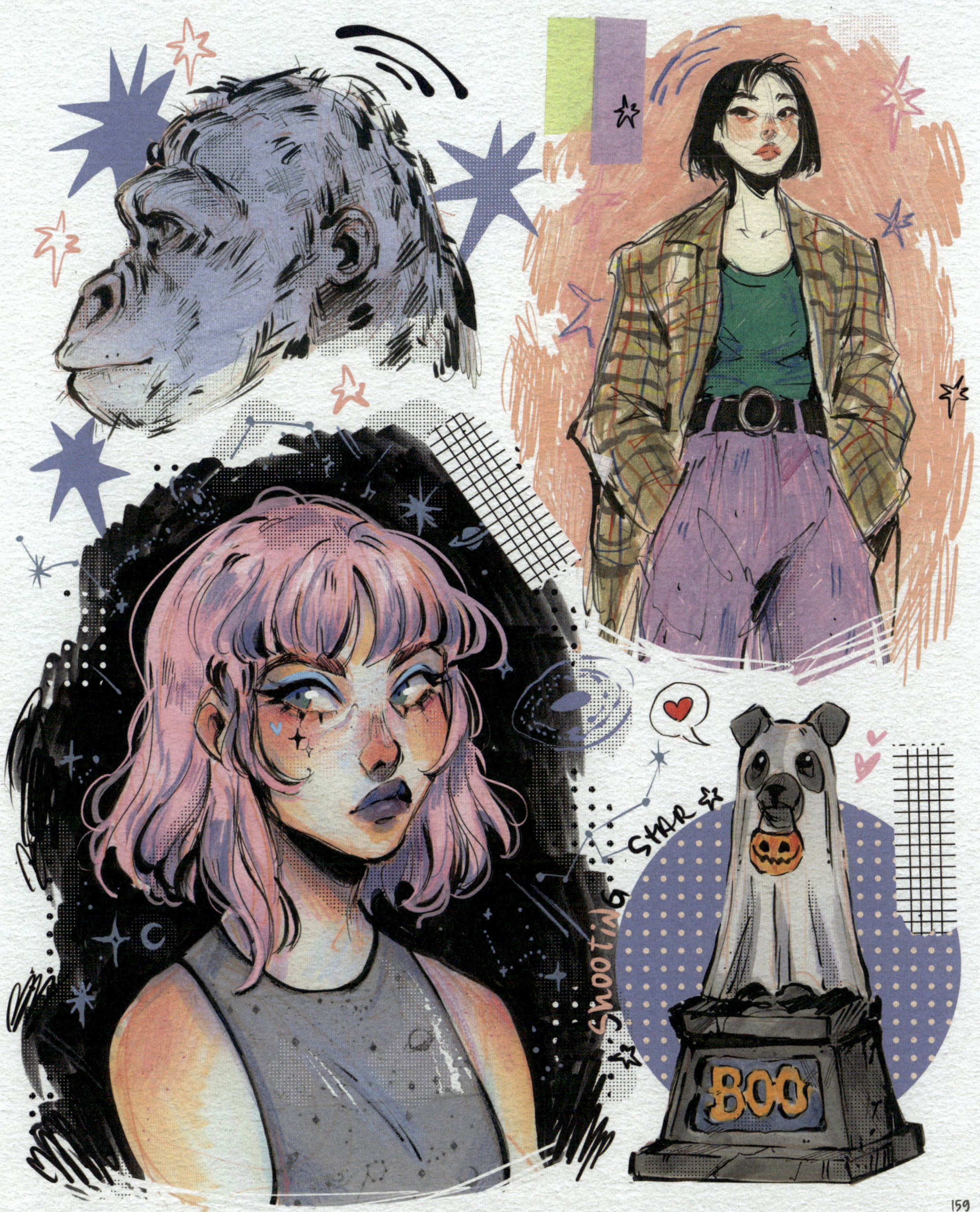
SHOOTING
STAR
BOO

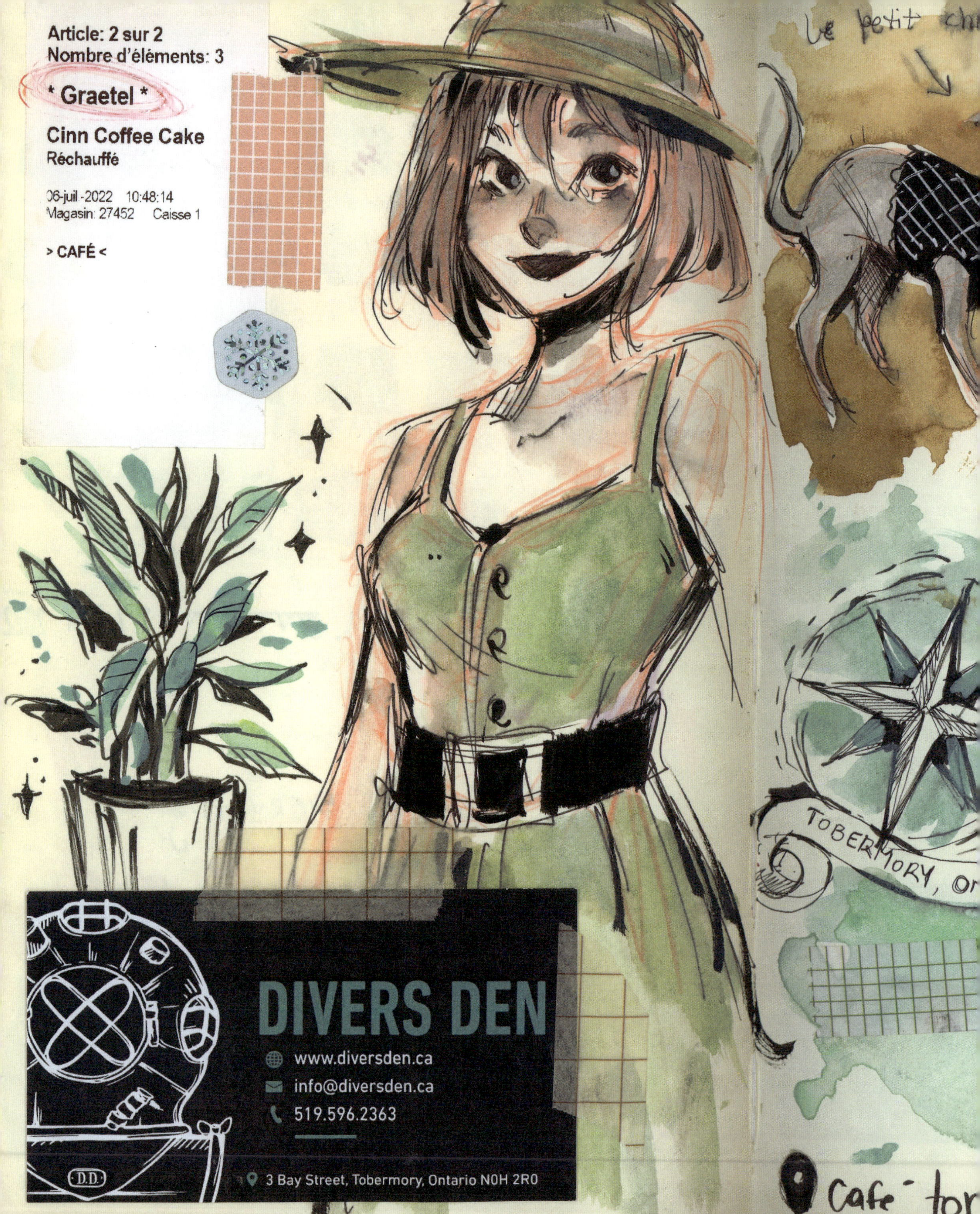

Article: 2 sur 2
Nombre d'éléments: 3
* Graetel *
Cinn Coffee Cake
Réchauffé
06-juil.-2022 10:48:14
Magasin: 27452 Caisse 1
> CAFÉ <
Le petit
TOBERMORY, O
DIVERS DEN
www.diversden.ca
info@diversden.ca
519.596.2363
3 Bay Street, Tobermory, Ontario N0H 2R0
D.D.
Cafe - tor

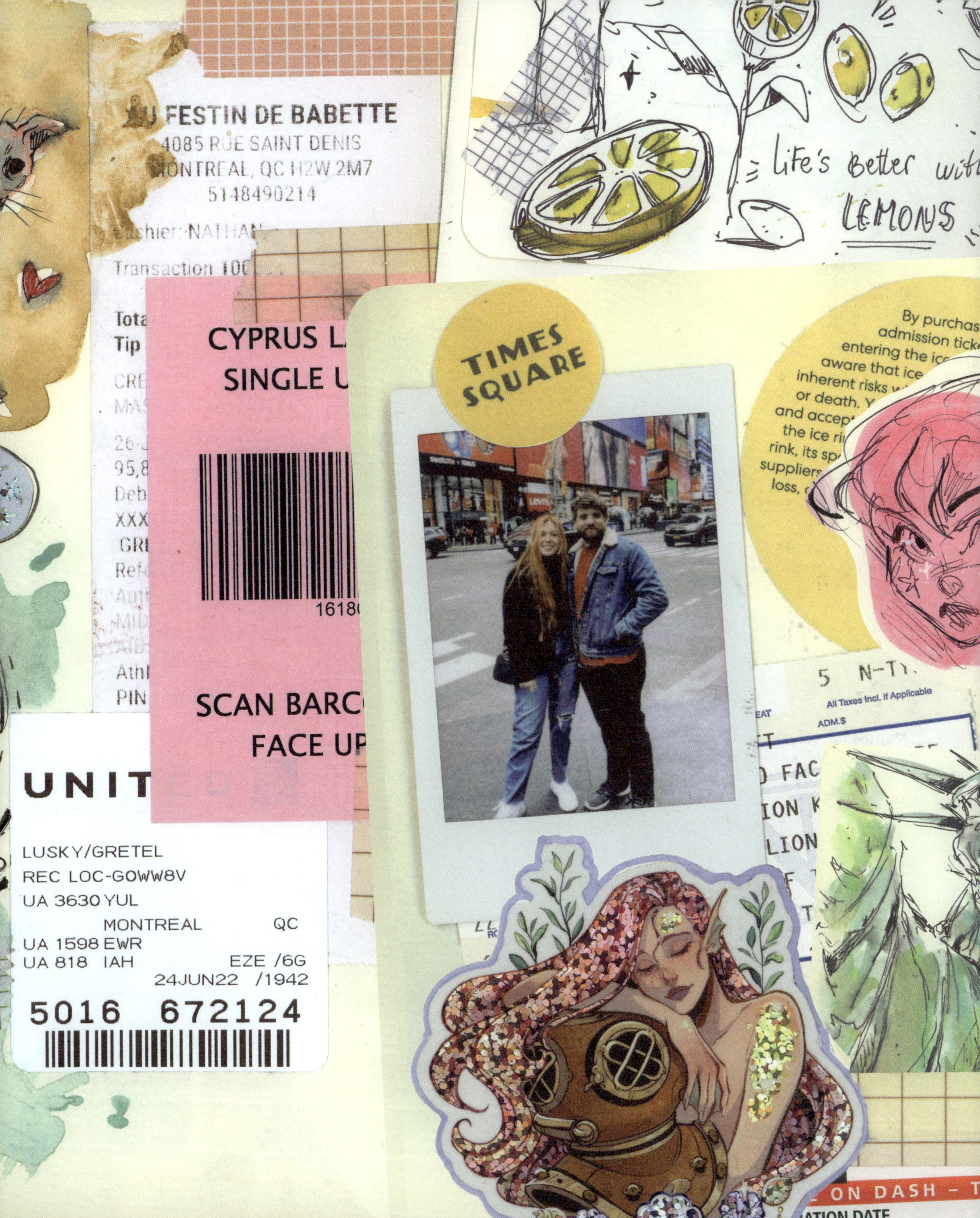

FESTIN DE BABETTE
4085 RUE SAINT DENIS
MONTREAL, QC H2W 2M7
5148490214
Cashier: NATHAN
Transaction 100
Life's Better with LEMONS
CYPRUS L
SINGLE U
SCAN BARC
FACE UP
TIMES SQUARE
By purchas
admission ticke
entering the ic
aware that ice
inherent risks
or death.
and accept
the ice ri
rink, its sp
suppliers
loss,
All Taxes Incl. If Applicable
ADM.$
UNIT
LUSKY/GRETEL
REC LOC-GOWW8V
UA 3630 YUL
MONTREAL QC
UA 1598 EWR
UA 818 IAH EZE /6G
24JUN22 /1942
5016 672124
ON DASH - T
ATION DATE

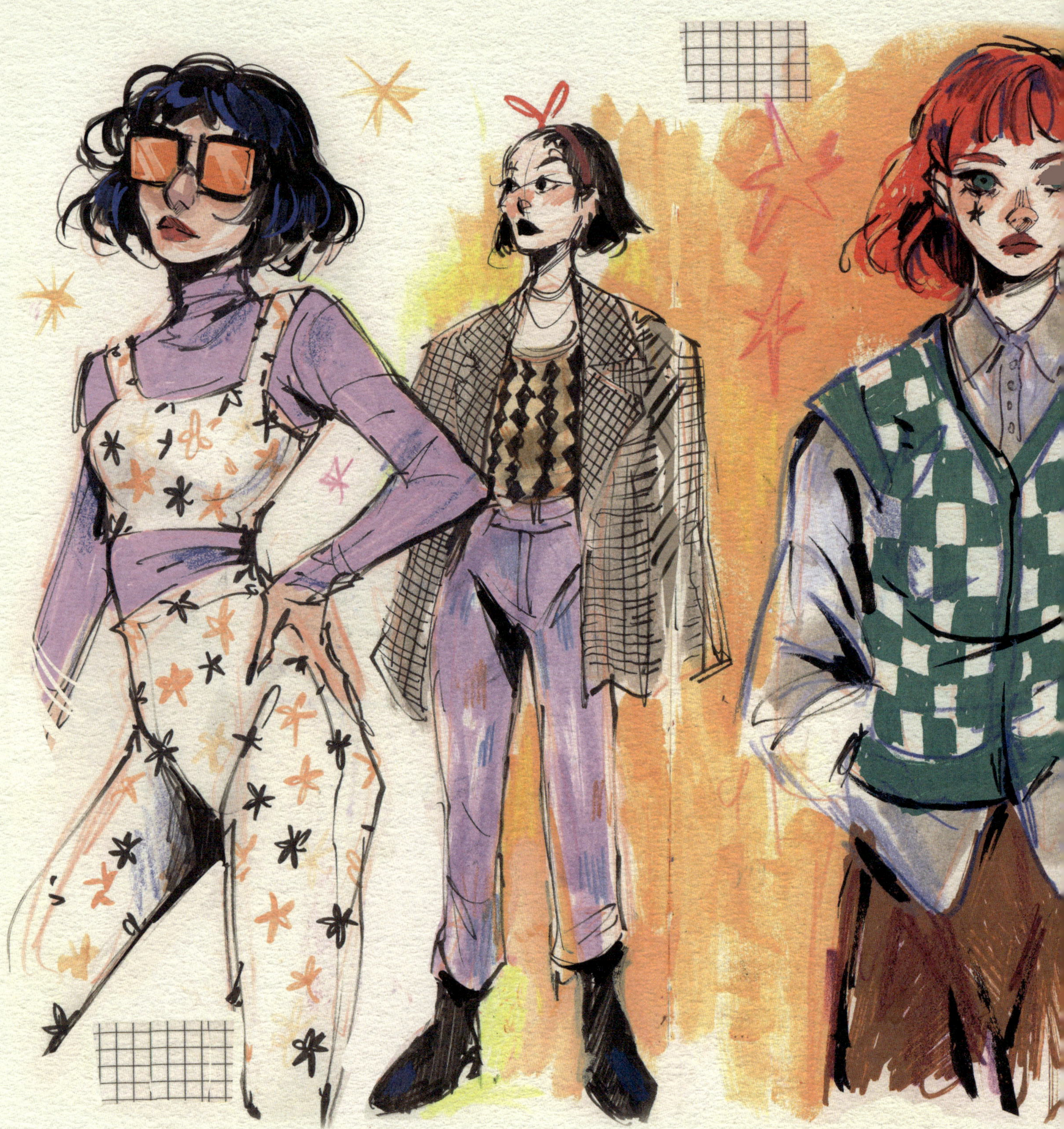

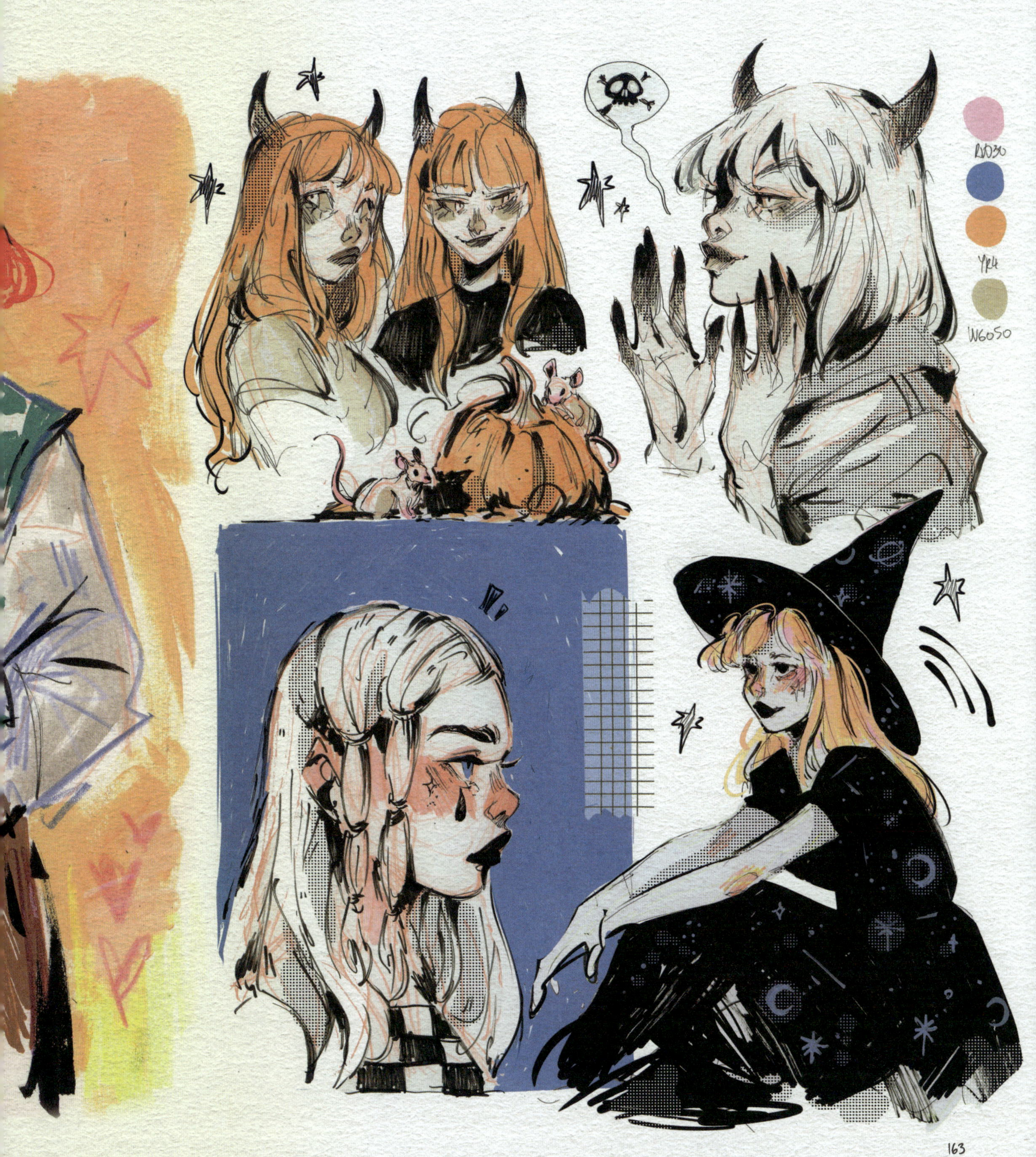
RV030
YR4
W6050

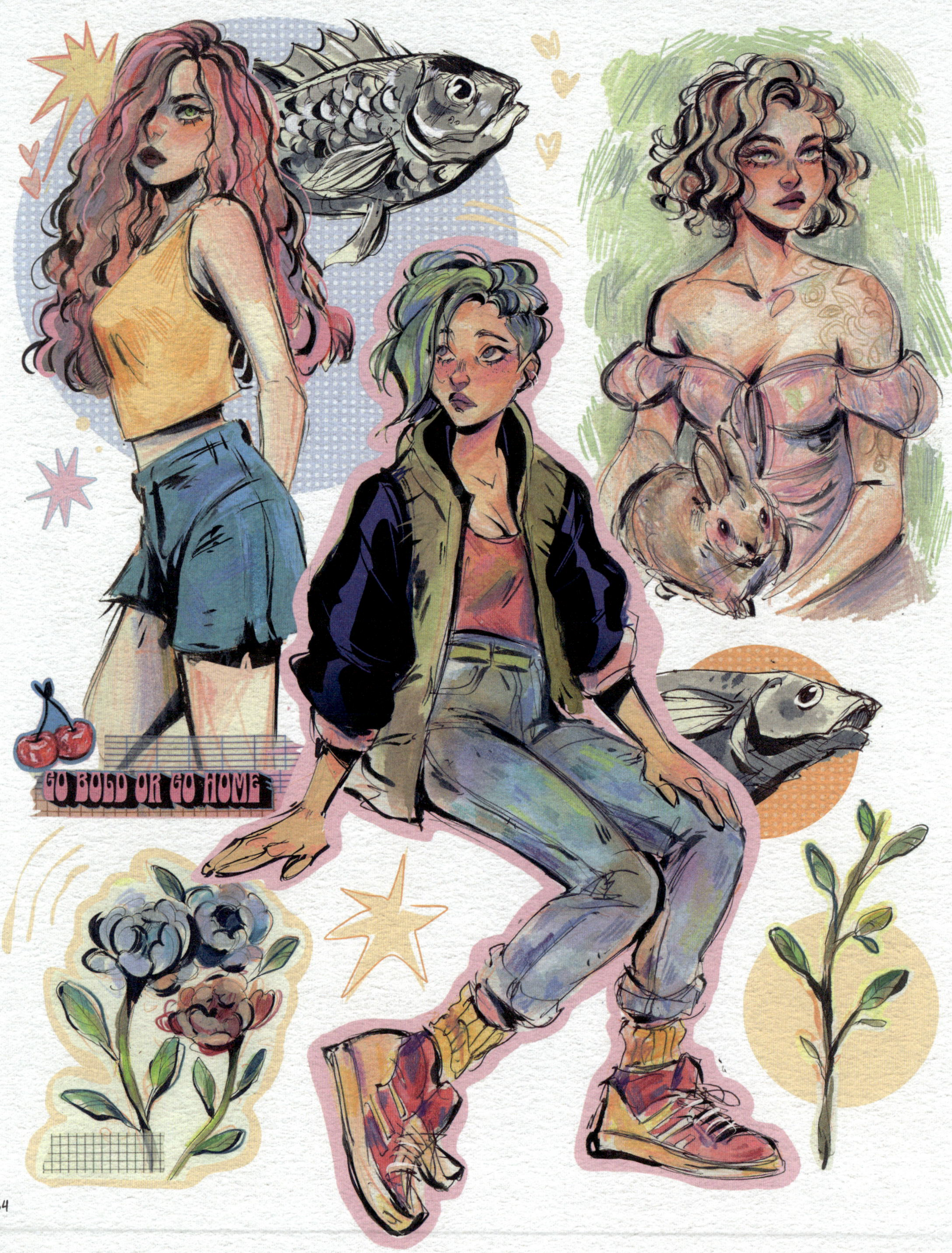
GO BOLD OR GO HOME

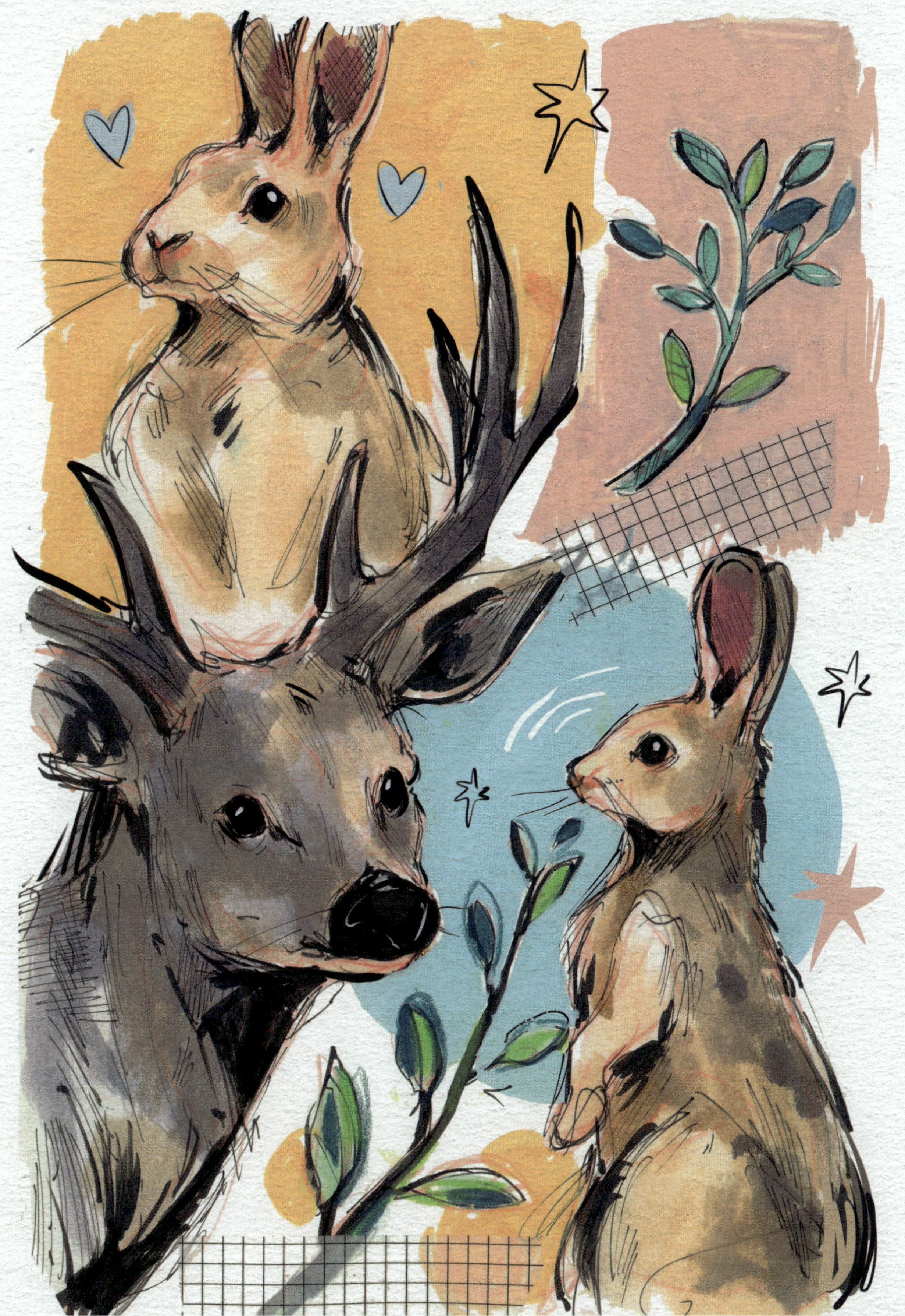

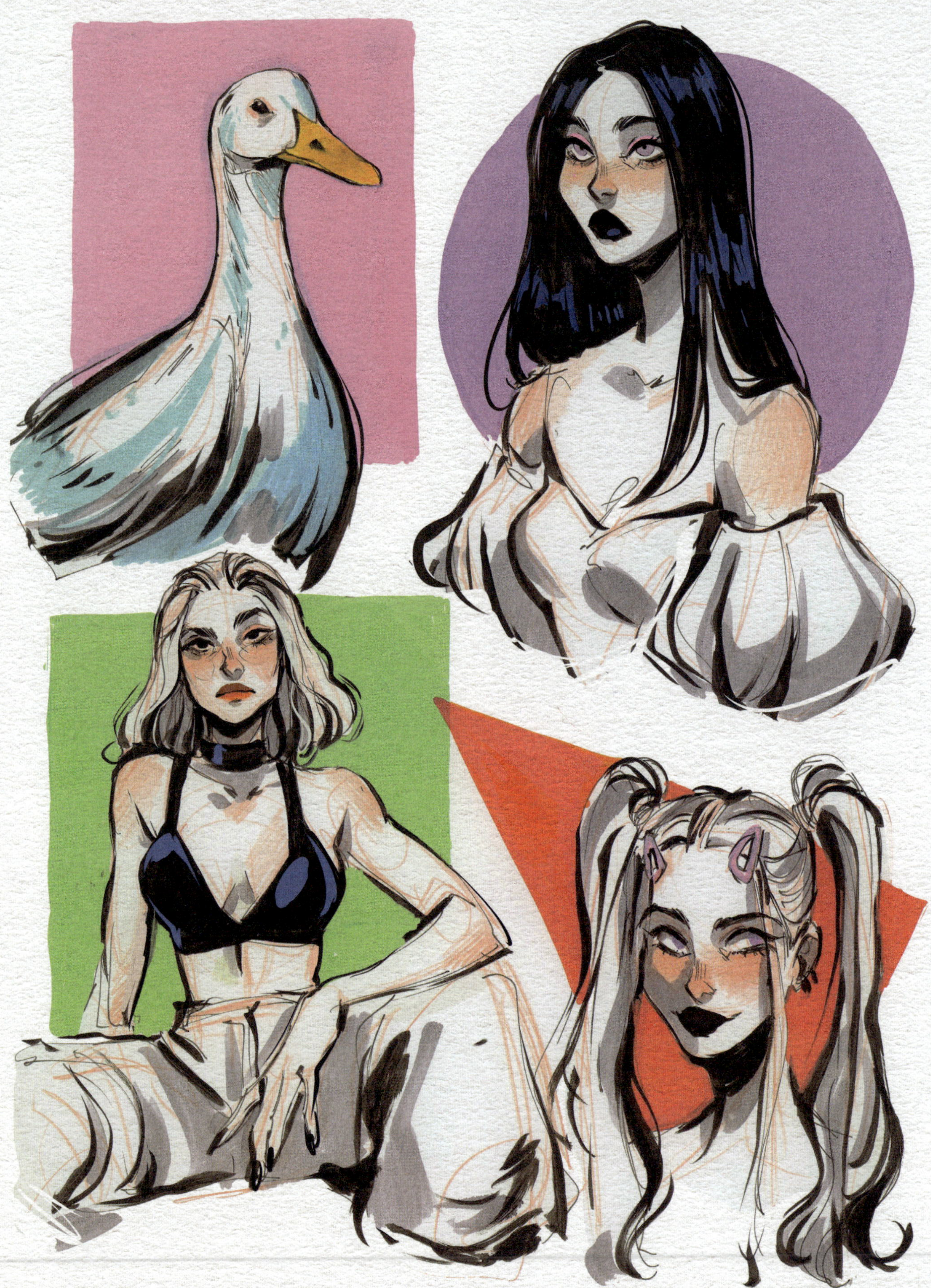

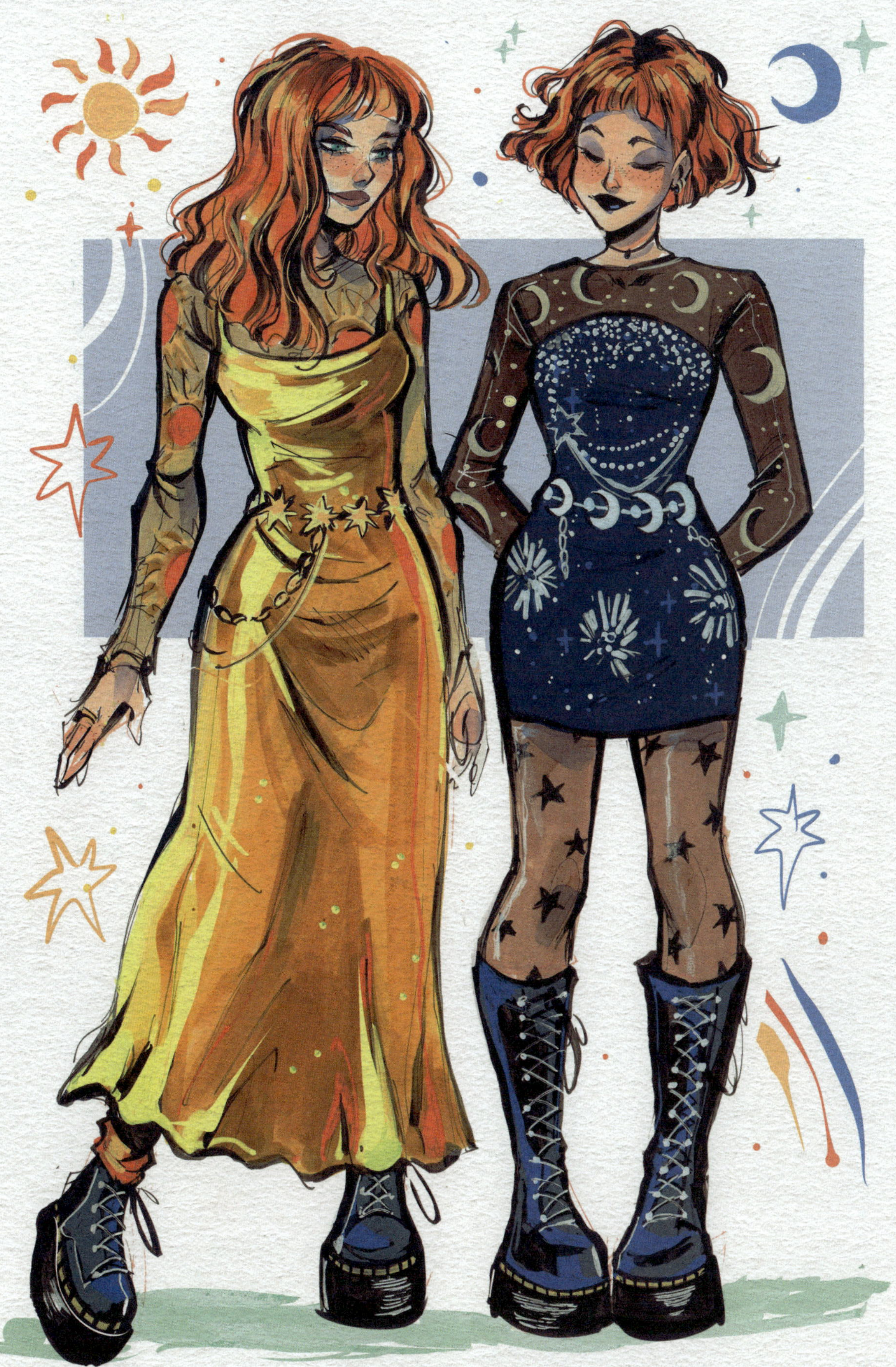

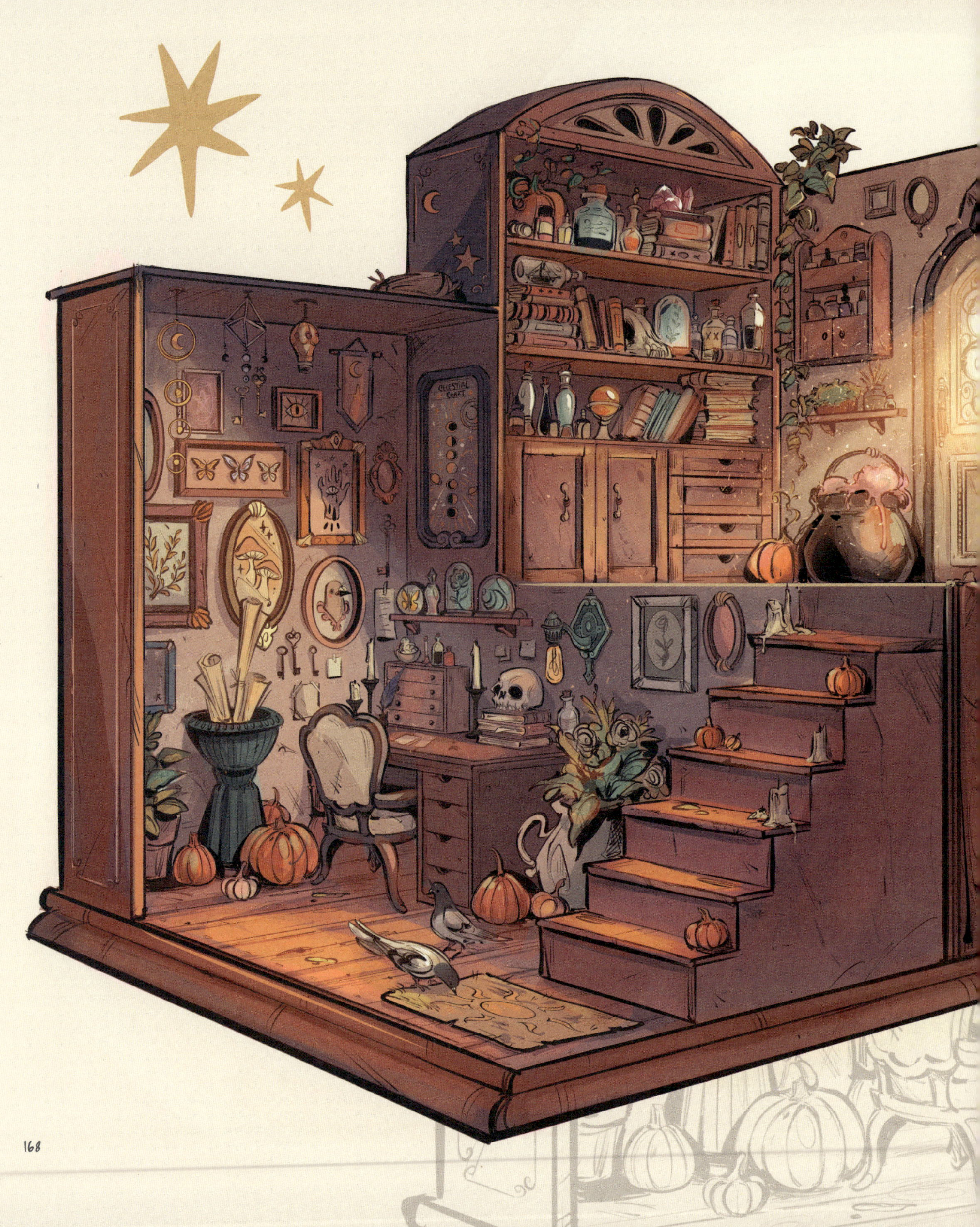
CELESTIAL
CHART

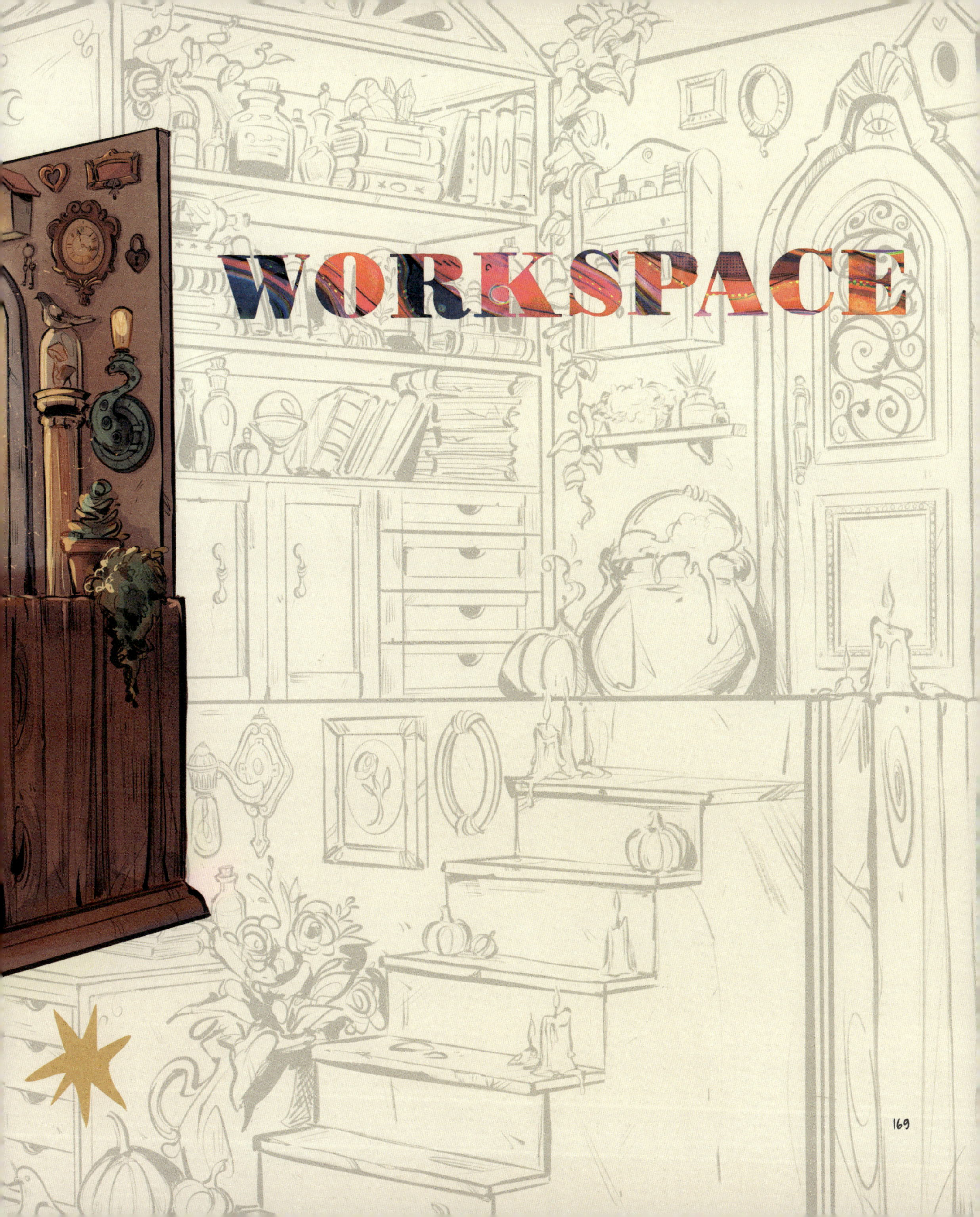

WORKSPACE

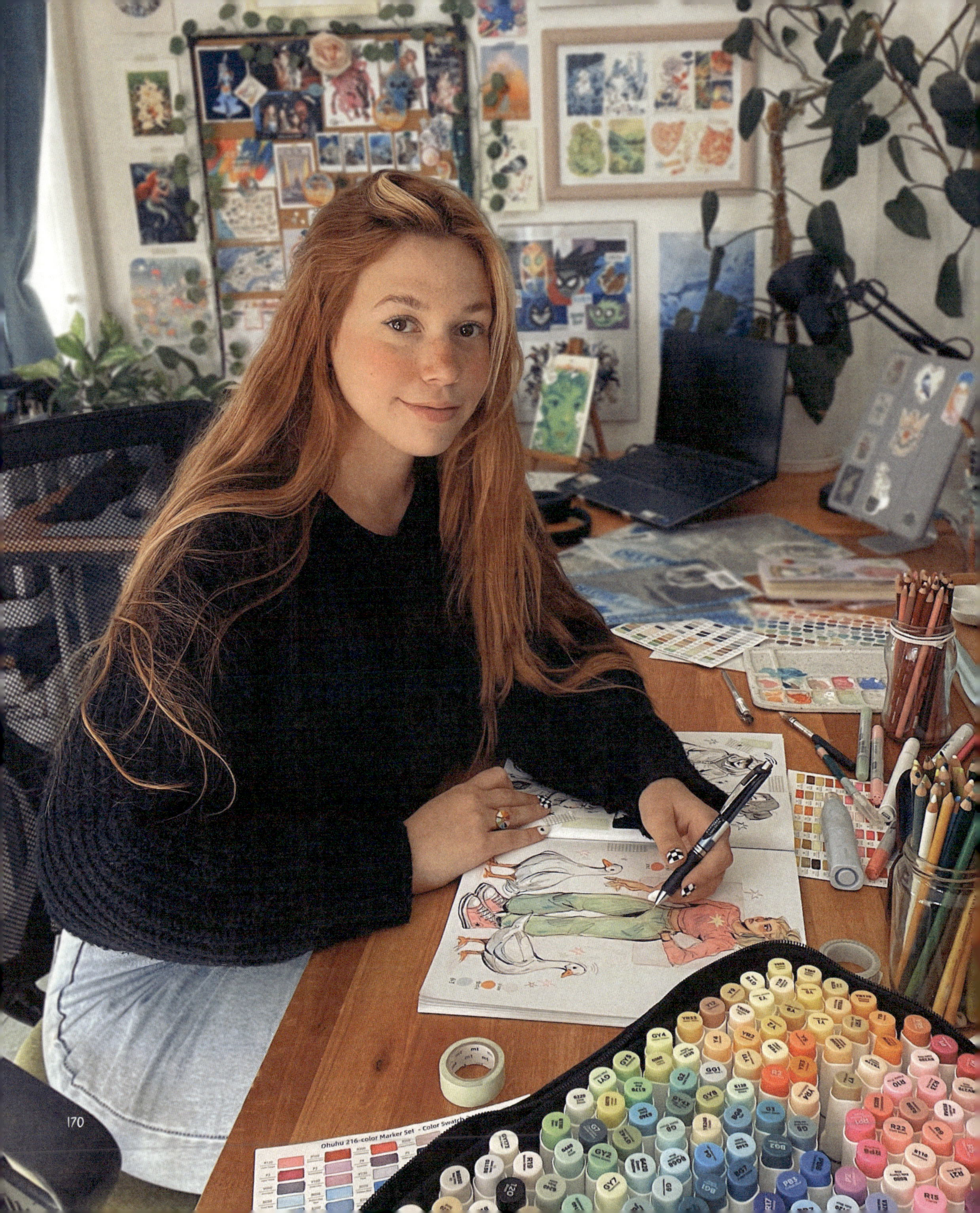
Ohuhu 216-color Marker Set - Color Swatch

STUDIO

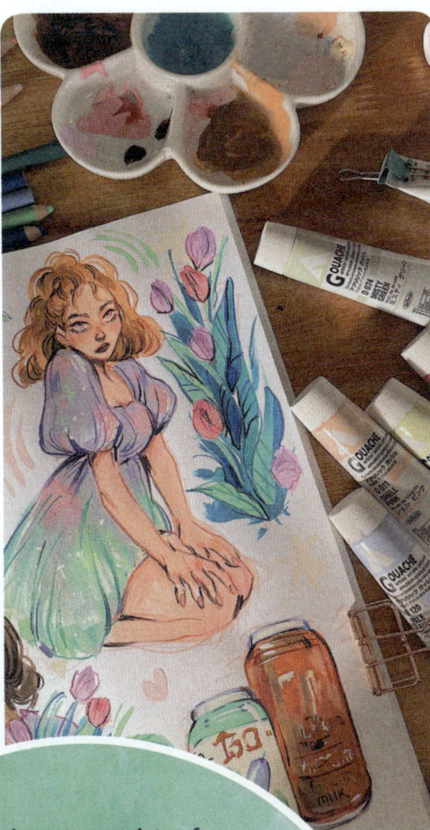

My workspace consists of an L-shaped desk situated in the brightest corner of my house. I like having a dedicated area for digital art with my tablet and laptop, as well as another larger space to work traditionally, where I can be as experimental as I want without worrying about making a mess. I'm not the most organized person, but I do make sure everything in my studio has a designated spot, always keeping the tools I use the most within reach. I spend a lot of time here, so I love filling the walls with inspiring art, decorating the room with plenty of plants, and having colourful fairy lights to give the space a cosy atmosphere at night!

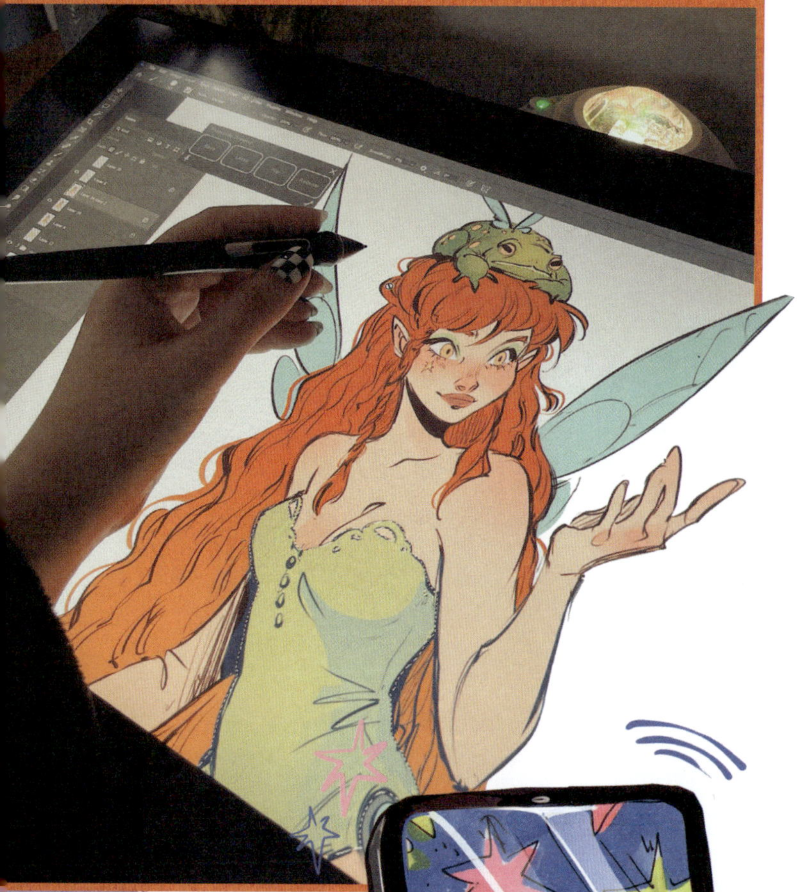

DIGITAL TOOLS

WACOM CINTIQ 22 + PHOTOSHOP

I've always been a laptop person because I like the idea of being able to work from anywhere. My current setup is a Dell laptop with a Wacom Cintiq that serves as a second, larger monitor. I've been using Photoshop ever since I received my first tablet, so I've built my entire workflow around that software. I also use Lazy Nezumi, which is a life-saver plugin for smooth lines, pen stability, perspective grids, and a bunch of other cool stuff.

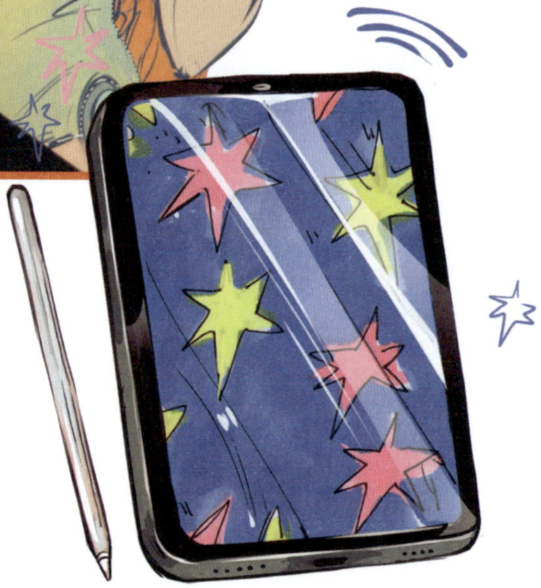

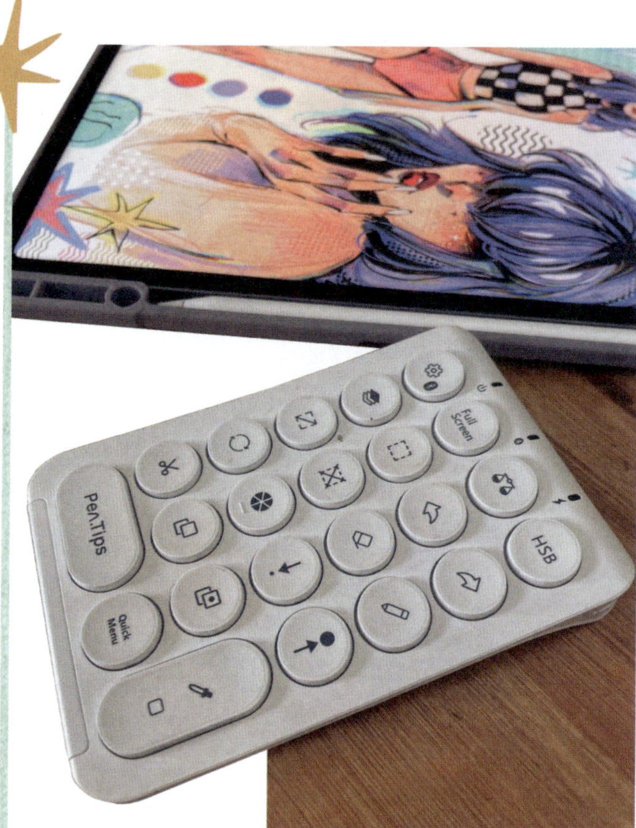

IPAD PRO 12 + PROCREATE

I absolutely adore the feel of drawing on an iPad to the point where I've tried to make it my sole tool for digital art. It's just tricky to make that switch because I'm so used to working in Photoshop. I use my iPad mostly for sketching, editing, quick colour tests for my traditional paintings, or if I'm travelling. I love how portable and convenient it is. My favourite Procreate brushes are the Dry Ink brush, Georg's Inktober brushes, and the Watercolor Maxpack.

KEYBOARD FOR PROCREATE

One of the things I found really hard about using Procreate on the iPad was the lack of shortcuts, which slowed down my workflow way too much. Investing in this little keyboard from PenTips was one of the best decisions and a huge time saver. It made my process of working in Procreate so much more enjoyable and efficient!

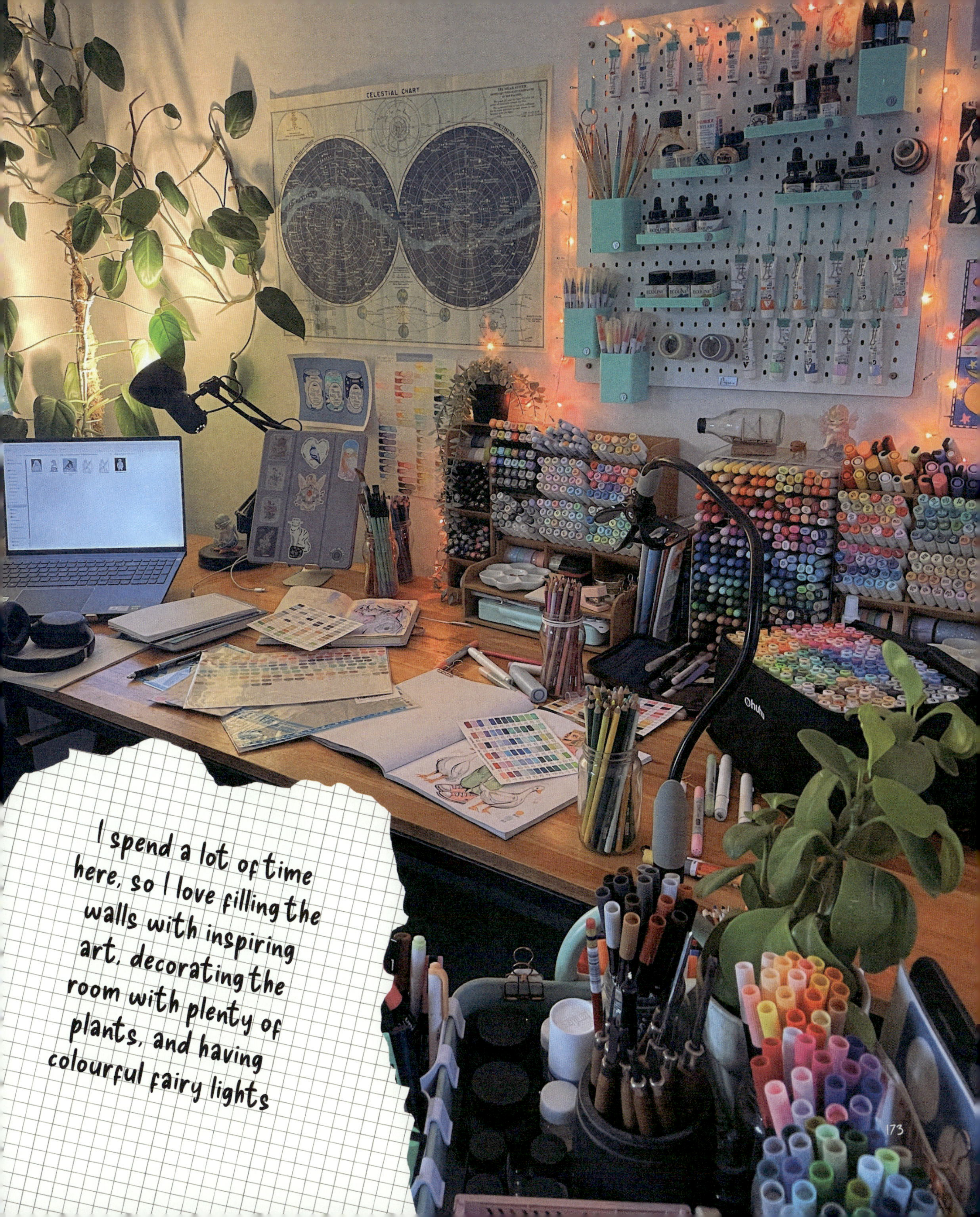

I spend a lot of time here, so I love filling the walls with inspiring art, decorating the room with plenty of plants, and having colourful fairy lights

TRADITIONAL TOOLS

I truly believe that creating amazing art doesn't require many fancy or expensive tools. It's completely possible to make great pieces using whatever materials you have available. As a mixed-media enthusiast, I've always been curious about experimenting with new tools and techniques. There's something about trying new art supplies that never fails to excite and inspire me to create. In the following pages, I'll be sharing all the traditional tools I've discovered over the years that have become my absolute favourites.

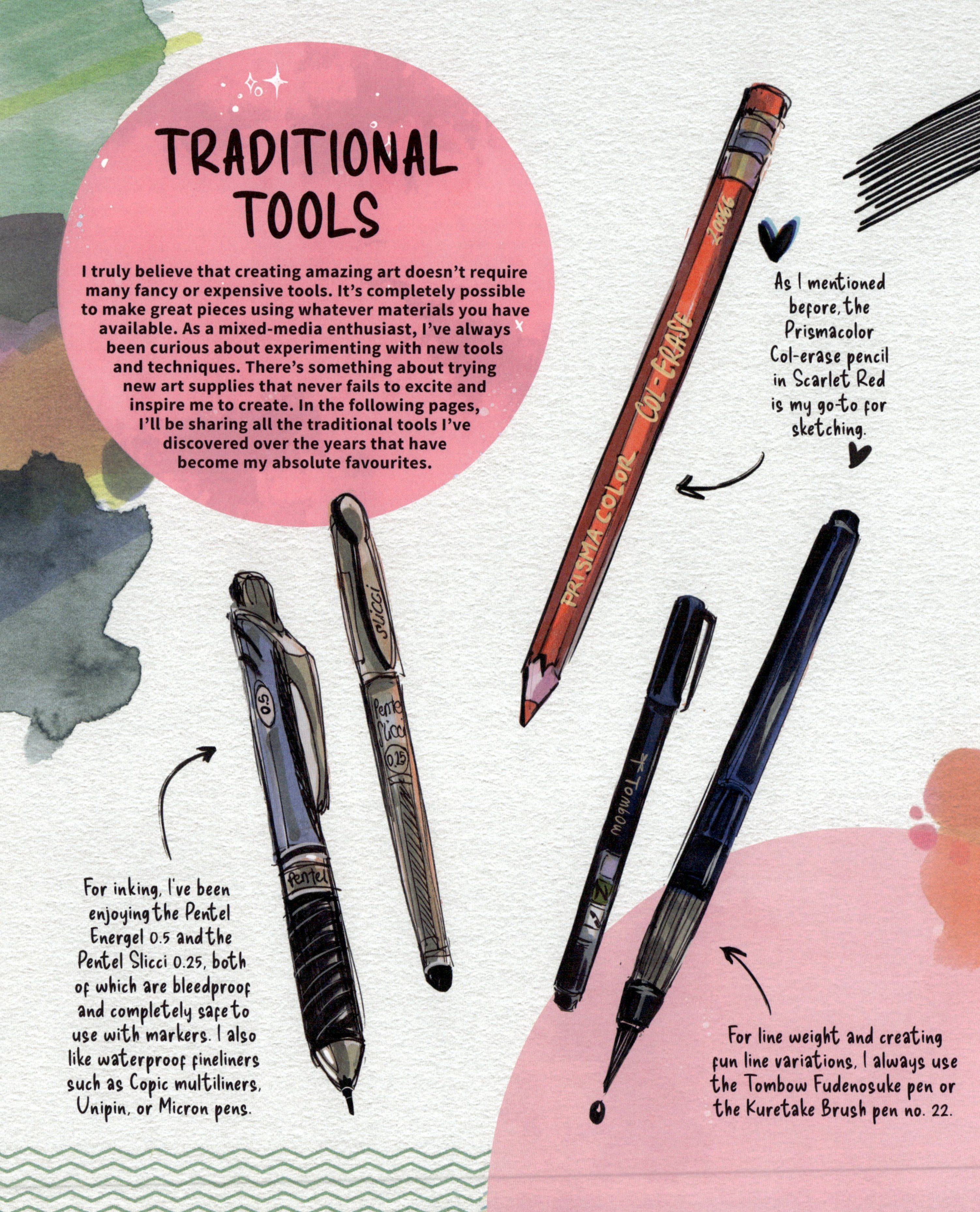

As I mentioned before, the Prismacolor Col-erase pencil in Scarlet Red is my go-to for sketching.

For inking, I've been enjoying the Pentel Energel 0.5 and the Pentel Slicci 0.25, both of which are bleedproof and completely safe to use with markers. I also like waterproof fineliners such as Copic multiliners, Unipin, or Micron pens.

For line weight and creating fun line variations, I always use the Tombow Fudenosuke pen or the Kuretake Brush pen no. 22.

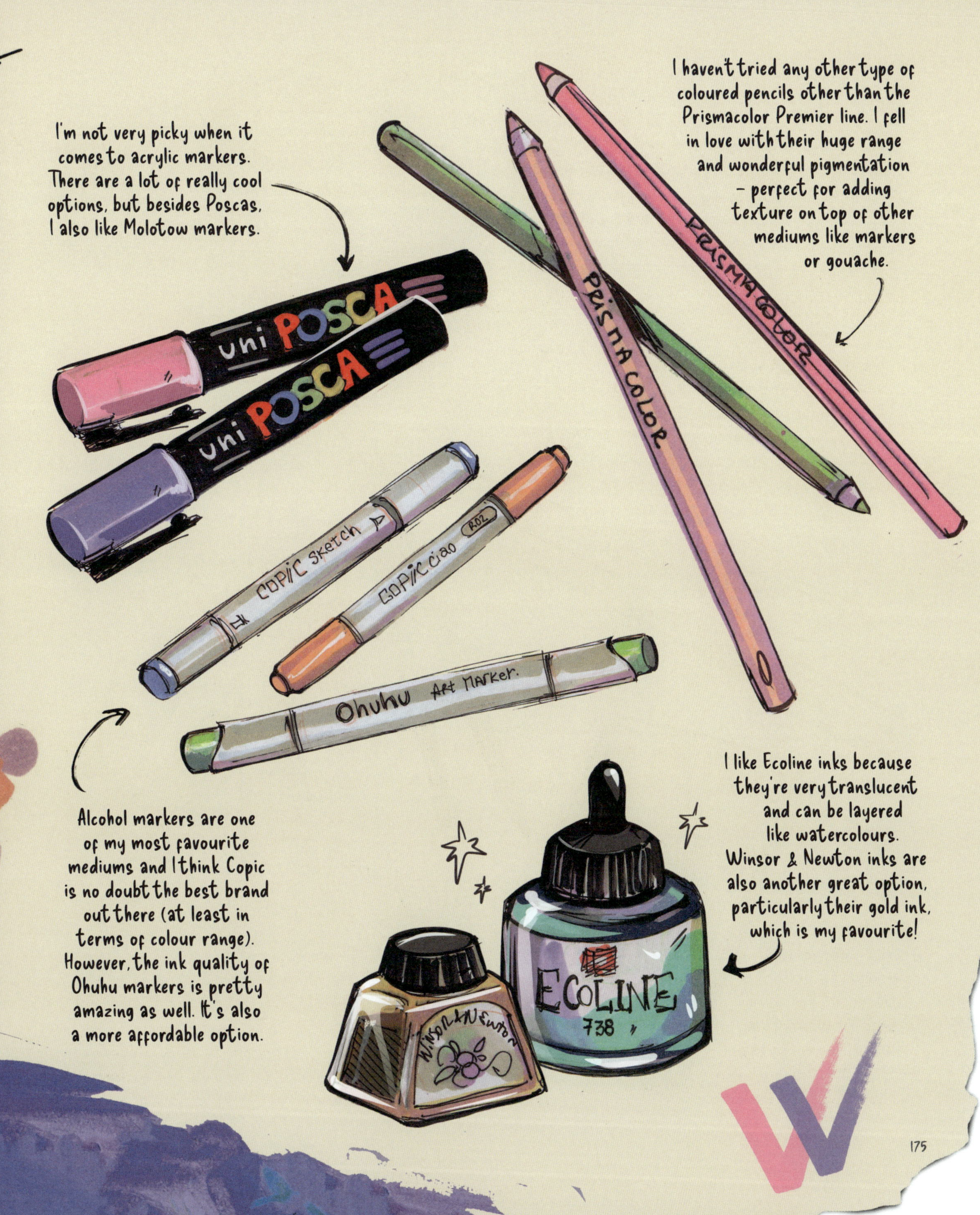
I'm not very picky when it comes to acrylic markers. There are a lot of really cool options, but besides Poscas, I also like Molotow markers.
I haven't tried any other type of coloured pencils other than the Prismacolor Premier line. I fell in love with their huge range and wonderful pigmentation – perfect for adding texture on top of other mediums like markers or gouache.
uni POSCA
uni POSCA
PRISMACOLOR
PRISMACOLOR
COPIC sketch
COPIC ciao
R02
Ohuhu Art Marker.
Alcohol markers are one of my most favourite mediums and I think Copic is no doubt the best brand out there (at least in terms of colour range). However, the ink quality of Ohuhu markers is pretty amazing as well. It's also a more affordable option.
I like Ecoline inks because they're very translucent and can be layered like watercolours. Winsor & Newton inks are also another great option, particularly their gold ink, which is my favourite!
ECOLINE
738
WINSOR & NEWTON

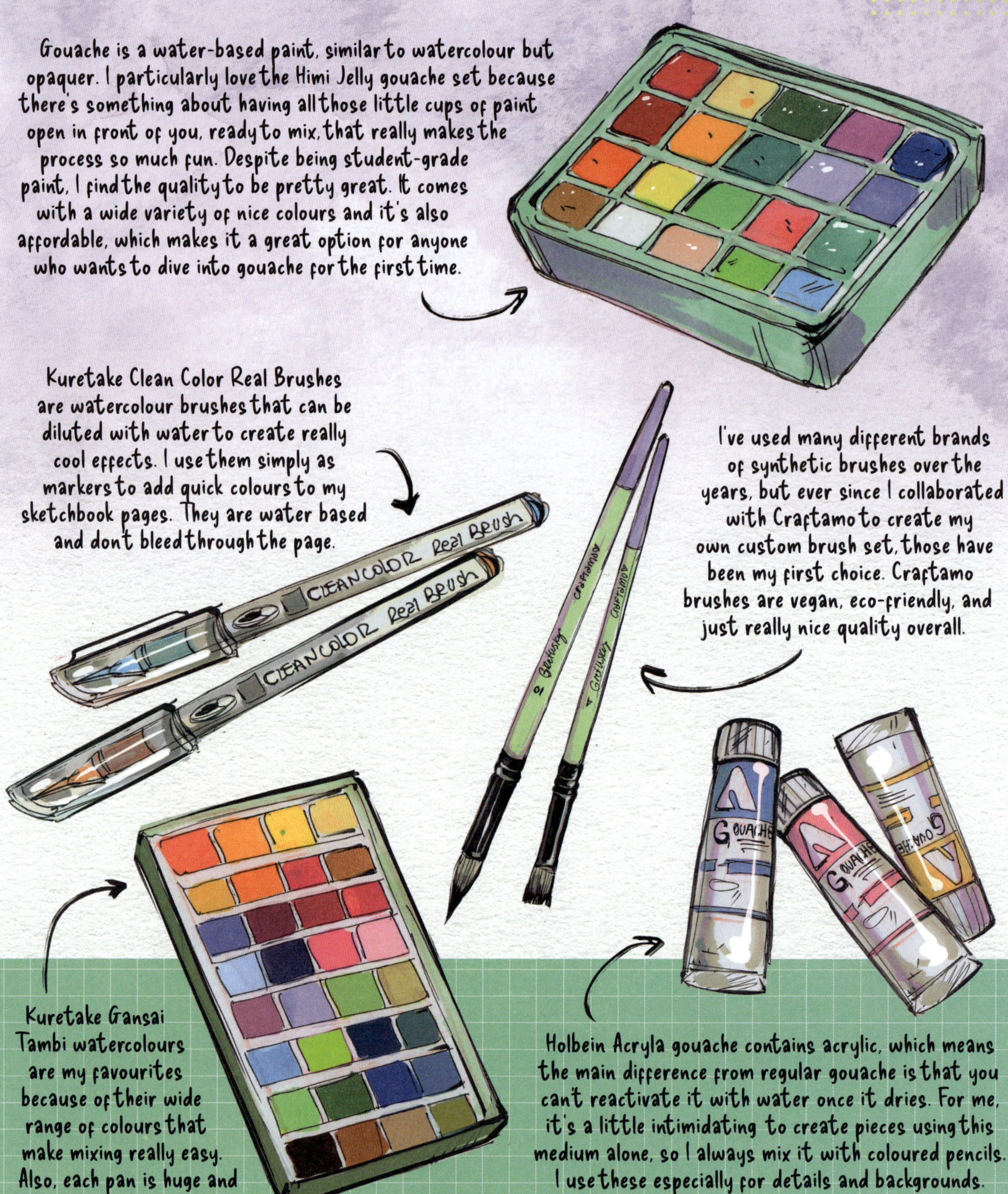

Gouache is a water-based paint, similar to watercolour but opaquer. I particularly love the Himi Jelly gouache set because there's something about having all those little cups of paint open in front of you, ready to mix, that really makes the process so much fun. Despite being student-grade paint, I find the quality to be pretty great. It comes with a wide variety of nice colours and it's also affordable, which makes it a great option for anyone who wants to dive into gouache for the first time.

Kuretake Clean Color Real Brushes are watercolour brushes that can be diluted with water to create really cool effects. I use them simply as markers to add quick colours to my sketchbook pages. They are water based and don't bleed through the page.

I've used many different brands of synthetic brushes over the years, but ever since I collaborated with Craftamo to create my own custom brush set, those have been my first choice. Craftamo brushes are vegan, eco-friendly, and just really nice quality overall.

Kuretake Gansai Tambi watercolours are my favourites because of their wide range of colours that make mixing really easy. Also, each pan is huge and will literally last a lifetime.

Holbein Acryla gouache contains acrylic, which means the main difference from regular gouache is that you can't reactivate it with water once it dries. For me, it's a little intimidating to create pieces using this medium alone, so I always mix it with coloured pencils. I use these especially for details and backgrounds.

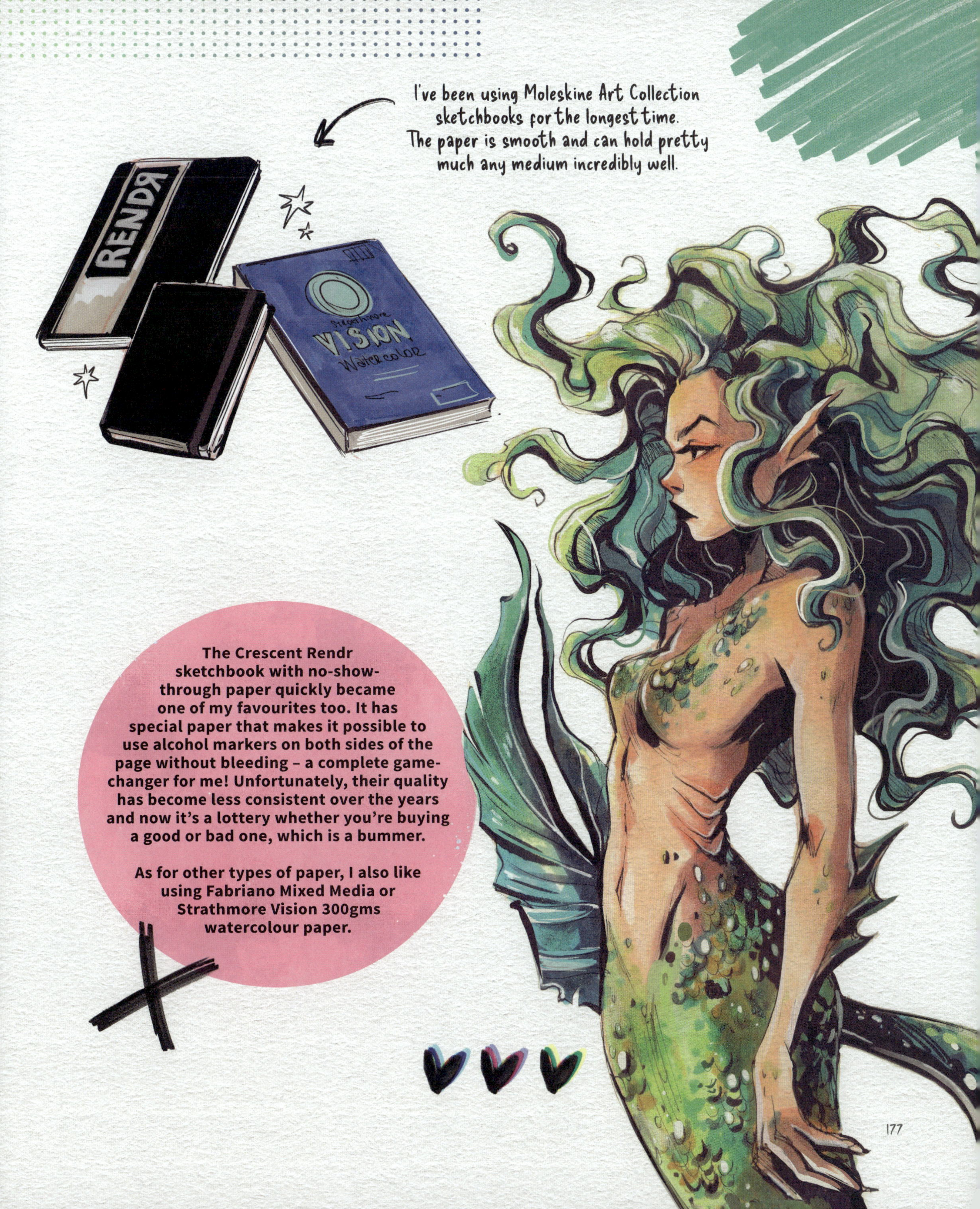

I've been using Moleskine Art Collection sketchbooks for the longest time. The paper is smooth and can hold pretty much any medium incredibly well.

The Crescent Rendr sketchbook with no-show-through paper quickly became one of my favourites too. It has special paper that makes it possible to use alcohol markers on both sides of the page without bleeding – a complete game-changer for me! Unfortunately, their quality has become less consistent over the years and now it's a lottery whether you're buying a good or bad one, which is a bummer.

As for other types of paper, I also like using Fabriano Mixed Media or Strathmore Vision 300gms watercolour paper.

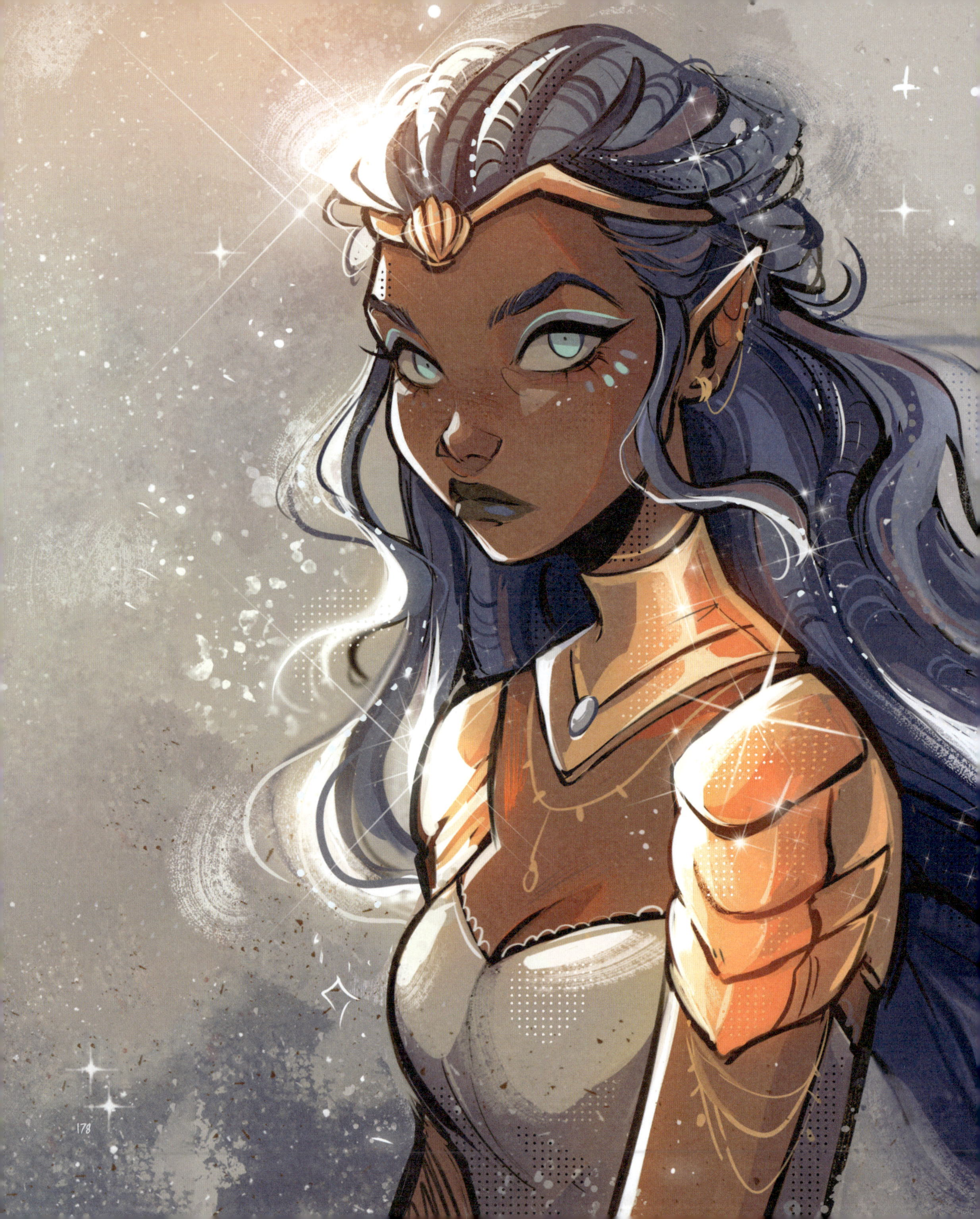

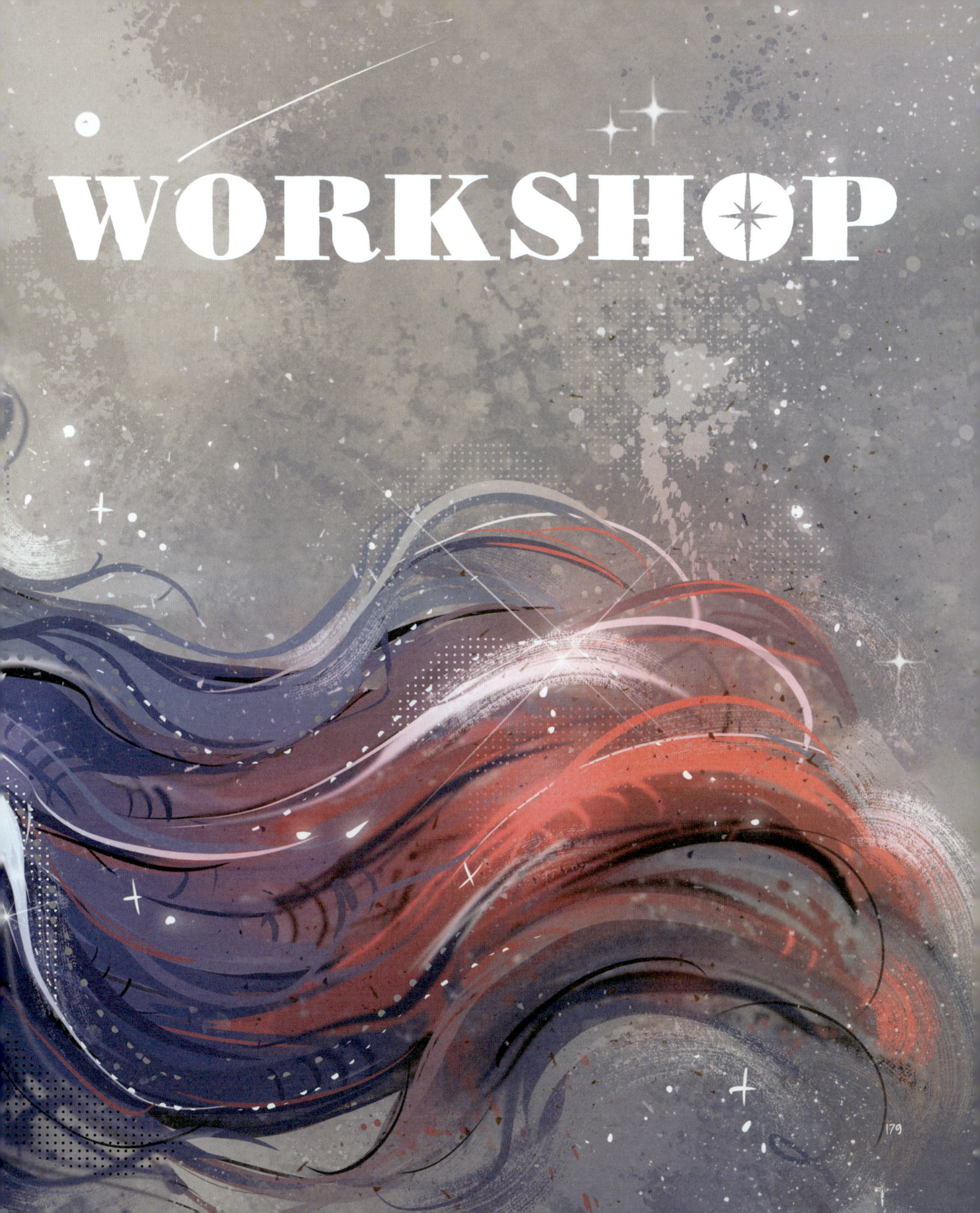

WORKSHOP

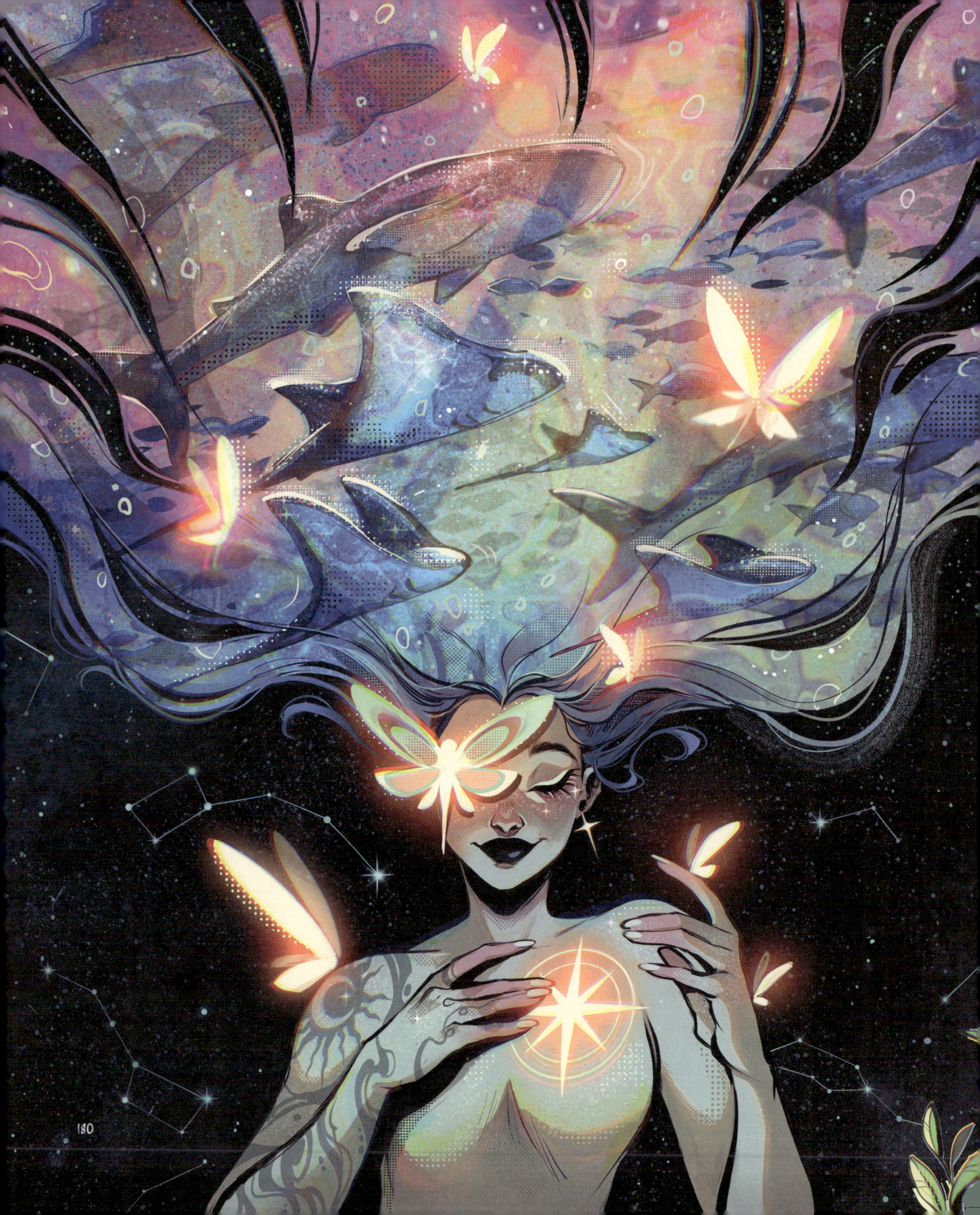

THE WAYFINDER: MAKING THE COVER

It was really important to create an illustration that felt truly special enough to be the cover of this project; something that reflected my art style, interests, and everything that this book means to me. I knew from the start that it was going to be a hard task, so I gave myself permission to explore a few ideas without any pressure. I decided to do a few sketches based on different subjects I liked, creating options inspired by nature, space, and the sea. The one thing I was adamant about incorporating was the symbolism of a compass in some way or another.

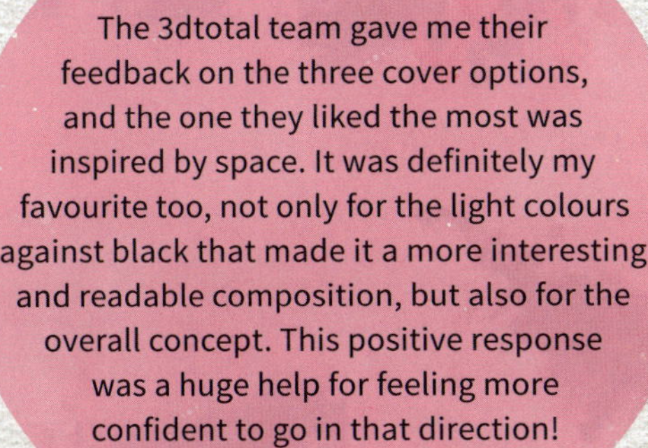

The 3dtotal team gave me their feedback on the three cover options, and the one they liked the most was inspired by space. It was definitely my favourite too, not only for the light colours against black that made it a more interesting and readable composition, but also for the overall concept. This positive response was a huge help for feeling more confident to go in that direction!

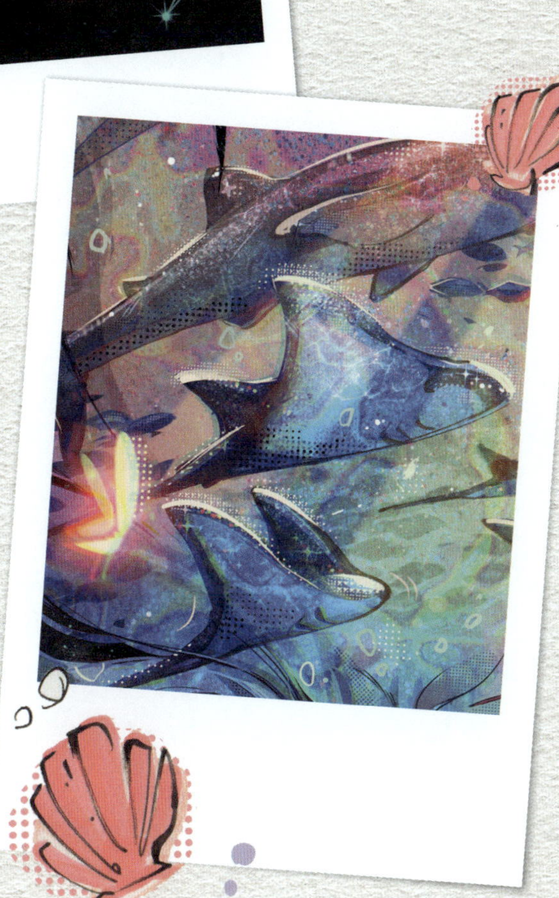

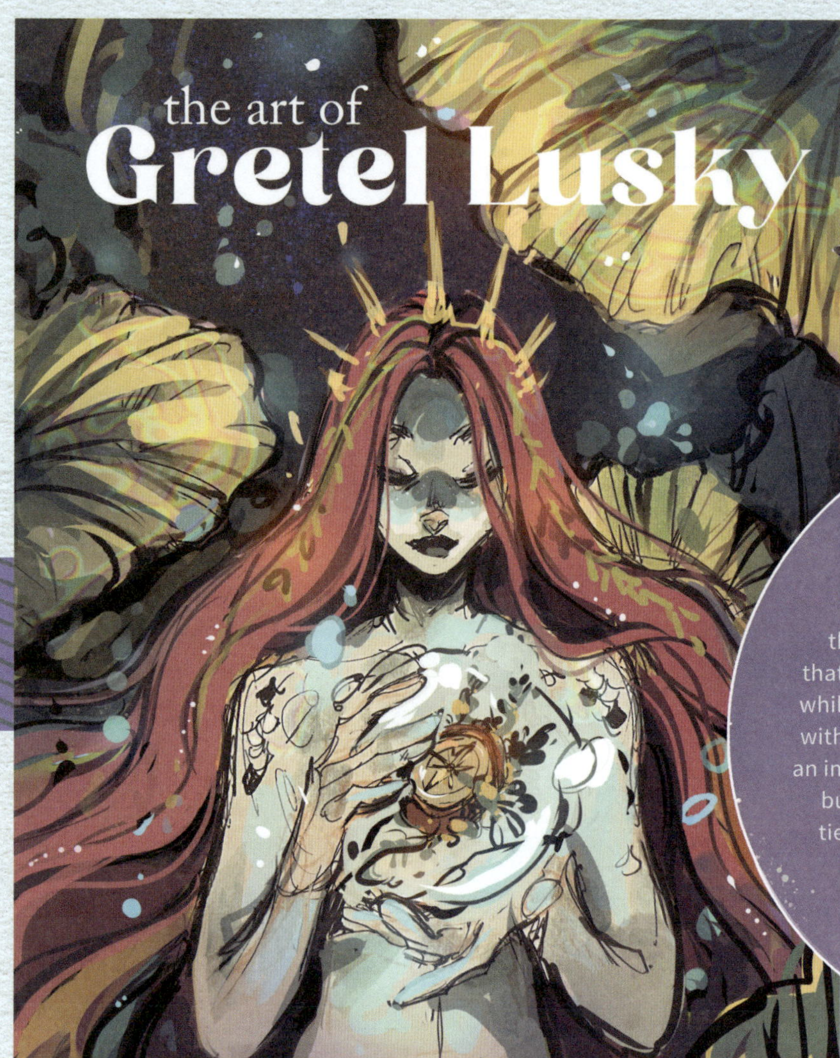

While working on the cover, I hadn't yet decided on a title for the book, but I knew I wanted to find a special word that complemented the illustration. It needed to be something that captured a sense of wonder and adventure while also representing my personal connection with art. At times, it felt like I was trying to solve an impossible puzzle; all the elements were there but I wasn't seeing the common thread that tied everything together. After so much back and forth, my partner came up with the word 'wayfinding' – a term I had heard before but had buried deep in my mind and forgotten.

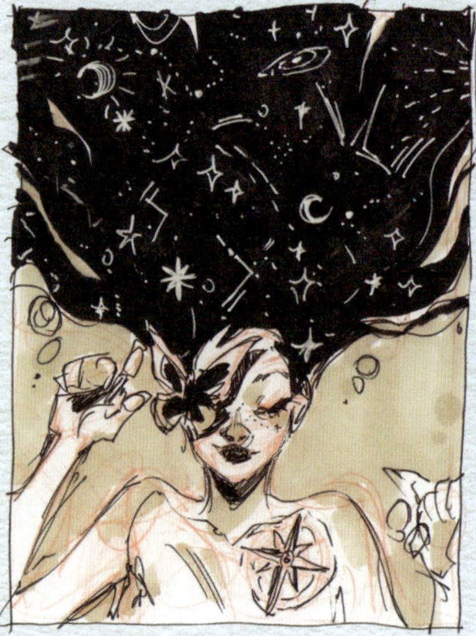

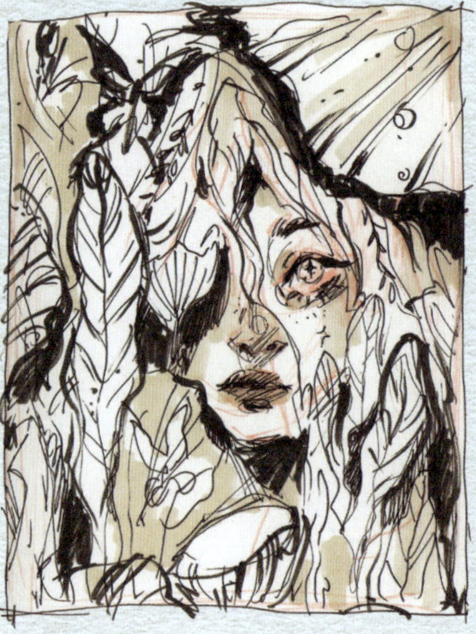

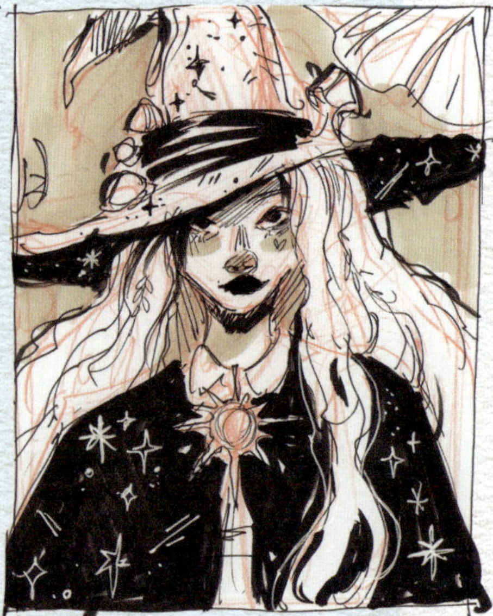

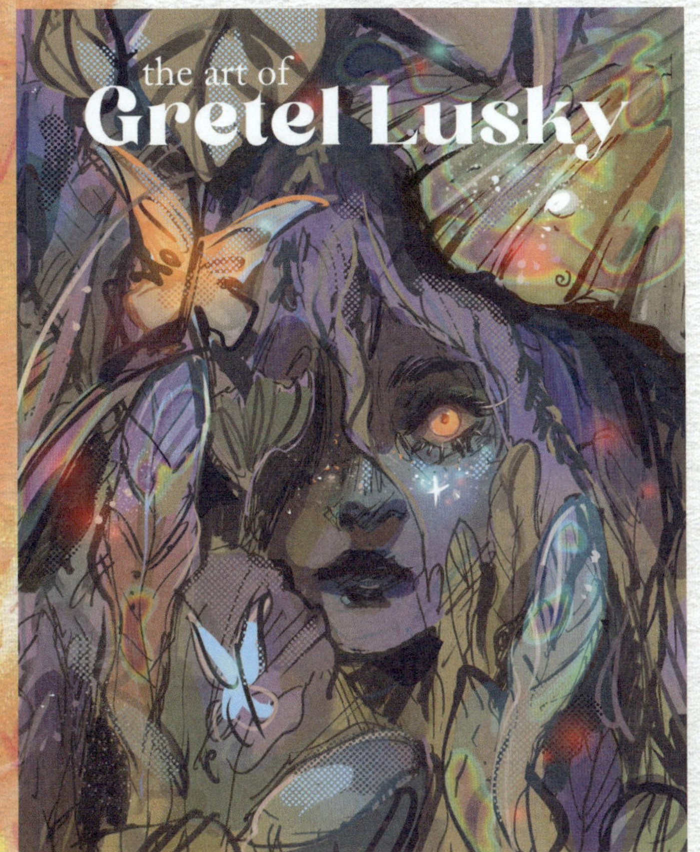

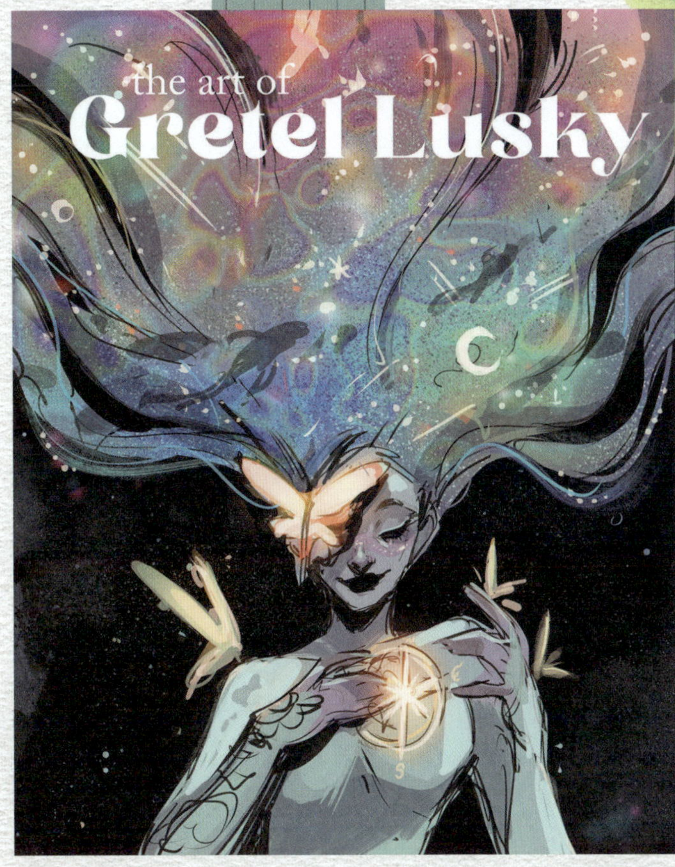

Wayfinding is the ancient Polynesian practice of navigating the vast open ocean by consulting the sky, stars, and swells of water to find direction. It combines pure observation with knowledge passed down from generation to generation. Not only do I find this fascinating, especially given its strong connection to the sea, but I love the more literal aspect of the word 'wayfinder' too – simply, someone who finds a way.

I decided to call this book *Wayfinder* because, like many of you, art was the thing that helped me find my way in life, time and time again. Art has been my north star since the very beginning and this book perfectly embodies that. The name also encapsulates that sense of exploration and discovery that I wanted to convey. It made all the essential elements – the stars, sea, compass heart, and butterflies guiding the way – fall beautifully into place.

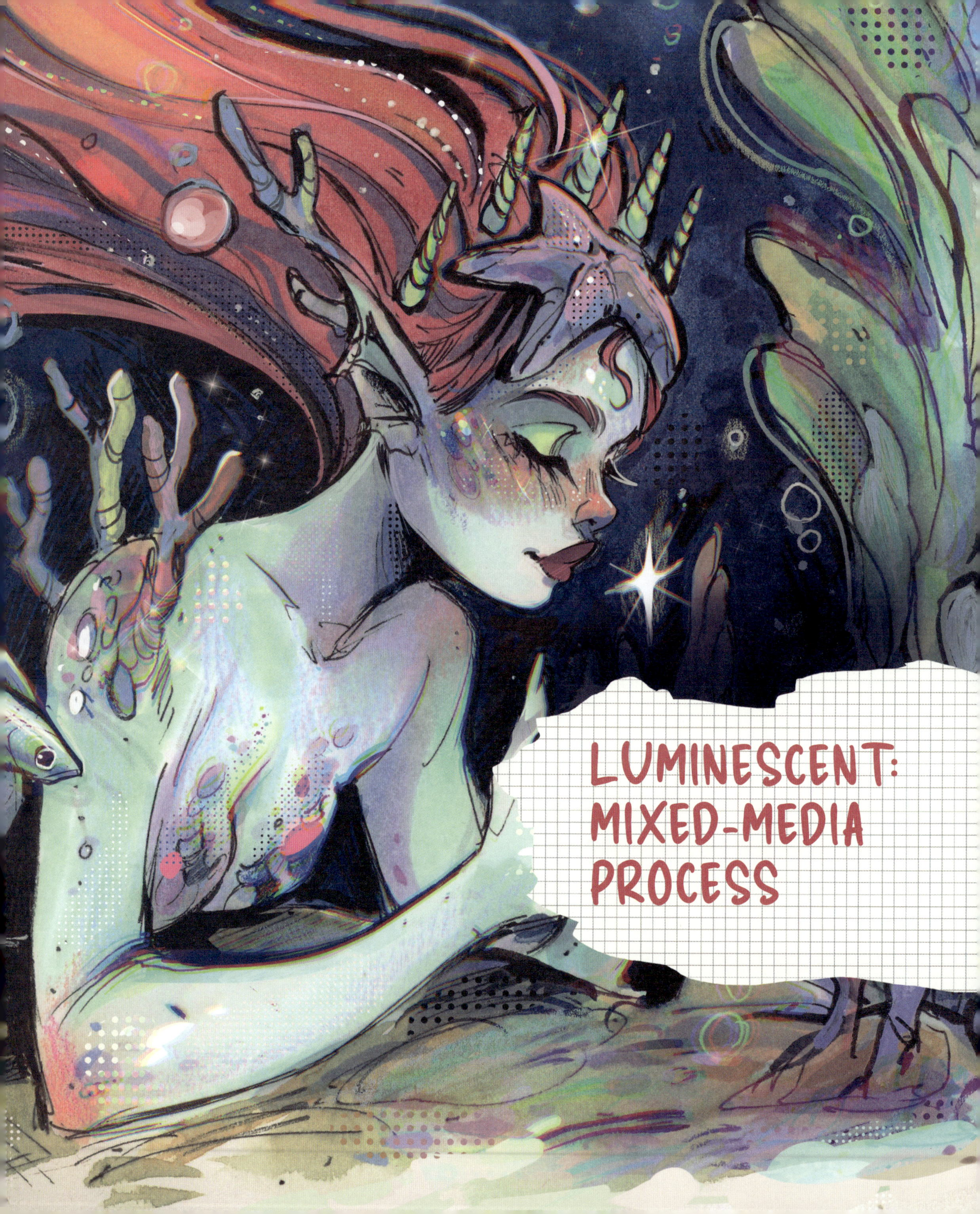

LUMINESCENT: MIXED-MEDIA PROCESS

When it comes to my traditional process, I don't often follow a rigid formula. However, I've tried to put together a mixed-media tutorial that encapsulates the majority of my workflow and creative decisions, from sketching and exploring different mediums, all the way to the final steps of scanning and digital editing. In this tutorial, I hope I can demonstrate how the unique strengths of both traditional and digital mediums can be blended together to discover new techniques, resulting in artwork that beautifully combines the best of both worlds.

The initial sketch

For this drawing, I decide to explore a few ideas and compositions using my iPad. Sketching digitally gives me the freedom to try different things without too much pressure, and I can easily adjust things until I'm completely satisfied.

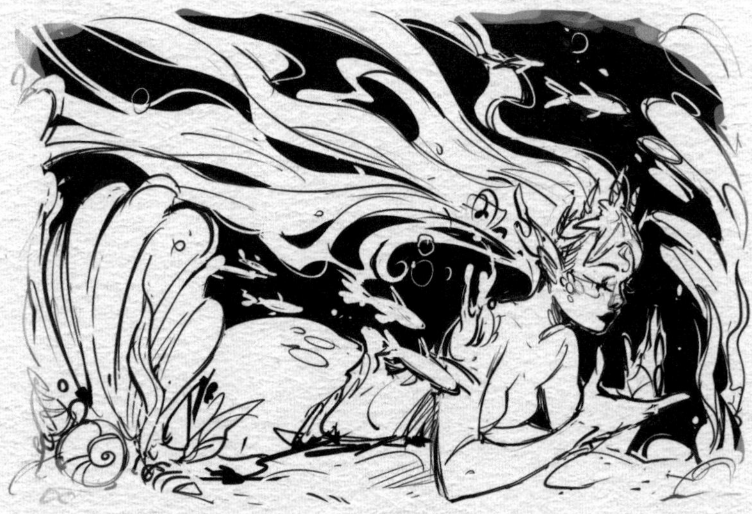

Transferring the sketch to paper

I have a few preferred methods when it comes to transferring a digital sketch onto paper. Sometimes, I print the sketch on regular paper and trace it with a pencil using my light pad. Other times, I opt to lower the sketch's opacity to around 7% and print it directly onto Fabriano Mixed Media 250gsm A4 paper. The second method usually saves me some time since the transferred sketch is ready to be inked without any additional steps. For reference, I have an Epson EcoTank L805 printer and I found that it's safe to work on top of printed sketches as the ink is completely bleedproof.

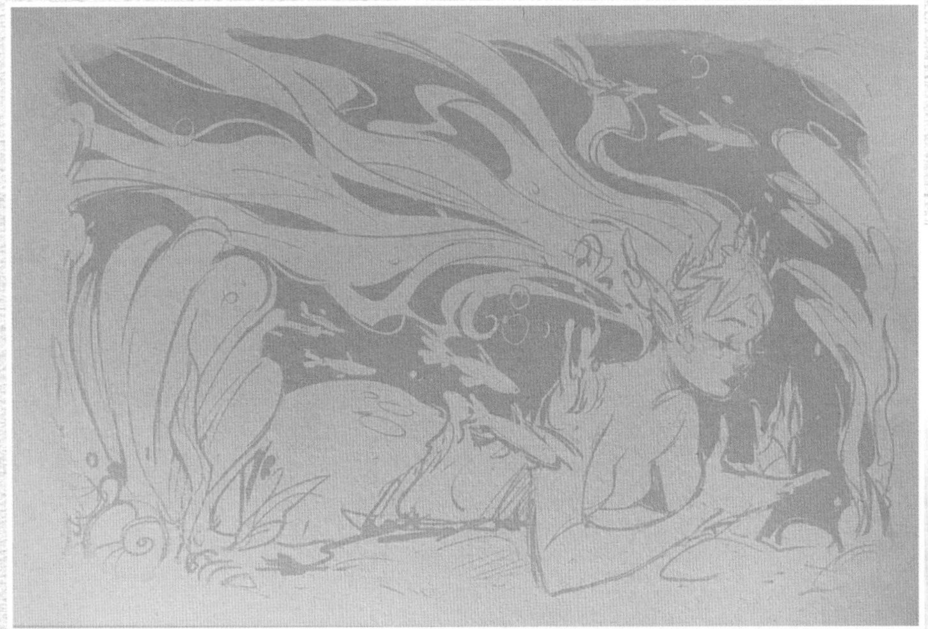

Inking

For the first pass of ink, I always start with a very thin tip – my favourite pen these days is the Pentel EnerGel 0.5. As I work on the line work, I go back and forth between the Pentel and the Tombow Fudenosuke pen, which has a thicker tip, to add some line weight and variation to certain areas. Although the printed sketch may still be slightly visible under the inks, it will be completely covered once I add colour.

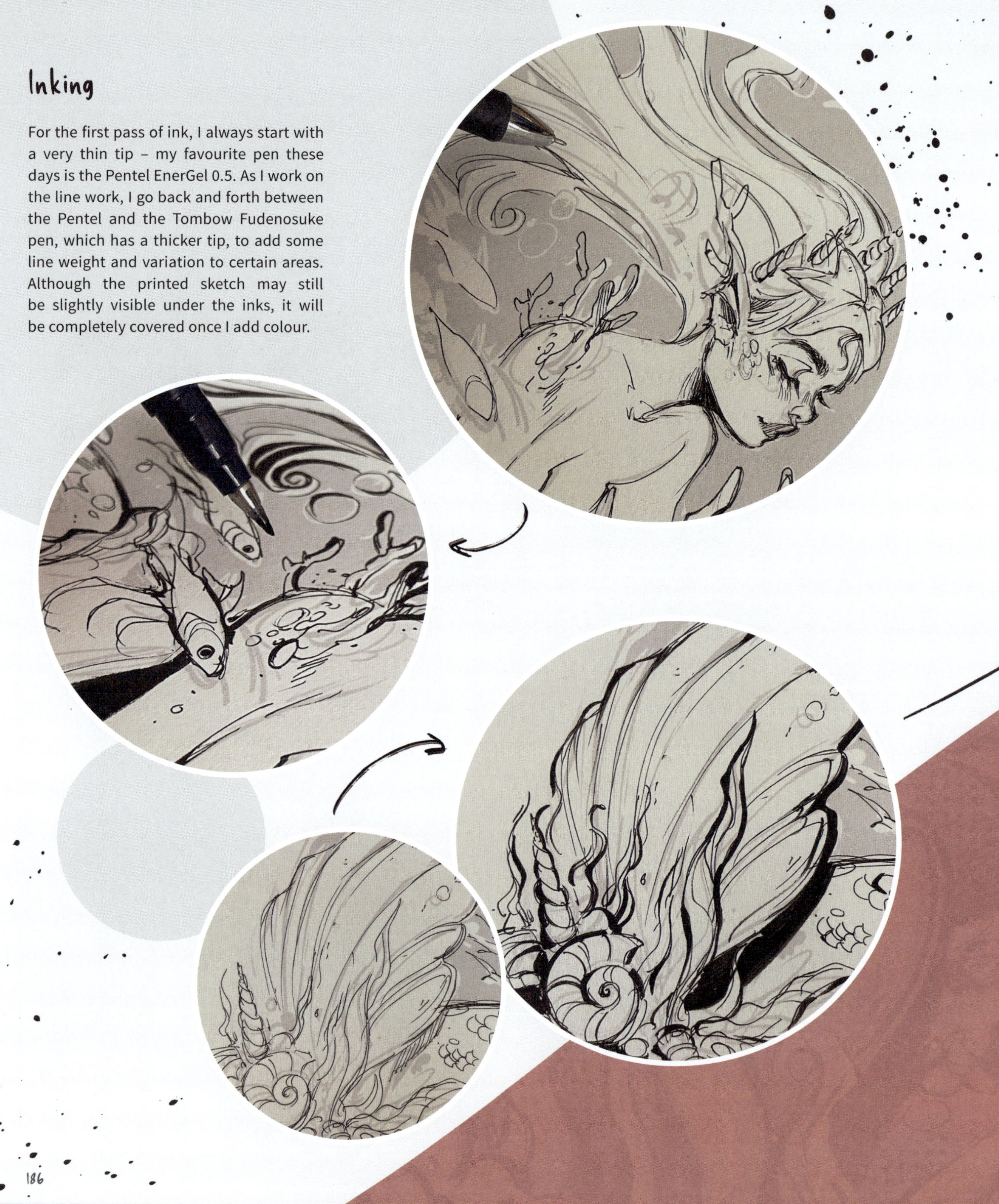

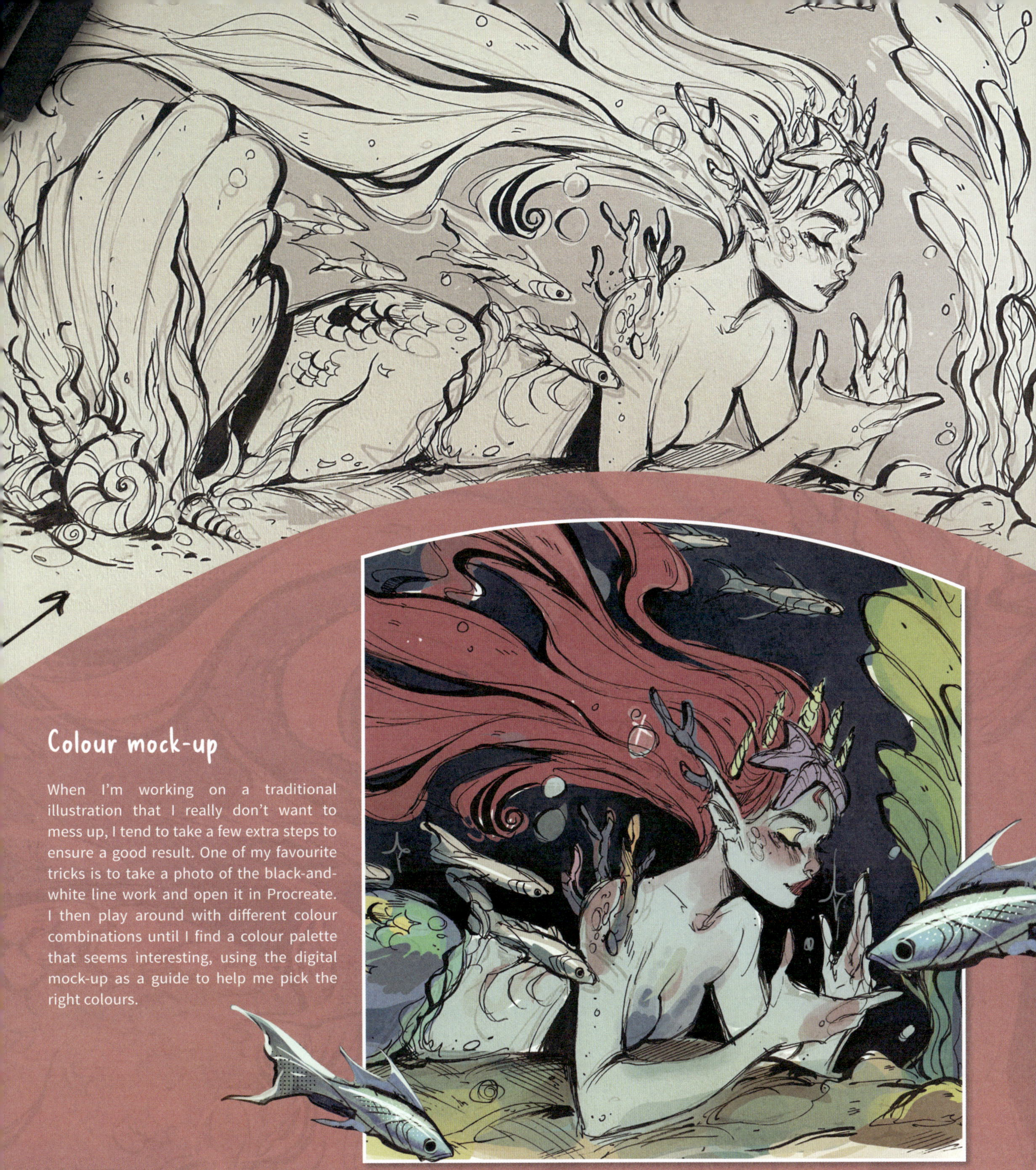

Colour mock-up

When I'm working on a traditional illustration that I really don't want to mess up, I tend to take a few extra steps to ensure a good result. One of my favourite tricks is to take a photo of the black-and-white line work and open it in Procreate. I then play around with different colour combinations until I find a colour palette that seems interesting, using the digital mock-up as a guide to help me pick the right colours.

Coat of watercolour

I like using watercolours to quickly lay down a base colour for most of my traditional work, before adding other mediums on top. I plan on doing a watercolour pass for the whole piece, but halfway through completing the background, I remember that the Pentel EnerGel ink tends to smudge if you apply too much water. These unexpected little accidents can happen when working with traditional mediums and sometimes you have to rethink your initial plan in order to adapt to the artwork's specific needs. I decide to carefully finish painting the background with watercolours and leave the remaining areas for another medium.

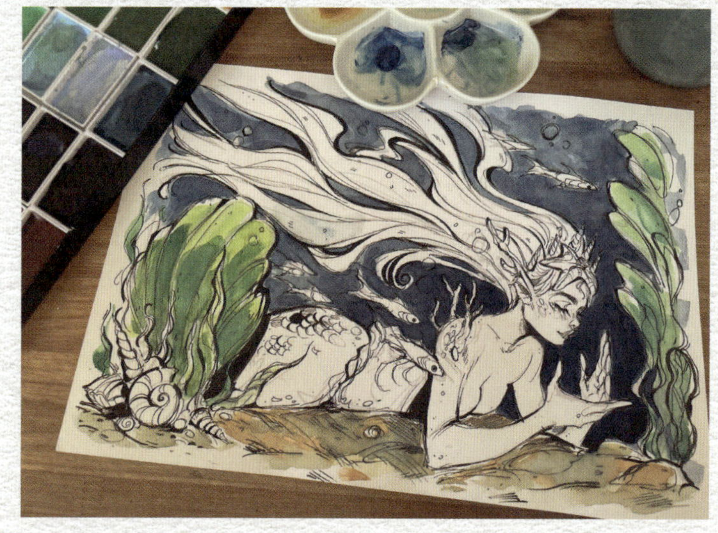

Painting with alcohol markers

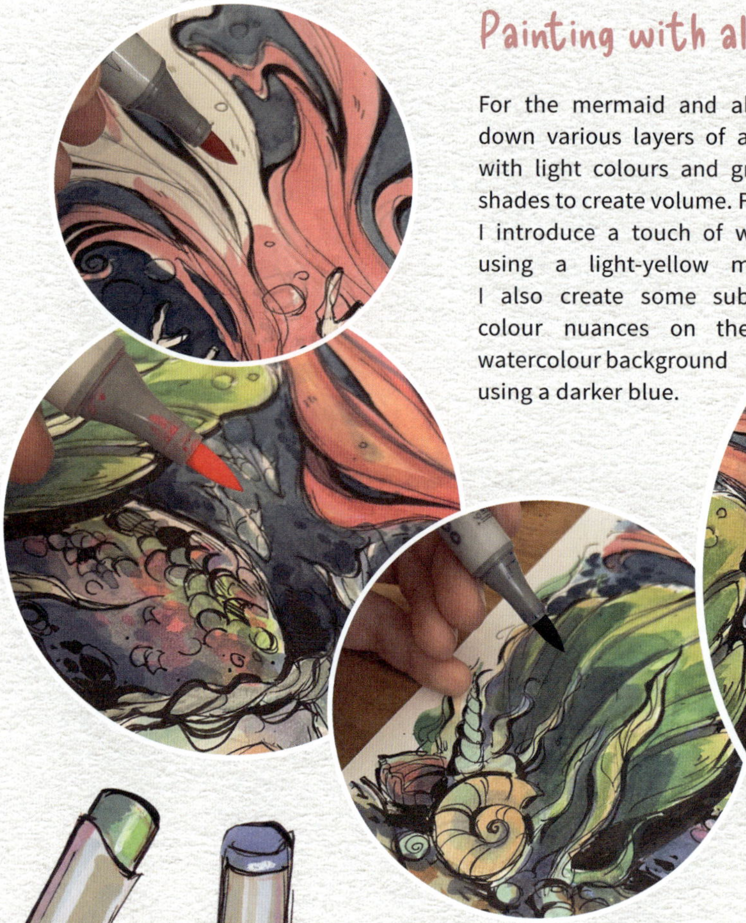

For the mermaid and all the remaining details, I lay down various layers of alcohol markers. I always start with light colours and gradually work towards darker shades to create volume. For the seaweed, I introduce a touch of warmth by using a light-yellow marker. I also create some subtle colour nuances on the watercolour background using a darker blue.

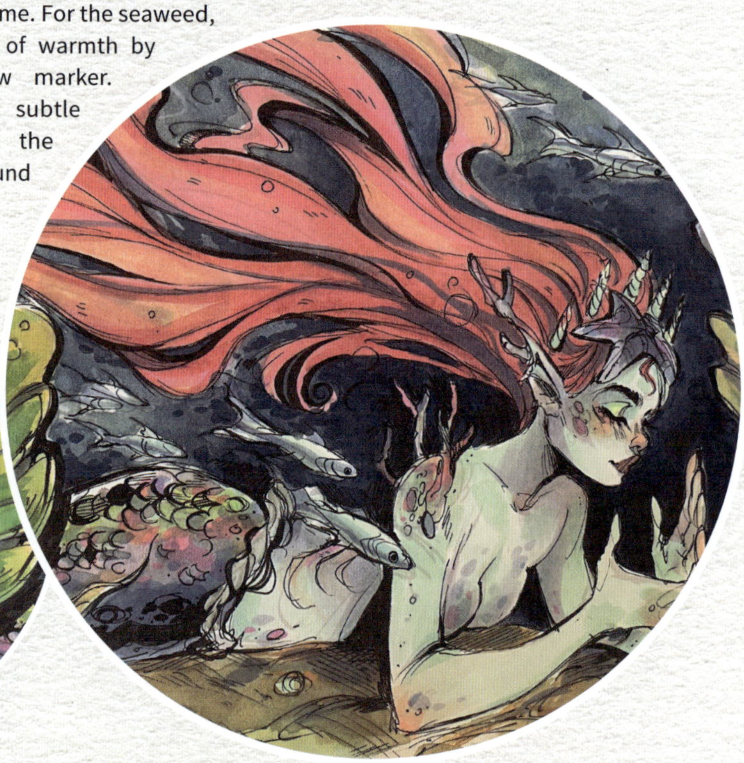

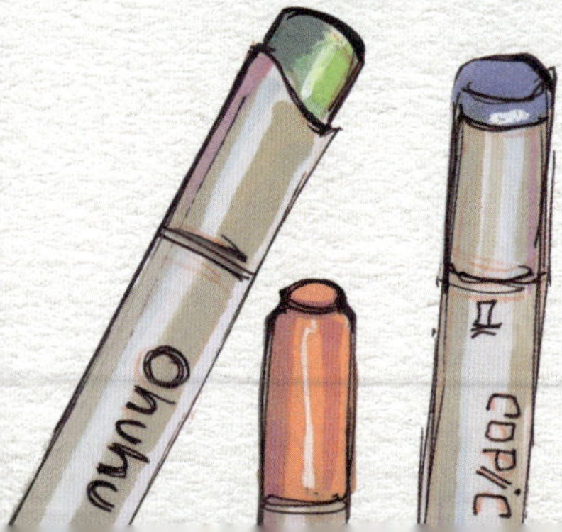

Refining with acrylic markers

As I mentioned earlier, the opaqueness of acrylic markers is perfect for bringing back any details or shapes that might have been lost or covered during the previous steps. It's also good for enhancing areas that need improvement. I use a few different colours – yellow, lavender, and pink, among others – to embellish the mermaid's tail with a few more scales. Next, I add hair strands and render the starfish, shell crown, and corals on her shoulder.

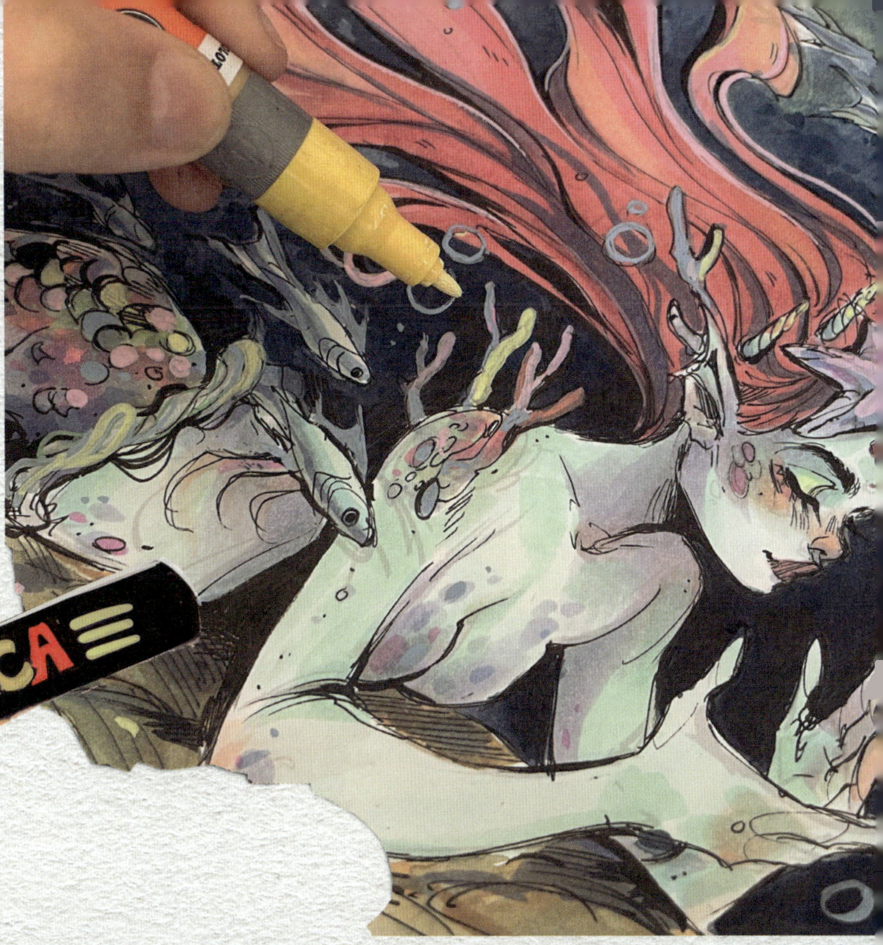

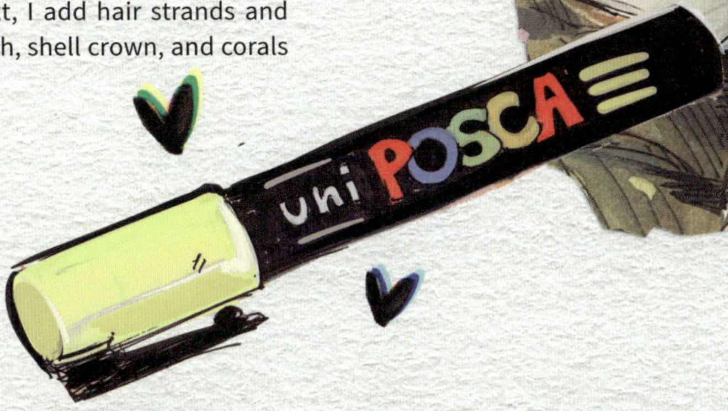

Little details

Using a white Sakura Gelly Roll pen, I add some of the surrounding bubbles.

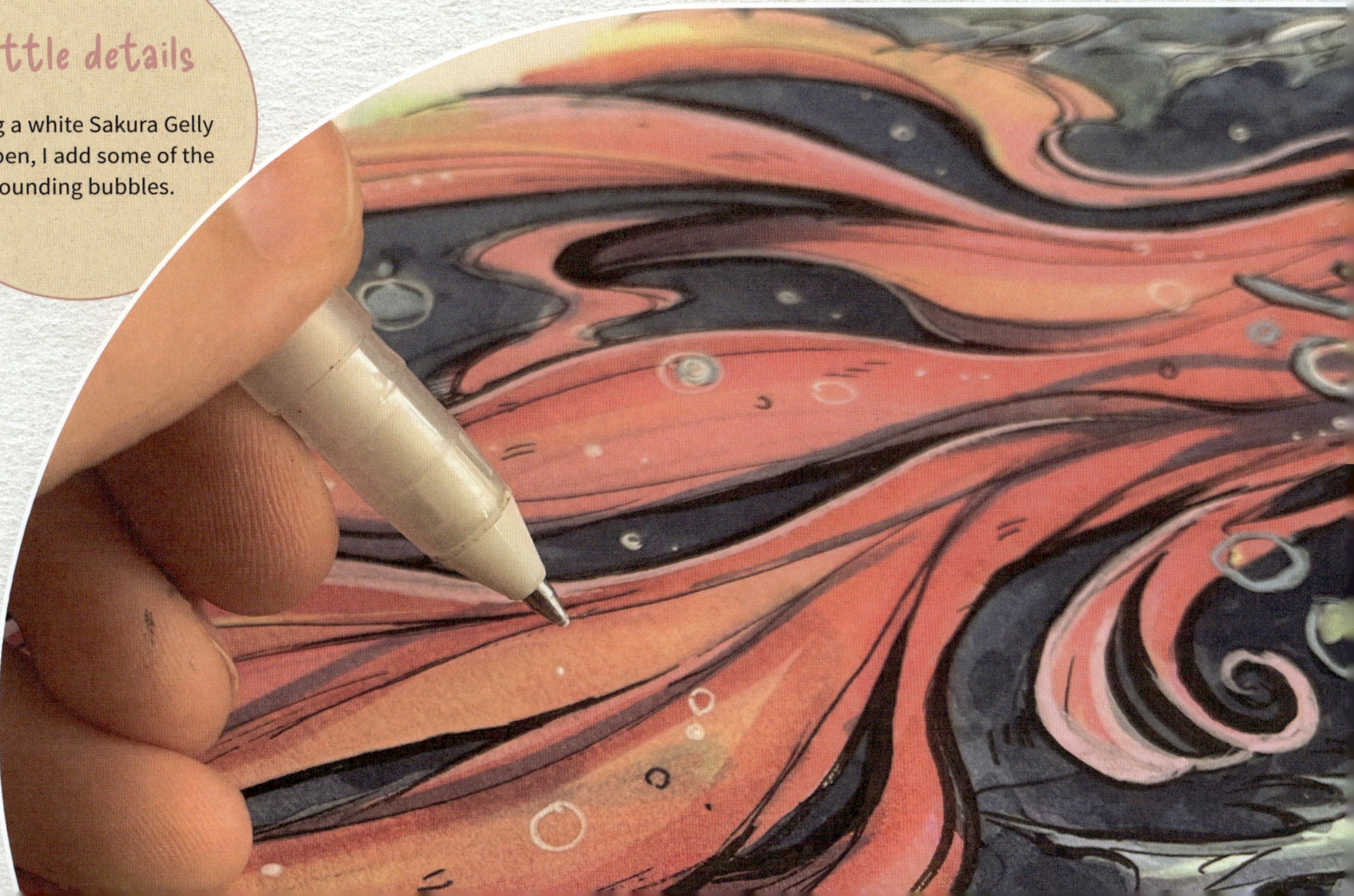

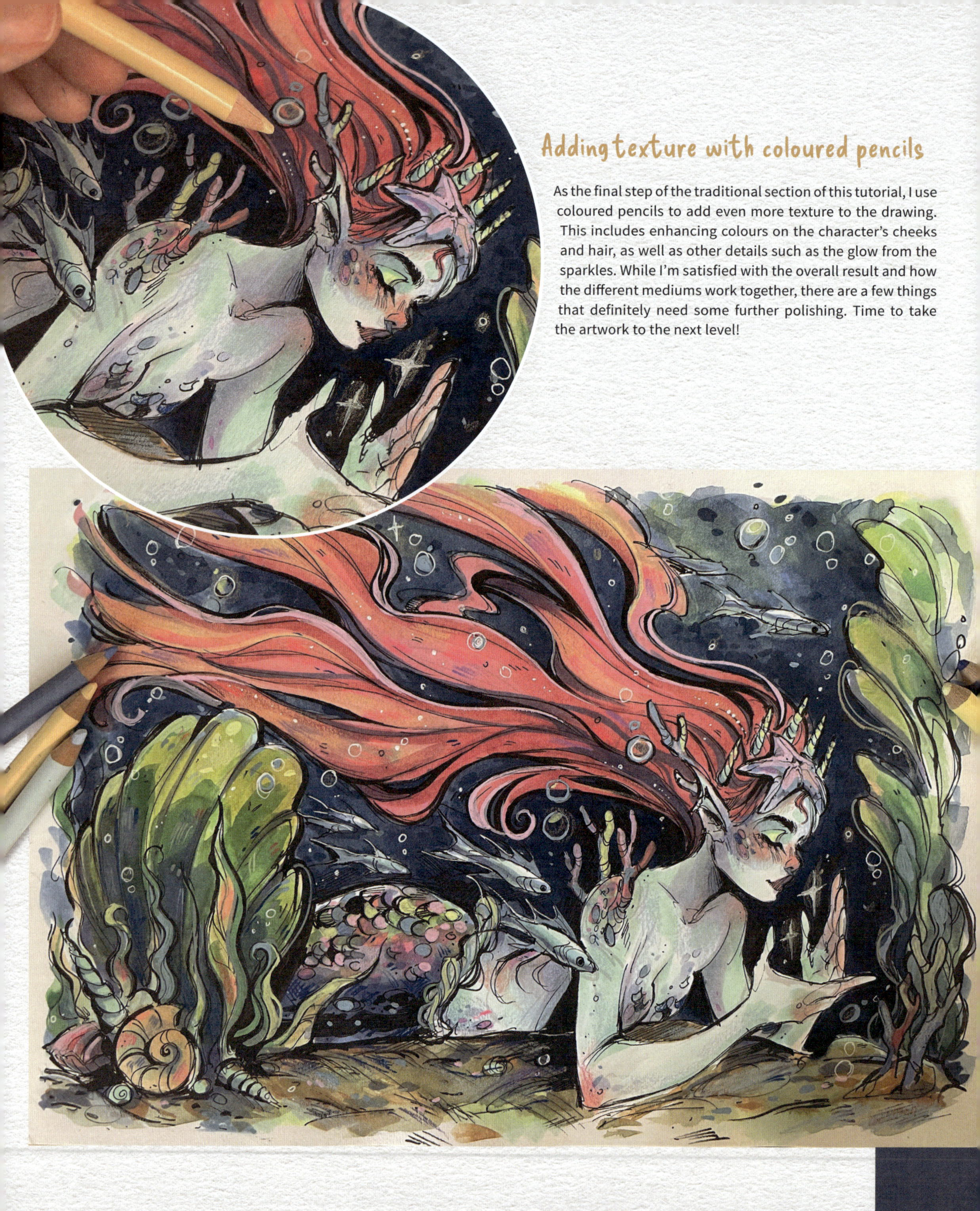

Adding texture with coloured pencils

As the final step of the traditional section of this tutorial, I use coloured pencils to add even more texture to the drawing. This includes enhancing colours on the character's cheeks and hair, as well as other details such as the glow from the sparkles. While I'm satisfied with the overall result and how the different mediums work together, there are a few things that definitely need some further polishing. Time to take the artwork to the next level!

Scanning the drawing

To begin the digital editing, I scan the image with an Epson Perfection V600 scanner at 500 dpi and open it in Photoshop. I adjust the colours slightly using the Selective Colour tool to deepen the blacks and increase the saturation by 10% to make the colours more vivid.

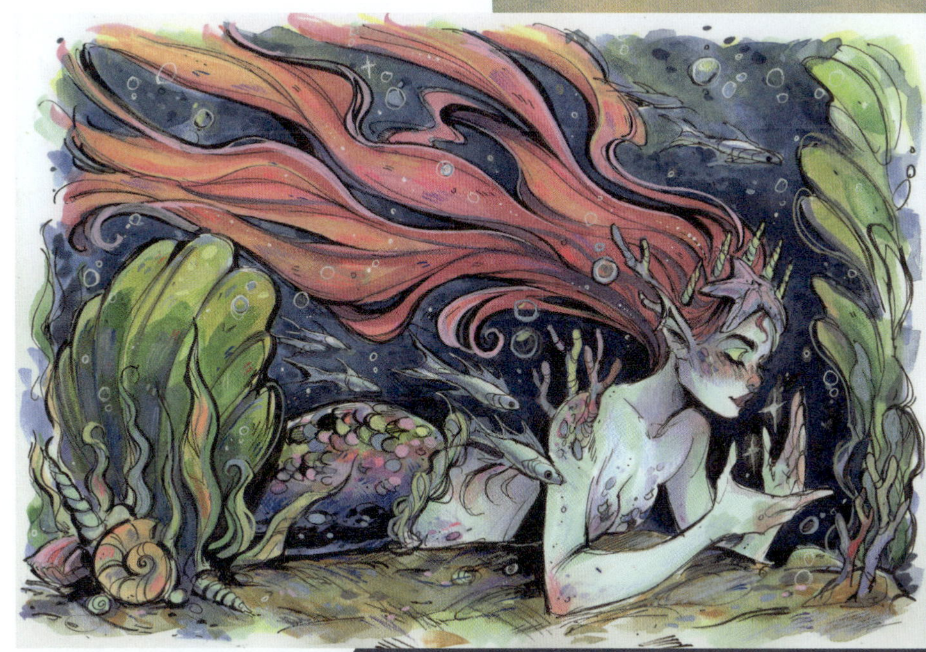

Digital touch-ups

Next, I create a new layer on top. Using a regular round brush, I start picking up the colours and rendering the whole image. I don't want to lose the traditional feel of the image, so I just focus on any intricate details that I couldn't achieve traditionally. It's not about covering; it's all about working with what is already there in order to elevate the whole piece. For this particular artwork, I pay close attention to the character's face and hair, softening her expression and adding more hair strands. I also clean up her silhouette so that everything reads better against the dark background. Additionally, I add more definition to the fish and surrounding coral.

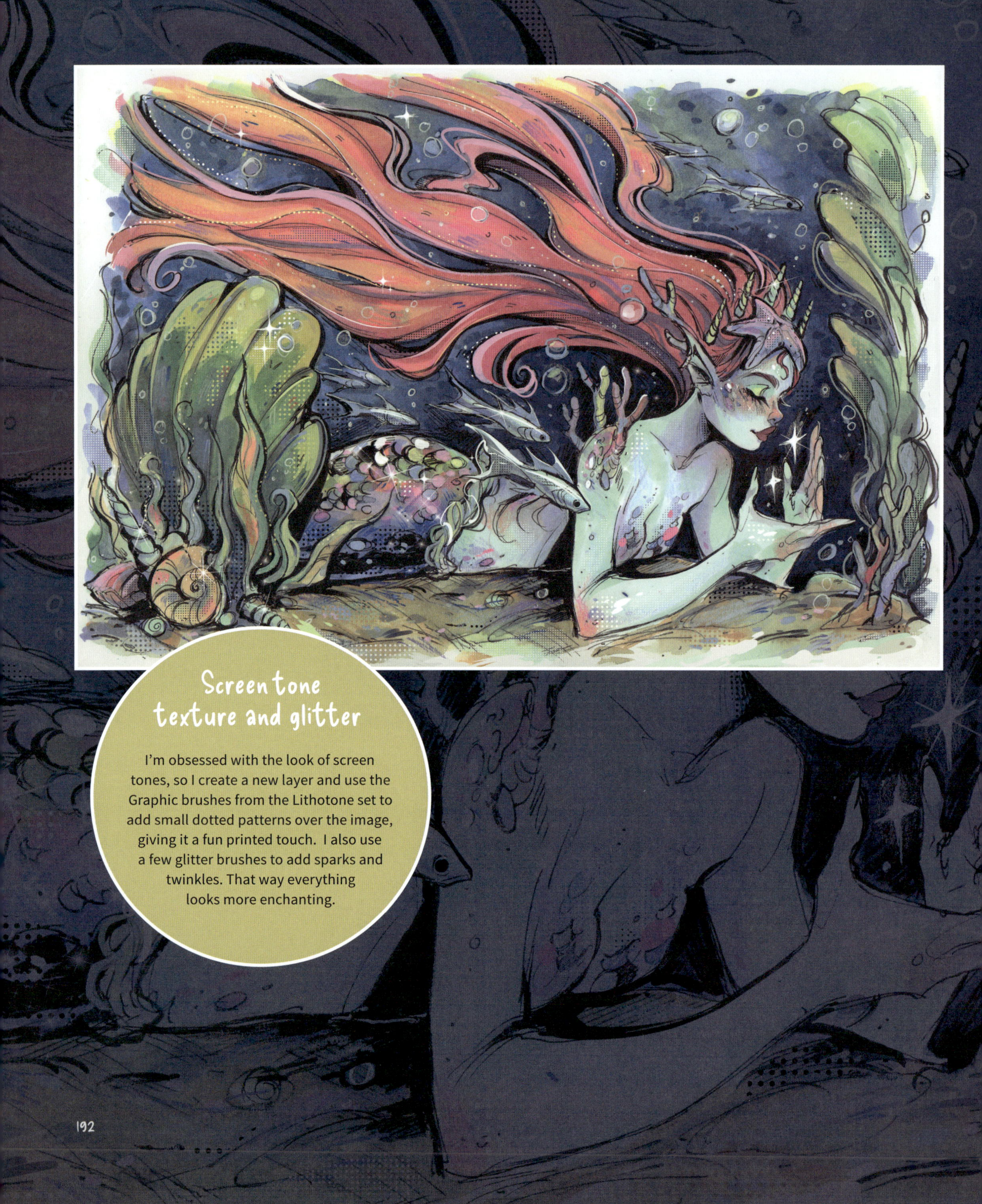

Screen tone texture and glitter

I'm obsessed with the look of screen tones, so I create a new layer and use the Graphic brushes from the Lithotone set to add small dotted patterns over the image, giving it a fun printed touch. I also use a few glitter brushes to add sparks and twinkles. That way everything looks more enchanting.

Adding atmosphere

I feel this drawing is lacking some depth and atmosphere, so I create a new layer and set it to Multiply to work on the shading using a light purple. I set another layer in Hard Light to apply a soft gradient at the top with a light-orange colour. These two layers help to reinforce the existing shadows and introduce a warm ambient light that adds a subtle sense of dimension.

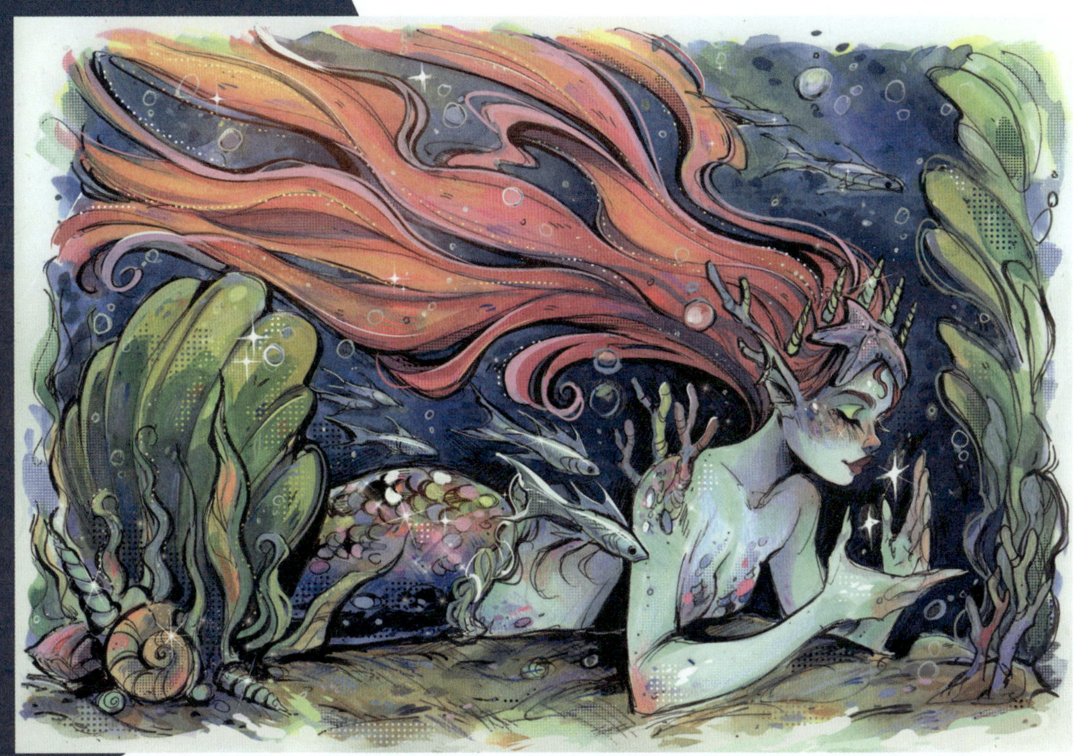

Chromatic aberation

Similar to my digital tutorial, I add a Chromatic-aberation effect using Procreate's integrated tool as a pencil. I repeat this process a few times to achieve different results by changing the direction of the lens effect.

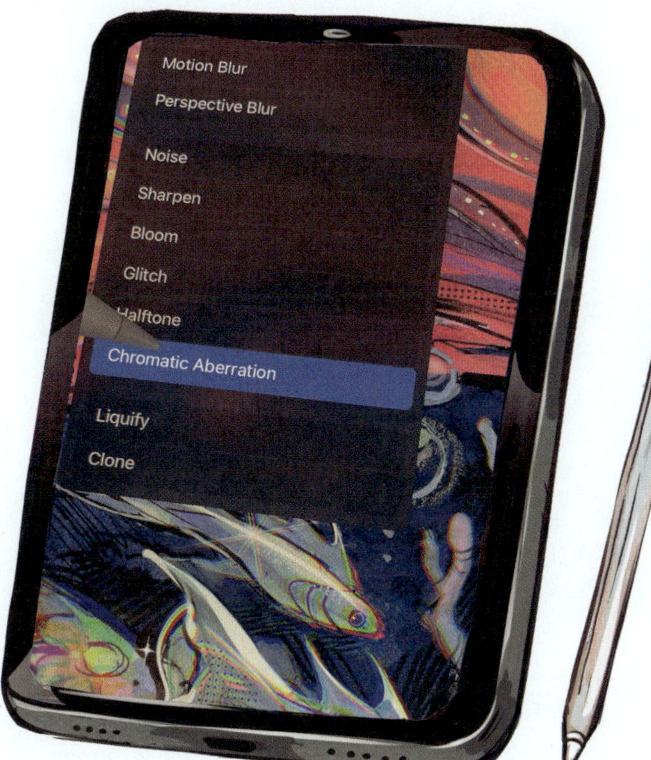

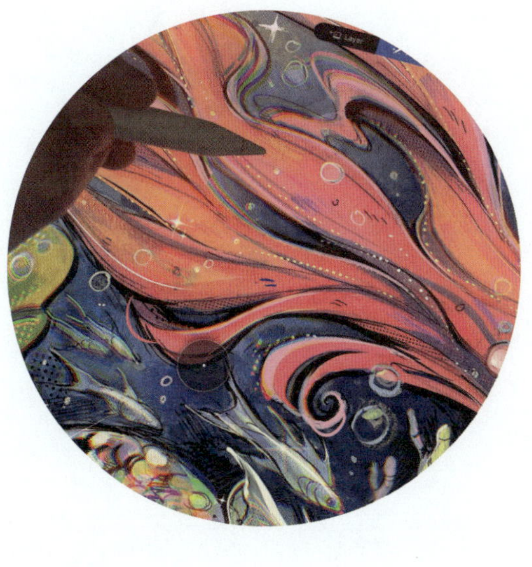

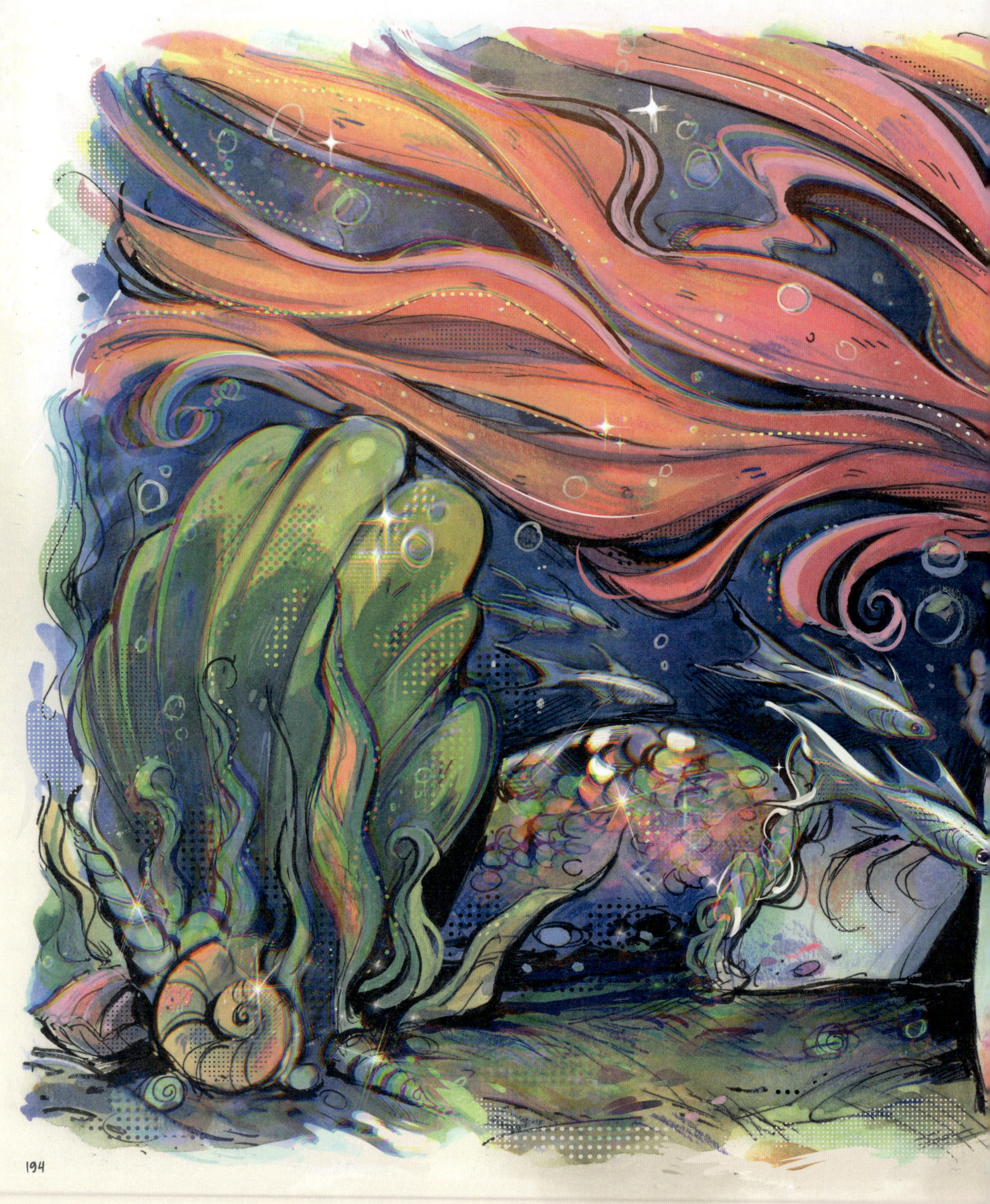

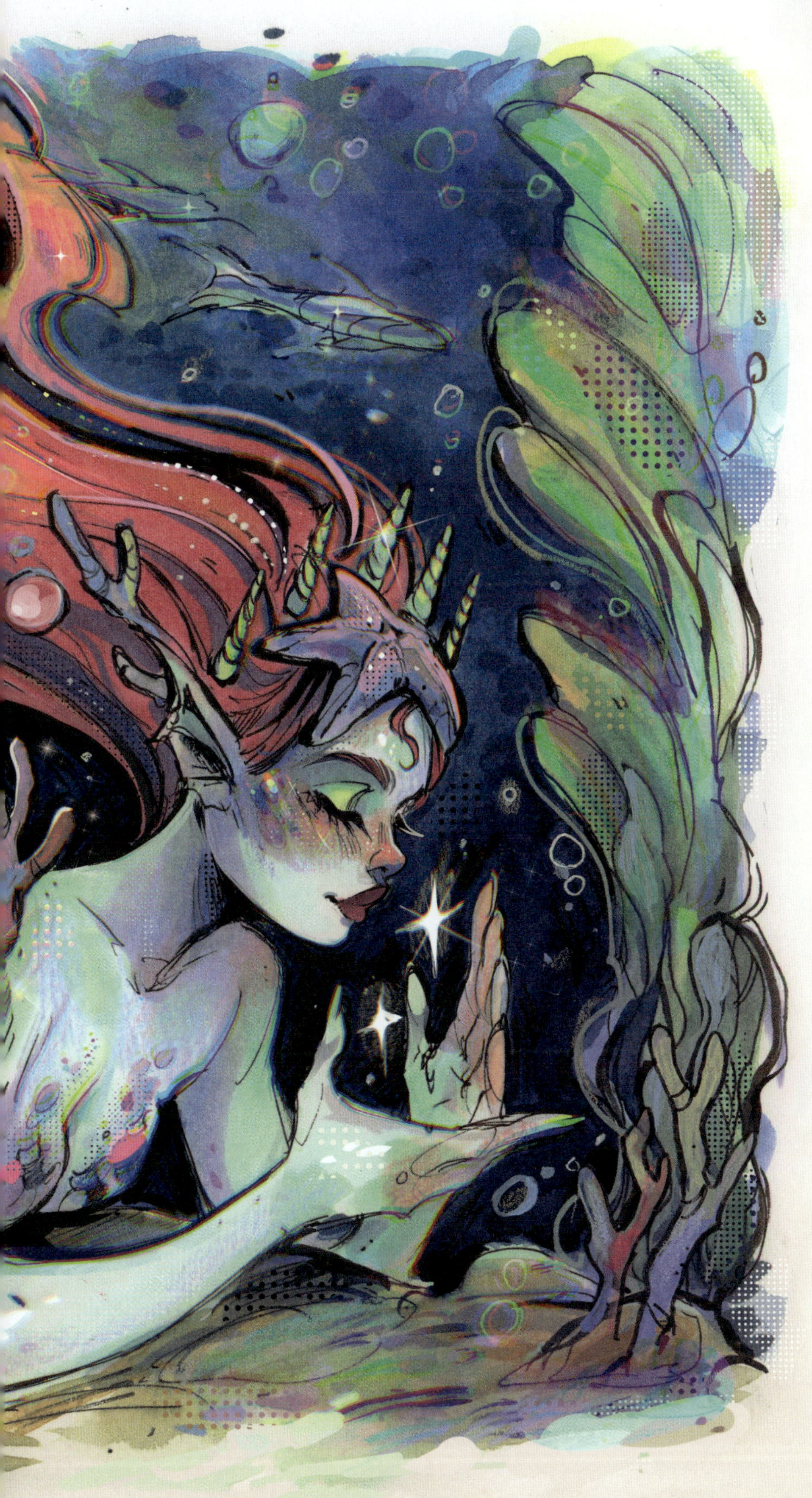

Finishing touches

Now, I take the illustration back to Photoshop and apply a little bit of Noise to unify the drawing. I also adjust the colours one last time. The final result showcases a harmonious blend of the organic and textured quality of traditional mediums with the precision and versatility of the digital tools, creating a unique visual richness that I couldn't have achieved with either medium alone.

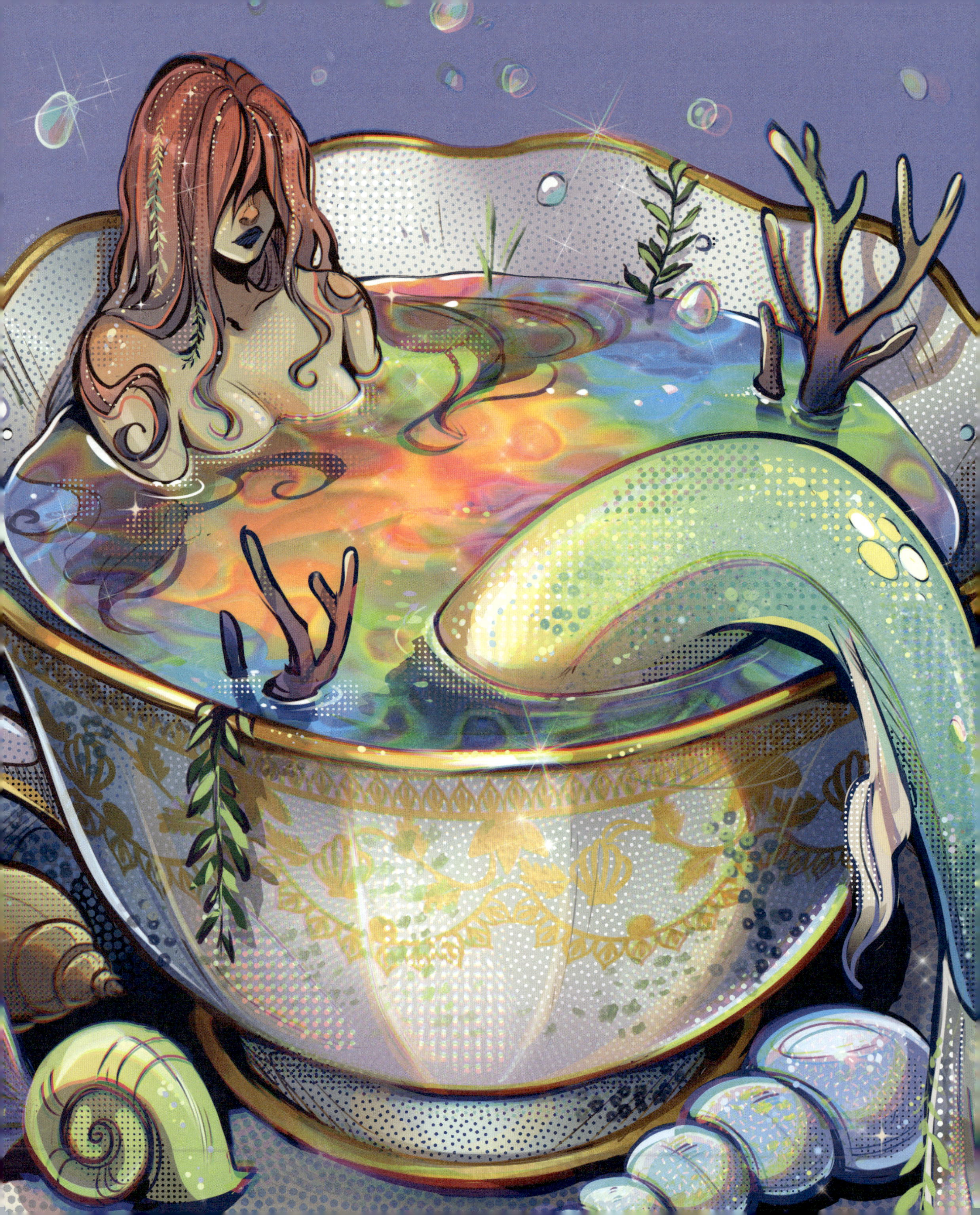

A CUP OF SEA
DIGITAL PROCESS

I wanted to revisit an old concept I came up with many years ago about a pensive mermaid inside a teacup. This new illustration had to look colourful and feel magical, so I chose to work on it digitally in order to have more control over the outcome. In this tutorial, I will walk you through all the steps of my process in Adobe Photoshop to create this digital piece from start to finish. Keep in mind that these steps can be applied to other software too.

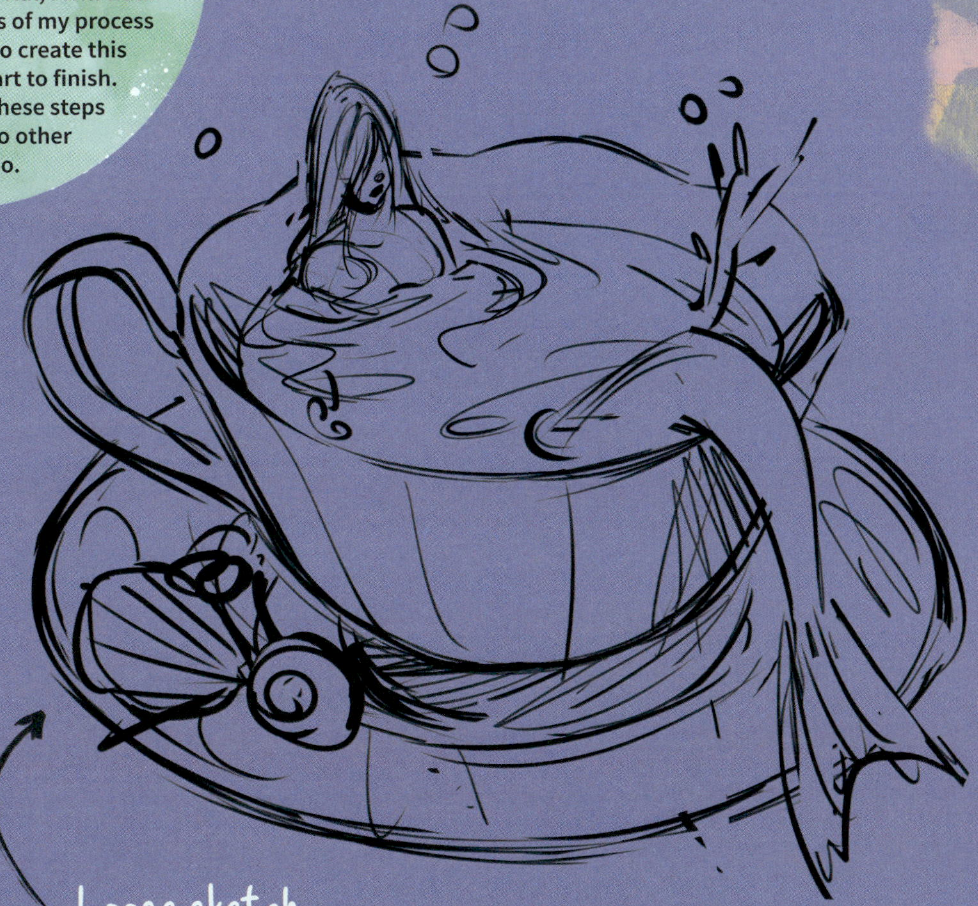

Loose sketch

My sketching process varies a lot. Sometimes an idea requires many little thumbnails and various compositions until I find the one I like most. Other times, the process is much more straightforward. With this particular drawing, I know exactly what I want to draw and how I want it to look, so this simple sketch is enough for me to visualize the whole piece.

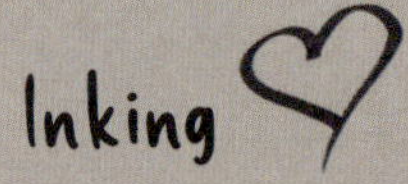

Using a hard round brush, I start refining my sketch and outlining all the elements of the drawing. At this stage, everything should be detailed instead of just 'implied', so I make sure to take as much time as necessary to create line work that is solid, readable, and expressive. I also make sure to look for references if I need them in order to better understand certain elements. In this case, I search for cup references as it is the most important element and I want to get it right!

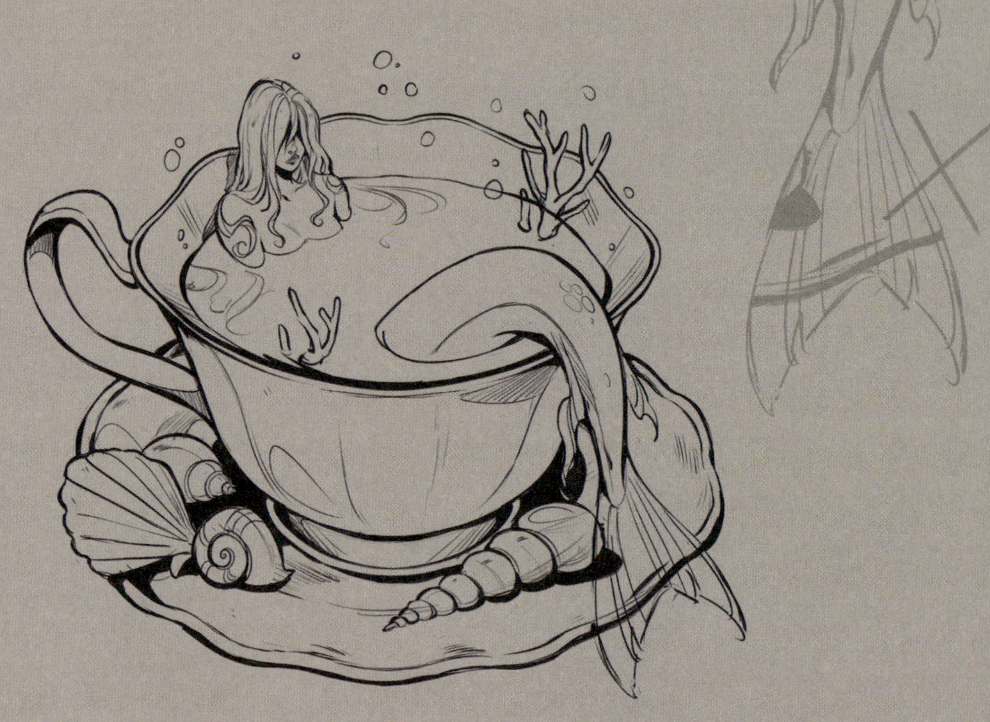

Laying down the base colours

I start the colouring process by focusing on all the base colours first. I'm not the type of artist who likes to use too many layers, so I only create a new one if the elements are overlapping to make the following steps much easier. For this step, I paint the cup, water, and mermaid on different layers and take my time playing around with different colour combinations until I find one that I like.

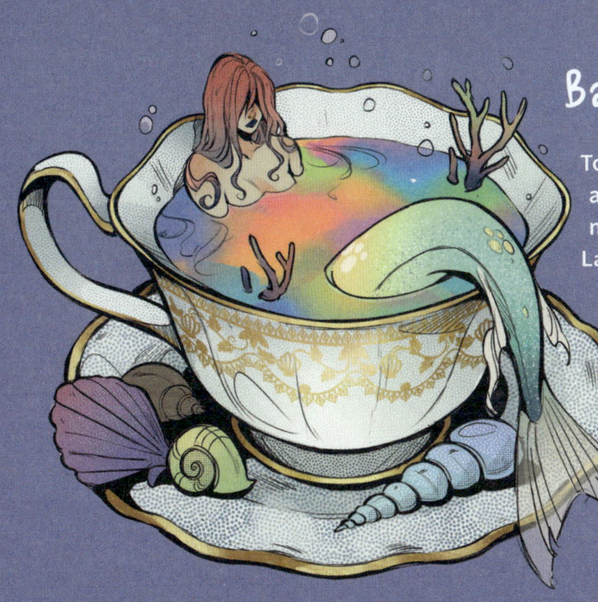

Background & texture

To make my base colours a bit more rich and interesting, I add texture and colour nuances at this early stage. I use the Lasso and Gradient tools to add colour variations and the Sprinkle and Noise brushes from True Grit Supply's Lithotone set to add grain and texture to the tail, cup, and seashells. I also paint gold details on the cup and choose a colour for the background to make everything more cohesive and harmonious. At this point, I consider the base colours good enough to move on to the shading part.

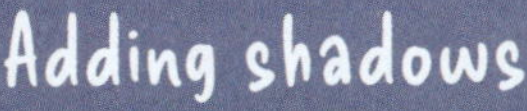

Adding shadows

My process for adding shadows is very simple. I create a new layer on top of each base-colour layer, convert them into clipping masks, and set them to Multiply. With a light violet or a soft blue, I start shading by painting directly with a hard round brush or by selecting areas with the Lasso tool and applying a radial gradient at 30% opacity.

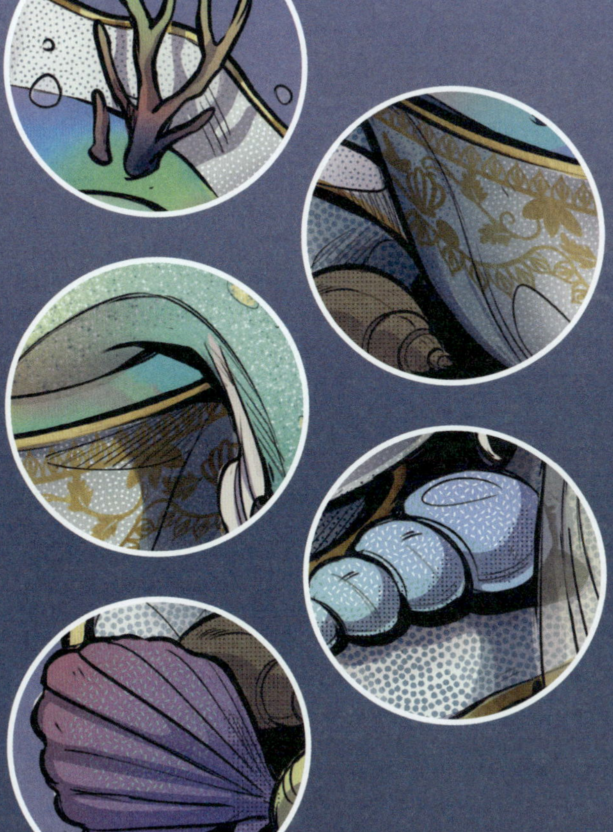

CLIPPING MASKS

Especially when painting shadows, clipping masks always come in handy. These allow you to link two layers together, so when you create a new layer on top of the base-colour layer and convert it into a clipping mask, the new layer will be affected by the shape below, making it easier to paint within that layer's limits. It's like putting a stencil on a piece of paper and only colouring within the stencil's boundaries.

Colouring the linework

I love inking with black and I don't normally feel the need to change the colour of my line work. However, sometimes black lines can look too overpowering, especially against a soft/pastel colour palette. I want to incorporate a sense of harmony into this piece, so I lock my line-work layer and paint it directly with a lighter colour so it matches the surrounding elements, making the dark lines more subtle while creating a more unified look.

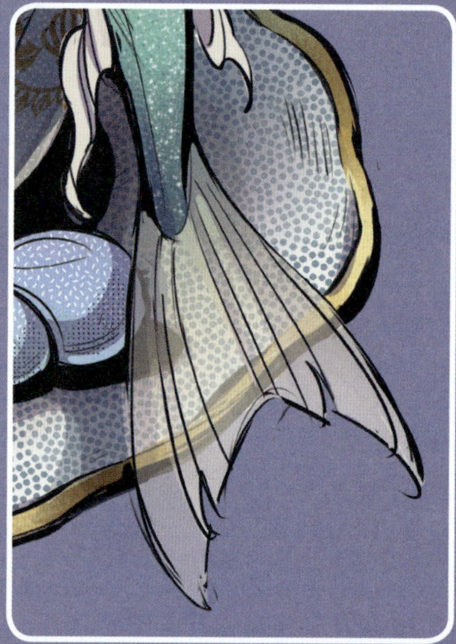

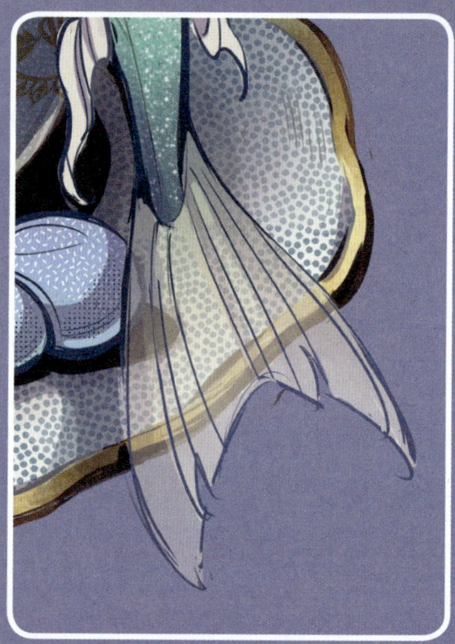

Painting the water

For the water, I use a fun and easy trick I learned from fellow artist Telthona! The iridescent effect is very versatile and can be used to add a unique touch to any illustration. I particularly like to use it for depicting the reflection of water in some of my pieces.

1. Create a new layer and double-click it. A new window called 'Layer Style' will pop up. Select the Outer Glow style. Change the blending mode to Overlay and change the solid option to a gradient.

2. Create a gradient similar to this one for an iridescent effect, or simply play around with any colour combinations you like.

3. Save the new style for future use. All the effects you create can be found on the Styles tab.

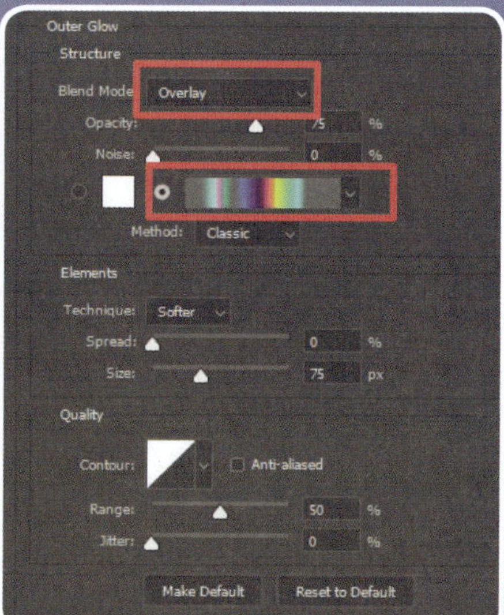

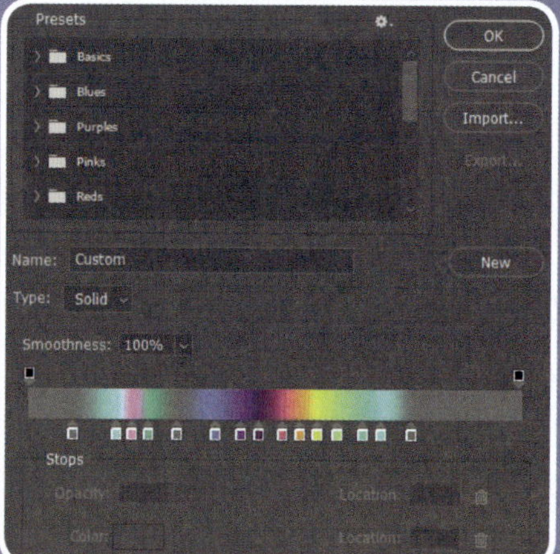

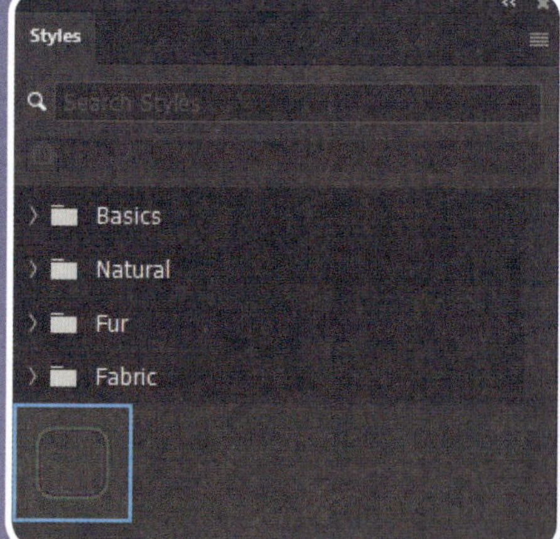

Once I create and save the new layer style, I use the same hard round brush to paint the effect on the surface of water. Notice all the different hues and colour nuances that are easily created thanks to the iridescent effect. I switch between the brush and the eraser to slowly create a pattern that I like.

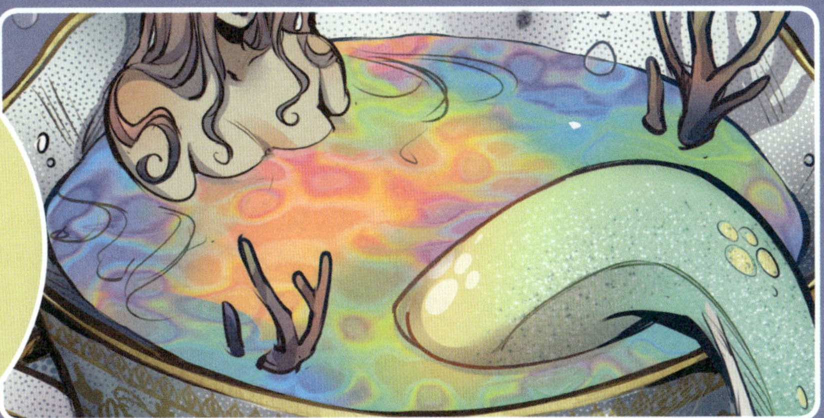

This is how the layer looks without the base colours. Since this effect is transparent, the final result will depend a lot on the colours beneath.

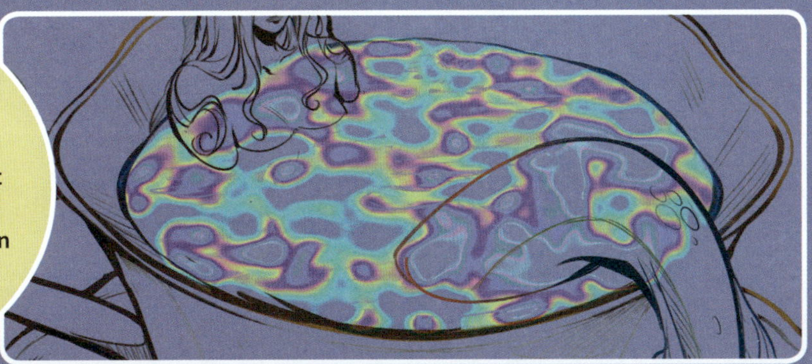

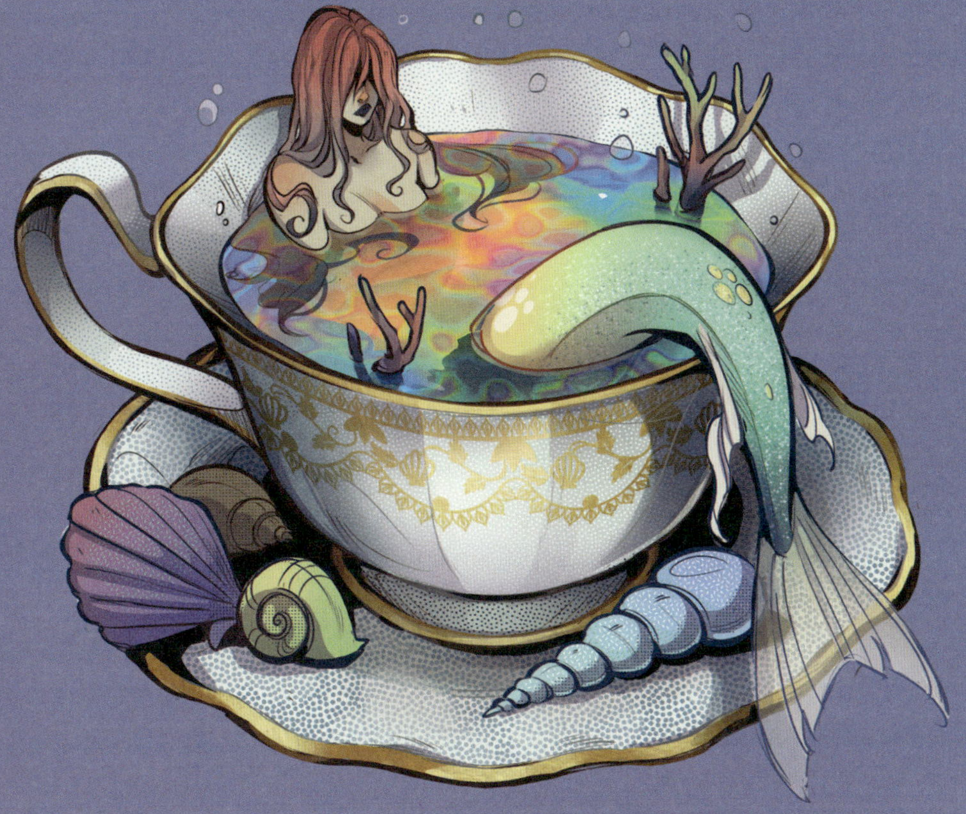

Shadow & depth

I create a new layer below the previous effect and set it to Multiply. With the Lasso tool, I create a wobbly, imperfect selection and apply a gradient to it using a blue colour. These shadows create a transparency effect on the water, giving the impression that part of the mermaid and the surrounding corals are submerged.

Working with highlights

Like the shading process, I create a new layer and set it to Overlay this time. I use the Lasso tool to quickly create some selections and apply a radial gradient using white. When you use white on an overlay layer, it lightens the underlying colours, resulting in a highlight effect that gives a sense of volume and light.

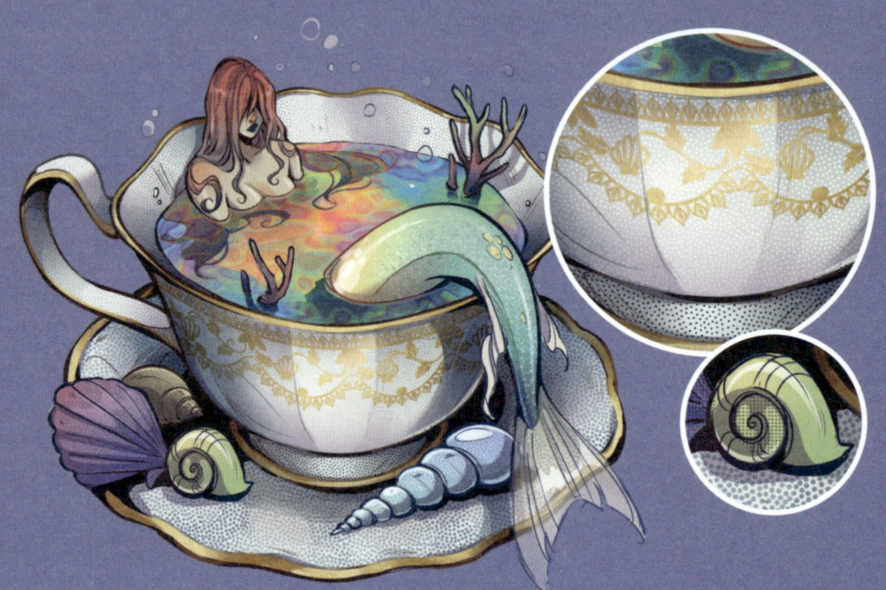

Rendering & refining

Once I have laid down the base colours and placed the shading and highlights, I create a new layer on top of everything and begin rendering the image, using the colour picker to grab the existing colours. This step is so much fun because everything starts coming together. I add details such as the highlights in the water, hair strands, rim lights, bubbles, and whatever other elements I feel are necessary to make everything look polished.

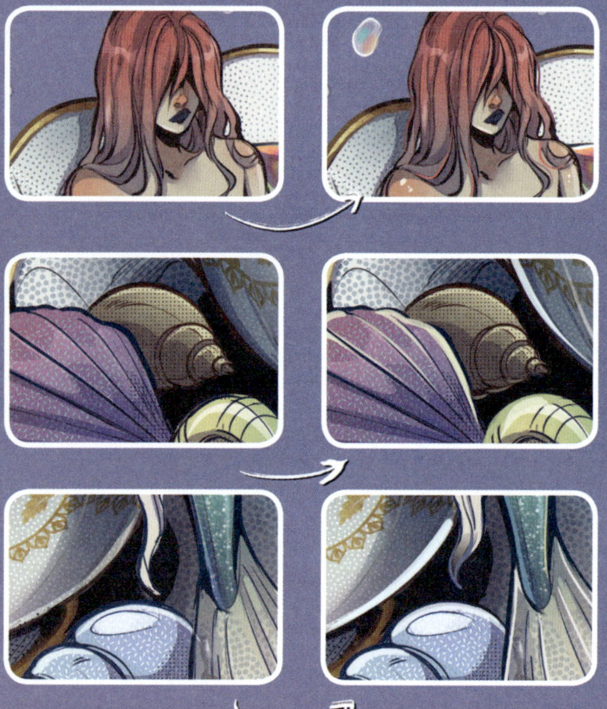

Adding a magic touch

Nothing says magic more than sparkles and glitter! This illustration was really asking for more of a shimmering look, so I use my favourite glitter-brush set to apply different types of sparkles and particles, focusing specifically on the gold details of the cup and the iridescent bubbles.

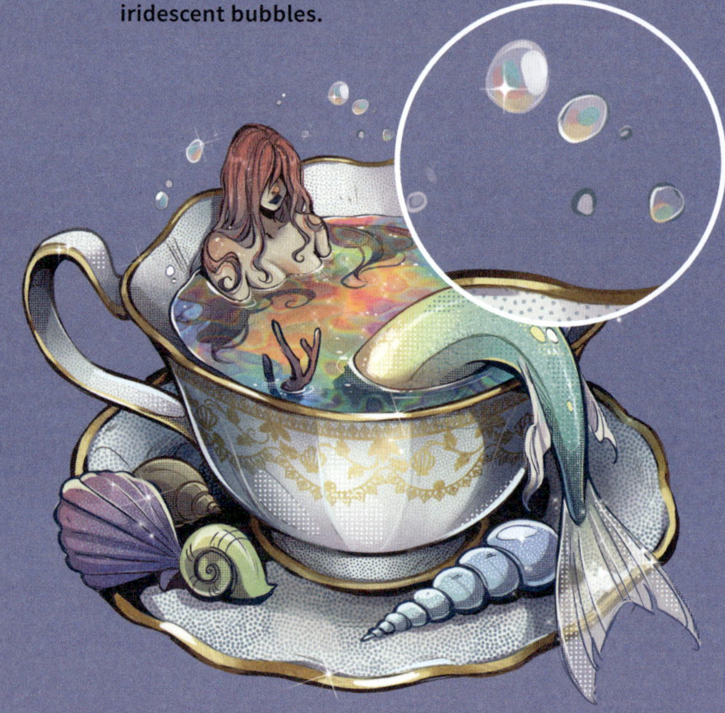

Colour adjustments

The colour adjustment decisions I make depend a lot on each illustration and the desired effects. Usually, I apply a little saturation to enhance the existing colours and also use the Selective Color tool in Photoshop if I want to slightly tweak certain colours (like all the reds within an image, for example) without modifying the other hues. It's incredibly helpful and one of my favourite tools.

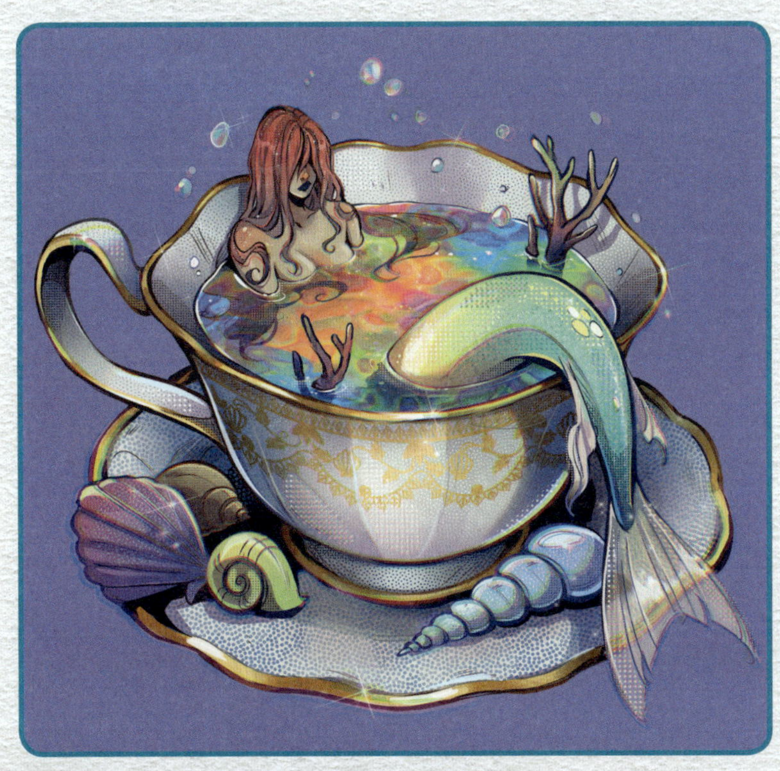

Adding warmth

With a new layer set in the Soft Light mode, I use a light orange to paint a soft rim on all the shadow edges. The yellow contrasts with the cold shadows, bringing a warm glow to the overall piece. This could be interpreted as the ambient light reflecting on the porcelain cup, but to be honest, I'm not interested in depicting light in a perfectly accurate way, so I don't usually rationalize these choices too much! If it feels right and it adds to the piece, then it works for me.

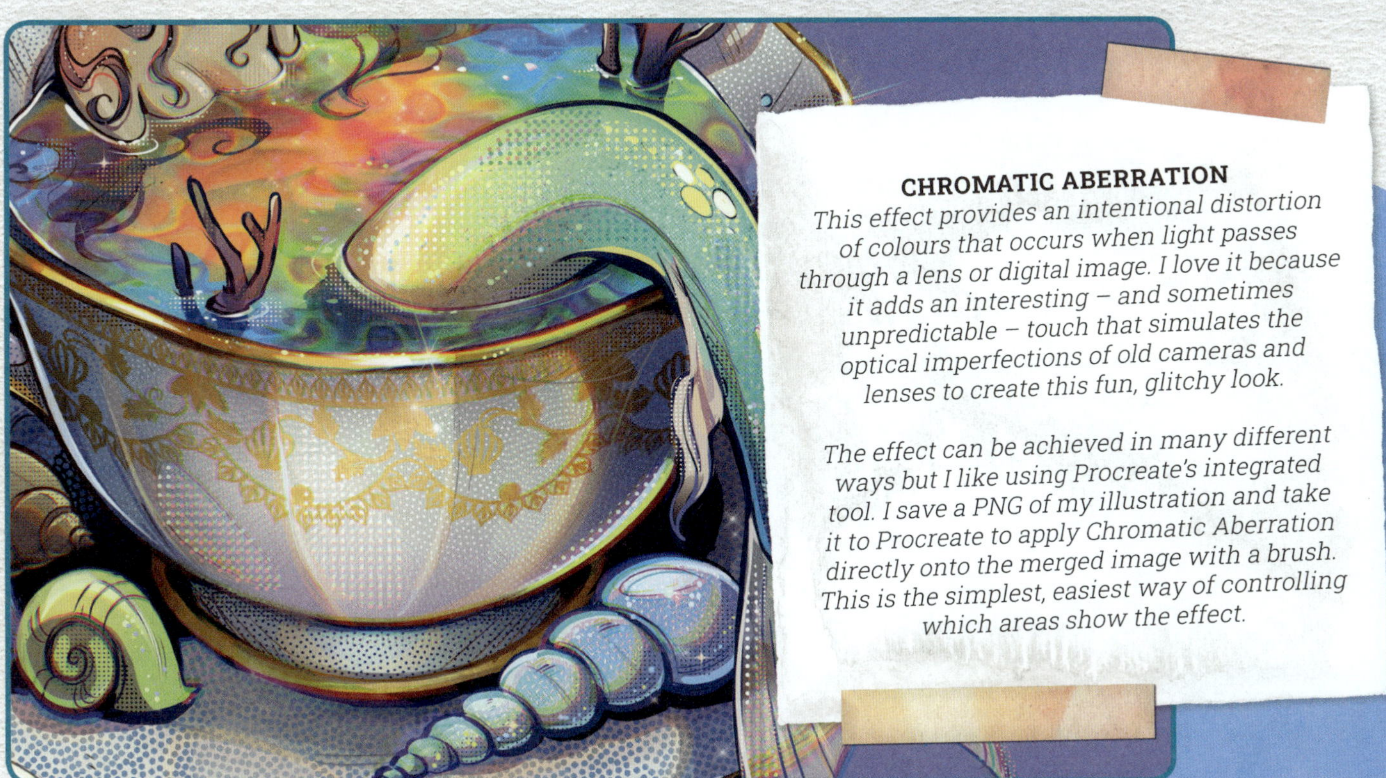

CHROMATIC ABERRATION

This effect provides an intentional distortion of colours that occurs when light passes through a lens or digital image. I love it because it adds an interesting – and sometimes unpredictable – touch that simulates the optical imperfections of old cameras and lenses to create this fun, glitchy look.

The effect can be achieved in many different ways but I like using Procreate's integrated tool. I save a PNG of my illustration and take it to Procreate to apply Chromatic Aberration directly onto the merged image with a brush. This is the simplest, easiest way of controlling which areas show the effect.

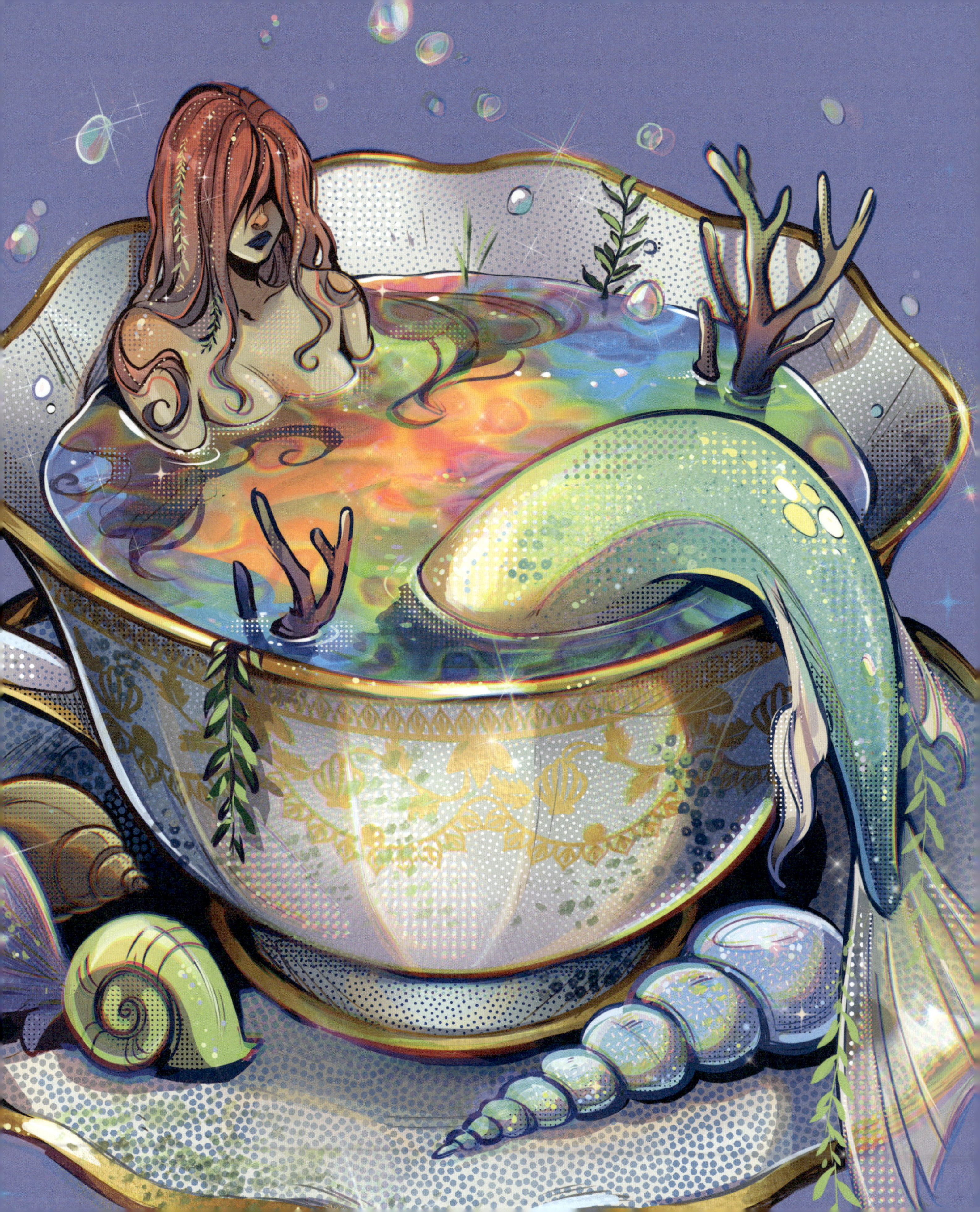

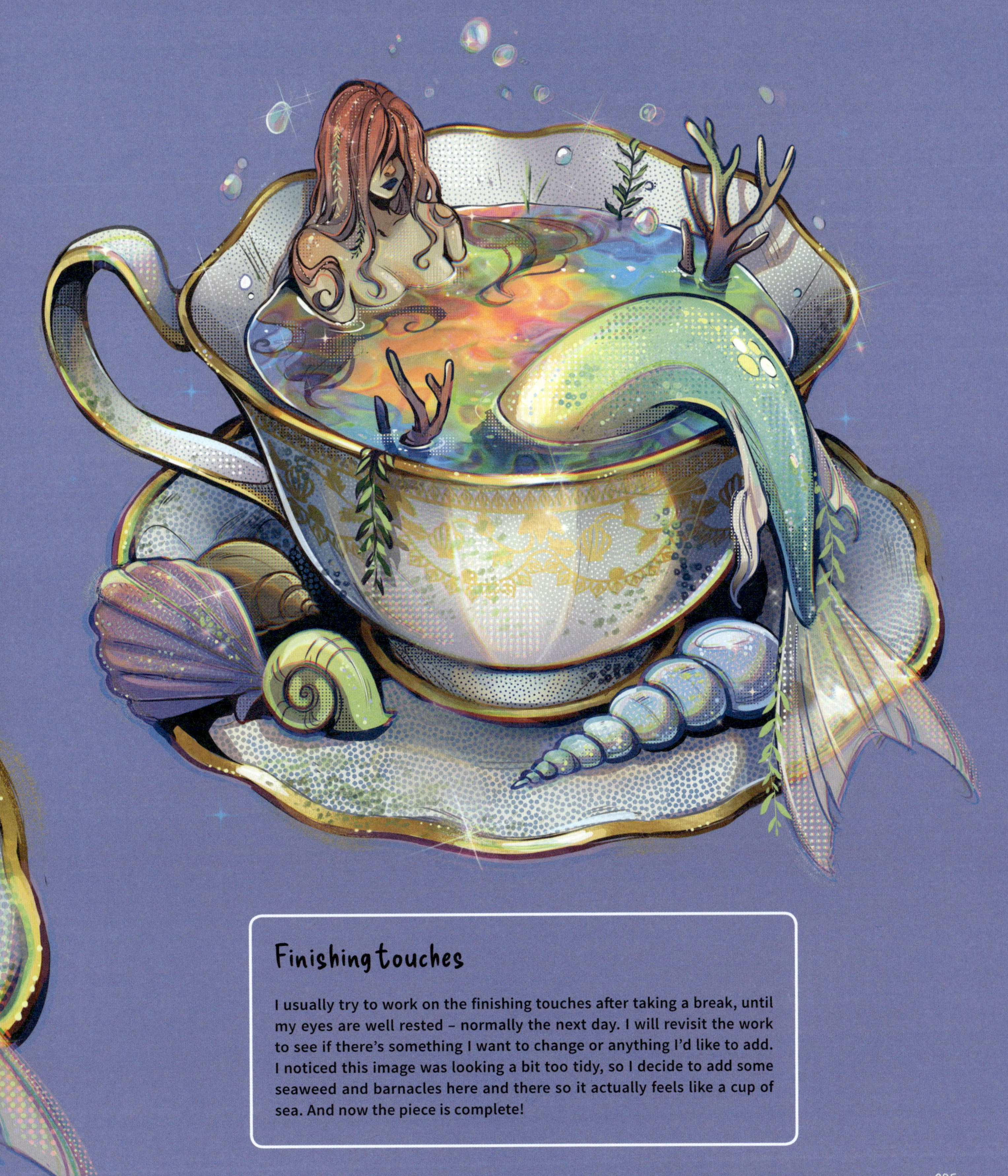

Finishing touches

I usually try to work on the finishing touches after taking a break, until my eyes are well rested – normally the next day. I will revisit the work to see if there's something I want to change or anything I'd like to add. I noticed this image was looking a bit too tidy, so I decide to add some seaweed and barnacles here and there so it actually feels like a cup of sea. And now the piece is complete!

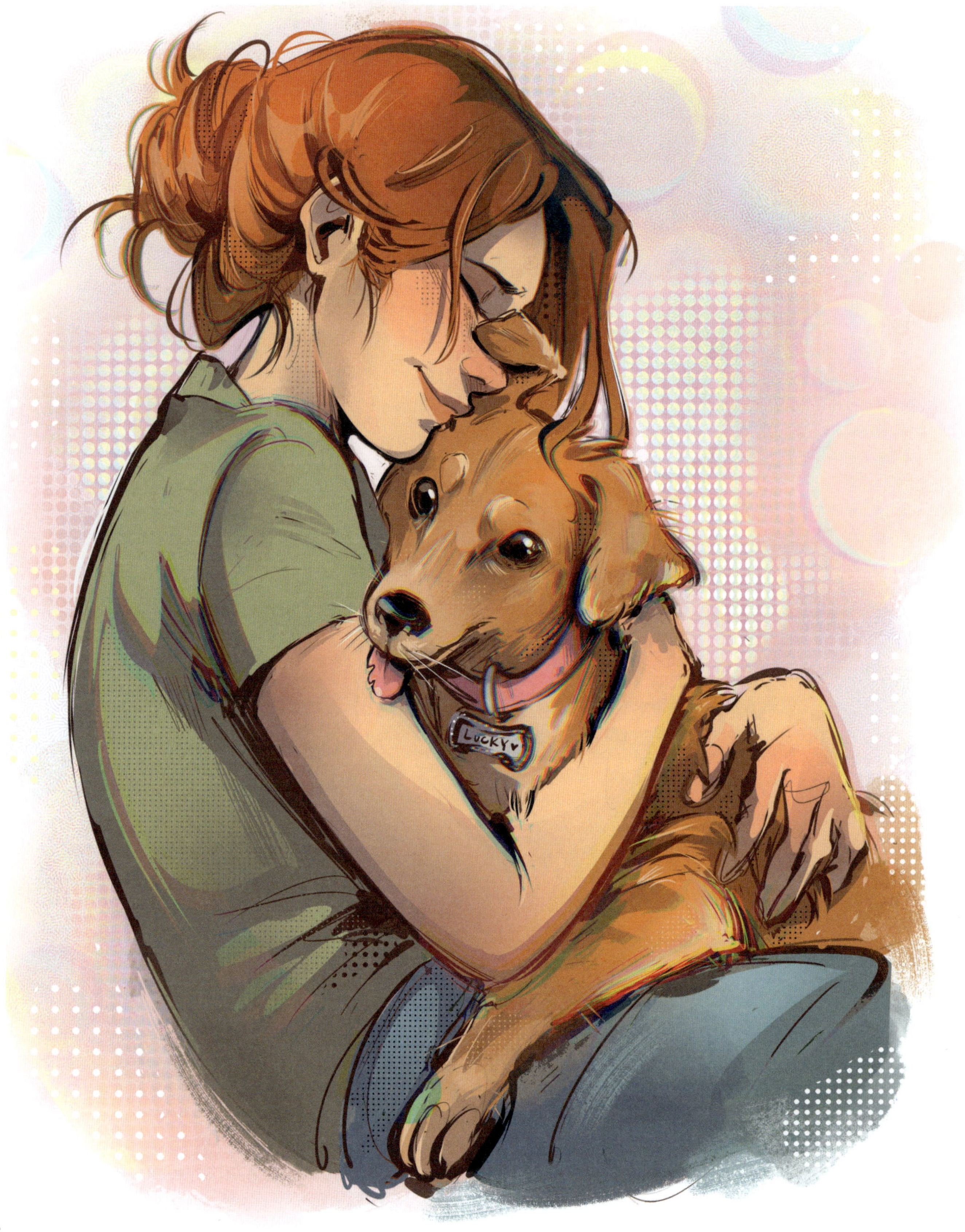
LUCKY♥

THANK YOU

A huge thank you to everyone who has supported me and followed my work throughout the years, from liking my posts and leaving a sweet message, to buying my art prints and joining my Patreon. You can't begin to know how much it has all impacted my life. You allowed me to build a career and I'm so incredibly grateful. This book was made for you and because of you.

Thank you to all of you who supported this project, whether it was by kindly backing the Kickstarter campaign, grabbing a copy in the store, or just spreading the word and sharing your enthusiasm. It truly means the world to me. As long as I am able, I will keep making art that I hope will brighten your day!

A special thanks to Simon for believing in my work and giving me the opportunity to work on this dream project. And thank you to the incredible 3dtotal team for their hard work and dedication to bringing this book to life, especially my editor Rhee, who was so kind and encouraging throughout the whole process, and Joe, for making everything look so great. Thanks for guiding me and helping me create something I feel very proud of.

To my family, who have always been there for me – thank you for being my number-one fans since the very beginning, never hindering my passion, and supporting me every step of the way. Big thanks to my friends and colleagues, who always saw the best in me and for motivating and inspiring me every day. And a big, big, *big* thank you to Nahu, my favourite person in this whole world, for being so loving and always cheering me on, even when I don't feel like cheering for myself. I'm so lucky to have you in my life.

Gret.♡

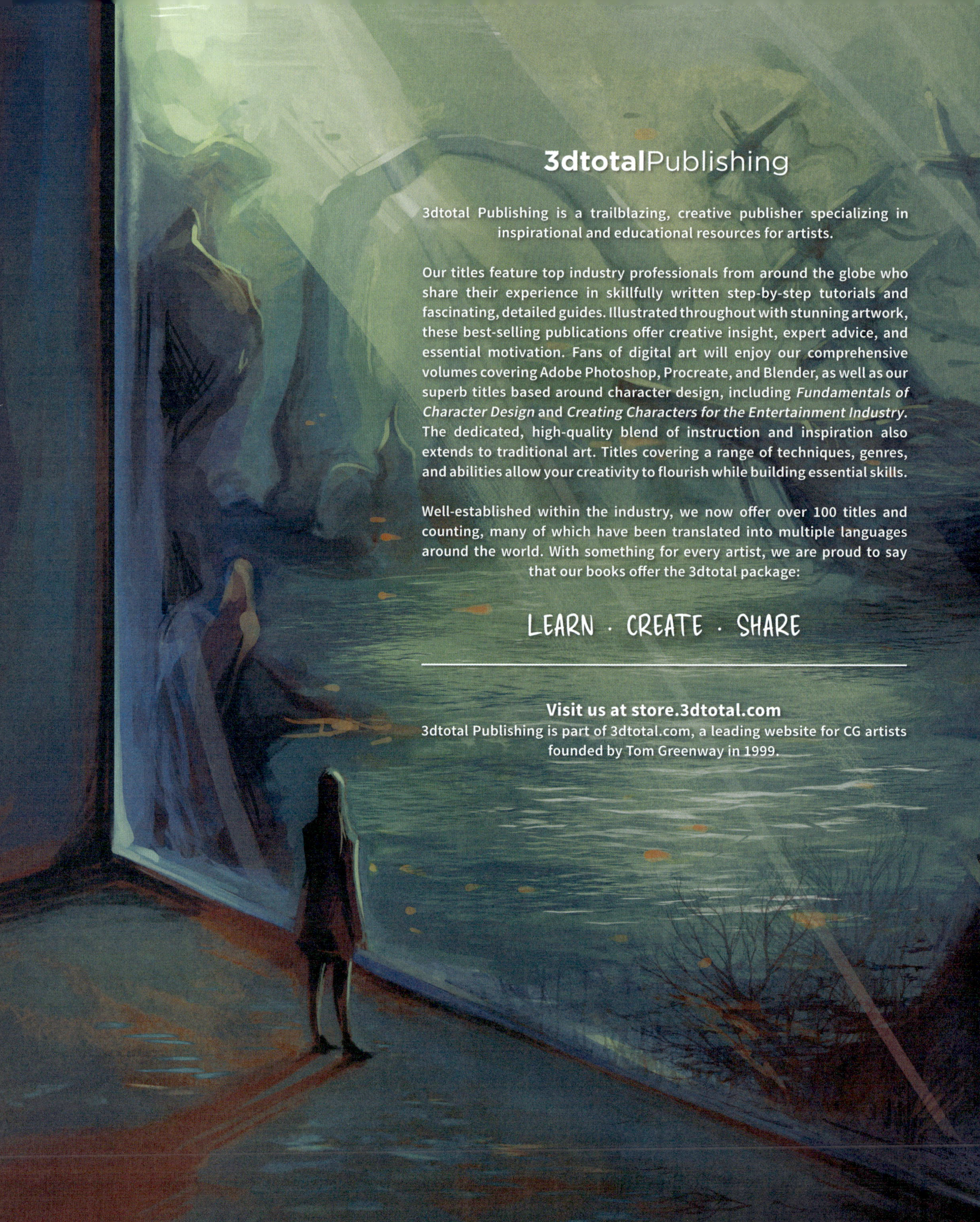
3dtotalPublishing
3dtotal Publishing is a trailblazing, creative publisher specializing in inspirational and educational resources for artists.
Our titles feature top industry professionals from around the globe who share their experience in skillfully written step-by-step tutorials and fascinating, detailed guides. Illustrated throughout with stunning artwork, these best-selling publications offer creative insight, expert advice, and essential motivation. Fans of digital art will enjoy our comprehensive volumes covering Adobe Photoshop, Procreate, and Blender, as well as our superb titles based around character design, including Fundamentals of Character Design and Creating Characters for the Entertainment Industry. The dedicated, high-quality blend of instruction and inspiration also extends to traditional art. Titles covering a range of techniques, genres, and abilities allow your creativity to flourish while building essential skills.
Well-established within the industry, we now offer over 100 titles and counting, many of which have been translated into multiple languages around the world. With something for every artist, we are proud to say that our books offer the 3dtotal package:
LEARN · CREATE · SHARE
Visit us at store.3dtotal.com
3dtotal Publishing is part of 3dtotal.com, a leading website for CG artists founded by Tom Greenway in 1999.

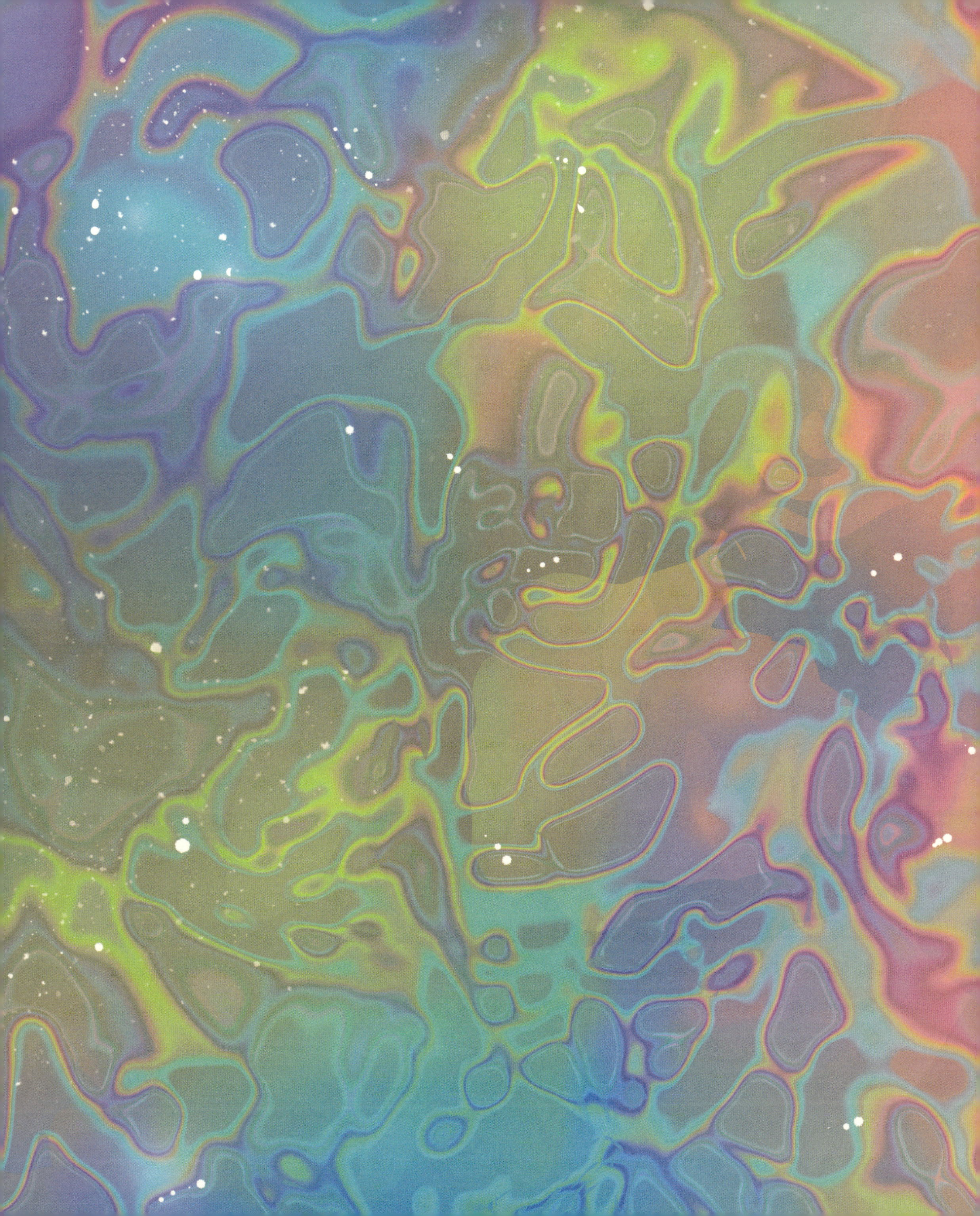

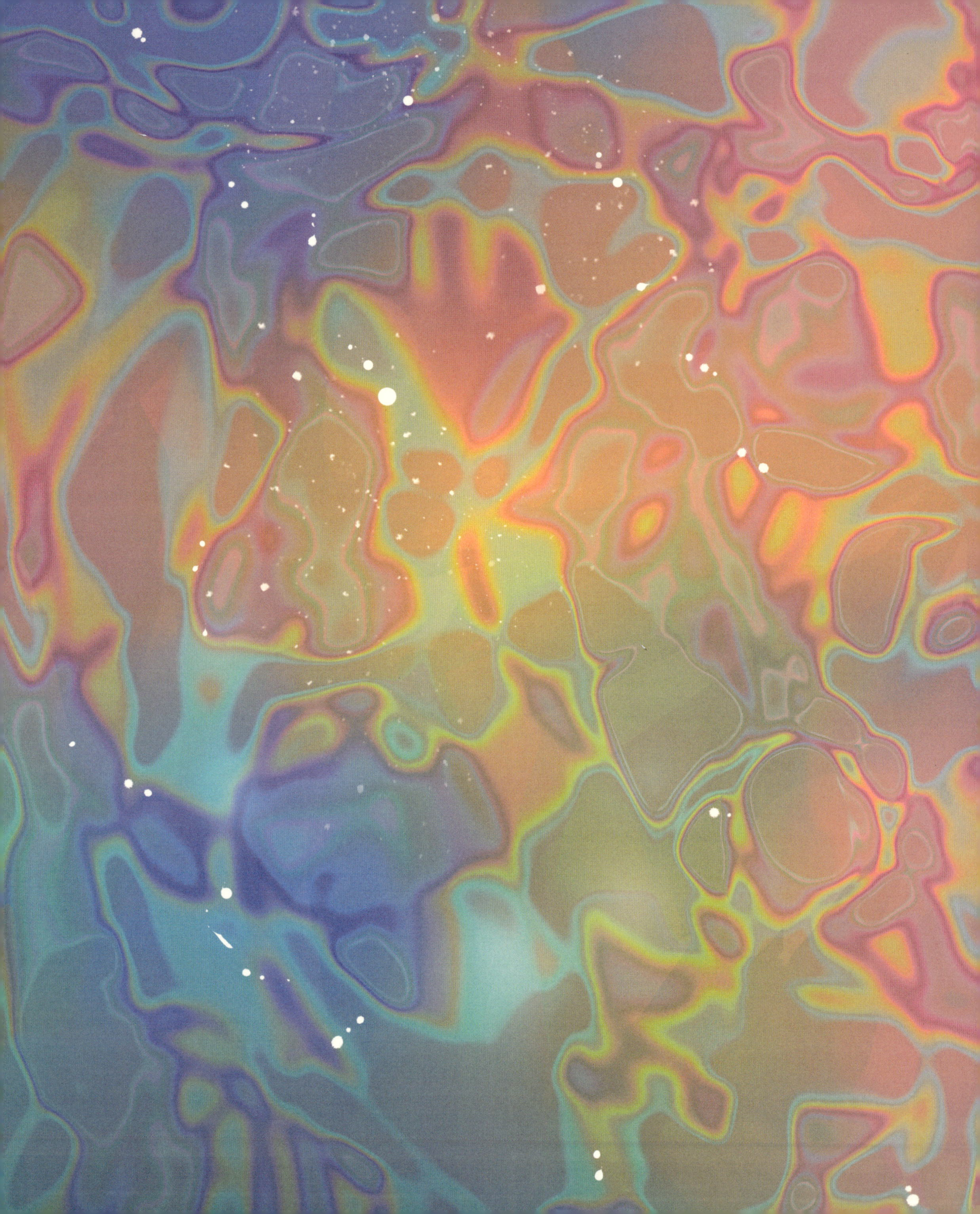